The Write Start with Readings

PARAGRAPHS TO ESSAYS

Second Edition

Gayle Feng-Checkett

St. Charles Community College

Lawrence Checkett

St. Charles Community College

PEARSON

Longman

New York Boston San Francisco
London Toronto Sydney Tokyo Singapore Madrid
Mexico City Munich Paris Cape Town Hong Kong Montreal

To our children: Kitaro Lawrence,
Brian Yi Chuan, and David Yi Shon.
Knowledge is life . . . pass it on.

Vice President and Editor-in-Chief: Joe Terry
Acquisitions Editor: Susan Kunchandy
Development Editor: Marion B. Castellucci
Senior Marketing Manager: Melanie Craig
Senior Supplements Editor: Donna Campion
Media Supplements Editor: Nancy Garcia
Production Manager: Ellen MacElree
Project Coordination, Text Design, and Electronic Page Makeup: Nesbitt Graphics, Inc.
Cover Design Manager: Wendy Ann Fredericks
Cover Designer: Maria Ilardi
Cover Photos (left to right): E.R. Degginger/Animals Animals/Earth Scenes; Ralph A. Reinhold/Animals Animals/Earth Scenes; E.R.
   Degginger/Animals Animals/Earth Scenes; and Jerry Young/Dorling Kindersley Media Library
Photo Researcher: Photosearch Inc.
Manufacturing Buyer: Lucy Hebard
Printer and Binder: Quebecor World/Taunton
Cover Printer: Coral Graphic Services

For permission to use copyrighted material, grateful acknowledgment is made to the copyright holders on pp. 459–460, which are hereby made part of this copyright page.

Library of Congress Cataloging-in-Publication Data

Feng-Checkett, Gayle.
   The write start with readings : paragraphs to essays / Gayle Feng-Checkett, Lawrence Checkett.— 2nd ed.
      p. cm.
   Lawrence Checkett's name appears first on the earlier edition.
   ISBN 0-321-14296-9
   1. English language—Rhetoric. 2. College readers. 3. Report writing. I. Checkett, Lawrence. II. Title.

PE1408 .F443 2004
808'.0427—dc22   2004005785

Please visit us at http://www.ablongman.com/checkett.

ISBN 0-321-14296-9 (Student Edition)

ISBN 0-321-14297-7 (Annotated Instructor's Edition)

1 2 3 4 5 6 7 8 9 10—WCT—07 06 05 04

BRIEF CONTENTS

PART 1

Getting Started: The Fundamentals   13

PART 2

Moving Forward: Strategies for Developing Essays   75

PART 3

Special Writing Situations   239

The Writer's Resources   293

Additional Readings   375

DETAILED CONTENTS

Chapter 6

The Concluding Paragraph   64

PART 2

Moving Forward: Strategies for Developing Essays   75

Chapter 7

The Descriptive Essay   77

Chapter 8

The Narrative Essay   94

The Writer's Resources 293

PREFACE

We would like to express our appreciation to all the instructors around the country who adopted the first edition of *The Write Start with Readings: Paragraphs to Essays,* and its companion volume, *The Write Start with Readings: Sentences to Paragraphs,* as their developmental writing texts. The feedback we have received has been overwhelmingly positive, supporting the approach we have taken with both texts. In this second book of the series, *Paragraphs to Essays,* we focus on writing paragraphs using the various modes of development and then on applying the techniques of the mode to the longer essay format. Grammar, sentence structure, and ESL concerns, while an integral part of all the writing exercises and assignments, are embedded in the chapters in a less noticeable way in this paragraph-to-essay text; instead, they are the primary focus of The Writer's Resources section at the end.

We have listened closely to suggestions as well as praise, and in this second edition we have made some significant changes that will make the series even more relevant to the writing demands and needs of your students.

What's New in the Second Edition

Most of the changes in this second edition are designed to expand and improve our treatment of the writing process and the interrelationship of reading, critical thinking, and writing. As a result, Chapters 2 through 6 have been given a major overhaul both in content and organization.

▼ **Chapter 2, Critical Thinking: The Connection Between Reading and Writing, has been completely rewritten to be more accessible for developing writers.** Terminology has been reduced and simplified, and concepts and examples have been changed to be more relevant to academic writing. We explain and model the use of four basic critical thinking questions to analyze a student essay, and then we provide a professional essay with critical thinking questions to apply and reinforce the instruction.

▼ **Prewriting instruction and activities have been moved to Chapter 3, which has been expanded to cover the entire writing process.** Explanations of drafting, revising, and proofreading have been added to the prewriting coverage, and the entire writing process is illustrated with a single paragraph at each stage, along with practice exercises.

▼ **An exciting addition to Chapters 4 (The Introductory Paragraph), 5 (The Body Paragraphs), and 6 (The Concluding Paragraph) is an essay modeled step-by-step from its prewriting stage through successive revisions and proofreading to its final version.** We think this essay will be an invaluable tool for both instructors and developing writers. In addition, we have provided a discussion of audience, coherence, and unity to give students a focus for developing their ideas.

In addition to the critical reading and writing process revisions we made in Chapters 2 through 6, we made changes in the remainder of the book to improve its effectiveness.

▼ **Critical reading questions now follow the essays in Chapters 7 through 15, which cover patterns of development in the various rhetorical modes.** These provide more opportunities for students to analyze and evaluate the essays.

▼ **Additional writing topics as well as writing checklists, both specific to the mode of development, have been added to Chapters 7 through 15.** These provide students with ideas for writing and specific guidance on the writing process..

▼ **About one-third of the professional essays in the Additional Readings section are new.** These were chosen for their interest as well as to better reflect the diversity of student populations. As we did for all the essays in the modes chapters, we added a new set of critical reading questions to all the essays in the Additional Readings section.

▼ **In The Writer's Resource section, the treatment of sentence problems has been expanded and many additional exercises have been added throughout.** These provide additional practice for students who need help with grammar, punctuation, style, and word choice.

The Write Start Series

The Write Start is a two-book series designed to meet the needs of students taking developmental writing courses. The first text, *The Write Start with Readings: Sentences to Paragraphs*, addresses the most basic writing skills: grammar, sentence and paragraph structure, the integration of reading and writing, the special concerns of students for whom English is a second language, the various modes of developing topics, and an introduction to the essay. This text, *The Write Start with Readings: Paragraphs to Essays*, is the second book of the series. It continues the developmental writing sequence first by focusing on writing paragraphs that express thoughts about a topic by using the various modes of development and then by expanding the topic by applying the techniques of the mode to the longer essay format. Grammar, sentence structure, and ESL concerns are dealt with in The Writer's Resources section at the end of the text.

Organization of the Text

We have organized the text in an effort to introduce the developing writer to the basic elements and skills necessary for writing effective essays in the academic environment. While these skills also will help students communicate more effectively in their personal and work correspondence, the primary focus is to ready developing writers for the rigors of their first college-level composition course (for credit) at the next level. Many developing writers are taking courses requiring college-level writing skills while concurrently enrolled in developmental writing courses, and as a result they face problems doing the written work that is expected of them. Thus we have attempted to illustrate the processes and skills necessary for effective writing in as simple and straightforward a manner as possible, so students can begin applying their new writing skills immediately to their work in other courses.

Introduction: Chapters 1 and 2

Chapter 1 reinforces the idea that writing is important. The developing writer might at first resist this idea, but it is our belief, through years of experience, that the developing writer knows this to be true. This chapter stresses the idea that writing is difficult, but like other skills, can be developed with the proper attitude, information, and work ethic. It emphasizes the important link between reading and writing, the need for writing presentable papers without significant grammar, punctuation, and sentence structure errors, the mature writing and thinking that comes from writing about topics in a variety of modes, and the techniques for making the transition from paragraphs to essays.

Chapter 2 introduces the developing writer to the elements of reasoning that underpin the critical thinking processes for analyzing and evaluating reading and writing. At the end of each essay in Chapters 7 through 15 and in the Additional Readings section, the developing writer is given a set of questions to answer based on the critical reading questions discussed in Chapter 2.

The Fundamentals: Chapters 3 Through 6

Chapters 3 through 6 focus on the total writing process, from prewriting to the final draft. Part 1 begins with an overview of the major elements of the essay: the sentence, the paragraph, thesis statement, topic sentences, support sentences, audience, unity, and coherence. Chapter 3 discusses the entire writing process: prewriting, drafting, revising, and proofreading. The chapter includes a sustained example of a paragraph in various stages of development as well as practice exercises.

Chapter 4 introduces the developing writer to the introductory paragraph, including lead-in techniques and the thesis statement. Chapter 5 describes the body paragraphs, including the topic sentence and support sentences. Part 1 closes with Chapter 6 and an examination of the concluding paragraph, focusing on several techniques to bring an essay to a successful end. Throughout Chapters 4 through 6, the developing writer will see a single essay as it is developed from the prewriting stage, through revisions of the rough draft, to the final proofread and corrected draft. This instruction will reinforce the rules and processes that have been introduced, and it will actually show how the processes help to create the essay.

Strategies for Developing Essays: Chapters 7 Through 15

These nine chapters introduce the developing writer to the modes of development for examining topics. Each chapter begins by using the paragraph to explain the basic concepts and techniques of the mode; then, the chapter shows students how to make the transition to the full essay. A list of transitional expressions is provided in each chapter to aid the developing writer in creating rhythm, connecting related ideas, and combining sentences. Student essays are used to model the concepts, techniques, and processes of each mode, as well as the thesis statement with essay map approach. In addition, professional essays are provided in each chapter to give students exposure to writing that has a less structured format. Each chapter ends with additional writing prompts, a writing checklist for that mode, and a review of the major points discussed in the chapter.

Special Writing Situations: Chapters 16 Through 18

Because this text focuses on preparing the developing writer for the rigors of academic writing—specifically the first college composition course—these chapters focus on writing the research paper, the in-class essay examination, and the literary analysis essay.

Chapter 16 introduces the developing writer to the steps involved in writing a paper that requires research in primary and secondary sources and in documenting that research using the Modern Language Association format. The chapter uses one student-written and one professionally written research paper to model the techniques and process for research writing.

Chapter 17 focuses on the key terms that developing writers should look for in the prompts they are given on examinations to help them organize an essay in just a few minutes. The thesis statement with essay map is offered as a technique to quickly identify and organize subtopics into a clearly defined approach in response to the overall topic parameters. A number of prompts from various disciplines are illustrated with accompanying thesis statements.

Chapter 18 examines the critical thinking process involved in literary criticism. The elements of literary analysis (character, plot, setting, time, theme, and technique) are discussed as complements to the six reporter's questions (who, what, where, when, why, and how), with which the developing writer is already familiar. Each of the elements of literary analysis is discussed in detail. Examples of the thesis sentence with and without the essay map are illustrated. The chapter ends with two models of literary analysis essays: one for the poem "After Apple-Picking" by Robert Frost and one for the novel *Sula* by Toni Morrison.

The Writer's Resources

The Writer's Resources section is a veritable warehouse of information on grammar, punctuation, usage, and spelling. Examples and exercises accompany the material for illustration, clarification, and additional practice. Material that is especially helpful to English as a Second Language (ESL) students is tagged by an ESL icon.

Additional Readings

To give developing writers more exposure to good writing, the Additional Readings section contains two professional essays to accompany each of the modes covered in Chapters 7 through 15. Each essay has its own apparatus, including vocabulary, writing technique questions, critical reading questions, and writing opportunities.

Limited Answer Key

An answer key provides half the answers to the in-chapter objective practices. Students can check their own work to see how their skills are developing. (A complete answer key is included in the Annotated Instructor's Edition.)

Glossary

At the end of *The Write Start*, a glossary of terms provides a convenient resource for students to look up the meanings of key terms used in the text.

Special Features of *The Write Start*

The features of *The Write Start with Readings: Paragraphs to Essays* have been carefully developed with the needs of developmental English students and instructors in mind.

▼ **Clarity and Simplicity.** Concepts and techniques are simply described and illustrated, with key terms boldfaced and defined in each chapter as well as in the end-of-book glossary. The writing style is friendly, clear, and easy for students to understand. The topical presentation is logically sequenced and flows easily from chapter to chapter, yet all chapters are entirely modular, allowing instructors to determine their own order of presentation and to structure their classes however they choose without having to worry about possible text usage problems. To support the clarity of the presentation, a simple, uncluttered, attractive design has been used.

▼ **Smooth Flow of Concepts Within Each Chapter.** In each chapter, concepts flow logically from the simple to the more complex. Students are presented with concepts in a fashion that allows them to understand a little at a time and build on what they have just learned.

▼ **Examples.** One of the best ways for developmental students to learn is through example, and examples are used liberally to illustrate all the concepts presented. Examples are screened to make them pop out for clear emphasis and easier reference.

▼ **Practices.** Numerous practices reinforce learning and help students apply what they've just read. The practices are narrowly focused on the content just covered, and they range from making lists, to writing sentences, to writing and rewriting paragraphs.

▼ **Highly Structured Presentation of the Essay as a Form.** Writing a good essay is a complex undertaking. To help students develop their essay writing skills, *The Write Start* first presents a five-paragraph essay structure (introductory paragraph with thesis statement and essay map, three body paragraphs, concluding paragraph) and then presents instruction on each essay mode (description, narration, etc.) using the five-paragraph essay as a structural model. Thus students can improve their organizational and writing skills within a highly structured form defined by the thesis statement with essay map. All the model student essays use the essay map and are written in this five-paragraph form to reinforce the instruction.

A Word about the Thesis Statement. Although this textbook uses the thesis statement with essay map as the tool for organizing the essay, you are free to use whatever thesis statement mechanism with which you feel comfortable. Some writing teachers complain that the essay map forces the writer into a mechanical style. We believe this to be untrue. In writing this text, we have made two assumptions, one about the developing writer and one about writing. First, we believe that the developing writer, to be successful in academic work, needs structure. The essay map in the thesis statement allows the developing writer to create a mini-outline of the essay, helping the writer to stay focused on the subtopic at hand and on the order in which the subtopics should be discussed. In fact, the feedback we have received from our students indicates that they rely on the thesis statement in many of their other classes, particularly during in-class essay exams. Second, we believe that mechanical writing results from the failure to make good use of techniques that promote a fluid, rhythmical style. In each of the modes chapters we illustrate the transitional devices that help connect related ideas, foster rhythm in the paragraphs, and combine sentences to reduce choppiness and introduce variety, a hallmark of good writing. In fact, many professionals use the essay map as the organizing tool in their writing, yet one would hardly call the writing styles of professional writers Ernst Mayr and Barbara Ehrenreich—each of whom has used the essay map—stodgy, stolid, or mechanical.

▼ **Focus on ESL.** The developmental writing market overlaps with the ESL market in that many ESL instructors need to use developmental texts and many developmental instructors have ESL students enrolled in their courses. Gayle Feng-Checkett is a certified ESL instructor, so much of the text was written with ESL students in mind. This book uses ESL research and pedagogy to the benefit of all developmental English students.

▼ **Critical Thinking Skills: The Connection between Reading and Writing.** Good writers are also good readers, and many of the skills used in reading are also used in writing. Chapter 2, on critical thinking, explains why critical thinking skills are important in today's informationoverloaded society, provides students with an explanation of key critical thinking skills, and models the use of the skills on a reading. The skills covered in this introductory chapter are picked up in the later essay modes chapters. In each of these chapters, a critical reading activity requires students to analyze the chapter's model essays using particular critical thinking skills.

▼ **Model Essays.** Each of the essay modes chapters has two model essays. The first is a student essay written in the five-paragraph essay structure on which the instruction is built. The second is a professionally written essay that departs from the five-paragraph structure and gives students exposure to less structured, but excellent, writing. All essays have been chosen not only for their technical merit but also because they are about high-interest topics.

▼ **Writing Technique Questions and Critical Reading Questions.** Each model essay in the chapters (as well as in the Additional Readings) is followed by a series of questions that help students analyze the techniques as well as the content of the essay.

▼ **More Topics for Writing.** At the end of each of the essay modes chapters are more suggested topics for essay writing. Students may choose a topic, or instructors may assign topics, as they prefer. In the more topics for writing activity, at least one of the choices is a photo on which an essay can be based.

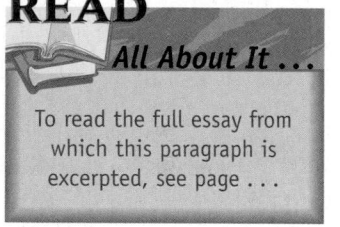

To read the full essay from which this paragraph is excerpted, see page . . .

▼ **Writing Checklists.** Writing checklists appear at the end of each of the essay mode chapters. These help students identify strategies and tasks needed to write an essay using that mode.

▼ **Read All About It.** Exercises in The Writer's Resources section are based on the readings that appear at the end of the text. An icon indicates the reading from which the exercise is excerpted so that students can refer to the complete essay for additional context.

The Teaching and Learning Package

Each component of the teaching and learning package has been crafted to ensure that the course is rewarding for instructors and students. In addition to the book-specific supplements discussed above, a series of other skills-based supplements is available for both instructors and students. All of these supplements are available either free or at greatly reduced prices.

For Instructors

Annotated Instructor's Edition This book is a replica of the student text, but it includes answers printed directly on the fill-in lines provided in the text. 0-321-06119-5.

Instructor's Manual with Transparency Masters. The Manual provides information on the following: *Using the Text, Syllabus Preparation, Answer Keys, Student and Professional Reading Selections, Thesis Sentences, Outlining, Proofreading Checklists, Peer Editing, English as a Second Language/English as a Foreign Language (ESL/EFL), Diagnostic Pre-Test, and Transparency Masters.* 0-321-06120-9.

Test Bank These tests provide a wealth of printed quizzes and additional practice exercises for each chapter in the text. The test bank is formatted in a way that simplifies copying and distribution. 0-321-06121-7.

Electronic Test Bank for Writing. The electronic test bank features more than 5,000 questions in all areas of writing, from grammar to paragraphing, through essay writing, research, and documentation. With this easy-to-use CD-ROM, instructors simply choose questions from the electronic test bank, then print the completed test for distribution. 0-321-08117-X. A printed version is also available.

Competency Profile Test Bank, Second Edition. This series of 60 objective tests covers ten general areas of English competency, including fragments, comma splices and run-ons, pronouns, commas, and capitalization. Each test is available in remedial, standard, and advanced versions. Available as reproducible sheets or in computerized versions. Free to instructors. Paper version: 0-321-02224-6. Computerized IBM: 0-321-02633-0. Computerized Mac: 0-321-02632-2.

Diagnostic and Editing Tests and Exercises, Seventh Edition. This collection of diagnostic tests helps instructors assess students' competence in Standard Written English for purpose of placement or to gauge progress. Available as reproducible sheets or in computerized versions, and free to instructors. Paper: 0-321-28041-5. CD-ROM: 0-321-28040-7.

CLAST Test Package, Fourth Edition. These two 40-item objective tests evaluate students' readiness for the CLAST exams. Strategies for teaching CLAST preparedness are included. Free with any Longman English title. Reproducible sheets: 0-321-01950-4. Computerized IBM version: 0-321-01982-2. Computerized Mac version: 0-321-01983-0.

TASP Test Package, Third Edition. These 12 practice pre-tests and post-tests assess the same reading and writing skills covered in the TASP examination. Free with any Longman English title. Reproducible sheets: 0-321-01959-8. Computerized IBM version: 0-321-01985-7. Computerized Mac version: 0-321-01984-9.

Teaching Online: Internet Research Conversation and Composition, Second Edition. Ideal for instructors who have never surfed the Net, this easy-to-follow guide offers basic definitions, numerous examples, and step-by-step information about finding and using Internet sources. Free to adopters. 0-321-01957-1.

ESL Worksheets, Third Edition. These reproducible worksheets provide ESL students with extra practice in areas they find the most troublesome. A diagnostic test and post-test are provided, along with answer keys and suggested topics for writing. Free to adopters. 0-321-07765-2.

For Students

Companion Website. The Companion Website to accompany *The Write Start: Paragraphs to Essays,* Second Edition (**http://www.ablongman.com/checkett**) offers chapter summaries, additional quizzes, readings, and Web-based activities for each chapter of the text. Students can also access annotated Web links to resources online to help further their studies.

The Longman Writer's Warehouse. The innovative and exciting online supplement is the perfect accompaniment to any developmental writing course. Developed by developmental English instructors specially for developing writers, The Writer's Warehouse covers every part of the writing process. Also included are journaling capabilities, multimedia activities, diagnostic tests, an interactive handbook, and a complete instructor's manual. The Writer's Warehouse requires no space on your school's server; rather, students complete and store their work on the Longman server and are able to access it, revise it, and continue working at any time. For more details about how to shrinkwrap a free subscription to The Writer's Warehouse with this text, please consult your Longman sales representative. For a free guided tour of the site, visit **http://longmanwriterswarehouse.com.**

www.myskillslab.com MySkillsLab opens the door to a world of dynamic multimedia resources and gives students all the multimedia solutions they'll need to develop reading and writing skills in one easy-to-use place. Here, students can gain access to Longman Writer's Warehouse, Reading Roadtrip, Exercise Zone, Research Navigator, Longman Vocabulary Website, Longman Study Skills Website, and Avoiding Plagiarism Tutorial. These tools allow students to practice grammar and usage, develop their reading skills, enhance their writing skills, improve their vocabulary, learn strategies to avoid plagiarism, develop their research skills, and learn strategies for college success.

The Dictionary Deal. Two dictionaries can be shrinkwrapped with *The Write Start* at a nominal fee. *The New American Webster Handy College Dictionary* is a paperback reference text with more than 100,000 entries. *Merriam Webster's Collegiate Dictionary*, tenth edition, is a hardback reference with a citation file of more than 14.5 million examples of English words drawn from actual use. For more information on how to shrinkwrap a dictionary with your text, please contact your Longman sales representative.

Newsweek Alliance. Instructors may choose to shrinkwrap a 12-week subscription to *Newsweek* with any Longman text. The price of the subscription is 59 cents per issue (a total of $7.08 for the subscription). Available with the subscription is a free "Interactive Guide to *Newsweek*"—a workbook for students who are using the text. In addition, *Newsweek* provides a wide variety of instructor supplements free to teachers, including maps, Skills Builders, and weekly quizzes. For more information on the *Newsweek* program, please contact your Longman sales representative.

Penguin Quality Paperback Titles. A series of Penguin paperbacks is available at a significant discount when shrinkwrapped with this text. Some titles available are Toni Morrison's *Beloved*, Julia Alvarez's *How the Garcia Girls Lost Their Accents*, Mark Twain's *Huckleberry Finn, Narrative of the Life of Frederick Douglass*, Harriet Beecher Stowe's *Uncle Tom's Cabin*, Dr. Martin Luther King, Jr.'s *Why We Can't Wait*, and plays by Shakespeare, Miller, and Albee. For a complete list of titles or more information, please contact your Longman sales consultant.

100 Things to Write About. This 100-page book contains 100 individual assignments for writing on a variety of topics and in a wide range of formats, from expressive to analytical. Ask your Longman sales representative for a sample copy. 0-673-98239-4.

Research Navigator Guide for English, H. Eric Branscomb & Linda R. Barr (Student/0-321-20277-5) Designed to teach students how to conduct high-quality online research and to document it properly, Research Navigator guides provide discipline-specific academic resources; in addition to helpful tips on the writing process, online research, and finding and citing valid sources. Free when packaged with any Longman text, Research Navigator guides include an access code to Research Navigator™, providing access to thousands of academic journals and periodicals, the NY Times Search by Subject Archive, Link Library, Library Guides, and more.

Longman Editing Exercises. Fifty-four pages of paragraph editing exercises give students extra practice using grammar skills in the context of longer passages. Free when packaged with any Longman title. 0-205-31792-8.

80 Practices. A collection of reproducible, ten-item exercises that provide additional practices for specific grammatical usage problems, such as comma splices, capitalization, and pronouns. Includes an answer key, and free to adopters. 0-673-53422-7.

The Longman Writer's Journal. This journal for writers, free with *The Write Start*, offers students a place to think, write, and react. For an examination copy, contact your Longman sales consultant. 0-321-08639-2.

The Longman Researcher's Journal. This journal for writers and researchers, free with this text, helps students plan, schedule, write, and revise their research project. An all-in-one resource for first-time researchers, the journal guides students gently through the research process. 0-321-09530-8.

A Guide for Peer Response, Second Edition. This guide offers students forms for peer critiques, including general guidelines and specific forms for different stages in the writing process. Also appropriate for freshman-level course. Free to adopters. 0-321-01948-2.

For Florida Adopters: Thinking Through the Test, by D. J. Henry. This special workbook, prepared specially for students in Florida, offers ample skill and practice exercises to help students prep for the Florida State Exit Exam. To shrinkwrap this workbook free with your textbook, please contact your Longman sales representative. Available in two versions: with and without answers. Also available: Two laminated grids (one for reading, one for writing) that can serve as handy references for students preparing for the Florida State Exit Exam.

For Texas Adopters: The Longman THEA Study Guide, by Jeannette Harris (Student/0-321-20271-6) Created specifically for students in Texas, this study guide includes straightforward explanations and numerous practice exercises to help students prepare for the reading and writing sections of THEA Test.

For New York Adopters: CUNY-ACT: Preparing for the CUNY-ACT, Reading and Writing Test, edited by Patricia Licklider (Student/0-321-19608-2) This booklet, prepared by reading and writing faculty from across the CUNY system, is designed to help students prepare for the CUNY-ACT exit test. It includes test taking tips, reading passages, typical exam questions, and sample writing prompts to help students become familiar with each portion of the test.

Acknowledgments

Thanks to everyone at Longman for their steadfast effort in bringing *The Write Start: Paragraphs to Essays* to life.

Our special thanks go to Senior Editor Steven Rigolosi, who shepherded the development of *The Write Start* series and who has moved on to other challenges, and a warm welcome and thanks to our new editor, Susan

Kunchandy. To our development editor, Marion Castellucci, we offer our praise and thanks. Her title is simply insufficient to describe the contributions she made to this text. Marion not only adds fresh approaches to age-old concepts, but her continued advice and creativity puts our initial ideas into a simple, clear, and comprehensible context. Having Marion as an editor is like having a third author. She has our unbounded gratitude.

To the staff at Longman . . . Kudos! Many thanks to Editorial Assistant Meegan Thompson, who sought the answers to all of our questions, even if the answers seemed obvious. A note of thanks to our Supplements Editor, Donna Campion, who kept her eye on a thousand details that make the text a whole, not just a series of unfinished and unrelated parts. And special thanks to Marketing Manager Melanie Craig.

As always, thanks to our students, who contributed paragraphs and essays to the text and whose special needs and superlative successes have kept us on our toes and given us immeasurable rewards.

We also owe many thanks to our colleagues and other devoted English instructors around the country who reviewed the text in all stages of its development. Thank you to all of the following for your corrections, advice, and spirited encouragement:

Cathryn Amdahl, Harrisburg Area Community College

Betty Bastankhah, San Jacinto College

Mary Anne Bernal, San Antonio College

Joseph Booker, Palo Alto College

Helen Chester, Milwaukee Area Technical College

Marianne Dzik, Illinois Valley Community College

Gene Fant, Mississippi College

Laura Gray-Rosendale, Northern Arizona University

Carlotta Hill, Oklahoma City Community College

Patsy A. Krech, University of Memphis

Irma Luna, San Antonio College

Judith McKenzie, Lane Community College

Margaret Murray, Western Connecticut State University

Raymond E. Mort, Oakland Community College

Andrew Nesset, Century College

Scottie Priesmeyer, St. Charles Community College

Linda C. Rollins, Motlow State Community College

Jennifer Scheidt, Palo Alto College

John N. Thornburg, San Jacinto College Central

Peter Van Leunen, St. Charles Community College

Suzanne Weisar, San Jacinto College South

Gayle Feng-Checkett
Lawrence Checkett

1 To the Student

As a college student, you face multiple demands each day, and writing is an integral part of most of these challenges. This book has been written to help you, the developing college writer, to reach your immediate and long-term goals. You have made the decision to go to college to learn the skills that will help you succeed in your learning, as well as help you secure a rewarding career. Whether or not you already know your career path, you will find that writing will play a large part in your successfully completing college work and in reaching your future work-related goals.

How This Book Can Help You Reach Your Goals

Good writing is hard, but good writing is achievable. People are not born good writers. With hard work, the right techniques, and helpful advice, you can master the skills of writing. This book will give you the tools, the strategies, and the advice that have been used successfully for years with students like you in classes just like yours.

This book will help you achieve your writing goals in the following ways.

▼ **By emphasizing the important link between reading and writing.** The student and professional essays in this book are used to model the writing techniques demonstrated in the instructional chapters. By understanding how these techniques are used in the readings, you will improve your own writing skills.

▼ **By helping you read and write with more depth and understanding through the use of critical thinking skills.** In Chapter 2, you will be introduced to the key critical thinking questions that will help you analyze and evaluate the information coming to you. Learning how to analyze what you read will help you improve your ability to communicate your own ideas to others. At the end of Chapters 7 through 15, you will find a number of writing opportunities based on critical thinking skill elements.

▼ **By introducing you to a variety of methods you can use to develop your ideas about specific topics.** Not every topic can best be developed using the same approach. One piece of information might be best presented by using definition, while another might be clarified using example, and another might be best explained by comparing or contrasting it to something else. In this book, you will be introduced to the traditional methods used for developing topics.

▼ **By teaching you a few techniques to develop a topic and write about it.** In Chapter 3, you will be introduced to the writing process: prewriting, drafting, revising, and proofreading. (1) Prewriting activities, such as brainstorming, clustering, and cubing, can help you develop subtopics to support your ideas concerning the main topic. For instance, you may want to write about investing (the main topic), but investing covers a lot of possible areas (the subtopics): investing for immediate income as opposed to investing for retirement, investing in stocks versus investing in bonds, or whether to do your own investing or let a brokerage firm do it for you. Prewriting activities will help you map out a variety of subtopics so that you can focus on those you think will best develop the main topic. (2) Drafting is the stage at which you write the first, rough version of your paragraph or essay. You write the draft to get your ideas down, however roughly. (3) Revising techniques can help you sharpen what you want to say, better organize and develop your thoughts, and express your ideas more clearly. You can revise at any time during the writing process. (4) Proofreading, however, takes place after you have written the final draft. When proofreading, you correct errors of misspellings, punctuation, poor word choice, and grammar. These distract from clear content and presentation.

▼ **By demonstrating how the different parts of an essay are written.** In Chapters 4 through 6, we will model the writing process using the introductory, body, and concluding paragraphs of an essay. This will help you get an overview of how an essay is written.

▼ **By showing you how to make the transition from writing the paragraph to writing the longer essay.** In Chapters 7 through 15, you will be introduced to different methods of developing a topic. At the start of each chapter, the method will be explained using the paragraph as the instructional model. The paragraph is used because it is short but still enables us to illustrate the key concepts of the method under discussion. Once the basic elements and techniques are demonstrated, the transition to a longer unit of writing, the essay, follows.

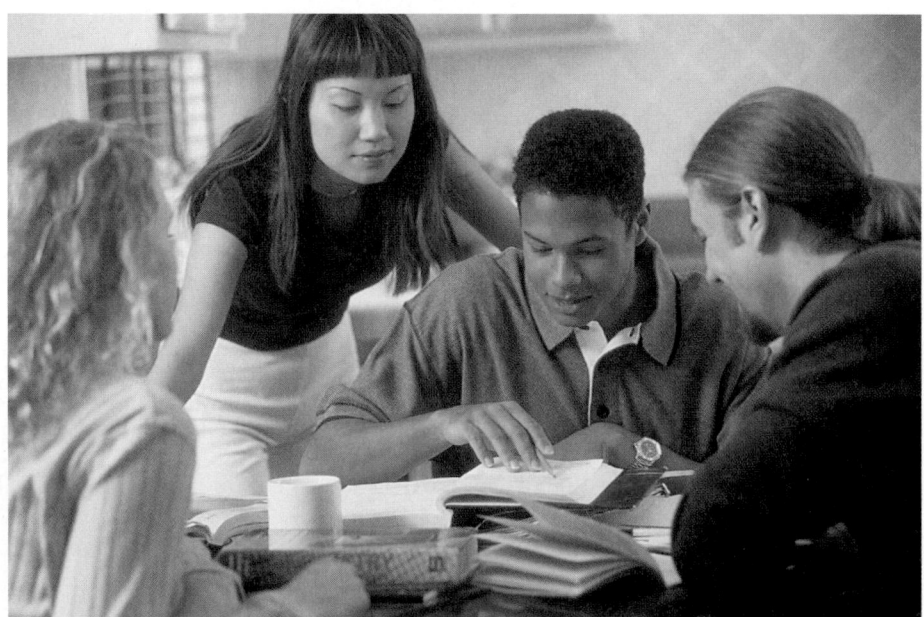

▼ **By helping you present your thoughts more professionally, using good grammar, punctuation, and sentence structure.** Constructing logical and reasonable content is only half of the writing process. The other half has to do with proper presentation. For instance, you might have the most talented mind in the world, but if you show up at a job interview wearing torn jeans and a shirt with food stains all over it, having unwashed and uncombed hair, and with a cigarette hanging out of the side of your mouth, you are not likely to get the job. You may have the right content, but your presentation is wrong. So it is with writing. If you have too many errors in punctuation or mechanics, your writing will not be successful, no matter how good the content is. The Writer's Resources at the end of the book is a complete guide to correct grammar, punctuation, and usage. It also contains information and helpful techniques for students whose first language is not English.

Writing Can Be Learned

People in academia and the business world view writing skills as essential, yet they have a growing concern about the writing abilities of the graduates they hire and work with. Teachers and executives have the same need for excellent communication skills on the part of their students and employees—to foster increased productivity and enhanced performance. Whether it is a term paper or a business report you are asked to complete, good writing skills are a necessity. This book will help you establish and maintain the skills necessary for good writing. Once again, writing is a skill that can be learned with practice and dedication. In this way, good writing is no different from any other skill you want to learn and improve upon. There is an old joke that captures the essence of this undertaking:

> A person carrying a violin case and walking along a street in New York City stops another person walking by and asks, "Excuse me, but how do I get to Carnegie Hall?" The second person answers sternly, "Practice, practice, practice."

Visit *The Write Start* Online!

For additional practice with the materials found in this chapter, visit our Website at

http://www.ablongman.com/checkett

The Website also features additional readings, quizzes, writing activities, and Internet links, as well as a bulletin board and interactive chat.

2 Critical Thinking: The Connection Between Reading and Writing

You often will be asked to write about a topic you have studied. In the academic world, this is the most common form of communication you will have with your instructors. However, before you can write about what you have learned and the conclusions you have come to, you first must think critically about what you have heard, read, observed, listened to, or discussed. An effective way to start the **critical thinking** process is to ask yourself some questions about the material you are reading.

The point of asking questions about the material you are exploring is so you do not blindly accept the opinions and conclusions of others. Every person and organization has an agenda with which you may or may not agree. It is necessary to understand the points of view of others in order to evaluate their arguments and conclusions. Once you have analyzed the points of view of others, you are in a better position to reach your own conclusions.

Questions for Thinking Critically

To assess a piece of information critically, ask the following four critical thinking questions. By doing so, you will come to a better understanding of why you are convinced or unconvinced by the material's point of view or conclusions. The critical thinking questions also will help you identify the major strengths and weaknesses of the material.

1. **What is the main idea?** The **main idea** is the writer's basic approach to the subject matter. The main idea is the most important aspect of the essay; it is the problem to be solved or the issue being raised for consideration. In an essay about the topic of national I.D. cards, for example, the main idea might be that the United States should consider issuing I.D. cards to residents. You can usually find the topic and main idea in the first paragraph of an essay.

2. **What conclusions are reached regarding the main idea?** The writer's conclusions might include steps to solve the problem or possibilities that might lead to a solution. In the national I.D. card essay, the writer might conclude that national I.D. cards would be useful because they would help combat crime and terrorism.

3. **What reasons or evidence does the writer give to support the conclusions?** *Reasons* is another word for *evidence*. Evidence can be personal

experience; the experiences of others; the ideas of experts regarding the topic; statistics; or information from articles, magazines, journals, books, lectures, videos, or other sources.

4. **Are the reasons or evidence fact or opinion?** Generally, *fact* is distinguished from *opinion* in the following way. Facts are accepted as *true*. Water freezes at 0° Celsius or 32° Fahrenheit—this is a fact. It cannot be disputed. That the United States is a member of the United Nations (UN) is also a fact in the same way. However, *opinions* are interpretations of the facts. While it is a fact that the United States is a member of the UN, is its membership positive or negative for you personally, for the nation as a whole, or for the international community? Do you think the United States' membership costs too much for the results produced? Should other countries bear more of the UN's operating costs? Do small nations have too much voice in UN decisions? While we all agree that it is a fact that the United States is a member of the UN, we will have a variety of opinions about whether that fact is good or bad.

Applying the Critical Thinking Questions

To help you see how asking the critical thinking questions work, we have provided an example. First, read the following excerpt from a student essay. Then, read through the brief model analysis that uses the four critical thinking questions.

▼
Sample Student Essay: ARE TWO MILLION AMERICAN INMATES TOO MANY?

Tom Weidemann

The following is an excerpt from an essay by student writer Tom Weidemann. In the essay, Tom is concerned with how the U.S. criminal justice system deals with people found guilty of committing minor drug-related crimes.   ⎤ main idea

Are Two Million American Inmates Too Many?

1   Crime has always been one of society's major concerns, as have the ways to deal with it. According to a report from the Government Accounting Office (GAO), as of February 15, 2000, an estimated two million Americans were doing jail time in the American penal system. And the number is increasing each year. The cost of housing, feeding, guarding, and providing medical care for inmates is spiraling upward. Columnist Neal Janny, in an article appearing in the editorial section of the Denver Post, states, "America has the largest prison population in the world, and an inordinate number of the prison population is comprised of black males serving time for minor drug-related crimes." Janny concludes that there is something dreadfully wrong when a wealthy, well-educated society handles a problem in such a ham-fisted and shortsighted way. Michael Cartine, in his book Mindless Revenge, explains,

"While black males represent only 5–6 percent of the American population, they represent 50 percent of the prison population." This kind of disproportionate outcome should be a flashing danger signal to all Americans and to the leaders of our judicial and penal systems. It is time to recognize that our society is wasting money and potentially productive lives by the way it handles criminals convicted of minor drug-related crimes. Imprisoning petty crooks is too costly and does little to change the adverse effects caused by both the crime and the incarceration.

2   Some people believe that placing small-time drug dealers in prison is a way to ensure the safety of the general public. They believe that it is necessary to separate criminals from society for the common good. In Sheila Adkins' article, "The Wrong Sentence," appearing in the journal American Prison Quarterly, she explains that both Japan and China have effectively reduced the drug problems in their countries by arresting and re-educating, not arresting and imprisoning, drug users and, thereby, ending the vicious supply and demand circle. Our prisons have not done a good job in rehabilitating inmates. Most inmates, after being paroled, return to prison within a short time. Adkins' solution is, then, one that should merit society's attention. America can help solve some of its drug problems by decriminalizing minor drug-related crimes and focusing on rehabilitating rather than imprisoning those found guilty of minor drug-related offenses. Decriminalization and rehabilitation would lower the cost of operating our penal system. It also would lead to a lower crime rate. Re-educating petty criminals also would deliver productive and law-abiding citizens rather than recycling yet another batch of criminals whose actions are to society's detriment.

Model Critical Thinking Analysis of "Are Two Million American Inmates Too Many?"

1. What is the main idea?

The topic of the essay is the treatment of people who commit minor drug-related crimes. In this case, there are several ideas in the opening paragraph.

The main idea is the one that specifies the essay's purpose. For instance, in the preceding excerpt, the paragraph begins with a broad concept, *Crime*, in the first sentence; moves to a more specific idea in the fourth sentence, *The cost of housing, feeding, guarding, and providing medical care for inmates is spiraling upward*; and finishes in the second to last sentence with the most specific and focused statement, one that announces a purpose, and, therefore, is the main idea: *It is time to recognize the fact that our society is wasting money and potentially productive lives by the way it handles criminals convicted of minor drug-related crimes.* The rest of the essay, then, will give the reader information on how society can save money and generate more productive lives by changing how it treats petty criminals convicted of minor drug-related crimes.

2. What conclusions are reached regarding the main idea?

One conclusion is stated in the second to last sentence of the first paragraph, that *society is wasting money and potentially productive lives by the way it handles criminals convicted of minor drug-related offenses;* other conclusions are found in paragraph 2, sentence 4, *Our prisons have not done a good job in rehabilitating inmates;* sentence 7, *America can help solve some of its drug problems by decriminalizing minor drug-related crimes and focusing on rehabilitating rather than imprisoning those found guilty of minor drug-related offenses;* sentence 8, *Decriminalization and rehabilitation would lower the cost of operating our penal system;* and sentence 9, *It also would lead to a lower crime rate;* and sentence 10, *Re-educating petty criminals also would deliver productive and law-abiding citizens rather than recycling yet another batch of criminals whose actions are to society's detriment.*

3. What reasons or evidence does the writer give to support the conclusions?

The evidence in paragraph 1 includes sentence 2, *an estimated two million Americans were doing jail time;* sentence 3, *the number* [of inmates] *is increasing each year;* sentence 4, *The cost of housing, feeding, guarding, and providing medical care for inmates is spiraling upward;* sentence 5, *the prison population is comprised of black males serving time for minor drug-related crimes;* and sentence 7, *While black males represent only 5–6 percent of the American population, they represent 50 percent of the prison population.*

The evidence in paragraph 2 includes sentence 3, *both Japan and China have effectively reduced the drug problems in their countries by arresting and re-educating, not arresting and imprisoning, drug users and, thereby, ending the vicious supply and demand circle;* and sentence 5, *Most inmates, after being paroled, return to prison within a short time.*

4. Are the reasons or evidence fact or opinion?

All of the evidence is factual. In paragraph 1, sentences 2, 3, and 4, the source of the evidence is the Government Accounting Office (GAO), not the author's opinion; in sentence 5, the source is a newspaper columnist, a professional expected to gather such evidence from reliable sources, not from personal opinion; in sentence 7, the evidence comes from a book and is statistical and, therefore, most probably taken from a study or survey done by a reputable organization; and, in paragraph 2, sentence 3, the information comes from a journal article and indicates an objective source other than the author's opinion. Finally, in sentence 7, the evidence is statistical in nature, and most likely was taken from a source other than the author's opinion.

Note that even if the source of factual evidence is not stated in the essay or references, it is still presumed that the author can produce the source if necessary. To make up information as if it came from a reliable source or to be unable to document factual evidence is considered a serious error in writing.

Finally, ask yourself how convincing are the evidence and conclusions in supporting the main idea. The answer to this question will vary from reader to reader, but you should examine all the information with this purpose in mind.

Using the four critical thinking questions will enable you to critically analyze information with depth and clarity, and it will allow you to communicate your thoughts about an essay clearly and confidently.

Questions for Thinking Critically

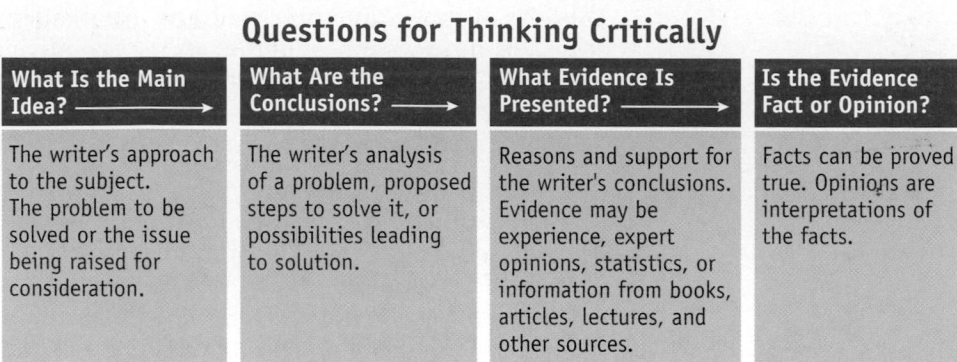

What Is the Main Idea? →	What Are the Conclusions? →	What Evidence Is Presented? →	Is the Evidence Fact or Opinion?
The writer's approach to the subject. The problem to be solved or the issue being raised for consideration.	The writer's analysis of a problem, proposed steps to solve it, or possibilities leading to solution.	Reasons and support for the writer's conclusions. Evidence may be experience, expert opinions, statistics, or information from books, articles, lectures, and other sources.	Facts can be proved true. Opinions are interpretations of the facts.

▼ Sample Professional Essay: DESIGNER BABIES

Sharon Begley

> In the following essay, *Newsweek* writer Sharon Begley looks at one of the potential consequences stemming from the Human Genome Project (the effort to map the genetic makeup of humans). What she finds is a disturbing possibility that may affect the very nature of evolution.

Vocabulary
Before you begin reading, look up the definitions of the following terms that appear in the essay. The number in parentheses after each term indicates the paragraph in which the term appears.

anecdotal (6)	eradicate (7)	presto (5)
bequeathed (2)	gene (1)	protocol (6)
chromosome (1)	insinuate (6)	quirk (4)
disposition (3)	in vitro fertilization (1)	Rubicon (2)
embryo (1)	momentous (2)	

Designer Babies

1   It is only a matter of time. One day—a day probably no more distant than the first wedding anniversary of a couple who are now teenage sweethearts—a man and a woman will walk into an in vitro fertilization clinic and make scientific history. Their problem won't be infertility, the reason couples

now choose IVF. Rather, they will be desperate for a very special child, a child who will elude a family curse. To create their dream child, doctors will fertilize a few of the woman's eggs with her husband's sperm, as IVF clinics do today. But then they will inject an artificial human chromosome, carrying made-to-order genes like pearls on a string, into the fertilized egg. One of the genes will carry instructions ordering cells to commit suicide. Then the doctors will place the embryo into the woman's uterus. If her baby is a boy, when he becomes an old man he, like his father and grandfather before him, will develop prostate cancer. But the cell-suicide gene will make his prostate cells self-destruct. The man, unlike his ancestors, will not die of the cancer. And since the gene that the doctors gave him copied itself into every cell of his body, including his sperm, his sons will beat prostate cancer, too.

2   Genetic engineers are preparing to cross what has long been an ethical Rubicon. Since 1990, gene therapy has meant slipping a healthy gene into the cells of one organ of a patient suffering from a genetic disease. Soon, it may mean something much more momentous: altering a fertilized egg so that genes in all of a person's cells, including eggs or sperm, also carry a gene that scientists, not parents, bequeathed them. When the pioneers of gene therapy first requested government approval for their experiments in 1987, they vowed they would *never* alter patients' eggs or sperm. That was then. This is now. One of those pioneers, Dr. W. French Anderson of the University of Southern California, recently put the National Institutes of Health on notice. Within two or three years, he said, he would ask approval to use gene therapy on a fetus that has been diagnosed with a deadly inherited disease. The therapy would cure the fetus before it is born. But the introduced genes, though targeted at only blood or immune-system cells, might inadvertently slip into the child's egg (or sperm) cells, too. If that happens, the genetic change would affect that child's children unto the nth generation. "Life would enter a new phase," says biophysicist Gregory Stock of UCLA, "one in which we seize control of our own evolution."

3   Judging by the 70 pages of public comments NIH has received since Anderson submitted his proposal in September, the overwhelming majority of scientists and ethicists weighing in oppose gene therapy that changes the "germline" (eggs and sperm). But the position could be a boulevard wide and paper thin. "There is a great divide in the bioethics community over whether we should be opening up this Pandora's box," says science-policy scholar Sheldon Krimsky of Tufts University. Many bioethicists are sympathetic to using germline therapy to shield a child from a family disposition to cancer, or atherosclerosis or other illness with a strong genetic component. As James Watson, president of the Cold Spring Harbor Laboratory and codiscoverer of the double-helical structure of DNA, said at a recent UCLA conference, "We might as well do what we finally can to take the threat of Alzheimer's or breast cancer away from a family." But something else is suddenly making it OK to discuss the once forbidden possibility of germline engineering: molecular biologists now think they have clever ways to circumvent ethical concerns that engulf this sci-fi idea.

4   There may be ways, for instance, to design a baby's genes without violating the principle of informed consent. This is the belief that no one's genes—not even an embryo's—should be altered without his or her permission. Presumably few people would object to being spared a fatal disease. But what about genes for personality traits, like risk-taking or being neurotic? If you like today's blame game—it's *Mom's fault* that you inherited her temper—you'll love tomorrow's: she intentionally stuck you with that personality quirk. But the child of tomorrow might have the final word about his genes,

says UCLA geneticist John Campbell. The designer gene for, say, patience could be paired with an on-off switch, he says. The child would have to take a drug to activate the patience gene. Free to accept or reject the drug, he retains informed consent over his genetic endowment.

5 There may also be ways to make an end run around the worry that is wrong to monkey with human evolution. Researchers are experimenting with tricks to make the introduced gene self-destruct in cells that become eggs or sperm. That would confine the tinkering to one generation. Then, if it became clear that eliminating genes for, say mental illness also erased genes for creativity, that loss would not become a permanent part of man's genetic blueprint. (Of course, preventing the new gene's transmission to future generations would also defeat the hope of permanently lopping off a diseased branch from a family tree.) In experiments with animals, geneticist Mario Capecchi of the University of Utah has designed a string of genes flanked by the molecular version of scissors. The scissors are activated by an enzyme that would be made only in the cells that become eggs or sperm. Once activated, the genetic scissors snip out the introduced gene and, presto, it is not passed along to future generations. "What I worry about," says Capecchi, "is that if we start messing around with [eggs and sperm], at some point—since this is a human enterprise—we're going to make a mistake. You want a way to undo that mistake. And since what may seem terrific now may seem naive in 20 years, you want a way to make the genetic change reversible."

6 There is no easy technological fix for another ethical worry, however; with germline engineering only society's "haves" will control their genetic traits. It isn't hard to foresee a day like that painted in last year's film "Gattaca," where only the wealthy can afford to genetically engineer their children with such "killer applications" as intelligence, beauty, long life or health. "If you are going to disadvantage even further those who are already disadvantaged," says bioethicist Ruth Macklin of Albert Einstein College of Medicine, "then that does raise serious concerns." But perhaps not enough to keep designer babies solely in Hollywood's imagination. For one thing, genetic therapy as done today (treating one organ of one child or adult) has been a bitter disappointment. "With the exception of a few anecdotal cases," says USC's Anderson, "there is no evidence of a gene-therapy protocol that helps." But germline therapy might actually be easier. Doctors would not have to insinuate the new gene into millions of lung cells in, say, a cystic fibrosis patient. They could manipulate only a single cell—the fertilized egg—and still have the gene reach every cell of the person who develops from that egg.

7 How soon might we design our children? The necessary pieces are quickly falling into place. The first artificial human chromosome was created last year. The Human Genome Project decoded all 3 billion chemical letters that spell out our 70,000 or so genes. Animal experiments designed to show that the process will not create horrible mutants are underway. No law prohibits germline engineering. Although NIH now refuses to even consider funding proposals for it, the rules are being updated. And where there is a way, there will almost surely be a will: none of us, says USC's Anderson, "wants to pass on to our children lethal genes if we can prevent it—that's what's going to drive this." At the UCLA symposium on germline engineering, two-thirds of the audience supported it. Few would argue against using the technique to eradicate a disease that has plagued a family for generations. As Tuft's Krimsky says, "We know where to start." The harder question is this: do we know where to stop?

▼ **PRACTICE**   **Using the Critical Thinking Questions to Evaluate "Designer Babies"**

1. What is the main idea?

_____

_____

_____

2. What conclusions are reached regarding the main idea?

_____

_____

_____

_____

_____

_____

_____

3. What are the reasons or evidence given to support the conclusions?

_____

_____

_____

_____

_____

_____

4. Are the reasons or evidence fact or opinion?

_____

_____

_____

_____

_____

Critical Reading Questions

At the end of each essay in Chapters 7 through 15 and the Additional Readings, you will find a set of Critical Reading Questions based on the critical thinking questions you have studied in this chapter: main idea, conclusions, reasons or evidence, and the nature of the reasons or evidence (fact or opinion). By answering the critical reading questions, you will improve your reading comprehension and thinking abilities, and your writing will become clearer and more meaningful.

CHAPTER REVIEW

▼ It's important to think critically about what you are reading so you can evaluate the point of view and conclusions of the writer.

▼ There are four main questions to ask when reading critically: (1) What is the main idea? (2) What conclusions are reached regarding the main idea? (3) What reasons or evidence does the writer give to support the conclusions? (4) Are the reasons or evidence fact or opinion?

▼ The topic is the subject matter of the essay. The main idea is the writer's basic point about the subject matter. Both are often found in the first paragraph of an essay.

▼ Conclusions about the main idea need to be supported by sound evidence and reasons.

▼ Evidence and reasons can be fact-based (accepted as true) or opinions (interpretations that may or may not be sound).

▼ Your evaluation of an essay's conclusions is based on your answers to the four critical thinking questions.

Visit *The Write Start* Online!

For additional practice with the materials found in this chapter, visit our Website at

http://www.ablongman.com/checkett

The Website also features additional readings, quizzes, writing activities, and Internet links, as well as a bulletin board and interactive chat.

Getting Started: The Fundamentals

While sentences are good for expressing short pieces of information, a longer format is necessary for longer, more developed ideas. The following four chapters will enable you to understand and write the basic paragraphs that make up an even longer format called the essay. Writing paragraphs is good practice, because paragraphs contain many of the elements you will find in longer pieces of writing, such as letters, reports, essays, and research papers.

Prewriting, Drafting, Revising, and Proofreading

When you begin writing a paragraph or essay, you should consider what needs to be done prior to drafting the paragraph or essay you hand in. In Chapter 3, with a few short examples, we will explain the **prewriting** strategies for getting started, the **drafting** stages, the need for **revising** to take your rough drafts to a final draft, and **proofreading** techniques that remove any technical errors in the finished draft.

After you have studied the short prewriting, drafting, revising, and proofreading examples in Chapter 3, you can follow an entire essay being written using these techniques in Chapters 4 through 6 as you study the introductory, body, and concluding paragraphs.

The Paragraph

A paragraph consists of a number of sentences that develop a single idea called a **topic**. In fact, you are reading a paragraph right now, and its topic is "the paragraph." Four to eight sentences is the length of most paragraphs, although they can be as short or as long as the topic or assignment demands. A good paragraph is long enough to develop the topic adequately but no longer.

On the page, a paragraph is formatted like this:

▼ The first sentence of a paragraph should be indented five spaces, or one tab stop.

▼ Each line of the paragraph should begin at the left margin, but each line does not have to end exactly at the right margin. Your computer will automatically adjust end of line spacing for you.

▼ If the last word of a line comes before the right margin, leave the remainder of the line blank.

Types of Sentences in Paragraphs

There are two basic types of sentences in a paragraph: the **topic sentence** and **support sentences.** The topic sentence tells the reader what the main idea, or topic, of the paragraph is. Although there is no set place in the paragraph for the topic sentence, making the topic sentence the first sentence in the paragraph will help you organize and develop the topic. The topic sentence is followed by support sentences that explain, clarify, and define the topic by using specific detail. Support sentences should demonstrate a variety of styles to show the relationship between the various pieces of information and to create rhythm.

To summarize the characteristics and elements of a paragraph:

▼ A topic sentence announces one main idea (the topic).

▼ Support sentences use specific details to develop the topic.

▼ Sentence variety connects related ideas and adds rhythm.

Let's look at an example paragraph that exhibits the characteristics and elements you have been reading about.

Example Paragraph

Edward Kennedy "Duke" Ellington was an American composer, pianist, and conductor greatly admired for bringing jazz from nightclubs into mainstream concert halls. "Sophisticated Lady" and "Mood Indigo" were two of his most famous shorter jazz pieces, but his longer compositions, such as *Paris Blues* and *Far East Suite*, were styled after the classical concerto form, modified for his jazz stylizations. This creativity led to appearances on radio and television, in theaters and nightclubs, and on worldwide tours. Even though Duke Ellington was so prolific, his music won critical acclaim worldwide.

▼ The first sentence is the topic sentence, and it announces the main idea of the paragraph (Duke Ellington) and what specific information will be used in the support sentences to explore the main idea. The specific support information also can be called the **controlling idea** (Ellington was greatly admired for his ability to make jazz appreciated by the mainstream public).

▼ The following three support sentences develop the topic and controlling idea by naming his most famous compositions (sentence 2), by explaining that critics and the public enjoyed his music (sentences 3 and 4), and by giving the vast numbers of venues in which he played his music (sentence 3).

▼ The sentences also exhibit variety. The second sentence is coordinated with the conjunction **but**; it also contains extra information between two commas. The third sentence is a simple sentence. The fourth sentence is subordinated by using an introductory dependent clause preceding the independent clause.

The Essay

Effective paragraph writing is useful for short pieces of communication, such as memos, short-answer exams, and brief writing assignments, but many business reports and longer college writing assignments require multiple paragraphs to explain many ideas.

Just as sentences are joined together to make paragraphs, paragraphs are used to make longer pieces of writing, including the **essay.** An essay is a number of related paragraphs that develop a particular topic. Essays can be developed using many of the techniques for developing the paragraph.

Although an essay can have any number of paragraphs, this book will use the five-paragraph model to introduce the basic elements of the essay.

The Essay Title

Almost all essays should have a title, one that should pique the reader's interest. It should be a catchy or dramatic phrase, usually comprising two to six words. Longer titles can become wordy and cumbersome to read. If you cannot come up with something clever or dramatic, use the main idea as your title. It's a good idea to wait until your essay is finished before you create a title. In that way, you give yourself enough time to fully understand the point of your essay and create the most appropriate title for it.

When writing your title, do the following:

▼ Capitalize all words except articles (a, an, the) and prepositions (of, on, to, in) unless the article or preposition is the first word of the title. First words of titles are always capitalized.

▼ Center the title on the page and leave two line spaces between it and the introductory paragraph.

Essay Elements

Most essays begin with the **introductory paragraph.** Its purpose is to introduce the reader to the topic of the essay. The paragraph consists of **introductory sentences** and the **thesis statement.** The purpose of introductory sentences (sometimes called "lead-in sentences") is to create a context that makes the topic interesting or important. The thesis statement clarifies the specific subject matter to be explored, and it gives the writer's attitude about the topic. The thesis statement also may outline how the subject will be explored by including an optional organizational idea, often called an "essay map" (a series of subtopics that will be used in the body paragraphs to explore the main topic).

After the introductory paragraph come the **body paragraphs.** Their purpose is to develop, support, and explain the topic idea stated in the thesis statement. Body paragraphs consist of a **topic sentence** followed by **support sentences.**

The essay ends with the **concluding paragraph.** Its purpose is to bring the essay to a conclusion that gives the reader a sense of completeness.

These essay elements will be discussed in detail in Chapters 4 through 6. Chapter 4 discusses the introductory paragraph, Chapter 5 discusses body paragraphs, and Chapter 6 discusses the concluding paragraph.

Audience

Before writing an essay, you should think about your **audience,** for whom you are writing. In college, you will almost always be writing for your professor. However, you also may be writing for other members of the class if peer reading and assessment is part of the assignment. In some cases, you will be writing for your employer, for someone in a company with which you want to do business, for members of a club to which you belong, or for a select group having special interest in your topic. Depending on your intended audience, you should think about the type, depth, and presentation of the information you want to include in your work. Consider the following points:

1. How much specific knowledge does your audience have about the topic?

For example, if you are writing about a new computer program, ask yourself how much your audience knows about computers. If you are writing for a group of novices—people who may not yet have a computer or have just recently purchased one—the information you provide will be very basic, and you will use simple wording and plenty of definitions for unfamiliar terms and, perhaps, many examples to illustrate what you mean. Conversely, if your audience is a group of computer programmers, who work every day with computer programs in a variety of applications, you will likely omit basic concepts that they are likely to know. Your word choices can be more sophisticated, and you will most likely use only a few examples to clarify information.

2. How much persuading do you need to do?

For instance, does the audience you are writing for agree or disagree with your ideas? If you know they agree with your position, typically you will use information that will assure them that their beliefs are acceptable. Your task is easy as long as you keep your audience comfortable and feeling good about themselves. You are, in essence, "preaching to the choir." If, however, you know that your audience disagrees or is uncomfortable with your topic, then your job becomes much tougher. You will need to present information to reduce the level of negative emotion and bias. You might want to begin by offering an olive branch to your audience. Instead of being confrontational—telling them in effect, that it is "your way or the highway"—you might concede that theirs is a legitimate point of view, and that people of good will can disagree without being disagreeable. In this way, you diffuse some of the opposition to your ideas before you actually dig into the substance of your position. Most often, you will never turn an audience completely to your side of things. However, if you can at least convince them to listen, to give you a reasonable hearing, you have done as much as you can do with a short piece of communication.

Unity

Unity means that each paragraph's topic sentence supports an essay's thesis statement, and each support sentence within a paragraph supports the paragraph's topic sentence. Ideas other than those that help develop, support, or clarify the topic and subtopics in the writing may not be introduced.

Example of a Paragraph without Unity

(1) When a space shuttle catastrophe occurs, funding of NASA's space program is threatened. (2) Many Americans consider space travel too dangerous, and they do not want Congress to

fund such programs. (3) Many members of Congress agree that the cost of manned space travel is too expensive, in terms of both money and loss of life. (4) Some astronauts come from the ranks of teachers. (5) When a crew of astronauts is lost in a tragic accident, the intense, widespread media coverage causes many viewers to have a negative emotional response toward NASA. (6) Opponents of space exploration use the incident and the emotional response as evidence that funding should be stopped.

The first sentence, the topic sentence, states the main idea: *space shuttle accidents threaten NASA funding.* The remainder of the support sentences in the paragraph must support this idea. Other ideas may not be introduced. Sentence number 4, then, should be removed from the paragraph because it does not develop, support, or clarify the main idea in the topic sentence.

▼ PRACTICE 1   Paragraph Unity

Read the following paragraph. If the paragraph is not unified, identify on the line provided the number of the sentence or sentences in the paragraph that should be removed.

(1) Owning guns should be illegal because they cause too much death. (2) Guns kill over 11,000 people each year in the United States. (3) There are more than 200 million guns held privately in America. (4) Men and women in the Armed Forces train regularly with firearms. (5) Polls suggest that almost everyone agrees the numbers of firearms should be reduced and stricter gun laws enforced. (6) Great Britain, for example, has very strict gun laws, and there are fewer than 100 gun-related deaths per year. (7) Some guns are specially made for buyers who keep them in expensive gun showcases. (8) Firearms should be treated as any other consumer product because most gun-related deaths occur between people who know each other. (9) As the saying goes, "Guns don't kill people. People kill people."

Coherence

Coherence means that the ideas expressed in your writing are presented so that the content is clear and convincing. Coherence keeps readers moving from idea to idea, keeps them focused on relevant information, and presents ideas with clarity and precision. Your thoughts should not be presented chaotically, in a random and confusing manner. Generally, you can order ideas by **time, space,** and **importance.**

Time Order

Time order means that ideas are arranged chronologically, either past to present or present to past. The time can be given in seconds, minutes, hours, days, weeks, months, years, decades, or centuries. Additionally, time can be divided into transitional expressions, such as "morning," "afternoon," and "evening," or with phrases such as "before breakfast," "after lunch," and "during dinner." "First," "second," "third," and "then," "next," and "finally" also are useful time-ordering transitional expressions. The important concept to remember is that presenting material in chronological order reduces the possibility of confusion.

Example of Poor Time Order

In the following paragraph, instructions for diffusing a bomb are given.

First, unscrew the nose cone. Second, remove the plastic housing covering the clock mechanism. Third, identify the black button with the red wire attached and the red button with the black wire attached. Fourth, press the black button. Fifth, before pressing the black button, make certain you first cut the black wire attached to the red button . . .

OUCH! You never got to instruction number 5! Instructions 4 and 5 should have been reversed. Using proper time order can be *extremely* important.

▼ **PRACTICE 2** | **Time Order**

To explain how to use an ATM for a cash withdrawal, arrange the following list in the proper sequence by numbering each item from 1 to 9.

_____ Remove cash

_____ Select Amount of Withdrawal

_____ Enter PIN Number

_____ Remove Card

_____ Select "Debit" or "Credit"

_____ Remove Receipt

_____ Insert Card

_____ Do You Want Another Transaction: Press "Yes" or "No"

_____ Select "Deposit" or "Withdrawal"

▼ **PRACTICE 3** | **Writing a Paragraph in Time Order**

Using the steps in Practice 2 that you have placed in chronological order, write a paragraph using transitional expressions to connect the steps in the process.

Space Order

If you describe a person, place, or thing from inside to outside, from back to front, from top to bottom, from right to left, and so on, you are using **space order.** Describing details about a subject using space order is very much like the experience of an audience watching a movie as the camera explores various people or places. The following paragraph is written with space order. It describes a house from outside to inside.

> ### Example of Space Order
>
> Whenever I think of the house I grew up in, I always envision myself coming home after school. The wooden gate in the front yard always squeaked when I pushed it. As I walked toward the porch, I skipped over each crack in the sidewalk because stepping on a crack was always considered bad luck. The smell of freshly baked cookies beyond the expanse of green lawn guided me up the porch steps, across the freshly painted wooden boards, and through the screen door with six small holes caused by my misplaced bow and arrow practice. My mouth was already watering by the time I stepped into the hallway. As I dropped my books on the hall table, I could hear sounds of my mother cooking in the kitchen. After passing through the living room in the center of the house, I would watch cartoons for a half hour in the den at the rear of the house. This is how I passed many a weekday afternoon after school in the warm comfort of my house.

In this paragraph, the writer describes his house by moving through it from outside to inside, from front to back. The space order follows a path from the front gate to the back den. The space order transitional expressions "front," "beyond," "across," "center," and "rear" assist the reader in following the journey.

▼ **PRACTICE 4** | **Writing a Paragraph Using Space Order**

Write a paragraph using space order. The paragraph can describe a person, a place, or a thing. Select a topic that interests you. Familiarity will help you select details and their arrangement. Use transitional expressions that enhance the details that you use.

Order of Importance

By beginning your writing with the most important point and finishing with the least important point, you are arranging your ideas by **order of importance.**

Example of Order of Importance

Many profound differences exist between upper management and middle management in terms of compensation. The most important difference is salary. While upper management salaries are generally six figures, middle managers usually do not break that barrier. The next factor is portfolio compensation. Most middle management must rely on company pension plans and IRAs for retirement, but upper management can increase retirement income with stock options, sick leave accrual buyouts, and post-employment "consulting" fees. Finally, middle management, after retirement, must find private health insurance, which is expensive and normally does not offer the same coverage as the plans they had with the company. In contrast, upper management is often given "paid for" policies for life, often including long-term and catastrophic coverage.

In this paragraph, the three ideas of importance are presented from most important to least important: salary, retirement compensation, and health insurance. The order of importance transitional expressions—"most important," "less likely," "next," and "finally"—help the reader connect ideas and move smoothly from one idea to the next.

You also can arrange ideas from least important to most important. The effect can be dramatic because the intensity builds to a climax.

PRACTICE 5   Rewriting a Paragraph Using Order of Importance

Rewrite the paragraph about upper and middle management compensation by reversing the order of importance from least important to most important. You will have to replace or move some of the transitional expressions to fit the new arrangement. After you have finished, compare the two paragraphs. Which do you think is the more powerful or convincing order?

3 The Writing Process

Ask almost any writer what is the hardest part of the writing process and the typical response will be "Getting started!" You've probably had problems getting started with some of your own writing assignments. Coming up with a topic is usually easy enough, but deciding what to write and how to say it can be paralyzing.

Over the years, writers have developed numerous **prewriting** methods for getting started with a piece of writing. Some of the more popular prewriting methods include **listing, clustering, cubing, cross-examination**, and **brainstorming.**

In this chapter, you will be introduced to these strategies to help you choose your topic, develop your thesis, and expand your ideas. Your instructor can probably suggest several other prewriting techniques. You might find that using one single method will work very well, or you might find it effective to use more than one strategy each time you write. The key is to experiment with as many prewriting methods as you need to get started writing.

In this chapter, you also will be introduced to three additional skills that will help you take the ideas you discovered in the prewriting processes through various stages of an essay's development to a finished product: **drafting, revising,** and **proofreading.**

By learning and practicing the techniques illustrated in this chapter, you can develop the skills that will allow you to approach any writing assignment with confidence. Nothing builds confidence like success, and nothing engenders success like confidence.

Prewriting

The prewriting techniques that follow will help you decide if there is enough to say about a particular topic to warrant writing about it. These techniques also will help you identify subtopics that will be developed in the body paragraphs of your essay.

Listing

Listing is exactly what it sounds like—making a list. Here's how it works. Take a blank piece of paper and write the topic at the top. If you are using a computer, write the topic at the beginning of the document. Next, as quickly as possible, write down any idea that pops into your head. Don't stop to think about how to develop each idea. This thinking technique is called *free association*. Let the words come fast, and write them down as they come. Remember, don't revise, correct, or edit your thoughts—just let them flow. A list of ideas on the topic of writing might look like this:

Example
Writing

assignment	thesis	paragraphs	content
grammar	topic	punctuation	analysis
sentences	spelling	development	conclusion
subtopics	coordination	essay	research
facts	opinion	title	body paragraphs

Continue listing for at least ten minutes, because one idea often inspires another. The act of writing helps the thinking process for most writers. When you have finished listing, see which ideas are related, and rearrange the items into groups. Your new page might look something like this:

Example
Writing

Group 1	**Group 2**	**Group 3**
grammar	sentences	thesis
spelling	paragraphs	topic
punctuation	conclusion	subtopics
	body paragraphs	

After you have put the ideas into lists of related terms, try to find a logical order for them, perhaps by chronology (what you would do first, then second, third, etc.) or by priority or importance (most important to least important, or vice versa). This step can help you outline your topic.

▼
PRACTICE 1   **Listing**

List at least ten words that come to mind about each of the following topics.

1. Your favorite vacation spot.

_____

_____

_____

2. A sport or sporting event.

_____

_____

_____

3. Ending a relationship.

_____

_____

_____

4. A memorable person.

_____

_____

_____

5. A phobia or fear (snakes, heights, spiders, enclosed spaces).

_____

_____

_____

Clustering (Mapping)

A technique similar to listing but more visual is **clustering**, or **mapping.** Clustering can help you see relationships among possible ideas more clearly. First, draw a circle at the center of your paper and write the topic inside it. Then, think of related topics and write them in circles around it. Link these to the topic circle by connecting lines. Next, focus on the new circles, one by one. Think of topics related to these, and put them in another layer of circles. Note the diagram on page 24. The main topic is educational television.

After studying the individual clusters, select the group that best develops the topic. You can expand on your options by continuing to add to the groups you have chosen. For instance, you could add Polynesian and Tex-Mex circles to the Cooking cluster. You could add Northern and Southern to the Italian circle. Then, you could write a paper about Northern Italian cooking versus Southern Italian cooking. The possibilities are as endless as the number of circles you can add to the clusters.

PRACTICE 2 Clustering or Mapping

Place each of the following topics in the middle of a piece of paper. As related ideas come to you, make clusters with lines connecting them to one another if the ideas are also related.

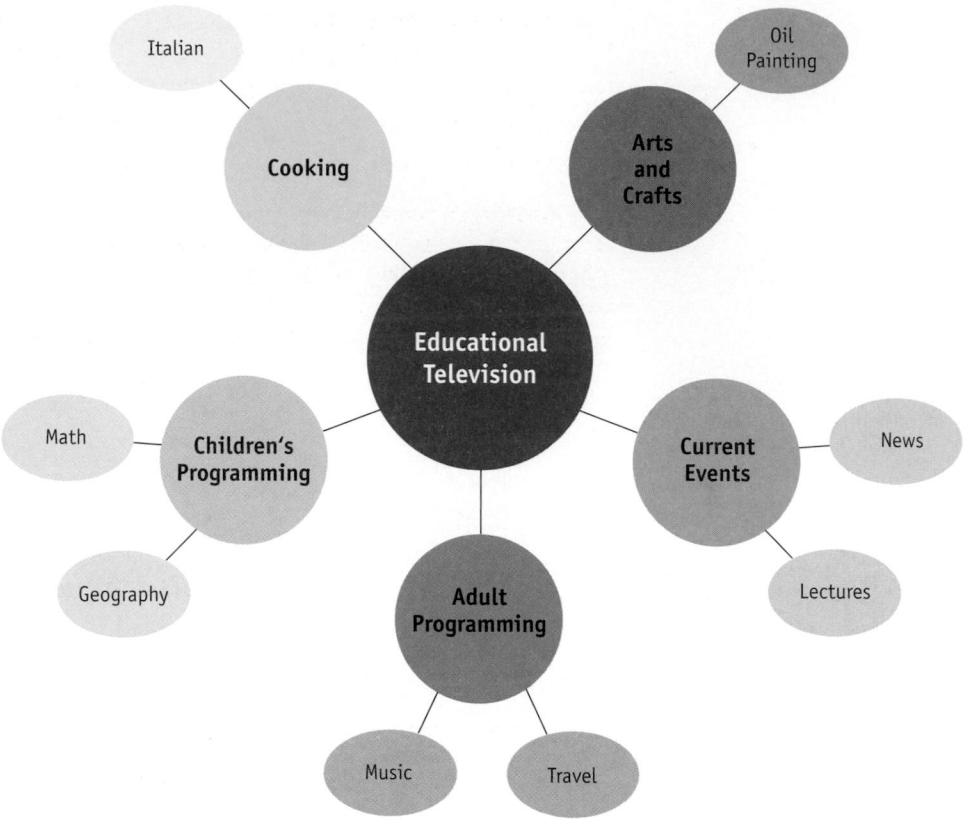

The Internet

Video games

Parenting

Cubing

Another method to generate new approaches to a topic is called **cubing.** To do this, imagine a cube with six sides with the following questions on each side:

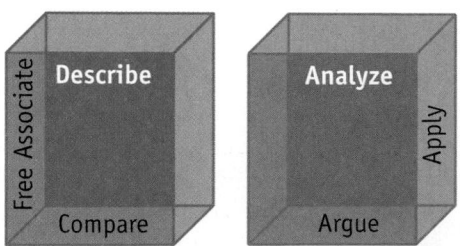

1. *Describe the topic:* What does the subject look like? What is the size, color, shape, texture, smell, and sound? Which details are unique?

2. *Compare or contrast the topic:* What is your subject like? How does it differ from other subjects? How is it similar? Give details.

3. *Free associate about the topic:* What does your subject remind you of? What further ideas can you think of?

4. *Analyze the topic:* What are the parts of the topic? How does each part function? How are the parts connected? What is the significance of the subject?

5. *Argue for or against the topic:* What are the arguments for and against your topic? What are its advantages and disadvantages?

6. *Apply the topic:* How can the topic be used?

Approach your topic from each of the six perspectives, freewriting your answers as with listing or clustering. Give yourself ten minutes to explore your ideas. Do not worry about topic development at this point. Just get your ideas down. Finally, review your responses. See if any are appropriate to your assignment. Sometimes, doing this will generate ideas for your writing assignment.

▼ **PRACTICE 3**   **Cubing**

Choose one of the following topics. Answer the questions on each side of the cube to develop ideas for the topic.

Ways to relax   A favorite room

A theatrical play   A type of music

An exciting city   Advertising a new product

1. Describe

_____

_____

_____

_____

2. Compare or contrast

_____

_____

_____

_____

3. Free associate

_____

_____

_____

_____

4. Analyze

_____

_____

_____

_____

5. Argue for or against

_____

_____

_____

_____

6. Apply

_____

_____

_____

_____

Cross-Examination

You can use cross-examination on your own or with a partner. Depending on the type of essay assignment or the type of essay you would like to write, the questions can be grouped differently. You can interview yourself or your partner regarding the topic, using the following sets of questions:

Definition
How is the subject defined or explained by the dictionary or encyclopedia?

How do most people define the topic informally?

How do I define the subject?

What is the history, origin, or background of the topic?

What are some examples of the topic?

Relationship
What is the cause of the topic?

To what larger group or category does the subject belong?

What are the values or goals of the subject?

What are the effects of the subject?

Comparison and Contrast
What is the subject similar to?

What is the subject different from?

What is the subject better than?

What is the subject worse than?

What is the subject opposite to?

Testimony

What do people say about the topic?

What authorities exist on this topic?

Has anything been written on this topic?

What are the important statistics?

Is there any further research on the topic?

Have I had any personal experience on this topic?

Circumstance

Is this subject possible?

Is this subject impossible?

When has this subject happened before?

What might prevent it from happening?

Why might it happen again?

Who or what is associated with the topic?

Of course, not all of these questions will apply to every topic. Choose those that help you develop your topic most thoroughly and effectively.

PRACTICE 4   Cross-Examination

For one of the following topics, quickly write down answers for as many of the questions in each category as you can. Don't hesitate to write down answers for questions that come to you that are not listed in the categories provided here.

Mandatory handgun registration   Parental control lockouts for the Internet

A prison without guards   Commercial-free television

1. Definition

_____

_____

_____

_____

2. Relationship

_____

_____

_____

_____

3. Comparison and contrast

_____

_____

_____

_____

4. Testimony

_____

_____

_____

_____

5. Circumstance

_____

_____

_____

_____

Brainstorming

Brainstorming can be done in a variety of ways. First, it can be accomplished through discussion with others: friends, family, or students engaged in a similar process. By brainstorming, you can expand your ideas about a topic by listening to one or two different perspectives and taking notes. Second, brainstorming can be done in writing using the techniques explored below, such as listing or freewriting. Following is a sample of verbal brainstorming focusing on notes a student has taken when presenting the topic of violence in society to a partner:

Example

Topic: Violence in Today's Society

Is it caused by television?	Movies are violent also.
Not everyone is affected by violence	Parent's role
What about guns, murders?	Why so many in America?
Is there more here than other places?	The cities more violent than the country?
Gun control	Constitutional Rights
What can reduce crime?	What is the effect of war?

Recent events	Columbine
Why do kids kill others?	Bullying?
What are we afraid of?	Racism

▼ **PRACTICE 5**   **Brainstorming**

In a classroom setting, students should break into small groups of two or three. Each student should present the topic they wish to explore to the other members of the group, and for five or ten minutes, the students should discuss what they think about each topic while the original author takes notes and joins in the discussion. After the assigned time period, the next student presents a new topic for a brainstorming session.

Freewriting

Freewriting is a warm-up technique similar to **listing** (already discussed). However, in freewriting, the writer chooses a topic and writes freely for five or ten minutes about whatever comes to mind, without an assigned structure or format, in order to explore any possible ideas that could be associated with the topic. The writer continues to write even when there is writer's block, saying honestly, "I don't know what else to say on the topic," or words to that effect. Additionally, the writer does not worry about grammar, punctuation, or spelling. The following is an example of a student's five-minute freewrite on the topic of "the environment."

Example

I am not sure what to say on the topic of the environment. It seems to me that people have been discussing ideas about how to improve the situation with the environment for a long time but there is not too much being done about it. No one in this country wants to really pay for new forms of energy. We want to drive the cars we like and we want to use electricity. I don't think we have done very much with solar power or wind power even though I think there are some people who try these things. I hear that there is a lot of pollution in the water and in the air. The problem seems so big that it is hard for us to think about how to solve this. I wonder why the ideas are not made into laws. Why do some cities have buses or subways and others rely on cars? It is overwhelming to think of what should be done regarding the environment.

▼ **PRACTICE 6**   **Freewriting**

To practice freewriting, take out several sheets of paper and choose one of the topics mentioned in the **listing** activity (pp. 22–23). Place the topic at the top of the first sheet of paper and write for five or ten minutes without stopping. If you have trouble thinking of what to write, write that down as well.

A Final Word About Prewriting

If you practice a variety of prewriting strategies, you are likely to find one or two with which you are most comfortable and that allow you to write with a sense of confidence. You'll probably learn which strategies best apply to different topics. Getting started on a writing project can be the most difficult part of the assignment, but using prewriting strategies can make the entire process get off the ground with less frustration and more success. Never forget that the goal of prewriting is *discovery,* not completion. Progress through your writing assignment step by step, don't get ahead of yourself, and you'll find the total experience much more enjoyable and worthwhile.

Drafting

When prewriting activities are completed, you are ready to begin writing your first **draft**. A *draft* is another word for *version*. In other words, you will write more than one version, or draft, of your ideas before handing in your work. You probably have heard the term *rough draft*. This is another name for an unfinished piece of writing, writing that must be revised and proofread before submission.

Focusing and Developing Ideas

In the clustering example on page 24, *educational television* is the overall topic being explored. If you write a paragraph about educational television, possible subtopics include *cooking, arts and crafts, current events, adult programming,* and *children's programming.* Let's say you have chosen *children's programming, adult programming,* and *current events* because all three have at least two items or subcategories within their grouping by which the topic can be developed. (Children's programming subdivides into "math" and "geography," and adult programming subdivides into "music" and "travel," and current events subdivides into "news" and "lectures.")

Writing the Paragraph's Topic Sentence

Now that you've chosen the topic and subtopics, you can write a topic sentence:

> *Educational television* [the main idea] *should be supported because children's programming, adult programming, and current events programming are valuable* [the focus the writer will use to explore the main idea].

Developing the Paragraph

The paragraph will be developed using the subcategories linked to the subtopics:

> *Children's programming—math* and *geography* to show how they support similar instruction children receive in school.
> *Adult programming—music* and *travel* to show how they can help make more enjoyable the lives of people who have a difficult time getting out because of physical limitations or illness.
> *Current events—news programming* and *lectures* to show how they help make the public better aware of happenings in the world.

Writing the Rough Draft Paragraph

To write the first draft of the paragraph, begin with the topic sentence, and follow it with the subtopic sentences.

Example 1: Rough Draft—The Basic Ideas

> Educational television should be supported because children's programming, adult programming, and current events programming are valuable. Children's programs help support instruction received at school. News programs and lectures by experts are essential. Adult shows make programming an enjoyable experience for a wider audience.

Of course, this is only the first draft. The next step on the road to the finished product is revising.

Revising the Rough Draft

Revising is not just another word for *rewriting*. **Revising** means to rewrite for both content and organization. As you reread and rewrite your assignment, you often will notice that one idea is not as good as another one that you have thought of. If so, you need to replace the initial idea with what you think will make the writing even better. The ideas in the paragraph should follow a plan—hopefully, the one stated in your topic sentence. Revising means to present your ideas in the best way possible to make them clear and interesting to the reader.

For example, in the first draft of the paragraph on educational television there are several flaws:

1. The organization does not follow the order given in the topic sentence: children's programming, adult programming, and current events programming. The writer has switched "news programming" and "adult programming." In the next draft of the paragraph, the writer should switch them back to their original sequence as stated in the topic sentence. Following a stated plan helps the reader to remain focused and clear about the paragraph's purpose.

2. The paragraph is not very well developed. The writer has not included information about the subcategories within each subtopic: "math and geography" in the *children's programming* subtopic, "music and travel" within the *adult programming* subtopic, and "news programming and lectures" within the *current events programming* subtopic.

Example 2: Rough Draft Revision—Developing the Basic Ideas

Using the revising notes, we rewrote the first rough draft, this time reordering the information and developing the paragraph by including the subcategory information:

> Educational television should be supported because children's programming, adult programming, and current events programming are valuable. Children's programs help support instruction received at school. Programs about math can include counting, addition, subtraction, multiplication, and division. Geography programming might include state capitals and countries around the world. Adult shows, such as those involving big band music, can help the elderly think about happier, carefree days of their youth; travel programs can take shut-ins and sick people to places they might not otherwise be able to travel to. Current events programming, both news and lectures, helps make viewers aware of important things worldwide. Worldwide ideas also are given, so the viewer is made aware that every issue has many people for it and against it.

This second draft of the paragraph is better than the first draft because it is easier to follow (the paragraph's organization follows that in the topic sentence), and the topic is more fully developed (additional, specific information is given about the topic). However, many of the ideas could be expressed more clearly with better word choices and a bit of sentence polishing to make the presentation better.

Example 3: Rough Draft Revision—Expanding the Content

You can use a thesaurus to locate more specific, descriptive nouns and verbs. Remember, one of your tasks as a writer is to choose language that makes your writing clearer and more interesting for the reader.

> Educational television should be supported because children's programming, adult programming, and current events programming are valuable. Children's programs help support instruction received in school. Programs about math can include counting, addition, subtraction, multiplication, and division. Geography programming ~~might~~ include state capitals and countries around the world. Adult shows, such as those involving ~~big band~~ "Big Band" music, can help the elderly ~~think about~~ remember [*reminisce* would even be a better choice] happier~~, carefree days of their youth~~ times [not all your readers might have been young when they listened to Big Band music, and they may have been listening to it all through the years, not just when they were young]; travel programs can ~~take~~ transport shut-ins and ~~sick people~~ the infirmed to ~~places~~ exotic locales they may not ~~have been able to get to~~ otherwise have been able to visit ~~travel to~~. Current events programming, both news and lectures, helps ~~make~~ keep viewers aware of important ~~things~~ happenings worldwide. ~~Worldwide~~ [don't repeat the same word after having just used it] International ~~ideas~~ points of view also are ~~given~~ presented, so the viewer is made aware that every issue has many ~~people for it and many people against it~~ supporters and opponents.

With the corrections and additions completed, compare the second rough draft with the third. The third draft's content is much more detailed and complete than in the earlier drafts, which enables the reader to comprehend and develop a better understanding of the topic.

Example 4: Rough Draft—Adding Transitional Expressions and Creating Sentence Variety

Now that the content is developed, we can add transitional expressions and create sentence variety. **Transitional expressions** accomplish three important things in good writing: They create rhythm within the writing, helping the communication flow from point to point in a smooth and enjoyable manner; they help to show relationships that exist between ideas, such as cause and effect, and comparisons and contrasts; and they can help create sentence variety.

Sentence variety is very important for communications to be clear and convincing. Simple sentences are fine for simple ideas, but complex ideas need to be presented in more sophisticated sentences. A paragraph consisting of nothing but simple sentences appears somewhat childlike in its presentation and rhythm, and it lacks the complexity to properly develop and show relationships between bits of information.

In a depressed economy, educational television should be supported because children's programming, adult programming, and current events programming are valuable. Children's programs help support instruction received in school**; for example,** programs about math can include counting, addition, subtraction, multiplication, and division. Geography programming might include state capitals and countries around the world. Adult shows, such as those involving "Big Band" music, can help the elderly remember happier times**; additionally,** travel programs can transport shut-ins and the infirmed to exotic locales they may not otherwise have been able to visit. Current events programming, both news and lectures, helps keep viewers aware of important happenings worldwide. **For instance,** international points of view also are presented, so the viewer is made aware that every issue has many supporters and opponents.

Notice how much more effective the paragraph is because the transitional phrases move the reader from idea to idea quickly and smoothly. The four transitional expressions also help the reader understand the content. "In a depressed economy," helps the reader understand why educational television, which is largely publicly funded, needs more help. When the economy is bad, governments earmark less money for organizations such as public television, which they do not consider as critical as national defense and highway improvement. "For example," "additionally," and "For instance" cue the reader that they are about to receive additional examples that will help them understand the topic more clearly and with more depth.

Proofreading—Catching the "Little" Errors that Can Mean "Big" Trouble

The final step in the writing process is **proofreading.** After your paper is written, you should read it two or three times, looking for the following types of errors:

▼ **Spelling**—Correct *misspelled words* (*liason* instead of *liaison*); *typos* (you hit the keys out of order, so *ball* looks like *blal*), and *sound-alike errors* (you meant to write *lean* meaning thin, but you wrote *lien* instead, a financial term). By the way, although most word-processing programs include a spellchecker, the program does not understand the context in which a word is used. The spellchecker, as its name implies, only checks to see if a word is spelled correctly.

▼ **Punctuation**—Check for *run on or fused sentence errors* (two independent clauses without punctuation between them) and *comma splice errors* (two independent clauses separated only by a comma), in addition to other punctuation errors.

▼ **Sentence fragments**—Look for *incomplete sentences* with a subject or verb missing from the independent clause or sufficient meaning missing from the clause, as is the case when a dependent clause is mistakenly used as a complete sentence.

▼ **Grammar**—Check for *grammatical errors* such as subjects and verbs that don't agree, pronouns with no antecedents, and other types of mistakes.

The "Final" Final Step

After you have proofread your paragraph or essay, print it in black ink on high-quality (20-pound white bond) paper. Make sure your name, class, and date appear on the printed paragraph or essay. Check to see if margins are consistent on each page. Make sure there are no ink smudges, wrinkles, or tears in the paper. The paper should look professional in every respect. After all, if it appears that you do not care for your work, why should the reader take it seriously?

From First Rough Draft to Finished Product

Look again at the first rough draft of the educational TV paragraph, and compare it with the final version. By using just a few techniques in a few drafts, the paragraph has evolved from an underdeveloped, unfocused, amateurish effort into a coherent, developed, and polished piece of professional-quality writing. Here is the first rough draft:

> Educational television should be supported because children's programming, adult programming, and current events programming are valuable. Children's programs help support instruction received at school. News programs and lectures by experts are essential. Adult shows make programming an enjoyable experience for a wider audience.

Now look at the finished product:

> In a depressed economy, educational television should be supported because children's programming, adult programming, and current events programming are valuable. Children's programs help support instruction received in school; for example, programs about math can include counting, addition, subtraction, multiplication, and division. Geography programming might include state capitals and countries around the world. Adult shows, such as those involving "Big Band" music, can help the elderly remember happier times; additionally, travel programs can transport shut-ins and the infirm to exotic locales they may not otherwise have been able to visit. Current events programming, both news and lectures, helps keep viewers aware of important happenings worldwide. For instance, international points of view also are presented, so the viewer is made aware that every issue has many supporters and opponents.

Writing is a learned skill. By practicing a few techniques and employing them in a few drafts, your writing can improve dramatically. Work the processes, and they will work for you.

▼

| PRACTICE 7 | Drafting, Revising, and Proofreading a Paragraph |

In the following exercise, use the techniques discussed in this chapter to develop a paragraph on a specific topic.

1. Choose a topic from the following list: The Power of Role Models; How Fear Affects Behavior; War as a Means of Solving International Disputes; Diplomacy as a Means of Solving International Disputes; The Value of a Positive Attitude; Stopping a Bad Habit; The Negative Effects of Eating Fast Food.

2. Apply one or more of the prewriting techniques to your topic to uncover subtopics; create a topic sentence; write a first draft; revise the first draft; develop the basic ideas; expand the content; add transitional expressions; proofread; and, finally, print your paragraph.

CHAPTER REVIEW

▼ Prewriting activities help you develop ideas for your writing. They include listing, clustering or mapping, cubing, cross-examination, freewriting, and brainstorming.

▼ Writing a rough draft of a paragraph or essay enables you to develop the content and organization of a piece based on your prewriting ideas. The rough draft may need several revisions.

▼ Revising a rough draft means evaluating its content and organization to ensure the ideas make sense and are presented in a way the reader will easily understand. Improvements to content and organization are made at this stage. Revising also includes improving the writing by using appropriate transitional expressions.

▼ Proofreading involves reading your paragraph or essay and correcting mistakes in spelling, punctuation, and grammar.

▼ The final step of your writing activity is to print the paragraph or essay, properly formatted, on good-quality paper. Use black ink.

Visit *The Write Start* Online!

For additional practice with the materials found in this chapter, visit our Website at

http://www.ablongman.com/checkett

The Website also features additional readings, quizzes, writing activities, and Internet links, as well as a bulletin board and interactive chat.

4

The Introductory Paragraph

In Chapter 3, you learned about the entire writing process. In this and the next two chapters, you will be introduced to the three major segments of the expository essay: the introductory paragraph in this chapter, the body paragraph in Chapter 5, and the concluding paragraph in Chapter 6. To illustrate the parts of the essay, an essay about the city of San Francisco will be developed one segment at a time at the end of these three chapters. The essay will go through the entire writing process, from prewriting activity, to rough draft revision, to proofreading, to final version.

We realize that there are as many methods of writing essays as there are different assignments. In this book, for ease and clarity of instruction, you will learn to write the five-paragraph model essay. All the student essays shown in the text are five-paragraph essays, although the professional essays vary in length. Each five-paragraph model essay contains an introductory paragraph, three body paragraphs, and a concluding paragraph. The five-paragraph model is used because it is short enough to demonstrate and keep you focused on the elements of good writing, and it is long enough to provide you with room to develop your ideas. Once you learn the elements of good writing using the five-paragraph model, you will be able to expand it to longer and more complex writing assignments.

The first part of an expository essay is the introductory paragraph, which introduces the reader to the essay's topic. It provides your first chance as a writer to engage your audience and set up the purpose of your essay. An introductory paragraph consists of a series of **introductory sentences** and a **thesis statement.**

The Thesis Statement

The thesis statement is the most important element in any essay because it sets the tone for the entire essay. It also provides a roadmap for the entire essay. It states what you are going to clarify, explain, or argue for or against about the topic. Although there is no rule about where to place the thesis statement in the introductory paragraph, it usually appears near the end. The thesis statement:

▼ announces the overall topic

▼ has only one topic, never more

▼ states the importance of the topic (the writer's attitude about the topic)

▼ limits the scope of the essay

▼ expresses the topic as an opinion that can be discussed

▼ can outline the organizational structure of the essay.

▼ does *not* express the topic as a fact

▼ does *not* express the topic as a question

The Attitude in the Thesis Statement

A thesis statement is the author's opinion about a particular subject. Opinion is not fact; it is a possible position that not everyone agrees with. An opinion opens the subject up for debate. Therefore, the thesis statement must contain a word or phrase that clarifies the writer's **attitude** regarding the subject. This expressed attitude prevents the thesis statement from being stated as a fact. The thesis statement, then, states how the writer feels about the subject; it is what makes the subject important or worth writing about. Readers do not have to agree with the writer's position, but they do have to understand clearly what the writer's position is.

A verb can be the basis of expressing your attitude about the topic. For example, the verbs *are/are not, is/is not, should/should not,* and *can/cannot* begin to tell the reader how you feel about a topic. Adjectives also can express the attitude about the topic. *Important, better,* and *more worthwhile* can suggest to the reader what the writer feels is important regarding the topic. Verbs and adjectives can work together to form the attitude in a thesis statement.

For instance, you might believe that reading to young children every day will make them more informed on a variety of subjects, thus making them better students. The thesis statement might read: *Parents should read to young children every day to make their children better students.* The verb *should read* begins to express your attitude about the topic. The adjective *better* also helps establish the writer's attitude about reading because doing so will make the children "better" students

The Controlling Idea in the Thesis Statement

Along with the topic and the attitude, the thesis statement should clarify how the topic will be discussed. This is called the **controlling idea** because it clarifies how the topic will be developed in the body paragraphs. In the thesis statement *Parents should read to young children every day to make their children better students,* "should read" and "better" are connected as the attitude toward the topic "parents reading to their children." The controlling idea is "make their children better students." Therefore, in the body paragraphs, the writer will discuss how parents reading to their young children should make the children better students.

As a writer, your attitude and controlling idea express not only why the subject is important to you, but also why it should be important to the reader.

Examples

In each of the following thesis statements, the attitude and controlling idea are italicized, with the attitude circled.

Lunch *is an important meal during the day.*

Psycho *is a scary movie because of the shower scene.*

Chevrolet *makes better trucks than Ford.*

> Tanning beds (do less) damage to your skin than the sun.
> Tanning beds (do as much) damage to your skin as the sun.
> Voting (should be important) to all 18- to 20-year-old citizens.
> Divorce (should not be) the first thought when problems surface in a marriage.

Providing readers with a thesis statement containing a clearly defined attitude and controlling idea will help them understand your focus before they begin reading the body of the essay.

PRACTICE 1   **Identifying the Topic and Controlling Idea**

In each of the following sentences, underline the attitude word or phrase once and the controlling idea twice.

Examples: The Rolls-Royce is considered by many as the finest car in the world.
The Lemonaire is not considered by anyone as the finest car in the world.

1. Reading a newspaper each day is important because it keeps you informed about current events.

2. Regular tune-ups can keep a car running efficiently for years.

3. Working while going to school should teach young people responsibility.

4. Laptop computers can make the workplace anywhere a worker happens to be sitting.

5. The Beatles remain popular, even after their breakup decades ago, because of their versatile musical style.

The Essay Map in the Thesis Statement

One easy way to make sure that your essay is well organized is to include an **essay map** in your thesis statement. The essay map lists the subtopics that will support your thesis in the body paragraphs. Each of the essay map items will become the topic for one of the three body paragraphs. The thesis statement with an essay map automatically organizes your essay and limits its scope. Because this book uses the five-paragraph essay model, with three body paragraphs, the essay map in the thesis statement will contain three subtopics.

In the following sentences, each element of the three-item essay map is identified by color. Notice that the essay map can be placed at the beginning, middle, or end of the thesis statement.

Examples

1. To prevent fires in the home, people should *hide matches from children, never smoke in bed,* and *keep a fire extinguisher in the kitchen.*
2. Practice, conditioning, *and a* proper diet *help athletes perform at a high level.*
3. Communist countries worldwide, because of *insufficient international trade strategies, poor farming methods,* and *excessive military budgets,* were not very successful.

PRACTICE 2 **Identifying the Essay Map**

Underline the three-item essay map in each of the following sentences.

1. Airlines, trucking companies, and railroads should be regulated by the federal government because they transport people and goods over state lines, they must ensure safe transportation, and the national economy depends on their remaining in business.

2. The aging process, talented newcomers, and constant travel make maintaining a sports career a difficult lifestyle.

3. Savings bonds, because of liquidity, safety, and interest, are a better investment vehicle than annuities.

4. A successful career often hinges upon hard work, dedication, and intelligence.

5. New York is an exciting city to visit because of its many points of historical interest, excellent music and theater, and fine restaurants.

Checking Your Thesis Statement

Your thesis statement must be constructed properly. Without a good thesis statement, the essay cannot succeed. To check your thesis statement, ask yourself these questions:

▼ Does the sentence introduce a single topic?
▼ Is my attitude toward the topic clearly stated?
▼ Have I included three supporting items in an essay map?

If the answer to any of these questions is "no," you need to rewrite your thesis statement.

Examples

Poor Voting and military service are important activities for all citizens. *(two topics with a clear attitude but no essay map)*

Better Voting is an important responsibility for all citizens. *(one topic and clear attitude but no essay map)*

Best	Voting is an important responsibility for all citizens because it gives people a voice in how the government is run, removes ineffective politicians from office, and influences political decision making. *(one topic, clear attitude, three-item essay map that supports the attitude about the subject)*
Poor	Many students work while going to school. *(statement of fact, no attitude, no essay map)*
Better	Working while going to school can teach students valuable lessons. *(one topic, clear attitude, but no essay map)*
Best	Working while going to school can teach students responsibility, organizational skills, and teamwork. *(one topic, clear attitude, three-item essay map that supports the attitude about the subject)*
Poor	Are regular automobile oil changes really necessary? *(the sentence is in the form of a question, not a clearly stated opinion, no attitude, no essay map)*
Better	Regular oil changes can keep a car running better. *(one topic, a clearly stated opinion, but no essay map)*
Best	Regular oil changes can keep a car running more efficiently, improve gas mileage, and reduce long-term maintenance costs. *(one topic, clear attitude, three-item essay map that supports the attitude about the topic)*

The essay map in the thesis statement is an easy and effective way to quickly organize thoughts about a topic developed in your essay.

PRACTICE 3: Identifying the Parts of a Thesis Statement

In each of the following thesis statements, underline the topic once, the attitude and controlling idea twice, and the essay map three times. On the line provided, indicate if any element is missing.

1. Fruits are a good source for vitamin C.

---

2. Fast serves, pinpoint lobs, and slice volleys make tennis an exciting sport to watch.

---

3. Many students make college a worthwhile experience by joining fraternities and sororities, playing intramural sports, and participating in student government.

---

4. Lightweight sleeping bags are good for camping trips.

---

5. Styling, construction, and value make the Breitling a popular wristwatch for collectors.

_____

6. Fuel cell cars should be an industry priority because of skyrocketing fuel costs, environmental pollution, and diminishing fuel reserves.

_____

7. Skydiving and bungee jumping are dangerous activities.

_____

8. The St. Louis Cardinals are a major league baseball team.

_____

9. *Star Trek* has been a long-running television series because of special effects, interesting characters, and fascinating stories.

_____

10. Cruises are a popular form of vacationing because of good food, entertainment, and stops in exotic places.

_____

▼ **PRACTICE 4**   **Rewriting Thesis Statements**

Rewrite the following thesis statements if the essay map items do not explain, clarify, or support the attitude expressed about the topic. If the essay map does explain, clarify, or support the attitude about the topic, write "Correct" in the space provided.

Example

The television program "Cops" is unfair to African- and Mexican-Americans because it shows their pets, kitchen appliances, and lawns.

Problem: The three essay map items do not support why the program is "unfair" to minorities. "Cops" is a show about crime. What do "pets," "kitchen appliances," and "lawns" have to do with crime and "unfair" treatment?

Revision: The television program "Cops" is unfair to African- and Mexican-Americans because it focuses on them as criminals, creates racial stereotypes, and distorts elements of their cultures.

In the revised sentence, the essay map items do explain why the program is unfair to African- and Mexican-American groups. Remember, readers do not have to agree with your position; however, they do have to understand where you stand on the issue.

1. A new car is superior to a used car because of better viewing, colors, and the neighbors.

   _____

   _____

   _____

2. Reducing air pollution, expanding the economy, and supporting education are good reasons to vote for a political candidate.

   _____

   _____

   _____

3. A successful small business, built on spectacular vistas, aromatic candles, and U.S. Grade A ground beef, is easy to franchise.

   _____

   _____

   _____

4. Hiring a housecleaning crew can help cure dizzy spells, make pets happier, and cause cars to get better gas mileage.

   _____

   _____

   _____

5. A professional wrestling career can be easier to attain by studying classical music, ballet, and the opera.

   _____

   _____

   _____

▼ PRACTICE 5   Writing Thesis Statements

Write a thesis statement for the following topics. Use the criteria for writing an effective thesis statement that you have learned.

1. A popular book.

_____

_____

2. A controversial movie.

_____

_____

3. Privacy on the Internet.

_____

_____

4. What makes a relationship work.

_____

_____

5. College drinking.

_____

_____

Introductory Sentences

In the introductory paragraph, the thesis statement is introduced by **introductory sentences,** also called **lead-in sentences.** The purpose of introductory sentences is to catch the reader's attention and clarify your **tone** (for example, humorous, serious, or satiric). Some effective techniques for introducing the thesis statement include using a shocking statistic or statement, posing a series of questions, or stating a common problem or misconception.

Examples

Shocking statistic or statement

One out of every three families is directly affected by alcoholism. Of the 50,000 people killed in automobile accidents each year, two-thirds have a direct link to drinking and driving. The numbers are increasing each year. _Place thesis statement here._

Series of questions

When is the last time you enjoyed the process of buying a car? Are you tired of worrying about whether you are going to end up with a lemon? Do you resent smooth-talking sales people who are more interested in their commission than concerned with your satisfaction? _Place thesis statement here._

Common problem or misconception
Most people define welfare as money going to the poor living in the inner city. However, many corporations receive tax abatements when they move to a new city or town. Military dependents receive free medical and dental coverage and discounted food and merchandise at base stores. Many college students receive money for tuition and living expenses that they do not have to repay. *Place thesis statement here.*

PRACTICE 6   Writing Thesis Statements

Write a thesis statement for each of the paragraph examples on pages 45–46. Don't forget to create an essay map that supports your attitude or controlling idea about the topic.

1. _____

_____

_____

_____

_____

2. _____

_____

_____

_____

_____

3. _____

_____

_____

_____

_____

PRACTICE 7   Writing Introductory Sentences

Write introductory sentences for each of the following thesis statements. Try to create at least three sentences using one of the introductory sentence techniques you have learned.

1. _____

_____

_____

_____

_____

_____

_____

Visiting foreign lands can make travelers appreciate their own country, understand other people's points of view, and learn more about current international issues.

2. _____

_____

_____

_____

_____

_____

_____

Canning fruits and vegetables, keeping the thermostat set at 68° in the winter, and making clothes can reduce monthly bills by half.

3. _____

_____

_____

_____

_____

_____

_____

Senior citizens who continue learning, have a hobby, and exercise regularly can live longer and happier lives.

Drafting an Introductory Paragraph for the San Francisco Essay

Prewriting Activities: Creating Ideas to Write About

To create some ideas concerning San Francisco, the writer has chosen the clustering technique:

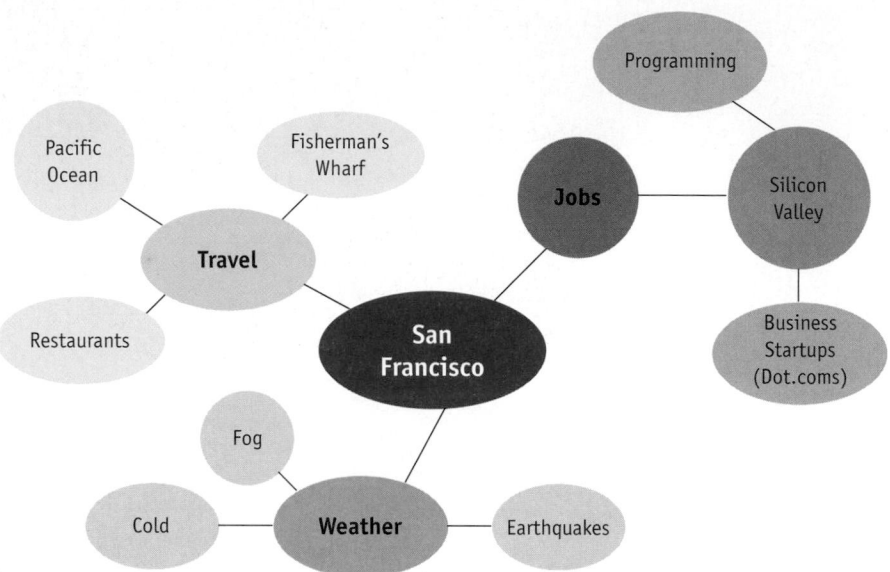

Possible topics to write about in regard to San Francisco are "Jobs," "Weather," "Expense," and "Travel." With "Jobs" as the organizational idea, the writer can perhaps explore "Silicon Valley," the center of computer-related jobs located nearby. If "Weather" is chosen, the writer can write about the cold current in the ocean, the well-known San Francisco fog, and the potential for serious earthquakes. However, because San Francisco is such a beautiful city with a variety of activities and attractions, "Travel" is selected as the reason for writing the essay.

To create ideas concerning travel, the writer can construct another cluster or use a different prewriting technique to explore this concept. You will see the listing technique demonstrated in Chapter 5, "The Body Paragraphs."

Drafting the Introductory Sentences

From personal experience, the writer knows that many people vacation at the same places each year. A trip to San Francisco, however, would be a very different and exciting experience. The writer explores the problem of boring vacations in the introductory paragraph by asking the reader a series of questions:

Example

Are you tired of going to see the same trees and hills year after year? Have you been going to the same time-share for so long that you have names for all the squirrels and chipmunks? Tired of hiking from museum to museum, until you become lost in a faceless crowd moving from one room to another? Thinking of separate vacations just so you can be assured of "not seeing the same old thing"? Well, if you want a memorable vacation, one packed with new experiences and invigorating activities, run— don't walk—to San Francisco.

In the introductory sentences, the writer has posed the problem (one lead-in technique) by creating a series of questions (another lead-in technique). More than one lead-in technique can be used in the introductory sentences.

Drafting the Thesis Statement

After posing the problem, *many vacations become boring because of familiarity,* the writer must state an opinion about how to solve the problem. This is the purpose of the thesis statement. By looking at the clustering diagram, the writer chooses the subtopics for the body paragraphs: Fisherman's Wharf, the Pacific Ocean, and Restaurants. These items will be the elements in the essay map in the thesis statement. Next, the writer must express an attitude about San Francisco that will be supported by the essay map items. While considering the Introductory Sentences, the writer used the word *exciting,* and that seems like an appropriate attitude about visiting San Francisco. Putting together the topic, attitude, and essay map, the writer creates the thesis statement:

San Francisco is an exciting city to visit because of Fisherman's Wharf, the Pacific Ocean, and fine restaurants.

The introductory paragraph is now in rough draft form:

> Are you tired of going to see the same trees and hills year after year? Have you been going to the same time-share for so long that you have names for all the squirrels and chipmunks? Tired of hiking from museum to museum until you become lost in a faceless crowd moving from one room to another? Thinking of separate vacations just so you can be assured of "not seeing the same old thing"? Well, if you want a memorable vacation, one packed with new experiences and invigorating activities, run—don't walk—to San Francisco. San Francisco is an exciting city to visit because of Fisherman's Wharf, the Pacific Ocean, and fine restaurants.

This paragraph is in rough draft form. It still needs to be revised and proofread for errors in grammar, punctuation, spelling, word choice, organization, and content. This will be demonstrated at the end of Chapter 6 when the entire rough draft essay is revised and proofread. The introductory paragraph is good enough to leave, for now, so that the body paragraphs can be drafted in Chapter 5.

CHAPTER REVIEW

▼ The thesis statement of an essay states the topic, the writer's controlling idea or attitude about the topic, and the essay map for the essay.

▼ In the thesis statement for a five-paragraph essay, the essay map has three subtopics. Each subtopic is developed by one of the body paragraphs.

▼ Introductory sentences usually precede the thesis statement. They catch the reader's attention and clarify the tone of the essay. Techniques for introductory sentences include using a surprising statistic or statement, posing a series of questions, or stating a common problem or misconception.

Visit *The Write Start* Online!

For additional practice with the materials found in this chapter, visit our Website at

http://www.ablongman.com/checkett

The Website also features additional readings, quizzes, writing activities, and Internet links, as well as a bulletin board and interactive chat.

5 | The Body Paragraphs

The purpose of the **body paragraphs** of an essay is to develop, support, and explain the thesis statement in the introductory paragraph. Each body paragraph's topic is based on one of the items in the essay map of the thesis statement. Body paragraphs follow the general organizational model for a paragraph as presented in Part 1: topic sentence and supporting sentences.

The Topic Sentence

The topic sentence of the body paragraph, like the thesis statement of the essay, has three parts: the **topic** (also called the **subject**), the **attitude,** and the **controlling idea.** Because this text demonstrates the essay map in the thesis statement, the subject of each topic sentence is taken from the items listed in the essay map. Sometimes, the subject or topic of a topic sentence also is called a **subtopic** when referring to the overall topic of the essay as stated in the thesis statement. If this sounds a bit confusing, think of it this way:

Thesis Statement Example

The controlling idea, also called the essay map, in the following thesis statement is underlined for instructional purposes: *Mutual funds are beneficial because of the need for college tuition, retirement income, and as a hedge against high taxation rates.*

Overall Topic of Essay ↓	Attitude ↓	Controlling Idea/Essay Map ↓

Mutual funds are beneficial because of the need for college tuition, retirement income, and as a hedge against high taxation rates.

Subtopic 1: Tuition ↓	Subtopic 2: Retirement ↓	Subtopic 3: Taxes ↓
The topic of the topic sentence in Body Paragraph 1	The topic of the topic sentence in Body Paragraph 2	The topic of the topic sentence in Body Paragraph 3

In this thesis statement, the controlling idea is an essay map, and the items in the essay map limit the scope of the information that can be used to develop, support, and explain the overall topic in the body paragraphs. New subjects or ideas cannot be introduced in the body paragraphs. They must follow the essay map items. For instance, in a paragraph about how novelists use description to create a violent atmosphere, the author cannot talk about other aspects of the novel, such as critical reviews, sales figures, or awards the novel may have won. The controlling idea forces the writer to talk only about those descriptive features that develop the violent aspects of the novel.

Just as a thesis statement without a controlling idea lacks focus, a body paragraph topic sentence without a clearly defined controlling idea lacks focus and specific direction. Without a controlling idea, the writer's thoughts or feelings about the subject may be unclear to the reader.

Examples

Poor topic sentences

Sammy Sosa is a baseball player.
(No controlling idea or attitude; this is simply a statement of fact)

Jogging is a popular form of exercise.
(No controlling idea)

Better topic sentences

Sammy Sosa's ability to hit home runs makes him an exciting baseball player.
(Controlling idea: *hit home runs*—Attitude: *exciting*)

Jogging is a popular form of exercise because it promotes cardio-vascular fitness.
(Controlling idea: *cardiovascular fitness*—Attitude: *popular*)

Again, the controlling idea in a thesis statement or a topic sentence does not have to be series of items (an essay map). However, because we are using the five-paragraph model with three body paragraphs, we are consistently demonstrating and referring to the three-item series (essay map) because it illustrates for the reader in advance the topics for the body paragraphs. The essay map is an optional tool to be used at your or your instructor's convenience.

PRACTICE 1   Improving Topic Sentences

The following sentences are inadequate as topic sentences because they lack a controlling idea and attitude. Turn them into topic sentences by adding a controlling idea and an attitude.

1. Commuters drive cars every day.

_____

_____

2. Marathoners wear running shoes.

_____

_____

3. Many young people attend rock concerts.

_____

_____

4. Jonathan attends precalculus classes.

_____

_____

5. The World Series is played during October.

_____

_____

6. Most businesses use computers.

_____

_____

7. Millions diet each day.

_____

_____

8. Voting in presidential elections takes place every four years.

_____

_____

9. A relationship exists between farming and the rainforest.

_____

_____

10. The police respond to emergency situations.

_____

_____

PRACTICE 2   Writing Topic Sentences

Write topic sentences for the following subjects. Don't forget to add a controlling idea and an attitude.

1. Clothes

_____

_____

2. Hurricanes

_____

_____

3. Political Races

_____

_____

4. Summer Jobs

_____

_____

5. Exercising

_____

_____

6. Soap Operas

_____

_____

7. Television Reruns

_____

_____

8. Rollerblading

_____

_____

9. Music

_____

_____

10. Astrology

_____

_____

Support Sentences

Support sentences follow the topic sentence in a body paragraph and help develop, support, and explain the subject by using specific facts, details, and examples. The supporting ideas must be consistent with the controlling idea and the attitude. The controlling idea and attitude help determine the kind of support ideas you can use in the support sentences.

> **Example**
>
> Teachers are most effective when helping students learn _how_ to learn.
>
> In this example, the topic is underlined once and the controlling idea and attitude are underlined twice.
>
> Support sentences for this topic would focus on _what_ teachers do to help students and might include teaching students the following activities:
>
> **a.** what information to take down as notes during a lecture
> **b.** what to identify as important information in reading assignments
> **c.** what techniques help make for effective studying

▼ **PRACTICE 3**   **Writing Topic Sentences**

Write a topic sentence with a controlling idea and an attitude for the support sentences in the following paragraphs.

1. _____

_____

First, the rafting trip down the river provided a thrill a minute as we hit the rapids. Next, the horseback ride along a winding trail took us through a dense forest filled with the sounds of many birds and other wildlife. After all the day's activities were complete, we sat around a roaring campfire and sang songs beneath a canopy of twinkling stars.

2. _____

_____

Monet's impressionistic paintings, with their muted colors and wispy, fog-like quality, seemed to be part of a dream. On the other hand, the shiny, brightly colored glass sculptures of Chihuly appeared like fantastic clouds plunging from the sky, and the rigid, metallic armor suits of the knights seemed to stand guard over the earthly domain.

3. _____

_____

Uncle Morgan seemed about ten pounds heavier than the last time the family got together. Twins Marleena and Marlaana, first cousins from Mom's side of the genealogy chart, were wearing their hair in long curls instead of their usual Peter Pan cut. The twinkle in Aunt Bessy's eyes had been replaced with a sad, almost mournful gaze.

4. _____

_____

China's population is already over 1 billion, and India's population will be over 1 billion in the near future. The total population for the United States, which has many well-advertised family planning organizations, has increased by 30 million in only a few decades. The rate at which the world's resources are being consumed is increasing at an alarming rate.

Drafting a Working Outline for a Body Paragraph

Before you begin writing your paragraph, you may want to sketch out the major ideas that will appear in your paragraph. This can help you discover whether or not you have a topic, a controlling idea, an attitude, and supporting ideas that work in unison for proper development. To create a working outline, you can write your topic, controlling idea, attitude, and support ideas in a ladderlike list. (For other prewriting techniques, see Chapter 3.)

Example	
Topic:	Smoking
Attitude:	can cause
Controlling idea:	harmful effects
Supporting ideas:	lung cancer
	emphysema
	gum disease

The paragraph outlined in the example will discuss the harmful effects of smoking. This topic will be developed and supported by using lung cancer, emphysema, and gum disease as the negative outcomes that smoking can produce. The finished paragraph might look like this:

Smoking can cause many harmful effects. It can lead to lung cancer, a potentially deadly condition for which cures are almost nonexistent. Emphysema, a chronic problem that worsens with time, is a disease wherein the air spaces in the lung increase, causing labored breathing and a susceptibility to infection. Additionally, smoking can cause excessive gum bleeding and gum cancer. Consult with a doctor for the best method to quit smoking.

PRACTICE 4   Outlining a Paragraph

To practice creating working outlines, create a controlling idea and an attitude for each of the topics listed below. List three specific support details that develop the controlling idea and attitude. After you have finished, you will have a list of all the basic ideas that will go into a paragraph on the topic. This is called a *working outline* because the paragraph is still unfinished.

1. Topic: The *Mission Impossible* movies

Controlling idea: _____

Attitude: _____

Supporting ideas:

   a. _____

   b. _____

   c. _____

2. Topic: Dating

Controlling idea: _____

Attitude: _____

Supporting ideas:

   a. _____

   b. _____

   c. _____

3. Topic: School violence

Controlling idea: _____

Attitude: _____

Supporting ideas:

   a. _____

   b. _____

   c. _____

4. Topic: Welfare

Controlling idea: _____

Attitude: _____

Supporting ideas:

a. _____

b. _____

c. _____

5. Topic: Recycling

Controlling idea: _____

Attitude: _____

Supporting ideas:

a. _____

b. _____

c. _____

▼
PRACTICE 5   Writing Paragraphs

Write a paragraph for each of the working outlines you created in Practice 4.

Writing the Body Paragraphs for the San Francisco Essay

In Chapter 4, we illustrated, step by step, the creation of the *Introductory Paragraph* with a *Thesis Statement* for an essay about reasons to visit San Francisco. Using the essay map items in the thesis statement, this section will develop the body paragraphs using the techniques you have studied.

Prewriting Activities: Creating Ideas to Write About

In Chapter 4, we demonstrated the clustering prewriting activity to uncover that "travel" was the focus of our attention in regard to the topic, and that the specific topics for our body paragraphs were Fisherman's Wharf, the Pacific Ocean, and restaurants. On the next page, the *listing or free association* prewriting technique is demonstrated to uncover the specific items to develop the topic in each body paragraph.

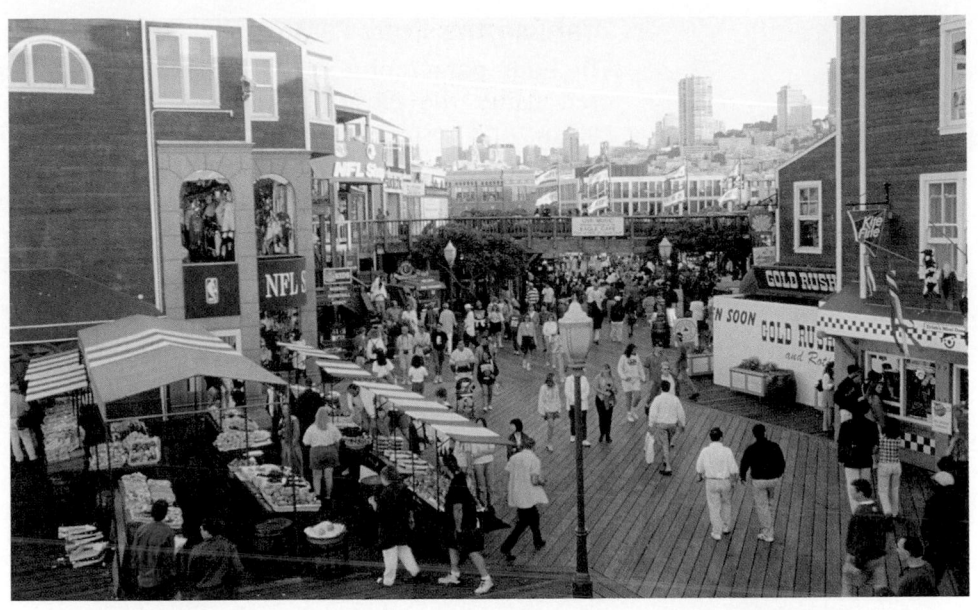

Listing or Free Association

Fisherman's Wharf	**Pacific Ocean**	**Restaurants**
Museums	Golden Gate Bridge	North Beach
Jefferson Street	Marinas	Chinatown
Pier 45	Fog	Italian food
Fishing fleets	Ships	Mission District
Ghirardelli Square	Museums	Russian delis
Specialty shops	Alcatraz	South American food
Sourdough bread	*Balclutha*	Richmond District
Medieval dungeon		
Submarine		
Wax museum		

Now that a significant number of ideas have been uncovered, the task of grouping the ideas into appropriate categories needs to be done. After the groups have been classified, other ideas can be added if they come to mind.

Fisherman's Wharf	**Pacific Ocean**	**Restaurants**
Museums	*Golden Gate Bridge*	*North Beach*
Wax museum	Fog	Italian food
Ripley's Museum	*Marinas*	California food
Medieval dungeon	Boat rental	*Richmond District*
Pier 45	Alcatraz	Russian delis
Submarine	*Museums*	*Chinatown*
Jefferson Street	Maritime museum	Mandarin
Fishing fleets	*Ships*	Szechuan
Specialty shops	*Balclutha*	Hunan
Ghirardelli Square	*Eureka*	*Mission District*
Specialty shops		Central American food
Sourdough bread		South American Food

Drafting the Body Paragraphs' Topic Sentences

The body paragraph topics are the essay map items we have already uncovered using the clustering prewriting activity: Fisherman's Wharf, Pacific Ocean, and restaurants. An attitude should be included in each topic sentence to support the overall attitude expressed in the thesis statement: "exciting." The controlling idea in the topic sentence is usually a word or phrase that can describe the elements that will clarify or explain the topic of the paragraph. These are the elements uncovered using the listing or free association prewriting activity above.

Body Paragraph 1

Topic: Fisherman's Wharf

Attitude: fascinating (supports "exciting")

Controlling idea: attractions

Topic sentence: Fisherman's Wharf offers the visitor a wide array of fascinating attractions.

Body Paragraph 2

Topic: Pacific Ocean

Attitude: unbelievable (supports "exciting")

Controlling idea: boating

Topic sentence: The Pacific Ocean, like an unbelievable expanse of blue glass, is a boater's paradise.

Body Paragraph 3

Topic: Restaurants

Attitude: delectable variety (supports "exciting")

Controlling idea: international cuisines

Topic sentence: The city's restaurants serve a delectable variety of international cuisines.

Checking the Outline

At this point in the drafting process, it is a good idea to check to make sure that your topic sentences actually support the thesis statement.

Thesis statement: San Francisco is an exciting city to visit because of fantastic Fisherman's Wharf, the incredible Pacific Ocean, and the extraordinary restaurants.

Topic sentence 1: Fisherman's Wharf offers the visitor a wide array of fascinating attractions.

Topic sentence 2: The Pacific Ocean, like an unbelievable expanse of blue glass, is a boater's paradise.

Topic sentence 3: The city's restaurants serve a delectable variety of international cuisines.

As illustrated in the outline above, the essay's body paragraphs are organized according to elements of the essay map in the thesis statement, and the "exciting" attitude regarding San Francisco will be supported in the body paragraphs as well. The next step is to write the body paragraph rough drafts using the items discovered in the listing or free association prewriting activity. If other items come to mind as the rough drafts are being written, feel free to include them.

Drafting the Body Paragraphs

Using the groups of items discovered in the prewriting activities, you can complete the rough draft of each body paragraph. Remember, if new ideas come to you during the rough-drafting process, feel free to use them.

Example of Body Paragraph 1

Fisherman's Wharf offers the visitor a wide array of fascinating attractions. The fishing fleets docks along the Jefferson Street promenade. An early morning stroll along "Fish Alley" **[new idea]** will allow you to see fishermen at work. Jefferson Street has a host of specialty shops and entertainment for the entire family. The Wharf has its share of museums, but they are a bit out of the ordinary. There's a wax museum, the Ripley's *Believe It or Not!* Museum, and a museum in the guise of a medieval dungeon. If you're not to claustrophobic, you can visit Pier 45 and tour the USS *Pampanito*, a retired WWII submarine. Also, you might want to visit Ghirardelli Square and pick a souvenier or two from the many specialty shops located there. Finally, before you leave the Wharf, make certain you take with you a loaf or too of San Francisco's famous sourdough bread. You'll probably want to visit Fisherman's Wharf several times before your vacation is over.

Example of Body Paragraph 2

The Pacific Ocean, like an unbelievable expanse of blue glass, is a boater's paradise. In San Francisco, boating enthusiasts can participate in activities in and out of the water. The San Francisco Maritime National Historical Pard contains four national landmark ships, including the famous square-rigger *Balclutha* and the ferry boat *Eureka*, which houses a collection of classic cars **[new idea]**. The park's Maritime Museum house a fascinating arry of model ships, figureheads, painting, photographs, and artifacts in an art deco building shaped to resemble a cruise ship **[new ideas]**. But, if it's the high seas you want, you can head for several marinas and rent a boat or take an excursion tour boat **[new idea]** out into the bay. Or, you can take a ferry to the infamous "Rock," Alcatraz island. The former maximum-security prison now offers guided tours, a self-guided hiking trail, and a slide show illustrating the penitentiary's notorious history. Or sail or motor out into the bay to view the enormous expanse of the Pacific Ocean and the incredible Golden Gate Bridge. Even when the fog is clouding and shrouding the enormous structure, the sight of fog rolling over the 1.2-mile-long bridge is both spectacular and haunting.

Example of Body Paragraph 3

The city's restaurants serve a delectable variety of international cuisines. The real difficulty is making a choice between so many delicious options. The Richmond district is well known for Russian delis. Chinatown offers traditional Mandarin, Szechuan, and Hunan food and an array of Asian restaurants, such Cambodian, Laotian, Burmese, and Indain **[new ideas]**. The North Beach area is famous for Italian and California cuisines, while Central and South American food is the specialy in the Mission District. To borrow from the Swedish—what a *smorgasbord*! If you like dining out, San Francisco is the place.

Note that the body paragraphs are not finished. They remain in a rough draft state, and they must be revised, proofread, and rewritten before the final draft is complete. This process will be illustrated at the end of Chapter 6. For now, however, the body paragraphs can be put aside, so the concluding paragraph can be drafted, as will be demonstrated in Chapter 6, "The Concluding Paragraph."

Additional Writing Assignments

The following paragraph writing assignments will help you practice the techniques you have learned. Create a working outline before you write each paragraph.

1. Write about an event: a public event such as an Olympic competition, a religious ceremony, a birthday or graduation party, an operation, an athletic event, or an historical event. The topic sentence should name the event and exhibit an organizational idea and attitude to be developed in the support sentences.

2. Write about a person: a parent, sibling, relative, friend, teacher, co-worker, or an historical figure. The topic sentence should identify the individual and clarify the organizational idea and attitude to be developed in the support sentences.

3. Write about a location: a room, house, school, workplace, or an historical location. The topic sentence should name the location, the organizational idea, and attitude to be developed in the support sentences.

4. Write about an important time: childhood, the teenage years, or a well-known time in history. In the topic sentence, clarify the timeframe, and include an organizational idea and attitude to be developed in the support sentences.

5. Write about why something happened: a recent event in the United States or in another country, or the reason something happened in history. In the topic sentence, name the reason for the occurrence, and write an organizational idea and attitude to be developed in the support sentences.

6. Write about how something happens or is done: a significant accomplishment by an individual or group, something that occurred in nature, or how something happened historically. In your topic sentence, name the process, and write an organizational idea and attitude to be developed in the support sentences.

CHAPTER REVIEW

▼ The body paragraphs of an essay develop and support the essay's topic as set forth in the essay map of the thesis statement.

▼ Each essay map item corresponds to a body paragraph topic.

▼ The topic sentence of a body paragraph states the topic, the controlling idea, and attitude toward the topic of the paragraph.

▼ Support sentences follow the topic sentence and help develop the topic by using specific facts, details, and examples.

▼ A working outline that states the topic, organizational and controlling idea and attitude, and support ideas can help you organize your paragraph.

Visit *The Write Start* Online!

For additional practice with the materials found in this chapter, visit our Website at

http://www.ablongman.com/checkett

The Website also features additional readings, quizzes, writing activities, and Internet links, as well as a bulletin board and interactive chat.

6 The Concluding Paragraph

Essays should not simply stop abruptly after the final body paragraph. Instead, you should leave your reader with a sense that your essay is complete. Use a **concluding paragraph** to bring a sense of completion to your essay and to reemphasize the central thesis. A concluding paragraph can simply be a summation of the points you've made, but it can also urge your readers to action, predict an outcome, or provide a warning based on the information in your essay. There are some things, however, that a concluding paragraph should *not* do.

▼ The concluding paragraph is not used to introduce new points; developing new points is the function of the body paragraphs.

▼ A concluding paragraph in a short essay should not simply restate your thesis sentence. Your reader is not likely to have forgotten the points you have developed in your body paragraphs. In a longer, more complex essay, restating the thesis in the concluding paragraph can be helpful because doing so reminds the reader of the major points that were used to support your ideas about the essay's topic.

There are several techniques you can use in the concluding paragraph to place emphasis on the points you have made throughout the essay. These include:

▼ call to action
▼ warning
▼ prediction
▼ evaluation

Call to Action

In a concluding paragraph that uses a call to action, the reader is asked to take some action—to do something based on the essay's content.

Example

New procedures are necessary to handle the burgeoning number of yearly visitors to national parks, but simply increasing entrance fees to generate more revenues is not an acceptable answer. <u>Write to senators and representatives and suggest that they need to hold hearings to determine what can be done to save these treasures.</u> If the destruction of national parks can be stemmed, future generations will be able to enjoy the natural beauty of America's great outdoors.

Warning

In some concluding paragraphs, the reader is warned that negative events might occur.

Example

Buying insurance on the Internet is becoming a commonplace practice. The amount of money spent online for insurance is doubling every year. The main reason for the popularity of buying insurance on the Internet is convenience. However, consumers should be careful when purchasing insurance online. <u>Make certain the company has an A+ Superior rating by a reputable rating service.</u> There have been cases where consumers paid for policies that didn't exist because the companies that sold the policies weren't actual insurance companies.

Prediction

A concluding paragraph may predict potential outcomes stemming from the discussion of the essay's topic. The writer looks into the future, so to speak.

Example

The new SUVs are becoming larger every year. They look like military humvee rejects. Families love the extra room, great for all kinds of shopping around town and vacationing with the children (pets included). However, handling the bigger vehicles can become a problem. Also, because their bumper height causes more damage to smaller cars, insurance companies are charging their owners higher premiums. <u>With the increasing popularity of SUVs, insurance rates will rise for all vehicles over the next few years.</u> It is incumbent upon the manufacturers of SUVs to plan for ways to reduce the spiraling insurance costs associated with these vehicles.

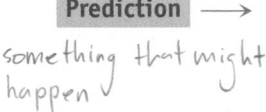

Evaluation

The importance of the overall topic may be summarized and judged in a concluding paragraph.

Example

Evaluation →

Evaluation →

Many bacteria that cause diseases are becoming resistant to antibiotics used to treat them. The rainforest provides many of the plants from which these antibiotics are made. But with so much of the rainforest being destroyed each year, a different method of producing antibiotics is necessary. New synthetic drugs can be effective in combating diseases currently resistant to natural drugs. Additionally, new synthetic derivatives can be created by studying both natural and existing synthetics. With assistance from the government, pharmaceutical companies should find new synthetic drug research a lucrative endeavor.

Drafting the Concluding Paragraph for the San Francisco Essay

While visiting San Francisco is certainly an exciting activity, big cities present some problems that visitors need to be aware of. With this in mind, a *warning* and a *call to action* seem appropriate techniques to use in drafting the concluding paragraph. A paragraph using these techniques might look like this:

As enjoyable as your vacation in San Francisco is likely to be, remember a few things. It's a big city, and it comes with the usual cautions. When you're in crowded places, keep your wallet in your front pocket, and hold onto your purse tightly. There are pickpockets in all large cities, and San Francisco is no different. Lock care doors, and don't leaving anything in plane sight. Discourage thieves from taking ad advantage of you. On a lighter but important topic, San Francisco, while blessed with a moderate climate, can get downright chilly at times. Remember, the city is quite far north, so always carry a widnbreaker, and wearing shorts is only encouraged if you have listen carefully to the local weather before you go out. With just a bit of planning and precaution, your vacation to San Francisco, the "City by the Bay," will be an experience that you and your family will remember for years to come.

In this paragraph, the *warnings* are twofold: Beware of pickpockets and consider the possibility of chilly weather. The *calls to action* advise the vacationer to keep valuables in secure places, lock car doors, and listen to local weather reports. Notice that the advice is presented in a matter-of-fact manner so as not to scare potential visitors. The writer is not attempting to alarm readers, just inform them about reasonable precautions to take while traveling. With the rough draft of the concluding paragraph finished, the first revision draft of the entire essay can begin. Remember, this is a rough draft of the concluding paragraph, and it still needs to be revised and proofread prior to producing the final draft.

Revising the First Rough Draft of the San Francisco Essay

As written, the first rough draft of the entire essay looks like this:

Are you tired of going to see the same trees and hills year after year? Have you been going to the same time-share for so long that you have names for all the squirrels and chipmunks? Tired of hiking from museum to museum until you become lost in a faceless crowd moving from one room to another? Thinking of separate vacations just so you can be assured of "not seeing the same old thing"? Well, If you want a memorable vacation, one packed with new experiences and invigorating activities, run—don't walk—to San Francisco. San Francisco is an exciting city to visit because of the Fisherman's Wharf, the Pacific Ocean, and the fine restaurants.

Fisherman's Wharf offers the visitor a wide array of fascinating attractions. The fishing fleets docks along the Jefferson Street promenade. An early morning stroll along "Fish Alley" will allow you to see fishermen at work. Jefferson Street has a host of specialty shops and entertainment for the entire family. The Wharf has its share of museums, but they are a bit out of the ordinary. There's a wax museum, the Ripley's *Believe It or Not!* Museum, and a museum in the guise of a medieval dungeon. If you're not to claustrophobic, you can visit Pier 45 and tour the USS *Pampanito,* a retired WWII submarine. Also, you might want to visit Ghirardelli Square and pick a souvenir or two from the many specialty shops located there. Finally, before you leave the Wharf, make certain you take with you a loaf or too of San Francisco's famous sourdough bread. You'll probably want to visit Fisherman's Wharf several times before your vacation is over.

The Pacific Ocean, like an unbelievable expanse of blue glass, is a boater's paradise. In San Francisco, boating enthusiasts can participate in activities in and out of the water. The San Francisco Maritime National Historical Pard contains four national landmark ships, including the famous square-rigger *Balclutha* and the ferryboat *Eureka,* which houses a collection of classic cars. The park's Maritime Museum house a fascinating arry of model ships, figureheads, painting, photographs, and artifacts in an art deco building shaped to resemble a cruise ship. But, if it's the high seas you want, you can head for several marinas and rent a boat or take an excursion tour boat out into the bay. Or, you can take a ferry to the infamous "Rock," Alcatraz island. The former maximum-security prison now offers guided tours, a self-guided hiking trail, and a slide show illustrating the penitentiary's notorious history. Or sail or motor out into the bay to view the enormous expanse of the Pacific Ocean and the incredible Golden Gate Bridge. Even when the fog is clouding and shrouding the enormous structure, the sight of fog rolling over the 1.2-mile-long bridge is both spectacular and haunting.

The city's restaurants serve a delectable variety of international cuisines. The real difficulty is making a choice between so many savory and delicious options. The Richmond District is well known for Russian delis. Chinatown offers traditional Mandarin, Szechuan, and Hunan fare and an array of Asian restaurants, such Cambodian, Laotian, Burmese, and Indain. The North Beach area is famous for Italian and California cuisines, while Central and South American food is the specialy in the Mission District. To borrow from the Swedish—what a *smorgasbord!* If you like dining out, San Francisco is the place.

As enjoyable as your vacation in San Francisco is likely to be, remember a few things. It's a big city, and it comes with the usual cautions. When you're in crowded places, keep your wallet in your front pocket, and hold onto your purse tightly. There are pickpockets in all large cities, and San Francisco is no different. Lock care doors, and don't leaving anything in plane sight. Discourage thieves from taking ad advantage of you. On a lighter but important topic, San Francisco, while blessed with a moderate climate, can get downright chilly at times. Remember, the city is quite far north, so always carry a widnbreaker, and wearing shorts is only encouraged if you have listen carefully to the local weather before you go out. With just a bit of planning and precaution, your vacation to San Francisco, the "City by the Bay," will be an experience that you and your family will remember for years to come.

In revising the first draft, eliminate poor noun and verb choices and unnecessary pronoun usage, and replace them with more specific nouns and verbs. Additionally, adding descriptive adjectives and adverbs helps to develop and clarify the content. Also, unless specifically assigned to do so, do not write in the first or second person; in other words, do not use "I," "me," "myself," "you," and "your." Substituting "person," "people," or "one" for these nouns and pronouns is not good writing, either. Use specific words to achieve developed, specific ideas that present clear content to your audience. As you focus on removing and replacing words, look for misspelled words, and correct them.

A revision of the first draft might look like this:

~~Are you~~ Many vacationers are tired of ~~going~~ looking ~~to see~~ **at** the same trees and hills year after year. ~~Have you been going to~~ Visiting the same time-share each summer can become so commonplace that the visitors give all the squirrels and chipmunks pet names! Tired of hiking from museum to museum? ~~until you~~ Upset at becom**ing** lost in a faceless crowd ~~moving~~ **shuffling** from one **overcrowded, stuffy** room to another? Thinking of separate vacations ~~just so you can~~ to be assured of "not seeing the same old thing"? Well, ~~if you want~~ for a memorable vacation, one packed with new experiences and invigorating activities, run—don't walk—to San Francisco. San Francisco is an exciting city to visit because of the **fantastic** Fisherman's Wharf, the **incredible** Pacific Ocean, and the ~~fine~~ **extraordinary** restaurants.

Fisherman's Wharf offers the visitor a wide array of fascinating attractions. The fishing fleets dock~~s~~ along the Jefferson Street promenade. An early morning stroll along "Fish Alley" ~~will allow you to see~~ **uncovers** fishermen at work. Jefferson Street has a host of specialty shops and entertainment for the entire family. The Wharf has its share of museums, but they are a bit out of the ordinary. There's a wax museum, the Ripley's *Believe It or Not!* Museum, and a museum in the guise of a medieval dungeon. If ~~you're not to~~ claustrophobi**a** ~~you can~~ **is not a problem,** visit Pier 45 and tour the USS *Pampanito,* a retired WWII submarine. Also,

~~you might want to~~ visit Ghirardelli Square and pick a souvenir or two from the many specialty shops ~~located there~~. Finally, before ~~you~~ leav**ing** the Wharf, ~~make certain you take with you~~ **buy** a loaf or ~~too~~ **two** of San Francisco's famous sourdough bread. ~~You'll probably want to~~ **V**isit Fisherman's Wharf several times before ~~your~~ vacation-**time** ~~is over~~ **runs out**.

The Pacific Ocean, like an unbelievable expanse of blue glass, is a boater's paradise. In San Francisco, boating enthusiasts can participate in activities in and out of the water. The San Francisco Maritime National Historical Par**k** contains four national landmark ships, including the famous square-rigger *Balclutha* and the ferryboat *Eureka*, which houses a collection of classic cars. The park's Maritime Museum houses a fascinating arr**a**y of model ships, figurehead**s**, paintings, photographs, and artifacts in an art deco building shaped to resemble a cruise ship. But, if ~~it's~~ the high seas ~~you want~~ **is a must-see**, ~~you can~~ head for several marinas ~~and~~ **to** rent a boat or ~~take~~ **board** an excursion tour boat **motoring** out into the bay. Or, ~~you can take~~ **ride** a ferry to the infamous "Rock," Alcatraz **I**sland. The former maximum-security prison now offers guided tours, a self-guided hiking trail, and a slide show illustrating the penitentiary's notorious history. ~~Or~~ **S**ail or motor out into the bay to view the enormous expanse of the Pacific Ocean and the incredible Golden Gate Bridge. Even when the fog is clouding and shrouding the enormous structure, the sight of fog rolling over the 1.2-mile-long bridge is both spectacular and haunting.

The city's restaurants serve a delectable variety of international cuisines. The real difficulty is ~~making a choice~~ **choosing** between so many savory and delicious options. The Richmond District is well known for Russian delis. Chinatown offers traditional Mandarin, Szechuan, and Hunan fare and an array of Asian restaurants, such **as** Cambodian, Laotian, Burmese, and Ind~~ai~~**i**an. The North Beach area is famous for Italian and California cuisines, while Central and South American food is the special**ty** in the Mission District. To borrow from the Swedish—what a *smorgasbord!* ~~If you like dining out,~~ San Francisco is "the place" for dining out**!**

As enjoyable as ~~your vacation in~~ **a** San Francisco **vacation** is likely to be, remember a few ~~things~~ **important points**. It's a big city, and it comes with the usual cautions. ~~When you're~~ **I**n crowded places, keep ~~your~~ wallet**s secured** in ~~your~~ front pocket**s**, and hold ~~onto your~~ purse**s** tightly. ~~There are~~ **P**ickpockets ~~in~~ **infest** all large cities, and San Francisco is no different. Lock car**e** doors, and don't leav~~eing~~ ~~anything~~ **packages or video equipment** in plain**e** sight. Discourage thieves ~~from taking ad advantage of you~~ **by being prepared in advance**. On a lighter but important topic, San Francisco, while blessed with a moderate climate, can ~~get~~ **become** downright chilly at times. Remember, the city is quite far north, so always carry a wind~~dn~~breaker, and wearing shorts is only encouraged if ~~you have listen carefully to~~ the local weather **channel has predicted a warm forecast** ~~before you go out.~~ With just a bit of planning and precaution, ~~your~~ **a** vacation to San Francisco, the "City by the Bay," will be an experience ~~that you and your~~ **any** family will remember for years to come.

In the first draft revision, the second person pronoun "you" has been removed, and bland verbs, such as *going, moving, make,* and *take* have been replaced. Descriptive adjectives, such as *fantastic, incredible, extraordinary, overcrowded, stuffy,* and *important* have been added. Misspelled words, such as *too* [*two*], *Indain* [*Indian*], and *Pard* [*Park*] have been corrected.

Revising the Second Rough Draft of the San Francisco Essay

In revising the second rough draft, correct punctuation errors. Additionally, create sentence variety by adding introductory phrases and clauses, and connect related ideas by using coordinating conjunctions, adverbial conjunctives, and transitional expressions. Finally, where applicable, help order information by using the "time," "space," and "ideas of importance" techniques you studied in Part 1 preceding Chapter 3.

The revised second rough draft might look like this:

Many vacationers are tired of looking at the same trees and hills year after year. Visiting the same time-share each summer can become so commonplace that the visitors give all the squirrels and chipmunks pet names! Tired of hiking from museum to museum? Upset at becoming lost in a faceless crowd, shuffling from one overcrowded, stuffy room to another? Thinking of separate vacations to be assured of "not seeing the same old thing"? **Well, for a memorable vacation,** one packed with new experiences and invigorating activities, run—don't walk—to San Francisco. San Francisco is an exciting city to visit because of the fantastic Fisherman's Wharf, the incredible Pacific Ocean, and the extraordinary restaurants.

Fisherman's Wharf offers the visitor a wide array of fascinating attractions. The fishing fleets dock along the Jefferson Street promenade. **First,** an early morning stroll along "Fish Alley" uncovers fishermen at work. Jefferson Street has a host of specialty shops and entertainment for the entire family. **Second,** the Wharf has its share of museums, **but** they are a bit out of the ordinary. There's a wax museum, the Ripley's *Believe It or Not!* Museum, and a museum in the guise of a medieval dungeon. **Third, if claustrophobia is not a problem,** visit Pier 45 and tour the USS *Pampanito,* a retired WWII submarine. **Also,** visit Ghirardelli Square, and pick a souvenir or two from the many specialty shops. **Finally, before leaving the Wharf,** buy a loaf or two of San Francisco's famous sourdough bread. Visit Fisherman's Wharf several times before vacation-time runs out.

The Pacific Ocean, like an unbelievable expanse of blue glass, is a boater's paradise; **consequently, in San Francisco,** boating enthusiasts can participate in activities in and out of the water. The San Francisco Maritime National Historical Park contains four national landmark ships, including the famous square-rigger *Balclutha* and the ferryboat *Eureka,* which houses a collection of classic cars. The park's Maritime Museum houses a fascinating array of model ships, figureheads, paintings, photographs, and artifacts in an art deco building shaped to resemble a cruise ship. **But, if the high seas are a must-see**, head for several marinas to rent a boat or board an excursion tour boat motoring out into the bay**, or** ride a ferry to the infamous "Rock," Alcatraz Island. The former maximum-security prison now offers guided tours, a self-guided hiking trail, and a slide show illustrating the penitentiary's notorious history. **S**ail or motor out into the bay to view the enormous expanse of the Pacific Ocean and the incredible Golden Gate Bridge. **Even when the fog is clouding and shrouding the enormous structure**, the sight of fog rolling over the 1.2-mile-long bridge is both spectacular and haunting.

The city's restaurants serve a delectable variety of international cuisines. **Initially,** the real difficulty is choosing between so many savory and delicious options. The Richmond District is well-known for Russian delis. **Next,** Chinatown offers traditional Mandarin, Szechuan, and Hunan fare and an array of Asian restaurants, such a**s** Cambodian, Laotian, Burmese, and Indian. **Then,** the North Beach area is famous for Italian and California cuisines, **while** Central and South American food is the specialty in the Mission District. **To borrow from the Swedish—**what a *smorgasbord!* San Francisco is "the place" for dining out!

As enjoyable as a San Francisco vacation is likely to be, remember a few important points. It's a big city**, and** it comes with the usual cautions. **In crowded places**, keep wallet**s** secured in front pocket**s, and** hold purse**s** tightly. Pickpockets infest all large cities**, and** San Francisco is no different. Lock car doors**, and** don't leave packages or video equipment in plain sight. Discourage thieves by being prepared in advance. **However, on a lighter but important topic**, San Francisco, while blessed with a moderate climate, can become downright chilly at times. **Remember**, the city is quite far north**, so** always carry a windbreaker**, and** wearing shorts is only encouraged if the local weather channel has predicted a warm forecast. **Lastly, with just a bit of planning and precaution**, a vacation to San Francisco, the "City by the Bay," will be an experience any family will remember for years to come.

In the second rough draft, sentence variety has been achieved through the use of introductory phrases and clauses, coordinating conjunctions, adverbial conjunctives, and transitional expressions. Punctuation errors have been corrected, and the ideas have been given a logical order through the addition of key words and phrases. Additionally, misspelled words have been corrected.

Now it is time to take one last look at the essay. The essay should flow rhythmically from sentence to sentence. The ideas should be organized logically and orderly. In other words, the essay should be professional in both content and presentation. The final draft would look like this:

▼ Sample Essay: SAN FRANCISCO OR BUST!

1   Many vacationers are tired of looking at the same trees and hills year after year. Visiting the same time-share each summer can become so commonplace that the visitors give all the squirrels and chipmunks pet names. Tired of hiking from museum to museum? Upset at becoming lost in a faceless crowd, shuffling from one overcrowded, stuffy room to another? Thinking of separate vacations to be assured of "not seeing the same old thing"? Well, for a memorable vacation, one packed with new experiences and invigorating activities, run—don't walk—to San Francisco. San Francisco is an exciting city to visit because of the fantastic Fisherman's Wharf, the incredible Pacific Ocean, and the extraordinary restaurants.

2   Fisherman's Wharf offers the visitor a wide array of fascinating attractions. The fishing fleets dock along the Jefferson Street promenade. First, an early morning stroll along "Fish Alley" uncovers fishermen at work. Jefferson Street has a host of specialty shops and entertainment for the entire family. Second, the Wharf has its share of museums, but they are a bit out of the ordinary. There's a wax museum, the Ripley's *Believe It or Not!* Museum, and a museum in the guise of a medieval dungeon. Third, if claustrophobia is not a problem, visit Pier 45 and tour the USS *Pampanito,* a retired WWII submarine. Also, visit Ghirardelli Square, and pick a souvenir or two from the many specialty shops. Finally, before leaving the Wharf, buy a loaf or two of San Francisco's famous sourdough bread. Visit Fisherman's Wharf several times before vacation-time runs out.

3   The Pacific Ocean, like an unbelievable expanse of blue glass, is a boater's paradise; consequently, in San Francisco, boating enthusiasts can participate in activities in and out of the water. The San Francisco Maritime National Historical Park contains four national landmark ships, including the famous square-rigger *Balclutha* and the ferryboat *Eureka,* which houses a collection of classic cars. The park's Maritime Museum houses a fascinating array of model ships, figureheads, paintings, photographs, and artifacts in an art deco build-

ing shaped to resemble a cruise ship. But, if the high seas are a must-see, head for several marinas to rent a boat or board an excursion tour boat motoring out into the bay, or ride a ferry to the infamous "Rock," Alcatraz Island. The former maximum-security prison now offers guided tours, a self-guided hiking trail, and a slide show illustrating the penitentiary's notorious history. Sail or motor out into the bay to view the enormous expanse of the Pacific Ocean and the incredible Golden Gate Bridge. Even when the fog is clouding and shrouding the enormous structure, the sight of fog rolling over the 1.2-mile-long bridge is both spectacular and haunting.

4   The city's restaurants serve a delectable variety of international cuisines. Initially, the real difficulty is choosing between so many savory and delicious options. The Richmond District is well-known for Russian delis. Next, Chinatown offers traditional Mandarin, Szechuan, and Hunan fare and an array of Asian restaurants, such as Cambodian, Laotian, Burmese, and Indian. Then, the North Beach area is famous for Italian and California cuisines, while Central and South American food is the specialty in the Mission District. To borrow from the Swedish—what a *smorgasbord!* San Francisco is "the place" for dining out!

5   As enjoyable as a San Francisco vacation is likely to be, remember a few important points. It's a big city, and it comes with the usual cautions. In crowded places, keep wallets secured in front pockets, and hold purses tightly. Pickpockets infest all large cities, and San Francisco is no different. Lock car doors, and don't leave packages or video equipment in plain sight. Discourage thieves by being prepared in advance. However, on a lighter but important topic, San Francisco, while blessed with a moderate climate, can become downright chilly at times. Remember, the city is quite far north, so always carry a windbreaker, and wearing shorts is only encouraged if the local weather channel has predicted a warm forecast. Lastly, with just a bit of planning and precaution, a vacation to San Francisco, the "City by the Bay," will be an experience any family will remember for years to come.

When you are satisfied that the essay is well organized and presents its ideas clearly, you can print it and hand it in. Then, and only then, can you consider your essay finished.

Essay Writing Technique Questions

1. What technique is used in the introductory sentences to introduce the thesis sentence?

   _____

2. Identify the thesis sentence, and write it on the lines below. Circle the subject. Underline each of the essay map items twice.

   _____

   _____

   _____

3. Identify the topic sentence in each of the three body paragraphs, and write the sentences on the lines below. Circle the subject of each topic

sentence. Are the subjects the same as the essay map items that you underlined twice in Question 2?

_____

_____

_____

_____

_____

4. Identify the techniques used in the concluding paragraph, and write your answer on the following lines. Then, answer this question: If you were thinking about traveling to San Francisco for a vacation, would the concluding paragraph affect your decision?

_____

_____

_____

_____

CHAPTER REVIEW

▼ The concluding paragraph of an essay brings a sense of completion to the essay and reemphasizes its general thesis.

▼ Techniques for writing a concluding paragraph include call to action, warning, prediction, and evaluation.

Visit *The Write Start* Online!

For additional practice with the materials found in this chapter, visit our Website at

http://www.ablongman.com/checkett

The Website also features additional readings, quizzes, writing activities, and Internet links, as well as a bulletin board and interactive chat.

Moving Forward: Strategies for Developing Essays

Now that you have learned the steps in the writing process and how to write introductory, body, and concluding paragraphs, it is time to put these skills together and construct a longer unit of writing called an essay, theme, paper, or composition. Essays are an important part of the college learning process because the essay helps you in three important respects: (1) writing an essay helps you to learn, (2) writing an essay helps you to learn about a topic from a variety of viewpoints, and (3) your essay tells your instructor what you have learned.

The Modes of Development

The different viewpoints from which you can write about a topic are called **modes of development.** *Mode* simply means method or process. You can develop a topic in more than one way, thereby learning something different about it each time, depending upon the mode of development you use.

In Part 2 of the text, you will be exploring, in order, the following modes of development:

Description: developing a topic through the use of vivid detail.

Narration: developing a topic through a recounting of events.

Example: developing a topic by using illustrations as clarification.

Classification: developing a topic by categorizing its characteristics.

Process: developing a topic by explaining how to do something or how something operates.

Comparison and Contrast: developing a topic by focusing on similarities and differences.

Definition: developing a topic by explaining what it is and, at times, is not.

Cause and Effect: developing a topic by focusing on why it occurs or the consequences or results of it occurring.

Persuasion: developing a topic by convincing the audience to agree with a particular point of view.

For instance, in an engineering course, your instructor might ask you to write an essay about a piece of machinery. The modes of development can guide you in making choices about your approach to the assignment. You can use *description* to tell about the physical dimensions and visual characteristics of the machine, or you can use *description* to give your reader an emotional sense of the machine: what it sounds like and feels like when you use it. You can use *process* to explain how the machine works. You can *compare* or *contrast* the machine to other machines with similar or different characteristics. A *cause and effect* essay might explore what effects the machine has had on product development, company profitability, or later developments in technology or commerce.

Of course, you can increase your essay's depth and vision by combining one or more of the modes of development. In fact, you will do this to some degree whether you plan to do it or not. That is, you cannot *describe, compare,* or show *cause and effect* about a person, place, or thing without *defining* it; likewise, it is difficult to *compare, contrast, define, describe,* or show *cause and effect* without using *examples.*

The modes of development are tools to assist you in writing your paper by helping you to choose your approach to the topic. By learning to use these techniques, your writing will become more developed in content and more varied in style—both signs of a mature, intelligent thinker and communicator.

Beyond the College Essay

In the chapters that follow, student essays are used to model the five-paragraph essay. While this essay format is useful in teaching developing writers the elements of effective essay writing for an academic setting, other formats are used by more advanced student writers and professional writers. There's an old saying that "form follows function." This means that the format the writing takes is usually created to best suit the ideas the author is trying to get across to the reader. For instance, while paragraphs in college essays usually are at least four or five sentences long, paragraphs in professional essays sometimes consist of a single sentence. Perhaps the writer wishes to emphasize a particular idea or image by presenting it in a stand-alone sentence. This focuses the reader's attention on the idea or image without the distraction of other ideas and images in other sentences in a longer paragraph. So, as you read the professional essays in Chapters 7 through 15 and in the Additional Readings section, be aware that their formats are designed specifically to present the author's ideas in the best manner.

7 The Descriptive Essay

All essays develop a topic. One method to build on a topic is by describing it in detail. Effective **description** creates images in the reader's mind by using specific details. Like a painter using color on a canvas, the writer uses words (the color) to create pictures in the reader's mind (the canvas).

Instead of merely writing

> The bowl contained three scoops of ice cream.

A writer using effective description might write

> The glistening white bowl, decorated with bright blue spirals, overflowed with three gigantic mounds of vanilla, chocolate, and strawberry ice cream covered by a thick layer of whipped cream and garnished with a bright red cherry.

The specific details help develop the word-painting that describes persons, places, things, and emotions.

Identifying Your Purpose

The purpose of writing a descriptive essay is to clarify, explain, or create a particular mood about a person, place, or thing. Sometimes you want to be objective (factual) in your description. For instance, **objective description** can be useful in describing a medical procedure, a legal concept, or a new piece of technological hardware.

Most of the time, you will use **subjective description** to create a more emotionally charged impression. For instance, a subjective (or impressionistic) description may relate how a medical advance will affect the lives of patients and their families, how a legal concept can affect an entire population, or how a technological advance can change the economic outlook of an entire industry.

At times, you will want to convey a feeling of sadness. At other times, you might want to evoke a feeling of happiness, or frustration, or hope, or sarcasm. Effective description evokes emotion and adds clarity and depth to your writing.

Objective versus Subjective Description

Objective description relies on factual detail without much embellishment. You write down what you see, hear, taste, smell, or touch without any emotional response or interpretation.

> The old mansion sat in the middle of the unkempt property.

From this objective description, it is difficult to recognize what emotion or impression the writer wants the reader to understand.

In contrast, subjective description creates an easily identifiable emotion or impression.

> The hulking, old mansion, its windows covered with broken spider webs and darkened by a thick covering of dust, sat like a lurking beast hiding in a yard overgrown with weeds and creeping vines.

From this subjective description, it is clear that the writer wants the site of the mansion to evoke a mysterious or dreadful emotion. Objective description describes what the writer actually perceives. Subjective description describes the writer's emotional response to what he or she encounters.

▼ PRACTICE 1   Writing an Objective Description

On a separate piece of paper, write a paragraph about the room you are now sitting in. Describe the room objectively by simply writing down, in four or five sentences, what you see, hear, smell, or touch.

Dominant Impression

Your descriptive writing will be clearer and more enjoyable if you focus on just one **dominant impression** (sometimes identified as the DI). The dominant impression is the overall feeling or emotional response you want the reader to take away from the description. When you write a descriptive paragraph, each support sentence should build on the dominant impression you create in the topic sentence. Be careful to add only those details that support the dominant impression. Do not add details that suggest a different impression, as in the following example.

> **Examples**
>
> *Poor dominant impression*
> On a bright, sunny day, Meiling played joyously with her frisky, new puppy until it fell into a drainage ditch full of sewage.
>
> *Better dominant impression*
> On a bright, sunny day, Meiling romped joyously with her frisky, new puppy, and she could not contain herself from laughing out loud at the cute little dog's frolicking antics.

In the first example, the reader will not know what dominant impression the writer is attempting to convey. Is the writer trying to convey a positive impression (Meiling playing joyously with her puppy) or a negative impression (the puppy falling into a ditch full of sewage)? The second example is more convincing and focused on the writer's intentions. The descriptions of the dog, its actions, and Meiling's responses are consistent with the same happy mood. The positive dominant impression is clear, supported by such word choices as "bright," "sunny," "romped," "joyously," "frisky," "laughing," and "frolicking."

Some Dominant Impression Words

aggressive	angry	bitter	boisterous	bumbling
cheerful	clumsy	cluttered	comfortable	cozy
crowded	dazzling	depressing	drab	dreadful
eerie	fierce	friendly	gaudy	generous
gigantic	inviting	peaceful	pessimistic	placid
restful	restless	romantic	rustic	shy
silent	snobbish	spacious	stuffy	sullen
tasteless	tense	ugly	uncomfortable	unfriendly

PRACTICE 2   Rewriting an Objective Description to Make it Subjective

In Practice 1, you wrote an objective description of a room. On a separate piece of paper, rewrite your paragraph subjectively. Focus on the dominant impression the room suggests to you, perhaps because of the room's color scheme, some object in the room, or the type of activity that happens in the room. After you have finished, compare the two paragraphs. Which one do you think paints a sharper, clearer image in the reader's mind? You can choose one of the dominant impression words from the preceding list if you cannot think of one.

Writing the Descriptive Paragraph

A descriptive paragraph has a topic sentence that conveys the dominant impression. It also includes details that describe sensory images, sometimes using figurative language to make comparisons.

The Topic Sentence in a Subjective Description Paragraph

The topic sentence in a subjective description paragraph states the topic to be discussed and clearly states the dominant impression that will be developed in the supporting sentences that follow. Topic sentences without a dominant impression are usually statements of fact; in other words, they are too objective for a subjective description paragraph.

Examples

Topic sentences without a dominant impression:

The parade passed down the street.

Sareena wore a dress to the prom.

The hockey game was played Saturday night.

Yoshi had an interesting personality.

Topic sentences with a dominant impression:

The parade passing down the street was **dazzling.**

The dress Sareena wore to the prom was **tasteless.**

The hockey game played Saturday night was **exciting.**

Yoshi's personality was **bitter.**

Resource Note: A useful type of book to help you select better dominant impression words is a *thesaurus*. This type of reference book contains lists of synonyms, homonyms, and antonyms for almost any word you can think of. You can buy an inexpensive paperback thesaurus at any bookstore or from an online book source, and some computer programs have a thesaurus built in. You can also access a thesaurus on the Internet.

▼
PRACTICE 3   Adding a Dominant Impression to Topic Sentences

Rewrite the following topic sentences by adding a dominant impression to each one.

1. William Jefferson Clinton was President of the United States.

_____

_____

2. Students use the Internet to find information.

_____

_____

3. Ecstasy is a drug used mostly by young people.

_____

4. Security police help keep order on campuses.

_____

_____

5. Date rape is a new crime.

_____

_____

Supporting Details: Sensory Images

Once you have decided on the dominant impression you wish to create, you need to choose language and details to develop that impression. Writers can choose from a rich array of language to create and support description, including **sensory images.** These sensory images are based on the five senses with which we are all familiar: sight, touch, smell, sound, and taste. Because description creates images, it can tell the reader what a person, place, or thing

- ▼ looks like
- ▼ feels like
- ▼ smells like
- ▼ sounds like
- ▼ tastes like

By using sensory images, writers can draw a more fully developed picture of what they are describing. Good description actually causes readers to remember similar persons, places, or things from their own experiences. This personal interaction between the reader and the writing is a wonderful and powerful process.

Examples

Sight

Nondescriptive: The sky was blue.

Descriptive: The sky was a **deep, azure blue, dotted** by **fluffy, white clouds.**

Touch

Nondescriptive: The hospital bedsheets were uncomfortable.

Descriptive: The hospital sheets were **stiff** and **scratchy,** like **sandpaper scraping** against my skin.

Smell

Nondescriptive: The cab of Miguel's truck smelled awful.

Descriptive: The cab of Miguel's truck smelled like a **gym locker stuffed** with a year's worth of **dirty socks.**

Sound

Nondescriptive: The jetliner was loud as it took off.

Descriptive: As it took off, the jetliner was so loud that it **made your teeth vibrate, as if a dozen motorcycles were passing by.**

Taste

Nondescriptive: The bagels tasted old.

Descriptive: The bagels **tasted musty, like moldy cheese** I remember eating at my brother-in-law's house last New Year's Eve.

▼ **PRACTICE 4**   **Adding Sensory Details to a Paragraph**

Using the subjective paragraph you completed in Practice 2, add sensory description to some of the sentences. Try to use at least two different sensory techniques. After you are finished, compare this new paragraph with your previous version. Are the images more vivid in your mind?

Supporting Details: Comparisons Using Figurative Language

Another device that writers can use to describe something is comparison. Comparisons to well-known or everyday objects or images provide descriptions that readers can immediately recognize. Many writers find comparison the easiest descriptive tool because comparisons allow writers to provide clear ideas to the reader by tapping into images and emotions that the reader has already experienced.

Figurative language is one tool writers use to make comparisons. Figurative language describes a person or thing in terms usually associated with something very different. The three most effective figurative language devices are **similes, metaphors,** and **personification.**

A *simile* is a comparison using either *like* or *as* to show a similarity between two dissimilar things. Notice how similar the words *simile* and *similarity* are.

Examples

The huge football lineman is **like** a mountain.

The clouds covered the city **like** a thick, wool blanket.

The workman is **as** strong **as** a bull.

The gymnast is **as** agile **as** a monkey.

A *metaphor* is a stronger comparison between two things without using *like* or *as.* The implication is that one thing "is" the same as the other.

Examples

The huge football lineman **is** a mountain.

The cloud cover **is** a thick blanket smothering the city.

The workman **is** a bull.

The gymnast **is** an agile monkey.

Personification gives human emotions or characteristics to animals, objects, or ideas.

Examples

The wind **howled** past my ears.

Love **danced** in their eyes.

The fox **cheated** the farmer by **stealing** eggs from the henhouse.

The candle in the window **winked** at the passing cars.

The sun **slept** as the moon **kept watch** over the campers.

▼ **PRACTICE 5**   **Using Figurative Language**

Using the completed paragraph from Practice 4, add several figurative language techniques to several ideas. After you are finished, compare the paragraph with the previous ones. Quite a difference, isn't there? Your paragraph illustrates the creative power of effectively written description.

Moving from Paragraph to Essay

Now that you have studied and practiced the techniques to create effective subjective description paragraphs, it is time to expand your ideas to a larger writing unit: the descriptive essay. The descriptive essay is a union of the paragraph techniques you learned in Part 1 regarding developing the essay and the subjective description techniques you have just learned. This might be a good time to return to Part 1 and review the techniques for developing the full essay.

Creating the Introductory Paragraph

Description often can seem free-flowing and without purpose. But a descriptive essay is a piece of writing—and all good writing has a purpose and a clearly defined organization. The thesis statement of the introductory paragraph should clearly indicate the purpose of the essay and how the essay will develop.

The thesis in a descriptive essay should blend naturally into the rest of the introductory paragraph. In the following example, notice how the thesis announces the topic (*storms*), the writer's controlling attitude—the dominant impression—toward the topic (*devastation*), and the essay map containing the body paragraph subtopics (*lightning, winds, and flooding*). The thesis statement is underlined for instructional purposes only.

> **Example**
>
> The sky darkened like a ceiling scorched by fire. Raindrops as big as marbles began to pelt the ground, hurling bits of mud and grass into the air as the banks of creeks began to overflow. The wind swirled and muscled trees into spaghetti-like shapes. Brilliant flashes of light split the air like a hot knife through butter. <u>Lightning, raging winds, and flooding all added to the storm's devastation.</u> Such was the storm's vengeance; all in its path was destroyed.

Notice how the specific detail and the figurative language all support the dominant impression of devastation. There are specific sensory details: *darkened, scorched, hurling, swirled, muscled, flashes, split, raging, vengeance, destroyed*. There are similes: *sky darkened like a ceiling scorched by fire; raindrops as big as marbles; flashes of light split the air like a hot knife through butter*. There is also personification: *the wind . . . muscled; such was the storm's vengeance*.

Creating the Body Paragraphs

For a paper describing a storm's devastation, the focus of the body paragraphs will be the paragraph topics listed in the thesis statement's essay map. The first body paragraph's topic will be about *lightning*, the second body paragraph's topic will be about *raging winds,* and the third body paragraph's topic will be about *flooding*. Remember, as you write about each of these topics, your focus should be that these elements *added to the storm's devastation*. Your focus should not be on how the National Weather Service tracks storms, or how local authorities marshal their forces to help victims, or how people take precautions when preparing for severe weather. Keep your focus on the controlling idea or attitude as stated in your thesis sentence.

Creating the Concluding Paragraph

The approach of the concluding paragraph should flow naturally from the essay's main topic. Because the essay's focus is on how various elements can make a storm devastating, *evaluating* each element that might be part of a devastating storm would seem an appropriate choice. You might describe how each different element (lightning, wind, and flooding) can affect people's lives and property. Whereas the body paragraphs were used to describe the effects of the elements, you can use the concluding paragraph to present the more personal effects of the storm on its victims.

Sample Student Essay: MR. ROGERS DON'T LIVE HERE

Blanche Wade

The following essay, "Mr. Rogers Don't Live Here," by student writer Blanche Wade, is an emotionally intensive look at her inner-city neighborhood. The essay relies on sharply honed images that capture the sense of danger and broken dreams the neighborhood symbolizes. The numerous descriptive images paint a picture recognizable to anyone who has lived in or near a big city.

Vocabulary

Before you start reading, use a dictionary to look up the definitions of the following words that appear in the essay.

fatalistic (3)	foreboding (4)	formidable (2)
imps (2)	neurotic (3)	shroud (1)
obscure (1)	paraphernalia (2)	wily (4)
spawn (3)	waning (1)	

Mr. Rogers Don't Live Here

1   On a night when the inky sky is wearing a shroud, and the moon eyes weary travelers, the wind is whistling through vacant spaces like a broken phonograph playing ghostly melodies. Sluggish souls tremble as supernatural organs play tunes of terror in the waning light. While thoughts swarm of "things that go bump in the night" and devilish demons dance, the green and yellow eyes of obscure creatures watch from the shadows. The neighborhood has become a dangerous jungle of broken bodies, vacant eyes, and wild creatures waiting to pounce on unsuspecting souls.

2   Broken buildings are like bodies that have been used and tossed aside. These hulking, crumbling structures fling concrete boulders from their rooftops; consequently, the fused stones, as if tossed by evil imps, become murderous missiles of destruction. The unsuspecting traveler, unaware of their formidable firing power, now wears a bandage on his head, a reminder of the neighborhood's ability to strike swiftly and painfully. Windows, framed but without glass, squint as they watch passersby stumble on rippled sidewalks. Snake-like cracks wait to ambush unsuspecting victims. The menacing walkways connect the vacant spaces of deserted lots and the streets that are as mean as lions chasing lambs. The neighborhood is littered with a variety of paraphernalia: the unfulfilled visions lost in bottles of drowned dreams and needles of forgotten promises, the obstacles to the art of survival.

3   Vacant eyes are connected to lost souls. Dealers of every type of drug are lurking in deepening shadows; buyers rushing in to purchase the ability to forget. Dreams are forever lost after these transactions, like Satan's spawn. Pushers are cackling witches during a late October's eve as they collect all debts due from hopeless junkies. The wasted eyes are only capable of searching for someone to rob. Fatalistic criminals are prepared to relieve hard working citizens of their pay, and ladies of the evening are sometimes the forgotten players in this hellish nightmare. Young and not so young women, neurotic and high-strung, slither through the damp and filthy ruins seeking profits in exchange for pleasure but not enjoying the trade; these ladies, driven by desperation, work doggedly for their needs. The malignant obsession of their addictions compels them to continually abuse their temples. The patchwork existence within the neighborhood resembles a puzzle with missing pieces.

4   Meanwhile, once tame animals, mirroring the fate of their former masters, hasten to sanctuaries filled with unrecognizable rubble. Rats like cats, large and fearless, move swiftly through the outer limits of decay; wily and foreboding, they strike terror as they sprint past. Dogs, fierce and beyond approach, snarl at any movement, real or imagined; thin, starving, unwanted and on the prowl for mayhem and deadly dealing, they are killers in a dangerous nightmare come to life. Little tabbies have mutated into ferocious, menacing beasts. These clawing, scratching, and sneaky assassins wait silently

and patiently for their next meal. Shrewd and able hunters, these night-stalkers patrol their concrete forest with survival skills matching that of any well-trained mercenary: stalk and kill!

5   Even closed eyes can see the possibilities of hopelessness. The lost community, the depressing statistics, and the war on drugs are all too real, not a horrible fantasy. Demons are within all of us; be aware that one neighborhood lost is one too many. Small children, if neglected, have the potential to become large and powerful monsters. There are no quick fixes to the many causes of despair. Only caring for our children and pets and tearing down houses so they cannot be used as hideouts for delinquents from responsibility can possibly slow the neighborhood decay.

Descriptive Technique Questions

1. Identify the thesis statement by listing the topic, the attitude, and the three-item essay map.

Topic:

_____

Attitude:

_____

Essay Map Items:

_____

_____

_____

2. The author uses personification to enhance the menacing tone of the essay. Point out instances of personification, and explain how they help create the essay's tone.

_____

_____

_____

3. Underline as many similes and metaphors as you can find. How do they help support the writer's attitude concerning the neighborhood?

_____

_____

_____

4. Point out as many sensory images as you can. How do they help develop the essay's tone?

_____

_____

_____

5. Sentence variety helps to create rhythm and to connect related ideas. Identify different types of coordinated and subordinated sentences.

_____

_____

_____

Critical Reading Questions

1. How does the title affect your understanding of the author's feeling about her neighborhood? Do you know what the reference to "Mr. Rogers" means? How did the title affect you before you read the story? Did it have more significance once you had finished the story?

_____

_____

_____

_____

2. What dominant impression do you think the author is trying to achieve?

_____

3. Beside people, the author uses buildings and animals to describe her neighborhood. How does her using these "nonhuman" elements help create the dominant impression?

_____

Descriptive Writing Exercises

1. Write a descriptive paragraph about your neighborhood. First, what is the dominant impression you have about your neighborhood? Pick out one person, place, or thing, and use it as the focus of your paragraph. How does the person, place, or thing represent your feeling about your neighborhood? Use descriptive adjectives, sensory images, and figurative language to describe the element you have chosen. Even though you are writing about your neighborhood, do not use the first or second point of view; in other words, no "I" or "you" writing. Both Blanche Wade and Mario Suarez (the author of the next essay) are writing about their neighborhoods, but neither uses the first or second person point of view from which to tell their story.

2. Now, write a descriptive essay about your neighborhood. Expand your vision by including descriptions of the two elements you did not use in exercise 1 as other paragraph topics to support the dominant impression you want to convey. Create images using the descriptive techniques as you did in exercise 1. Remember, do not use first or second person point of view.

Sample Professional Essay: EL HOYO

Mario Suarez

> Although written in his first year of college at the University of Arizona, this essay by Mario Suarez is as professional as any you will ever read. It was published in the *Arizona Quarterly*. Suarez's audience was probably not very familiar with the Latino culture and some of the words he uses. Also, some of the words, like *barrio*, probably had negative connotations for the reader. To create a more positive image of the Latino culture, Suarez builds one positive event upon another with unrelenting descriptive imagery until the dignity of the chicano shines through the rubble and the squalor.

Vocabulary

Before you start to read, use a dictionary to look up the definitions for the following words appearing in the essay.

benevolent (2)	bicker (1)	conquistador (3)	famine (1)
imply (1)	inundated (1)	solace (2)	solicited (2)

See the Glossary at the end of the story for an explanation of words marked with an asterisk (*).

El Hoyo

1   From the center of downtown Tucson the ground slopes gently away to Main Street, drops a few feet, and then rolls to the banks of the Santa Cruz River. Here lies the section of the city known as El Hoyo. Why it is called El Hoyo is not very clear. In no sense is it a hole as its name would imply; it is simply the river's immediate valley. Its inhabitants are chicanos who raise hell on Saturday night and listen to Padre Estanislao on Sunday morning. While the term chicano is the short way of saying Mexican, it is not restricted to the paisanos who came from old Mexico with the territory or the last famine to work for the railroad, labor, sing, and go on relief. Chicano is the easy way of referring to everybody. Pablo Gutierrez married the Chinese grocer's daughter and now runs a meat department; his sons are chicanos. So are the sons of Killer Jones who threw a fight in Harlem and fled to El Hoyo to marry Cristina Mendez. And so are all of them. However, it is doubtful that all these spiritual sons of Mexico live in El Hoyo because they love each other—many fight and bicker constantly. It is doubtful they live in El Hoyo because of its scenic beauty—it is everything but beautiful. Its houses are simple affairs of unplastered adobe, wood, and abandoned car parts. Its narrow streets are mostly clearings which have, in time, acquired names. Except for some tall trees which nobody has ever cared to identify, nurse, or destroy, the main things known to grow in the general area are weeds, garbage piles, dark-eyed chavalos,* and dogs. And it is doubtful that the chicanos live in El Hoyo because it is safe—many times the Santa Cruz has risen and inundated the area.

2   In other respects living in El Hoyo has its advantages. If one is born with weakness for acquiring bills, El Hoyo is where the collectors are less likely to

find you. If one has acquired the habit of listening to Octavio Perea's Mexican Hour in the wee hours of the morning with the radio on at full blast, El Hoyo is where you are less likely to be reported to the authorities. Besides, Perea is very popular and sooner or later to everyone "Smoke in the Eyes" is dedicated between the pinto beans and white flour commercials. If one, for any reason whatever, comes on an extended period of hard times, where, if not in El Hoyo, are the neighbors more willing to offer solace? When Teofila Malacara's house burned to the ground with all her belongings and two children, a benevolent gentleman carried through the gesture that made tolerable her burden. He made a list of 500 names and solicited from each a dollar. At the end of a month he turned over to the tearful but grateful señora* $100 in cold cash and then accompanied her on a short vacation. When the new manager of a local store decided that no more chicanas were to work behind the counters, it was the chicanos of El Hoyo who, on taking their individually small but collectively great buying power elsewhere, drove the manager out and the girls returned to their jobs. When the Mexican Army was en route to Baja California and the chicanos found out that the enlisted men ate only at infrequent intervals, it was El Hoyo's chicanos who crusaded across town with pots of beans and trays of tortillas to meet the train. When someone gets married, celebrating is not restricted to the immediate friends of the couple. Everybody is invited. Anything calls for a celebration and a celebration calls for anything. On Memorial Day there are no less than half a dozen good fights at the Riverside Dance Hall. On Mexican Independence Day more than one flag is sworn allegiance to amid cheers for the queen.

3   And El Hoyo is something more. It is this something more which brought Felipe Suarez back from the wars after having killed a score of Vietnamese with his body resembling a patchwork quilt to marry Julia Armijo. It brought Joe Zepeda, a gunner, . . . back to compose boleros.* He has a metal plate for a skull. Perhaps El Hoyo is proof that those people exist, and perhaps exist best, who have as yet failed to observe the more popular modes of human conduct. Perhaps the humble appearance of El Hoyo justifies the indifferent shrug of those made aware of its existence. Perhaps El Hoyo's simplicity motivates an occasional chicano to move away from its narrow streets, babbling comrades, and shrieking children to deny the bloodwell from which he springs and to claim the blood of a conquistador while his hair is straight and his face beardless. Yet El Hoyo is not an outpost of a few families against the world. It fights for no causes except those which soothe its immediate angers. It laughs and cries with the same amount of passion in times of plenty and of want.

4   Perhaps El Hoyo, its inhabitants, and its essence can best be explained by telling a bit about a dish called capirotada. Its origin is uncertain. But, according to the time and the circumstance, it is made of old, new or hard bread. It is softened with water and then cooked with peanuts, raisins, onions, cheese, and panocha.* It is fired with sherry wine. Then it is served hot, cold, or just "on the weather" as they say in El Hoyo. The Sermenos like it one way, the Garcias another, and the Ortegas still another. While it might differ greatly from one home to another, nevertheless it is still capirotada. And so it is with El Hoyo's chicanos. While being divided from within and from without, like the capirotada, they remain chicanos.

Glossary of Terms	
chavalo = young man; lad	bolero = a type of dance
señora = Mrs.; woman	panocha = corn

Descriptive Technique Questions

1. Suarez describes El Hoyo by examining many aspects of the community. Point out examples of where El Hoyo is located, who lives there, how the inhabitants live, and why.

_____

_____

_____

_____

_____

_____

2. In the last paragraph, Suarez describes chicanos by comparing them to something else. Describe the details of the comparison. In what other parts of the essay do you find details to support your answer?

_____

_____

_____

_____

_____

3. Considering all the description about El Hoyo, what dominant impression do you think Suarez is trying to create in the reader's mind?

_____

Critical Reading Questions

1. What do you think Suarez's purpose is for writing the essay? Is his thesis implied, or can you find a sentence that states his thesis?

_____

_____

_____

2. How do you think Suarez feels about El Hoyo? Is the image he creates positive or negative? Support your answer with specific details from the essay.

_____

_____

_____

3. How does Blanche Wade's description of her neighborhood differ from Suarez's? What does Wade focus on that Suarez does not, and vice versa? Does Suarez's essay feel more like a story? Does it appear more "realistic"? If so, why?

_____

_____

_____

Descriptive Writing Exercises

1. Create a thesis statement with a three-item essay map for "El Hoyo." Use the dominant impression you chose for your answer in Question 3 above as the attitude in the thesis statement.

2. One of the important elements in thinking critically is to have a *purpose* to your writing. Suarez's essay is not simply a description of a neighborhood with which he is familiar. For instance, he may be attempting to familiarize his readers with an environment with which they might not be familiar or about which they may have a misunderstanding. He might be describing the neighborhood with an eye toward convincing his readers that this environment is not one we need to fear but one that could use our financial help or some other kind of understanding.

   Write an essay describing a neighborhood or area with which you are familiar. This can be a place where you once lived or the one in which you currently reside. You will most likely want to include descriptions of the houses or apartment buildings, the businesses, the surrounding neighborhood and environs, and the people living there. After you have completed your prewriting techniques, create a thesis statement that expresses the underlying purpose for writing your descriptive essay.

More Topics for a Descriptive Essay

Here are some possible topics for descriptive writing assignments. Remember, descriptive writing has purpose, so don't forget to create a thesis statement with an appropriate attitude. Use an essay map to organize the topics for your body paragraphs. Be certain that all specific information supports your topic sentences.

1. A spectacular event, such as a fireworks display or a lightning storm, or a famous event in history (the attack on Pearl Harbor or the marriage of Britain's Prince Charles and Diana).

2. A messy desk.

3. A piece of art, such as a painting or sculpture.

4. A holiday event, such as Christmas or Thanksgiving.

5. A bustling office.

6. An ethnic restaurant.

7. A busy street or intersection (this can be a famous location, such as London's Piccadilly Circus or New York's Times Square).

8. A nature setting.

9. A famous building or monument.

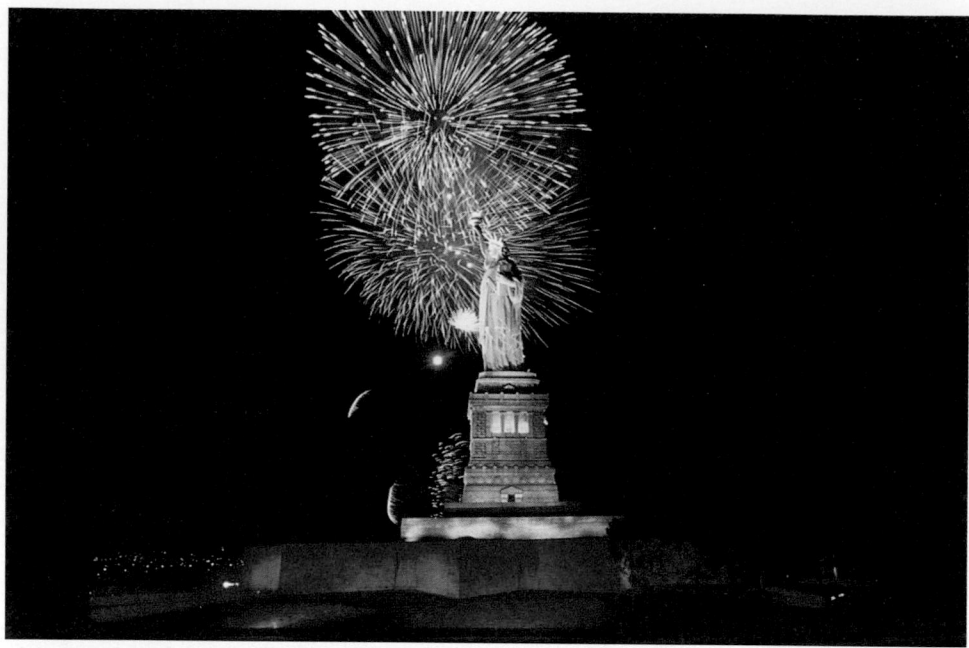

10. An interesting or unusual person (this can be a famous historical person).

11. A description of what you have seen under a microscope in a biology class (for example, blood cells, amoebae or paramecia, a strand of hair, or an insect's wing).

☑ Writing Checklist for a Descriptive Essay

❏ **1.** Choose a topic.

❏ **2.** Explore the topic using one or more of the prewriting techniques you studied in Chapter 3.

❏ **3.** Choose two to five (or whatever number the assignment calls for) of the characteristics you've uncovered during the prewriting phase as the topics for the body paragraphs (or as your essay map items).

❏ **4.** Create a dominant impression about the topic that can be supported by the body paragraph topics.

❏ **5.** Create the thesis statement.

❏ **6.** Use descriptive adjectives, sensory images, and figurative language to develop your topic and the dominant impression.

❏ **7.** Write a first draft of the introductory, body, and concluding paragraphs.

❏ **8.** Revise the first draft.

❏ **9.** Proofread the final draft.

❏ **10.** Print or type the essay and submit it.

CHAPTER REVIEW

▼ Description is a technique that creates images in the reader's mind by using specific details. Description can be objective or factual, or it can be subjective, evoking an emotion or mood. Good descriptive writing makes a dominant impression, creating a single mood or emotion.

▼ The topic sentence of a subjective description paragraph states the dominant impression, and all the details support the dominant impression. Supporting details in descriptive writing include sensory images and figurative language—similes, metaphors, and personification.

▼ In the introductory paragraph of a descriptive essay, the dominant impression is the controlling idea or attitude to the topic as a whole, and the body paragraphs focus on the items in the essay map. Evaluation is often used as the approach to the concluding paragraph.

Visit *The Write Start* Online!

For additional practice with the materials found in this chapter, visit our Website at

http://www.ablongman.com/checkett

The Website also features additional readings, quizzes, writing activities, and Internet links, as well as a bulletin board and interactive chat.

8 The Narrative Essay

To use **narration** is to tell a story, either to entertain or to inform. Narration can be made up, like a short story or novel, or it can be nonfiction, the retelling of an incident that actually happened. When you listen to a news program, the anchor narrates the day's events to you, perhaps reporting how an airplane disaster was averted, or explaining the background of the Supreme Court's latest legal decision. If you read a novel, you are reading a narrative.

Identifying Your Purpose

In college, you will be asked to write narrative essays quite frequently. In English classes, your instructor might ask you to retell an incident from your own life. In a science class, you might be asked to recount how a famous experiment led to an important discovery, such as Marie and Pierre Curie's discovery of radium. In a history course, you might be asked to write about a famous event, such as Germany's invasion of Poland that started World War II. Whatever the writing assignment, the narrative, like all writing, must have a purpose.

Writing the Narrative Paragraph

In addition to recounting events, the narrative paragraph must indicate why the events are important. Techniques for writing an effective narrative paragraph include using the six reporters' questions to focus the narrative and using transitional expressions to sequence the events being recounted.

The Topic Sentence and the Point of the Story

There must be a point to every narrative paragraph; otherwise, the reader will lose interest in it. Narrative writing, then, must have a clear point or purpose. This might seem obvious, but too many writers lose sight of it. The topic sentence of a narrative paragraph should announce the subject and clarify what is interesting about the subject. That interest is the **point of the story** as shown in Exhibit 8.1.

**Exhibit 8.1
The Point of
the Story**

Topic Sentence ⟶

Subject: abuse
Point of the story: abuse can change the victim's life

The Paragraph:

From the first moment I felt his large, cold hand strike my face, my life changed forever. For the first six months of our marriage, I truly believed he was my dream partner for a lifetime. I had done nothing wrong—I thought I was the perfect wife. I worked a 40-hour-a-week job, did the food shopping, house cleaning, cooking, and even made snacks for his weekly poker parties. He was tall, dark, blonde with blue eyes, and at first he seemed as perfect as a person could be but, at the end of six months, he was the devil in disguise. I have never been able wholly to trust another person since.

PRACTICE 1   Writing Narrative Topic Sentences

Write a narrative topic sentence for each of the following subjects. Be certain that the sentence expresses the point of the story, the idea that will keep the reader's interest. You will have to make up the point of each story.

1. Visiting a new place

_____

_____

_____

2. An important event

_____

_____

_____

3. An important person

_____

_____

_____

Supporting Details: The Six Reporters' Questions

Once you have chosen the subject and the point of the story, you must decide how to develop the subject. What details, facts, and examples will develop the ideas and get the point of the story across? The simplest method to develop the subject and maintain focus is to use the six reporters' questions: who, what, where, when, why, and how.

For the topic sentence example in Exhibit 8.1, the developing focus could be any of the following.

Examples

Who: Who was affected by the abuse?

As the topic sentence states, the writer was.

What: What was the abuse?

The abuse was physical, but the paragraph might also detail emotional abuse.

Where: Where did the abuse take place?

Although the inference is "in the home," abuse at other locations might be explored.

When: When did the abuse take place?

In this paragraph, the abuse took place early in the marriage.

Why: Why did the abuse take place?

The writer states that she did not do anything to cause the violence. Something in the husband's experience may have to be examined.

How: How did the abuse happen?

The abuse may have happened spontaneously, or a pattern of behavior may have preceded it.

From the list of examples, the answers to *who, where,* and *when* may be fairly obvious or they may be the least important of the factors. Thus, they probably do not need to be developed. The most important factors to develop would be *what* (the emotional abuse might be even more damaging over the long run than the physical abuse), *why* (why did the abuse occur), and *how* (what were the patterns of behavior that led up to the abuse). Other ideas might come to your mind as you ask these questions, and you can pick and choose depending upon your own experience.

Model Paragraphs

The three model paragraphs that follow were developed for the topic sentence in Exhibit 8.1 using the three focus questions *what, why,* and *how.*

Focus on What: developing the emotional effects stemming from the physical abuse.

Topic Sentence ⟶ The daily physical beatings took their toll. Their effects were short-lived compared to the devastating emotional effects that remain with me till this day. I used to be a very trusting individual. I would lend my car or give money to almost anyone if they were in need. My first thoughts about people were that they were as kind and generous as I was. If I showed kindness to someone, I expected the same in return. Now I am suspicious of everyone. It doesn't matter how good or nice they are to me. In the back of my mind there is a fear of what monster might crouch hidden behind the friendly mask looking at me. People have become like the famous creature of literature—Dr. Jekyll and Mr. Hyde.

In this paragraph, the topic is developed by those details that support the "what" focus question: the narrator used to be trusting; she would lend her car or money; she thought people were as kind and generous as she was; but now she is suspicious; she sees everyone as having a hidden personality.

Focus on Why: developing the reasons for the abuse.

Topic Sentence ⟶

From the beginning, I couldn't figure out why he was abusing me. I had done everything possible to please him and to keep a good home. It wasn't until after the divorce that his sister confided in me. My husband had been physically abused when he was a child. It turns out that his father was an alcoholic who had trouble keeping a job. He took his troubles out on Dennis. I have since learned that almost all abusers were abused as children—a terrible cycle of pain for everyone involved.

In this paragraph, the topic is developed by those details that support the "why" focus question: at first, the narrator could not figure out why the abuse was occurring; later she learned that her husband had been abused by an alcoholic father and that abused children grow up to be adults who abuse.

Focus on How: developing the patterns of behavior that led to the abuse.

Topic Sentence ⟶

Thinking back about how each of the horrible attacks occurred, I have come to the conclusion that each encounter was preceded by my husband being angry about something else, not me. He struck me when we had been discussing what bills to pay immediately and what bills could wait. He was angry that we couldn't pay them all at once. An attack came immediately after he had returned home from work. His boss had chewed him out because he had shipped some materials to the wrong buyer. Each time something made him angry, he took his anger out on me. It could be something as big as his boss threatening to fire him or something as small as bird droppings on his car. It didn't matter. I became the object of his anger.

In this paragraph, the topic is developed by those details that support the "how" focus question: the attacks were preceded by the husband being angry at things other than his wife, such as not being able to pay all the bills, his boss getting angry at him, and bird droppings on his car.

The important thing to remember is that each paragraph develops the same general topic—abuse—yet the topic is developed using information that places emphasis on a different aspect of the abuse.

PRACTICE 2   Writing Narrative Paragraphs

Using the narrative topic sentences you created in Practice 1, write a narrative paragraph for each. Choose one of the six reporters' questions (who, what, where, when, why, and how) to develop the topic for each paragraph.

Using Transitional Expressions to Order Events

Narrative writing tells a story. Therefore, it is important to present the events of the story in proper order so that the reader can remain focused without being confused about the sequence of how things happened. To help keep track of the chronological order of events, you need to use **transitional expressions.** Transitional expressions connect related ideas appropriately, and they also add rhythm to your writing.

Transitional Expressions for Narration		
after	first, second, . . .	soon
afterward	last(ly)	then
as	later	thus
as soon as	meanwhile	upon
before	next	when

Transitional expressions are simply words and phrases that indicate when one event happens in relation to another. When transitional expressions are added to the Focus on How paragraph, they help keep the events in chronological order, add rhythm, and connect related ideas.

Example

Thinking back about how each of the horrible attacks occurred, I have come to the conclusion that each encounter was preceded by my husband being angry about something else, not me. The **first** time he struck me was **when** we had been discussing what bills to pay immediately and what bills could wait. He was angry that we couldn't pay them all at once. The **next** attack came immediately **after** he had returned home from work. **Upon** arriving at work, his boss had chewed him out because he had shipped some materials to the wrong buyer. **Afterward,** each time something made him angry, he took his anger out on me. It could be something as big as his boss threatening to fire him, or something as small as bird droppings on his car. It didn't matter. I became the object of his anger.

PRACTICE 3   Using Transitional Expressions

Add at least three transitional expressions to each of the paragraphs you wrote in Practice 2. Choose the expressions that help order the events chronologically and connect related ideas appropriately.

Moving from Paragraph to Essay

Now that you have studied and practiced the techniques to create effective narration, it is time to expand your ideas by writing a narrative essay. The narrative essay is a union of the techniques you learned in Part 1 regarding developing the essay paragraphs and the narration techniques you have just learned. Return to Part 1 if you need to review the instruction concerning writing the essay.

Creating the Introductory Paragraph

Even though narration is the retelling of an event, don't let the reader become lost in a myriad of details, facts, and examples. Be certain that the purpose of the story remains the focus of the story. Your story should have a thesis around which the events unfold.

The thesis in the narration essay should blend naturally into the rest of the introductory paragraph. In the following introductory paragraph for a narrative essay, the thesis identifies the topic (drinking and driving), the writer's attitude about the topic (negative consequences arise from this activity), and the essay map containing the subtopics that will be developed in the body paragraphs (risking your life, risking the lives of others, and the possibility of a lifelong injury). The thesis statement in the example is underlined for instructional purposes only.

Example

It started out as a night full of anticipation. My four best friends and I were driving to a high school graduation party. We knew there would be some drinking at the party, but we never suspected how it would impact our lives. Why would we? We were young and fearless—invincible! We had all of our lives ahead of us. At least that's what we thought as we began the evening looking forward to another rite of passage. But risking your life, risking the lives of others, and the possibility of a lifelong injury are negative consequences of drinking and driving.

Notice that while the story will be about the night of revelry by the group of graduating high school seniors, the point of the story (the story's purpose) will be the negative consequences of drinking and driving.

Creating the Body Paragraphs

For an essay on drinking and driving, the focus of the body paragraphs will be the paragraph topics listed in the thesis statement's essay map. The first body paragraph's topic will be "risking your life," the second body paragraph's topic will be "risking the lives of others," and the third body paragraph's topic will be "the possibility of a lifelong injury." Remember, as you write about each of these topics, your focus should be that these are the *negative consequences of drinking and driving*. Your focus should not be on medical expenses or the need for tougher national drunk driving laws. Keep your focus on the point of the story: the negative *physical* possibilities stemming from driving drunk.

Creating the Concluding Paragraph

The approach of the concluding paragraph should flow naturally from the essay's main topic. Because this essay's focus is the negative consequences stemming from drinking and driving, a *warning* would seem an appropriate choice for the concluding paragraph. You might identify other negative consequences that might come from driving under the influence. Unlike the body paragraphs, the concluding paragraph is the proper place to mention medical expenses, the effects on family and friends should you be killed, or the potential legal problems that can occur if you are convicted of a related crime in a court of law. Other, more positive narrative essay topics might lend themselves to *prediction* rather than warning in the concluding paragraph. (Refer to Chapter 6 for other approaches for concluding paragraphs.)

▼

Sample Student Essay: SMALL-TOWN VIEWS

Matt Grant

> The following essay, "Small-Town Views," by student writer Matt Grant, recounts the author's trip to a small town on the U.S.-Canada border. Having lived his entire life in large cities, the author, like most Americans, believed that small towns were very different from large ones. Instead of vast differences, what he found were many similarities making the differences more exaggerated than they would otherwise seem.

Vocabulary
Before you begin reading, use a dictionary to look up the definitions of the following words that appear in the essay.

majestic (1)	obscurity (3)	perceptions (1)
propane (3)	quaint (3)	sprawling (2)

Small-Town Views

1   Perceptions of a small town all too often are the same. Moviemakers create the ideal vision of what a rural American town should look like, and society believes what moviemakers create: a single, white, steepled church in the middle of town surrounded by a few streets, mostly named for the majestic trees that front small brick and clapboard houses. No brightly lit neon signs, no high-rise office buildings, and no multiplex cinema showing twelve movies almost twenty-four hours a day. I've lived in a large town most of my life; my experience with small towns only involves driving by them on vacation. What I've seen during my "passerby" trips has given me the same perception as most of society. However, all that would change after I made my first extended visit to a small town on the U.S.-Canada border. The buildings in the town, my relative's house where I stayed, and the streets and roads in and around town forever altered my view of the small town.

2   The town of Sault Ste. Marie (pronounced Soo Saint Marie) appeared small, at first. But soon, a drive down the main four-lane road through town revealed a McDonalds, a Burger King, a Wendy's, an Arby's, an Applebees, and a Cracker Barrel. Then, as I continued on, I saw separating the national

restaurant chain outlets a variety of stores and businesses, including four car and two boat dealerships. So far, I could be back home, driving down any main drag in any sprawling suburban area. Next, a fairly new Wal-Mart stood out as one of the larger buildings. On top of a large, grassy hill, Lake Superior State College sat facing the divided highway that passed by the edge of town. Meanwhile, to the north, the Soo Locks controlled the busy and bustling river port traffic on the St. Mary River. The town was as cosmopolitan as St. Louis or Cincinnati.

3   Later, I drove from the center of town to my aunt and uncle's house, where I would be staying for the week. Their "house" turned out to be a quaint two-bedroom trailer among a whole subdivision of trailers. Not exactly the turn-of-the-century, solidly built homes one would expect from looking at movies depicting small-town America. After dinner, they took me for a walk. The homes lined a white rock road, and each house sat on a small lot set back a little ways into the woods that surrounded the trailer park. Gas lines were unavailable, so a large propane gasoline tank flanked each home. Without cable television, satellite dishes sprouted in the back yards like some strange, mutant plant. Upon returning to their house, we sat on the small, concrete patio and watched as millions of stars twinkled brightly without the obscurity of city lights; moreover, the silence was deafening. Suddenly, I wasn't in Kansas City anymore, Toto.

4   As soon as I awoke, I went for a drive. Unlike objects in your rearview mirror, objects at a distance appear smaller and, at fifteen miles out, the town seemed to disappear. I began to notice things that would not be seen in a large town. The roads leading away from the highway, like "6 mile," were named for the number of miles the road was from the town center. Subdivisions with miles of winding concrete streets did not exist. The homes were either located on acres of land out by the highway or, like my aunt and uncle's place, cramped together on small lots no bigger than half a basketball court lining a gravel strip that looked more like a dried-up creek bed than a thoroughfare. Traffic did not seem to exist at any time of day or night even though there were only two roads leading in and out of town.

5   When my week's stay was up, I said my good-byes and headed toward town. I grabbed lunch at one of the fast food drive-thrus and parked alongside the river. I watched as the lake freighters locked down and passed

through the narrow channel as they headed up river. As I drove away on the southbound highway, Sault Ste. Marie seemed a bit of a puzzle to me. When I was driving through the town, it seemed fairly large, but the more I drove away from it, the smaller it seemed. I guess that's the magic of illusion. It all depends on your perspective.

Narrative Technique Questions

1. Identify the thesis statement. What is the author's attitude about the topic?

_____

_____

_____

_____

2. Which of the six reporters' questions does the writer use most often to develop the story? Give examples.

_____

_____

_____

_____

_____

_____

_____

3. Identify the three essay map subtopics in the thesis statement. Are they clearly stated in the topic sentence of each body paragraph?

_____

_____

_____

_____

_____

4. The writer uses many transitional expressions. List at least five of them. How does each transitional expression help order the events chronologically?

_____

5. Sentence variety helps to create rhythm and to connect related ideas. Identify different types of coordinated and subordinated sentences.

_____

_____

_____

_____

_____

_____

_____

Critical Reading Questions

1. What do you think is the point of the story?

_____

_____

_____

2. How do the specific references to "fast food" restaurants in paragraph 2 convey his sense of surprise about Sault Ste. Marie?

_____

_____

_____

_____

3. The author often mentions "perception," "illusion," and "reality" when talking about the differences and similarities of big cities and small towns. How are these concepts explained in reference to his experiences in cities and towns?

_____

_____

_____

_____

Narrative Writing Exercises

1. Write a narrative paragraph about a commonly held assumption about a place (for example, Las Vegas, New York City, Paris, or Moscow) and whether the assumption is generally true or not.
2. Expand the ideas in the paragraph you wrote for exercise 1, and write a narrative essay. Don't forget to formulate a clearly defined thesis statement. Expand your vision by using more of the *six reporter's questions* to develop ideas for the body paragraphs.

▼

Sample Professional Essay: MY HIPS, MY CADERAS

Alisa Valdes

> In the following essay, "My Hips, My Caderas," written by Pulitzer Prize nominee Alisa Valdes, the author expresses a dilemma shared by many members of immigrant families in America. They are pulled in two different directions at once: they are judged by two cultures—the one of their heritage and the culture of their newly adopted country. Valdes writes specifically about how her two cultures, Latino and Caucasian, prefer different aspects of "outer" beauty and how she overcame expectations that cause problems for so many.

Vocabulary

Before you start to read, use a dictionary to look up the definitions for the following words appearing in the essay.

albino (5)	bandanas (3)	cleft (1)	imprudent (10)
metronome (7)	naive (5)	stigma (5)	voluptuous (2)

My Hips, My Caderas

1   My father is Cuban, with dark hair, a cleft in his chin and feet that can dance the Guaguanco. My mother is white and American, as blue-eyed as they come.

2   My voluptuous/big hips are both Cuban and American. And neither. Just like me. As I shift different halves of my soul daily to match whichever cultural backdrop I happen to face, I also carefully prepare myself for how differently my womanly/fat hips will be treated in my two realities.

3   It all started 15 years ago, when my hips bloomed in Albuquerque, New Mexico, where I was born. I went from being a track club twig—mistaken more than once for a boy—to being a splendidly curving thing that Chicano men with their bandanas down low whistled at as they drove by in their low-riders. White boys in my middle school thought I suddenly had a fat ass, and had no problem saying so.

4   But the cholos loved me. San Mateo Boulevard . . . I remember it well. Jack in the Box on one corner, me on a splintered wooden bench with a Three Musketeers bar, tight shorts, a hot summer sun, and those catcalls and woof-woofs like slaps. I was 12.

5   My best friend Stacy and I set out dieting right away that summer, to lose our new hips so boys from the heights, like the nearly albino Tim Fairfield

with the orange soccer socks, would like us. In those days, I was too naive to know that dismissing the Chicano guys from the valley and taking French instead of Spanish in middle school were leftovers of colonialism. Taking Spanish still had the stigma of shame, like it would make you a dirty wetback. So Stacy and I pushed through hundreds of leg lifts on her bedroom floor, an open *Seventeen* magazine as a tiny table for our lemon water, and the sound of cicadas grinding away in the tree outside.

6   In Spanish, the word for hips is caderas—a broad term used to denote everything a real woman carries from her waist to her thighs, all the way around. Belly, butt, it's all part of your caderas. And caderas are a magical sphere of womanhood. In the lyrics of Merengue and Salsa, caderas are to be shaken, caressed, admired and exalted. The bigger, the better. In Spanish, you eat your rice and beans and sometimes your chicharrones because you fear your caderas will disappear.

7   In my work as a Latin music critic for a Boston newspaper, I frequent nightclubs with wood-paneled walls and Christmas lights flashing all year long. I wear short rubber skirts and tall shoes. There, I swing my round hips like a metronome. I become fierce. I strut. In the red disco lights, my hips absolutely torture men. I can see it on their faces.

8   "Mujeron!" they exclaim as I shimmy past. Much woman. They click their tongues, buy me drinks. They ask me to dance, and I often say "no," because I can. And these men suffer. Ironically, this makes the feminist in me very happy. In these places, my mujeron's hips get more nods than they might at a pony farm.

9   In English, your hips are those pesky things on the sides of your hipbones. They don't "menear," as they do in Spanish; they "jiggle." In English, hips are something women try to be rid of. Hips are why women bruise themselves in the name of liposuction.

10   My mother's people hate my hips. They diet. My aunt smokes so she won't eat. And in the gym where I teach step aerobics—a habit I took up in the days when I identified more with my mother's than my father's people—I sometimes hear the suburban anorexics whisper in the front row: "My God, would you look at those hips." Sometimes they walk out of the room even before I have begun teaching, as if hips were contagious. In these situations, I am sad. I drive home and examine my hips in the mirror, hit them for being so imprudent, like great big ears on the side of my body. Sometimes I fast for days. Sometimes I make myself puke up rice and beans. Usually I get over it, but it always comes back.

11   Sociologists will tell you that in cultures where women are valued for traditional roles of mother and caregiver, hips are in, and that in cultures where those roles have broken down and women try to be like men were in traditional societies—i.e., have jobs—hips are out.

12   So when I want to be loved for my body, I am a Latina. But most Latino men will not love my mind as they do my body, because I am an Americanized professional. Indeed, they will feel threatened, and will soon lose interest in hips that want to "andar por la calle come un hombre" (carry themselves like a man).

13   When I want to be loved for my mind, I flock to liberal intellectuals, usually whites. They listen to my writings and nod . . . and then suggest I use skim milk instead of cream. These men love my fire and passion—words they *always* use to describe a Latina—but they are embarrassed by my hips. They want me to wear looser pants.

14   In some ways I am lucky to be able to move between two worlds. At least my hips get acknowledged as beautiful. I can't say the same for a lot of my bulimic friends, who don't have a second set of standards to turn to. But still, I dream of the day when bicultural Latinas will set the standards for beauty and success, when our voluptuous caderas won't bar us from getting through those narrow American doors.

Narrative Technique Questions

1. Many of the paragraphs in the essay are very short, unlike those you find in most essays. In order to give the reader a clearer sense of the topic and the author's attitude about the topic, which paragraphs would you combine?

   _____

   _____

   _____

   _____

   _____

2. In narrative writing, many sentences begin with "I." Would the essay have been more effective if the author had used "I" less often? Would combining sentences using transitional expressions to add rhythm and connect related ideas have been effective? Point out some examples where this would have added to the essay's effectiveness.

   _____

3. Narrative essays tell a story, but they also should have a purpose. Why do you think the author wrote this story about her life? Point out several ideas that support your answer.

   _____

Critical Reading Questions

1. What do you think is the point of the story? Which ideas in the story lead you to this conclusion?

   _____

   _____

   _____

2. In the story, the author states that women in traditional roles, such as housewives and mothers, are valued if they have big hips and figures. Does this still hold true? What about working women? Do the size and shape of their figures influence how they are seen, as beautiful or not?

   _____

   _____

   _____

3. How does Valdes's Cuban-American cultural heritage cause her problems? Point out some specific examples.

_____

_____

_____

Narrative Writing Exercises

1. Write a paragraph about how your weight or some other aspect of your body has caused you problems. If the reasons for the problems are cultural, include this in your paragraph.
2. Using the topic of your paragraph in exercise 1, write an essay. Expand your ideas by including how media and peer pressure influence how society judges you and how you see yourself.

More Topics for a Narrative Essay

Here are some possible topics for narration writing assignments. Remember, your narrative essay should have a clearly defined point or purpose.

1. Being different than others (at work, school, or in a specific neighborhood).
2. Being insensitive to another's needs.
3. An incident that challenged opinions.
4. A trip or place that triggers a change in self-awareness.
5. A pet's meaningfulness.
6. A happy or lonely time.
7. Heroism during an event.
8. The positive and/or negative effects of an accident, treatment, and recovery.
9. How stories, movies, and plays affect people.
10. How an acquaintance's lifestyle can affect family, loved one, and friends.

☑ Writing Checklist for a Narrative Essay

❑ **1.** Choose a topic.

❑ **2.** Explore the topic using one or more of the prewriting techniques you have studied, or use the six reporters' questions to uncover topics for the body paragraphs (or as your essay map items).

❑ **3.** Create the thesis statement.

❑ **4.** Write your narrative essay, remembering to use transitional expressions to create rhythm, to connect related ideas, and to order the events.

❑ **5.** Revise the first draft.

❑ **6.** Proofread the final draft.

❑ **7.** Print or type the essay and submit it.

CHAPTER REVIEW

▼ A narrative essay tells a story, fictional or true. An effective narrative has a point, a reason that the story is important.

▼ Techniques for writing narrative paragraphs include stating the point of the narrative in the topic sentence, using the six reporters' questions to focus the narrative, and using transitional expressions to order events.

▼ In a narrative essay, the thesis statement should state the point of the story as well as lay out the essay map. The body paragraphs pick up the topics of the essay map. The last paragraph can use any of the techniques for concluding paragraphs, but warning and prediction are often suitable for concluding a narrative essay.

Visit *The Write Start* Online!

For additional practice with the materials found in this chapter, visit our Website at

http://www.ablongman.com/checkett

The Website also features additional readings, quizzes, writing activities, and Internet links, as well as a bulletin board and interactive chat.

The Example Essay

Using **example** is one of the most popular and effective methods for developing an essay topic. Good examples can help focus the reader's attention and illustrate a topic quickly and clearly. Maybe you've heard a friend say, "School isn't any fun!" Your first thought might be to ask why your friend feels this way. You might ask her what specifically makes her feel the way she does. Your friend will probably respond by giving you examples: the teachers are uncaring, there's too much homework, the tests are too difficult, and the teachers assign too many papers. By giving you specific examples, your friend supports and clarifies her general critical view about her school experience.

Identifying Your Purpose

Detailed examples are used to illustrate, clarify, convince, or make concrete a general idea about a subject. Most people find specific, concrete examples easier to understand than general concepts. For instance, the topics in Exhibit 9.1 are accompanied by a list of examples that can be used to develop the subject.

**Exhibit 9.1
Detail Through
Examples**

Topic	Examples
clothing	formal, casual, athletic
food	ethnic, holiday, diet
airplanes	acrobatic, commercial, military
politicians	mayors, presidents, senators
glasses	reading, bifocals, sun

▼ **PRACTICE 1** **Writing an Example Paragraph**

Using one of the other topics in Exhibit 9.1, make a list of three examples that you could use to develop the subject you have chosen. Use one or more of the prewriting techniques you have studied to discover subtopics to use in the body paragraphs to develop your thesis about the topic. Next, write a paragraph using your chosen examples to develop the topic.

Writing the Example Paragraph

An example paragraph should include both the general topic under discussion as well as the examples that develop the topic. Prewriting techniques can be used to focus the discussion, and transitional expressions can help identify examples.

The Topic Sentence in an Example Paragraph

The topic sentence in an example paragraph states the general topic to be discussed and the controlling idea and attitude that will guide the development of the paragraph.

The controlling idea is a statement that tells the reader what your focus will be as you develop the topic and how you feel about it (your attitude). In Exhibit 9.2, the topic is *airplanes*, and the controlling idea is that *they have many uses besides transporting travelers.*

**Exhibit 9.2
The Adaptable
Airplane**

Exhibit 9.2 is an example paragraph using one of the topics and specific examples taken from Exhibit 9.1.

Topic Sentence ⟶ Airplanes have many uses besides transporting travelers. At county fairs and Fourth of July celebrations, the festivities often include a demonstration of aerial acrobatics. Usually, either a single biplane or a team of biplanes will dive and tumble their way through a series of flight patterns designed to bring "oohs" and "aahs" from the crowd below. Airplanes, since early in the 20th century, have been used to deliver mail. Big companies, such as FedEx and UPS, owe much of their success to the airplane because it allows them to deliver mail overnight, instead of the normal three to five days. Of course, no one uses the airplane more extensively than the military. Fighters, bombers, refueling tankers, cargo transports, and communication jets are only a few of the planes the armed services use to complete their varied missions.

▼ **PRACTICE 2**   **Identifying The Topic and Controlling Idea**

Underline the topic once and the controlling idea or attitude twice in the topic sentences that follow.

 1. Cybersex is becoming a popular activity.

2. Religion is an important aspect of most people's lives.

3. Binge drinking at parties is increasing.

4. Date rape is hard to prove in court.

5. A positive attitude can help fight illness.

6. Plagiarism defeats the purpose of writing assignments.

▼ **PRACTICE 3**   **Writing an Example Paragraph**

Using one of the topic sentences in Practice 2, select one of the prewriting techniques, and use it to discover subtopics you will use to develop the controlling idea. Second, make a list of three examples that explain the focus you've chosen for developing the controlling idea. Third, write one or more sentences for each of the examples you have chosen. Finally, rewrite your sentences into standard paragraph form.

Using Transitional Expressions to Connect Examples to the Topic

While each example helps to clarify, explain, and develop the topic, **transitional expressions** help to connect the examples to the topic, and they add rhythm to the paragraph. Use transitional expressions so that the examples don't appear merely as a list. Examples should act in unison to develop the subject expressed in the topic sentence.

> **Transitional Expressions for Example**
>
> | | |
> |---|---|
> | a case in point is | for example |
> | another example of | for instance |
> | another instance of | to illustrate |
> | another illustration of | specifically |

Look how using transitional expressions can help identify examples, connect related ideas, and add rhythm to the paragraph from Exhibit 9.2.

> Airplanes have many uses besides transporting travelers. **For instance,** at county fairs and Fourth of July celebrations, the festivities often include a demonstration of aerial acrobatics. Usually, either a single biplane or a team of biplanes will dive and tumble their way through a series of flight patterns designed to bring "oohs" and "aahs" from the crowd below. Airplanes, since early in

the 20th century, have been used to deliver mail. **To illustrate,** big companies, such as FedEx and UPS, owe much of their success to the airplane because it allows them to deliver mail overnight, instead of the normal three to five days. Of course, no one uses the airplane more extensively than the military. **For example,** fighters, bombers, refueling tankers, cargo transports, and communication jets are only a few of the planes the armed services use to complete their varied missions.

In the example paragraph above, the transitional expressions "for instance," "to illustrate," and "for example" are used to announce to the reader that an example is forthcoming. This technique helps to keep the reader focused on the specific example you are using to explain, clarify, and develop the topic.

▼ PRACTICE 4   Using Transitional Expressions

Using the paragraph you wrote for Practice 3, add at least three transitional expressions to connect related ideas, add rhythm, and announce upcoming examples. After you have finished, compare the two paragraphs. The paragraph with the transitional expressions should be easier to read and understand.

Moving from Paragraph to Essay

Now that you have studied and practiced the techniques to create effective example paragraphs, it is time to expand your ideas to a larger writing unit: the example essay. You will use the techniques you learned in Part 1 regarding developing the essay paragraphs and the example techniques you have just learned to create the example essay. This might be a good time to return to Part 1 and review the techniques for developing the full essay.

Creating the Introductory Paragraph

Because examples are such good devices to clarify ideas, it is easy for a writer to think that there needn't be any special concern regarding the organization and focus of an example essay. However, an example essay is writing, and all writing has specific purpose. Therefore, an example essay needs clearly defined purpose and organization. The thesis statement in an example essay should state the essay's purpose and organization.

The thesis in an example essay should blend naturally into the rest of the introductory paragraph. In the following introductory paragraph, notice how the thesis statement announces the topic (*required courses*), the writer's controlling idea about the topic (*are essential to a student's education*), and the essay map containing the body paragraph topics (*refining communication skills, developing a wide range of interests,* and *building practical skills*). The thesis statement in the example is underlined for instructional purposes only.

Freshman students attending college each fall soon discover that they have few choices in putting together their class schedule. Regardless if they have declared a major field of study, all students find out that they are required to take a minimum number of hours in general course work (introductory courses in history, civics, sociology, and writing, for example) before they can receive a degree. Many students think taking these courses is a waste of time because they have already taken these courses in high school. However, the amount of material covered and the specialized knowledge of college professors makes these courses valuable assets to college students as they prepare themselves for life in college and beyond. <u>Required courses are essential to a student's education because they help refine communication skills, develop a wide range of interests, and build practical skills.</u>

While this essay's topic is *required courses,* the focus of the essay is the idea that the required courses are essential to a student's education.

Creating the Body Paragraphs

For a paper on the "required courses" topic, the focus of the body paragraphs will be the topics listed in the thesis statement's essay map. The first body paragraph's topic will be "they help refine communication skills," the second body paragraph's topic will be "they help develop a wide range of interests," and the third body paragraph's topic will be "they help build practical skills." Remember, as you write about each of these topics, giving examples, your focus should be that required courses *are essential to a student's education.*

Creating the Concluding Paragraph

The concluding paragraph should flow naturally from the essay's main topic. Because the essay's focus is that required courses are essential for a student's education, a *prediction* would seem an appropriate choice. You might point out that students should not resent taking required courses; rather, if they apply themselves to their required course work, their educational development will be substantially rewarded. The concluding paragraph is the proper place to mention rewards other than those mentioned in the body paragraphs, such as nomination to honor societies, reference letters from teachers, and teaching assistantships during graduate studies.

Sample Student Essay: OPPORTUNITIES IN THE ARMED FORCES

Jennifer Staggs

In today's world of corporate downsizing and job insecurity, many young people are not prepared for the competitive world of job hunting and retention. Even college graduates can find it difficult to find employment because they lack specific skills. In this essay, student writer Jennifer Staggs, who spent four years in the Navy immediately following high school, suggests that many young people would benefit from a tour in the armed forces. While this particular essay uses many examples to support the thesis, it also uses many descriptive adjectives to help bring the examples to life.

Vocabulary

Before you start reading, use a dictionary to look up the definitions of the following words that appear in the essay.

acquiring (1)	apprehension (1)	burden (1)
distinct (4)	encounter (2)	impeccable (4)
initial (3)	invigorating (2)	propel (5)
rigorous (2)	sculpting (2)	sufficient (4)

Note: Icarus, in Greek mythology, was the son of Daedalus. Trapped in a labyrinth, Icarus attempted to escape by flying out of the labyrinth with wax wings. Although he thought he was properly prepared to be successful, he flew too close to the sun, the wax wings melted, and he fell into the ocean and was drowned.

Opportunities in the Armed Forces

1   Since the days of Icarus, young people have awaited the day to spread their wings and gain freedom and independence; however, although the future may seem sunny and bright, dark clouds can quickly appear on the horizon. An uncertain unemployment environment and the economic burden of college can also create apprehension in both student and parent. Even college graduates have difficulty acquiring employment because they may lack specific skills. Many of these young people do not have the proper advice and guidance from more experienced adults, and they also are unaware of an

Thesis Statement with Essay Map → exciting world awaiting discovery. Because of discipline, travel, and work experience, young people should consider enlisting in the military.

Topic Sentence → 2   In the armed forces, a new recruit will encounter many forms of discipline. During basic training, lasting eight to 13 weeks, trainees learn rigorous, invigorating exercises for achieving fitness and sculpting the body's shape. Maintaining a nutritious diet helps to fuel the vigorous routine that the trainee

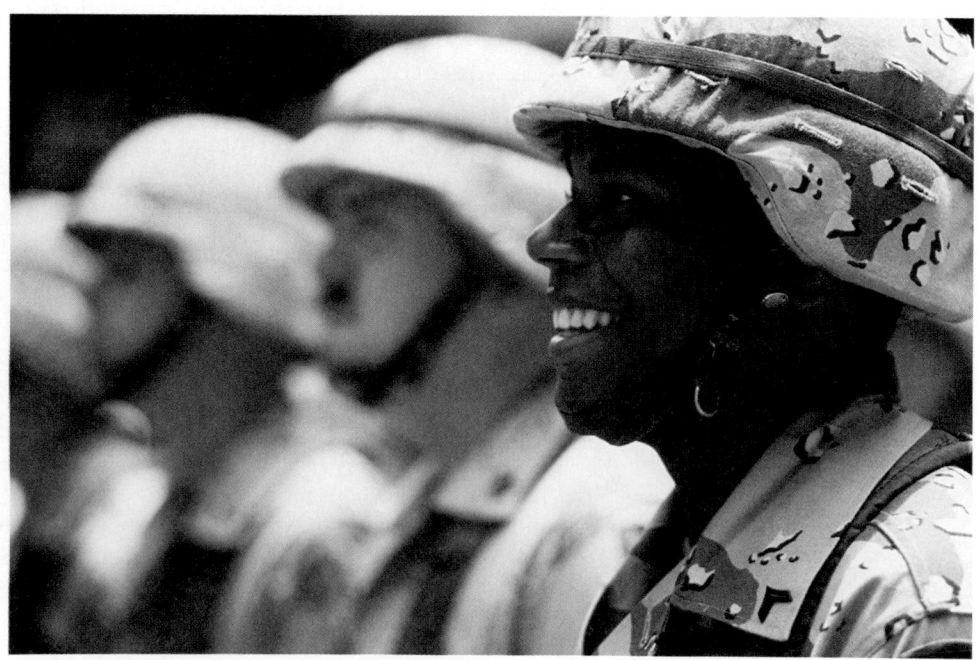

meets with each new day. The recruit will eat three balanced meals each day, including plenty of fruit and fresh vegetables—no more junk food! Most important, the trainee will learn to respect authority and to understand the life-saving elements of teamwork. There is no "I" in "team."

Topic Sentence → 3   After initial training, overseas assignments or other travel opportunities often become available. Imagine experiencing the mysteries of the Far East, the breathtaking landscapes of Ireland, or the magnificent Rhineland castles of Germany! Gourmet foods, exotic dress, and colorful arts and crafts are just some of the many aspects that make other cultures so fascinating. All the branches of the armed forces have duty stations worldwide that broaden the horizons of military personnel.

Topic Sentence → 4   The armed forces have an impeccable record of sending veterans out into the civilian world with superior work experience and skills. Because of sufficient funding, the military has some of the best equipment and training in the world. Many veterans return to civilian businesses with the knowledge and experience to operate or repair some of the most up-to-date and sophisticated machinery and electronic equipment in existence. Veterans of the military, because of their operating within a distinct chain of command, bring excellent communication abilities, organization strengths, and teamwork readiness to be successful in whatever work environment they enter. Employers find these "ready-to-work" veterans an invaluable resource for their companies.

5   Following a successful enlistment period, men and women are better prepared for the future. In addition to receiving the best education, honor is bestowed upon those serving the people of the United States. In the past, many young people have used their military experience to propel themselves into careers in business, industry, and politics. Most of our past and present congresspersons, senators, and presidents have served honorably and proudly in the military. All in all, from any employer's perspective, a veteran is a well-rounded person, an outstanding worker, and a trustworthy citizen.

Example Technique Questions

1. What lead-in technique(s) does the author use to introduce the thesis statement?

_____

2. The writer's attitude toward military service is that young people "should consider" it. What are some of the examples the writer uses in the body paragraphs to develop and support this attitude?

_____

_____

_____

_____

_____

_____

_____

_____

_____

_____

_____

_____

_____

_____

_____

_____

3. List some occupations that young people not going to college might consider exploring. What examples does the writer point out that could help
young people have a better chance at success in these occupations?

_____

_____

Critical Reading Questions

1. How does the reference to Icarus help the writer establish the seriousness
of the topic?

_____

_____

2. Underline the adjectives in the essay. How do they enhance and support
the writer's attitude that serving in the military can be a rewarding experience for young people?

_____

_____

_____

_____

Example Writing Exercises

1. In her essay "Opportunities in the Armed Forces," student writer Jennifer Staggs points out a *problem* that she notices about many young people (a lack of proper advice and guidance from adults and a lack of awareness of an exciting world around them). Her attempt to answer the problem is to introduce young people to the opportunities in the armed forces that help solve the problem. Write an example paragraph that explains how to solve a problem you see affecting young people or those in your age group. Some problems might be voting apathy, distrust in working for a large corporation, or a feeling that a high school or college degree is not important.

2. Expand the ideas in the paragraph you wrote in exercise 1, and write an example essay. Don't forget to formulate a clearly expressed thesis statement. Discover subtopics by using one or more of the prewriting techniques you have studied.

▼
Sample Professional Essay: DARKNESS AT NOON

Harold Krents

> The following article originally appeared in the *New York Times* in 1976. Author Harold Krents, blind from birth, was a lawyer and writer who never allowed his "handicap" to stand in the way of his accomplishments. In the article, Krents points out many examples of discrimination that he had to endure as a result of his being blind.

Vocabulary
Meaning comes primarily from words. Before you start reading, use a dictionary to look up the meanings of the following words that appear in the essay.

converse (2)	cum laude (15)	dependent (1)
disposition (13)	enunciating (2)	graphically (5)
intoned (12)	invariably (3)	narcissistic (1)

Darkness at Noon

1   Blind from birth, I have never had the opportunity to see myself and have been completely dependent on the image I create in the eye of the observer. To date it has not been narcissistic.

2   There are those who assume that since I can't see, I obviously cannot hear. Very often people will converse with me at the top of their lungs, enunciating each word very carefully. Conversely, people will also often whisper, assuming that since my eyes don't work, my ears don't either.

3   For example, when I go the airport and ask the ticket agent for assistance to the plane, he or she will invariably pick up the phone, call a ground hostess and whisper: "Hi, Jane, we've got a 76 here." I have concluded that the

word "blind" is not used for one of two reasons: Either they fear that if the dread word is spoken, the ticket agent's retina will immediately detach, or they are reluctant to inform me of my condition of which I may not have been previously aware.

4   On the other hand, others know that of course I can hear, but believe that I can't talk. Often, therefore, when my wife and I go out to dinner, a waiter or waitress will ask Kit if "*he* would like a drink" to which I respond that "indeed *he* would."

5   This point was graphically driven home to me while we were in England. I had been given a year's leave of absence from my Washington law firm to study for a diploma in law degree at Oxford University. During the year I became ill and was hospitalized. Immediately after admission, I was wheeled down to the X-ray room. Just at the door sat an elderly woman—elderly I would judge from the sound of her voice. "What is his name?" the woman asked the orderly who had been wheeling me.

6   "What's your name?" the orderly repeated to me.

7   "Harold Krents," I replied.

8   "Harold Krents," he repeated.

9   "When was he born?"

10   "When were you born?"

11   "November 5, 1944," I responded.

12   "November 5, 1944," the orderly intoned.

13   This procedure continued for approximately five minutes, at which point even my saint-like disposition deserted me. "Look," I finally blurted out, "this is absolutely ridiculous. Okay, granted I can't see, but it's got to have become pretty clear to both of you that I don't need an interpreter."

14   "He says he doesn't need an interpreter," the orderly reported to the woman.

15   The toughest misconception of all is the view that because I can't see, I can't work. I was turned down by over forty law firms because of my blindness, even though my qualifications included a cum laude degree from Harvard college and a good ranking in my Harvard Law School class.

16   The attempt to find employment, the continuous frustration of being told that it was impossible for a blind person to practice law, the rejection letters, not based on my lack of ability but rather on my disability, will always remain one of the most disillusioning experiences of my life.

17   I therefore look forward to the day, with the expectation that it is certain to come, when employers will view their handicapped workers as a little child did me years ago when my family still lived in Scarsdale.

18   I was playing basketball with my father in our backyard according to procedures we had developed. My father would stand beneath the hoop, shout, and I would shoot over his head at the basket attached to our garage. Our next-door neighbor, aged five, wandered over into our yard with a playmate. "He's blind," our neighbor whispered to her friend in a voice that could be heard distinctly by Dad and me. Dad shot and missed; I did the same. Dad hit the rim; I missed entirely; dad shot and missed the garage entirely. "Which one is blind?" whispered back the little friend.

19   I would hope that in the near future when a plant manager is touring the factory with the foreman and comes upon a handicapped and nonhandicapped person working together, his comment after watching them work will be, "Which one is disabled?"

Example Technique Questions

1. Is there a thesis statement in the essay? If you identify one, does it have an essay map?

   _____

   _____

2. The author uses humor to describe the situations that he found himself in. Point out some examples, and relate how the humorous tone affects your feelings toward the essay.

   _____

   _____

   _____

   _____

   _____

   _____

   _____

3. Examples sometimes are expressed in the form of dialogue. Explain why this is an effective method to develop Krents's main points.

   _____

   _____

   _____

Critical Reading Questions

1. Krents expresses that there are many common misconceptions about blind people. Point out three examples.

   _____

   _____

2. Even though the author uses humor throughout the essay, how do you know his attitude about being handicapped is serious?

_____

_____

_____

_____

_____

Example Writing Exercises

1. In his essay "Darkness at Noon," writer Harold Krents points out a misconception that people have about blind persons—that they cannot work. Have you ever been in a situation in which you were temporarily handicapped? Have you ever been confined to a wheelchair, had an arm in a sling or a leg in a cast? Have you ever had your eyes dilated at the optometrist's so that someone else had to drive you home? Write an example paragraph about how it would feel to be disabled. Give examples of how the handicap might affect daily life and if others empathize with those that are truly handicapped.

2. Using the topic of your paragraph in exercise 1, write an essay. Expand your ideas by including how the media and peer pressure influences how society judges the handicapped.

More Topics for an Example Essay

Here are some possible topics for example writing assignments. Remember, you must use examples for a purpose, so don't forget to create a thesis statement with an appropriate attitude and controlling idea. One option is to use the essay map to organize the subtopics for your body paragraphs. Be certain that all specific information supports your topic sentences.

1. Tattooing.

2. Dropping out of high school.

3. Role models.

4. Premarital sex.

5. Violence in video games, movies, or television.

6. Working for a large corporation.

7. Male and female homosexuality.

8. Interracial marriage.

9. Fraternities and sororities.

10. Body piercing.

☑ Writing Checklist for an Example Essay

❏ **1.** Choose a topic.

❏ **2.** Explore the topic using one or more of the prewriting techniques you have studied to discover topics for your body paragraphs (or as your essay map items).

❏ **3.** Create the thesis statement. Do not forget to include an attitude about the topic and a controlling idea (this can be an essay map).

❏ **4.** Write a first draft of the introductory, body, and concluding paragraphs of the essay.

❏ **5.** Be sure to include examples.

❏ **6.** Remember to use transitional expressions to create rhythm and sentence variety and to show relationships between ideas.

❏ **7.** Revise the first draft.

❏ **8.** Print or type the essay and submit it.

CHAPTER REVIEW

▼ In an example essay, detailed examples are used to illustrate, clarify, convince, or make concrete a general topic.

▼ The topic sentence of an example paragraph states the general topic and the controlling idea that guides the development of the paragraph. The six reporters' questions can be used to focus the discussion. Transitional expressions help identify examples, connect related ideas, and add rhythm to the paragraph.

▼ In an example essay, the thesis statement states the general topic, the controlling idea, and the essay map with subtopics. All the examples given in the body paragraphs should support the controlling idea of the essay.

Visit *The Write Start* Online!

For additional practice with the materials found in this chapter, visit our Website at

http://www.ablongman.com/checkett

The Website also features additional readings, quizzes, writing activities, and Internet links, as well as a bulletin board and inter-active chat.

10 | The Classification Essay

Some topics you will be assigned to write about are very complex. A simple definition or description of these topics often is not sufficient to adequately explain them. How, then, do you approach a large, complex subject so your reader has a full understanding of the point you are trying to make? One possibility is **classification,** the separation of smaller points from a larger concept and the arrangement of these smaller concepts into easily recognized groups.

These groups can be based on shape, kind, color, function, or any other category your reader will easily understand. For example, you can classify chefs as specializing in regional cooking: French, Southwest American, Northern Italian, Cajun; you can categorize birds by color: blue, red, yellow; you can group geometric figures by shape: rectangles, circles, triangles, hexagons.

Identifying Your Purpose

The purpose of classification, as for all writing, is to either inform, entertain, or persuade. When the subject is sufficiently complicated, classification is one method of making a complex subject easier to write about and easier for your reader to understand.

Suppose you were to write about William Shakespeare and that your focus was his genius. You would not be able to find out his IQ and his SAT scores because such testing did not exist in the 16th and 17th centuries. You could try to find out what his contemporaries and later critics said about him. Unfortunately, not many comments from his contemporaries have survived, and the analyses of later critics are too numerous for you to read every one.

You might look at Shakespeare's writings. He was a prolific writer, and we have plenty of his works. In fact, because so many of his plays have survived and are still produced and studied worldwide, this might give you your focus.

> **Example**
>
> William Shakespeare can be considered a genius because of his prolific writings in so many forms. Shakespeare wrote sonnets, histories, comedies, tragedies, dark comedies, and romances. Many of his plays are still produced both on the stage and in films. Courses of study in Shakespeare's writings remain a staple in colleges and universities worldwide.

▼ **PRACTICE 1**   **Creating Categories**

Separate each of the following topics into three classifications or groups. They can be based on shape, color, size, kind, or any other category that helps explain the topic. The first one is done as a sample.

Fish:	arctic	tropical	oceanic
Clothes:	_____	_____	_____
Music:	_____	_____	_____
Movies:	_____	_____	_____
Storms:	_____	_____	_____
Dates:	_____	_____	_____
Ice cream:	_____	_____	_____

Writing the Classification Paragraph

A classification paragraph should indicate the general topic being discussed as well as explain the categories into which it is divided. One or more of the prewriting techniques you have studied can be used to focus the discussion, and transitional expressions can provide signposts for guiding the reader.

The Topic Sentence in a Classification Paragraph

In a classification paragraph, the topic sentence must state the subject, how the subject will be divided, and why classifying the subject is important. Here is an example of a topic sentence for a classification paragraph shown in Exhibit 10.1.

**Exhibit 10.1
Classification
Topic Sentence**

> **Topic Sentence:** The negative effects of discrimination can be more easily understood if its targets are classified by race, gender, and age.
>
> **Subject:** discrimination
>
> **Categories:** race, gender, age
>
> **Controlling idea
> and attitude:** to learn about discrimination's negative effects

▼ **PRACTICE 2**   **Writing Topic Sentences**

Write a topic sentence for each of the subjects you classified in Practice 1. Remember, your topic sentence must state the subject, the classification categories, and why it is important to divide the topic into groups.

Using Supporting Details

To develop the controlling idea, use the subtopics you have discovered with the prewriting technique. They will help you focus on how you will develop the categories in which you have divided the subject. In Exhibit 10.1, the controlling idea and attitude that discrimination has negative effects focuses on people who most often suffer the effects of discrimination: people of color, women, and older adults. While other aspects might be expressed in the paragraph, such as events that have happened and the reasons for those occurrences, the people involved will be the main focus.

A paragraph based on the categories of race, gender, and age might look like the following, as shown in Exhibit 10.2.

**Exhibit 10.2
Supporting Details**

  The negative effects of discrimination can be more easily understood if its targets are classified by race, gender, and age. Although some progress has been made, racial discrimination is still evident in our culture. Hate groups still march in parades on Main Street, and with the advent of the Internet, they have filled cyberspace with their special brand of hatred against all people of color. Women are still expected by many men to stay home and take care of the house and the children (and of the husband's needs). In the workplace, men still get promoted faster, and men are still paid more for the same work as women. Older adults often are not hired because they are perceived as less dynamic and less willing to learn since they are set in their ways. Additionally, many older adults are downsized because younger workers can take their place at a lower salary rate. Discrimination knows no limits. It can strike almost anyone, anytime, and anywhere.

PRACTICE 3 Writing a Classification Paragraph

Using one of the topics from Practice 1, write a classification paragraph. Develop the paragraph by focusing on the three categories into which you divided the subject. Use the topic sentence you created in Practice 2 as the first sentence of the paragraph.

Using Transitional Expressions to Identify Classifications

While developing each category or group helps to inform, entertain, or persuade the reader, **transitional expressions** help to connect related ideas and add rhythm to the paragraph. Use transitional expressions in your classification paragraph so that the categories don't appear merely as a list. The groups or categories should work together to develop the subject and the controlling idea.

CONNECTS
RELATED IDEAS
AND ADDS
RHYTHM

Transitional Expressions for Classification		
can be categorized	can be classified	can be divided
can be grouped	the first/second category	the first group
the first/second kind	the first/second type	the last

See how adding transitional expressions can help make the paragraph in Exhibit 10.2 more readable and understandable.

> The negative effects of discrimination can be more easily understood if its targets are **classified** by race, gender, and age. Although some progress has been made with the **first group,** people of color, racial discrimination is still evident in our culture. Hate groups still march in parades on Main Street, and with the advent of the Internet, they have filled cyberspace with their special brand of hatred against all people of color. **The second group** targeted by discrimination is women. Women are still expected by many men to stay home and take care of the house and the children (and of the husband's needs). In the workplace, men still get promoted faster, and men are still paid more for the same work as women. Members of **the last category,** the elderly, are often downsized because younger workers can take their place at a lower salary rate. Discrimination knows no limits. It can strike almost anyone, anytime, and anywhere.

In the classification paragraph above, the transitional expressions "are classified," "the first group," "the second group," and " the last category" also are used to announce that the next group to be discussed is forthcoming. The technique helps to keep the reader focused on the specific categories being used to develop the topic and the controlling idea and attitude.

▼
PRACTICE 4   **Adding Transitional Expressions to a Classification Paragraph**

Using the paragraph you wrote in Practice 3, add at least three transitional expressions to connect related ideas, add rhythm, and announce upcoming categories. After you have finished, compare the two paragraphs. The paragraph containing the transitional expressions should be easier to read and understand.

Moving from Paragraph to Essay

Now that you have studied and practiced the techniques to create effective classification, it is time to expand your ideas to a larger writing unit: the classification essay. Using the techniques you learned in Part 1 regarding developing the essay paragraphs and the classification techniques you have just learned, you can write a classification essay. This might be a good time to return to Part 1 and review the techniques for developing the full essay.

Creating the Introductory Paragraph

Some writers think that once they have divided their topic into distinct categories their job is complete. Nothing could be further from the truth. All writing has to have a purpose, and that purpose must be clearly expressed. The thesis statement of a classification essay must state the topic, announce the writer's attitude toward the topic, and state the controlling idea that will clarify the organizational format of the essay.

The thesis in a classification essay should occur naturally as the introductory paragraph unfolds. In the following introductory paragraph, taken from the sample student essay to follow, notice how the thesis statement announces the subject (*selecting beneficiaries in a will*), his attitude about the process (*it makes the selections easier*), the writer's controlling idea about the topic (*categorizing the beneficiaries*), and the essay map containing the categories to be developed in the body paragraphs (*the disorderly, beggars, and friends*). The thesis statement is underlined for identification purposes only.

Example

Year after year, many Americans go through the dreadful task of preparing a will. Whether using the family attorney or the family computer, the question of who gets the house and who gets the loot needs to be answered clearly in black and white. Documents of this nature can get very complex and detailed, needing a linguist for translation, but choosing kin for determining who's in and who's definitely out of the legal instrument shouldn't be difficult at all. <u>Placing relatives into three categories, the disorderly, the beggars, and the friends, eases the process of selecting beneficiaries.</u>

Using the thesis statement with an essay map makes the contents and organizational structure clear for both writer and reader. As we shall see below, the essay will continue by developing the essay map items in their respective body paragraphs.

▼ PRACTICE 5   Writing a Thesis Statement for a Classification Essay

Create a thesis statement with an attitude and controlling idea and a three-item essay map using the topic idea in the paragraph you created for Practice 3. Make certain that the three essay map items you choose will be able to develop the topic as the controlling idea suggests. (See the sections titled "The Attitude in the Thesis Statement" and "The Controlling Idea in the Thesis Statement" in Chapter 4 if you need to review this information.)

Creating the Body Paragraphs

For an essay on preparing a will, the focus of the body paragraphs will be the paragraph topics listed in the thesis statement's essay map. The first body paragraph's topic will be about the "disorderly" relatives, the second body paragraph's topic will be about the "beggars," and the third body paragraph will be about "friends." Thus each of the body paragraphs in a classification essay focuses on one of the categories into which the topic has been divided. Remember, as you write about each of the topics, your focus should be on the attitude and controlling idea; in this case, the combined attitude and controlling idea is that *classifying potential beneficiaries makes the process of writing the will easier.*

Creating the Concluding Paragraph

The approach of the concluding paragraph should flow naturally from the essay's main topic. Because the essay's focus is placing potential beneficiaries into categories in order to make the overall process of selecting the actual beneficiaries easier, an evaluation of the main points in each category would seem appropriate. You might discuss how to be more precise in the classification of the disorderly, the beggars, and the friends. You could classify them further by age, schooling, how many times they've been arrested, or how distant they are on the branches of the family tree. You could further classify them by how many family functions they've attended, how many times they've asked for money, or how many times they've sued members of the family over property, possessions, or money. (Refer to Chapter 6 for other approaches for concluding paragraphs.)

▼
Sample Student Essay: LEFT OUT

Randy Raterman

In the essay "Left Out," student writer Randy Raterman takes a humorous and somewhat sarcastic look at making a will. The problem isn't so much a question of whether or not to leave possessions to relatives; the problem turns out to be deciding which relatives should be mentioned in the will. Raterman divides the potential recipients into three groups, two of which are decidedly on the "left out" list, making it easier to identify those on the "in" list. Notice how many adjectives the author attaches to nouns in order to bring them to life.

Vocabulary

Before starting to read, use a dictionary to look up the definitions of the following words that appear in the essay.

amplify (5)	beneficiaries (4)	commendable (4)	linguist (1)
mendicant (3)	ominous (5)	proverbial (3)	riffraff (2)

Left Out

1   Year after year, many Americans go through the dreadful task of preparing a will. Whether using the family attorney or the family computer, the question of who gets the house and who gets the loot needs to be answered clearly in black and white. Documents of this nature can get very complex and detailed, needing a linguist for translation, but choosing kin for determining who's in and who's definitely out of the legal instrument shouldn't be difficult at all. Placing relatives into three categories, the disorderly, the beggars, and the friends, eases the process of selecting beneficiaries.

Thesis Statement with Essay Map —→

Topic Sentence —→ 2   The first group to be eliminated from the selection of beneficiaries is the disorderly. Almost every family has individuals fitting this category. Kinfolk of this kind should include the uncontrollable creatures hanging from the branches of the family tree. This prevents the disobedient, undisciplined, unruly, rebellious, and violent souls from inheriting one red cent. If an entire branch is infested with precarious parasites, pruning is essential. Additionally, the pesky rodents burrowing in the tree roots may fill the void left by the branchless trunk. Tending to legalities is imperative because related riffraff have no problem dragging heirs through the legal system in search of a gold mine. Even though the timid and light of heart may be hesitant, constructing this category is highly effective for excluding unworthy, vulture-like inheritors.

Topic Sentence ⟶ 3   The second category, the beggars, also needs to be eliminated from consideration. Recording names of kinfolk in this second group may be the most challenging; numerous leeches will befriend the benefactors while simultaneously desiring particular heirlooms. Nonetheless, some mendicant pests are easy to identify. If receiving inescapable phone calls from long-lost family members gives rise to the question: "What did that misfit want? We haven't heard from him in years," simply jot down the callers' names. If several members possess a needy personality that seems only satisfied if they amass more objects than those listed in the will, put them on the list. Members of the proverbial family tree exhibiting sponge-like characteristics (never losing absorbency for family possessions) appropriately fit the category as well. Consequently, individuals in this group are notorious for dragging legitimate recipients to court, so double check all legal documents for erroneous entries. Unmentioned kin clearly belong with the uncontrollable creatures, parasites, and pesky rodents, or they (and their legal team) will think they are rightful recipients.

Topic Sentence ⟶ 4   The final category of potential, worthwhile inheritors contains the names of preferable kin. When composing the list, focus on relatives having friendly traits. Jot down the names of those who are truly close and dear; immediate loved ones would be devastated if they were accidentally left out or inherited the dirty sock collection, so double check to make sure these names have been inscribed. A truly considerate benefactor would include names of kin who have come to the rescue in time of need, no questions asked. Many relatives may at first seem helpful, but excluding those who want a crispy, new Ben Franklin for a couple hours of babysitting will leave just a handful of good-natured, kindhearted, and loving souls. Obviously, the most difficult task is still at hand. Who from the roster will be the recipients, and what will the recipients receive? Nonetheless, legally protecting the beneficiaries from the leeches, sponges, parasites, pesky rodents, and uncontrollable creatures inhabiting the family tree would be commendable.

5   Unfortunately, most Americans pass away each year having not completed a will or any other legal instrument that indicates how they want their possessions distributed to family. Occasionally, the goods get turned over to the state, leaving opportunities for the unworthy, ominous family members to inherit entire estates. Unpleasant as it may be, a few affectionate, kindhearted kin will be grieving the loss of a family member, so don't amplify the grief by not having a will or estate plan. Numerous little family squabbles may break out after the departure of the benefactor if legalities haven't been resolved, so heed the warning to exclude wicked, unworthy family members from the list of recipients.

Classification Technique Questions

1. How does the writer categorize potential beneficiaries?

_____

_____

_____

2. What other categories can you think of that might fit in the essay?

_____

_____

3. Underline as many of the classification transitional expressions that you can find, and list them below.

_____

_____

_____

Critical Reading Questions

1. What do you think is the writer's purpose for writing the essay?

_____

_____

_____

2. How do the transitional expressions help create a more effective essay?

_____

_____

_____

3. One form of alliteration is the intentional repetition of consonant sounds at the beginning of words or in stressed syllables (*p*etulant *p*uppies, *w*ithering *w*illows). Point out some examples of alliteration in the essay. How does Raterman's use of alliteration support the humorous aspect of the essay?

_____

_____

_____

_____

Classification Writing Exercises

1. Write a paragraph about how friends and relatives might be classified at home, school, and work. Don't forget to state an attitude and controlling idea in your topic sentence.

2. Expand the ideas in the paragraph you wrote for exercise 1, and write a classification essay. Discover categories for each subtopic by using one or more of the prewriting techniques you have studied. Use transitional expressions to create rhythm and sentence variety, and to connect related ideas.

▼
Sample Professional Essay: WHY I WANT A WIFE

Judy Brady-Syfers

The following essay, first published in *Ms.* magazine under the name Judy Syfers, is a satiric look at a woman's traditional, social role as a servant to her husband's needs. The author divides this major role into distinct categories as she comments on the female situation in respect to her husband, herself, and the society at large.

Vocabulary
Before you start reading, use a dictionary to look up the definitions of the following words that appear in the essay.

adherence (7)   dependent (3)   entail (7)   hors d'oeuvres (6)

monogamy (7)   nurturant (3)   rambling (5)   replenished (6)

Why I Want a Wife

1   I belong to that classification of people known as wives. I am a Wife. And, not altogether incidentally, I am a mother.

2   Not too long ago a male friend of mine appeared on the scene fresh from a recent divorce. He had one child, who is, of course, with his ex-wife. He is looking for another wife. As I thought about him while I was ironing one evening, it suddenly occurred to me that I, too, would like to have a wife. Why do I want a wife?

3   I would like to go back to school, so I can become economically independent, support myself, and, if need be, support those dependent upon me. I want a wife who will work and send me to school. And while I am going to school I want a wife to take care of my children. I want a wife to keep track of the children's doctor and dentist appointments. And to keep track of mine, too. I want a wife to make sure my children eat properly and are kept clean. I want a wife who will wash the children's clothes and keep them mended. I want a wife who is a good nurturant attendant to my children, who arranges for their schooling, makes sure that they have an adequate social life with their peers, takes them to the park, the zoo, etc. I want a wife who takes care of the children when they are sick, a wife who arranges to be around when the children need special care, because, of course, I cannot miss classes at school. My wife must arrange to lose time at work and not lose the job. It may mean a small cut in my wife's income from time to time, but I guess I can tolerate that. Needless to say, my wife will arrange and pay for the care of the children while my wife is working.

4   I want a wife who will take care of *my* physical needs. I want a wife who will keep my house clean. A wife who will pick up after my children, a wife who will pick up after me. I want a wife who will keep my clothes clean, ironed, mended, replaced when need be, and who will see to it that my personal things are kept in their proper place so that I can find what I need the minute I need it. I want a wife who cooks the meals, a wife who is a *good* cook. I want a wife who will plan the menus, do the necessary grocery shopping, prepare the meals, serve them pleasantly, and then do the cleaning up while I do my studying. I want a wife who will care for me when I am sick and sympathize with my pain and loss of time from school. I want a wife to go along when our family takes a vacation so that someone can continue to care for me and my children when I need a rest and change of scene.

5   I want a wife who will not bother me with rambling complaints about a wife's duties. But I want a wife who will listen to me when I feel the need to explain a rather difficult point I have come across in my course of studies. And I want a wife who will type my papers for me when I have written them.

6   I want a wife who will take care of the details of my social life. When my wife and I are invited out by my friends, I want a wife who will take care of the babysitting arrangements. When I meet people at school that I like and want to entertain, I want a wife who will have the house clean, will prepare a special meal, serve it to me and my friends, and not interrupt when I talk about things that interest me and my friends. I want a wife who will have arranged that the children are fed and ready for bed before my guests arrive so that the children do not bother us. I want a wife who takes care of the needs of my guests so that they feel comfortable, who makes sure that they have an ashtray, that they are passed the hors d'oeuvres, that they are offered a second helping of the food, that their wine glasses are replenished when necessary, that their coffee is served to them as they like it. And I want a wife who knows that sometimes I need a night out by myself.

7   I want a wife who is sensitive to my sexual needs, a wife who makes love passionately and eagerly when I feel like it, a wife who makes sure that I am satisfied. And, of course, I want a wife who will not demand sexual attention when I am not in the mood for it. I want a wife who assumes the complete responsibility for birth control, because I do not want more children. I want a wife who will remain sexually faithful to me so that I do not have to clutter up my intellectual life with jealousies. And I want a wife who understands that *my* sexual needs may entail more than strict adherence to monogamy. I must, after all, be able to relate to people as fully as possible.

8   If, by chance, I find another person more suitable as a wife than the wife I already have, I want the liberty to replace my present wife with another one. Naturally, I will expect a fresh, new life; my wife will take the children and be solely responsible for them so that I am left free.

9   When I am through with school and have a job, I want my wife to quit working and remain at home so that my wife can more fully and completely take care of a wife's duties.

10   My God, who *wouldn't* want a wife?

Classification Technique Questions

1. Most sentences begin with "I want a wife." Is this repetitious form effective? Why or why not?

_____

_____

2. The author lists a staggering number of wife-duty categories. Are they related in any particular way? Explain.

_____

_____

3. What is the effect of the author's continual use of "my" in the essay?

_____

_____

Critical Reading Questions

1. What is the purpose of Brady's essay?

_____

_____

_____

2. This essay was written in 1972. Is it still relevant today? Why or why not?

_____

_____

3. In the last line of the essay, Brady-Syfers asks, "My God, who *wouldn't* want a wife?" How would you answer this question, and why?

_____

_____

Classification Writing Exercises

1. Write a paragraph about the many roles that people have to assume and how those roles are perceived by others. The perceptions can be by individuals, groups, or society as a whole.
2. Examine the roles people play in their lives, such as student, friend, parent, and worker, and how the various roles make them feel. Take one person, playing three roles, and write an essay explaining how the person acts and feels in each role.

More Topics for a Classification Essay

Here are some possible topics for classification writing assignments. Remember, your essay must have a purpose, so don't forget to create a thesis statement with an appropriate attitude. Use the essay map to organize the subtopics for your body paragraphs. Be certain that all specific information supports your topic sentences.

1. Thrill-seeking activities
2. Television sit-coms
3. Sports
4. Movies
5. Pets
6. Summer jobs
7. Dates
8. Types of discipline
9. Phobias
10. Parties

☑ Writing Checklist for a Classification Essay

❑ **1.** Choose a topic that can be broken down into categories.

❑ **2.** Explore the topic and its categories using one or more of the prewriting techniques you have studied.

❑ **3.** Choose the categories to be used for the body paragraphs.

❑ **4.** Create the thesis statement and essay map.

❑ **5.** Write your essay, remembering to use transitional expressions to create rhythm and sentence variety and to connect related ideas.

❑ **6.** Revise the first draft.

❑ **7.** Proofread the final draft.

❑ **8.** Print or type the essay and submit it.

CHAPTER REVIEW

▼ In a classification essay, a large, complex topic is approached by breaking it into categories that the reader can easily grasp.

▼ The six reporters' questions can be used to help develop the categories into which the topic is divided, and transitional expressions can identify the classifications.

▼ In the five-paragraph classification essay, the introductory paragraph introduces the topic, states the categories that frame the discussion, and indicates the controlling idea and attitude. Each of the body paragraphs expands on one of the categories presented in the thesis statement.

Visit *The Write Start* Online!

For additional practice with the materials found in this chapter, visit our Website at

http://www.ablongman.com/checkett

The Website also features additional readings, quizzes, writing activities, and Internet links, as well as a bulletin board and interactive chat.

11 The Process Essay

Have you ever had to explain how something works or how you did something? Perhaps you had to explain how to install a computer program or how you made chocolate fudge. Think about how you would explain these activities in writing. You would have to describe a step-by-step **process** to develop these topics.

Identifying Your Purpose

Explaining the steps involved in completing an operation, a procedure, or an event is called process writing. Process is an important method in developing ideas, especially for science, history, sports, medicine, and business. In a science class, you might be assigned to explain how you did a specific experiment. In a history class, you might have to explain how an historical event happened. In a business class, you might have to explain how a product's advertising campaign was carried out. All of these writing situations involve explaining a process. The following paragraph outlines some steps necessary to the process of becoming a better college student.

> **Example**
>
> In order to use time more effectively, the student should buy a schedule-planner. Write the subjects for each day in the planner, and then add the time it will take to study each subject per day. Studying immediately after class can be an effective method for remembering information because it already is fresh in the mind. Don't forget to schedule a 15 to 20 minute break between studying each subject, or take a break if a particular problem or passage is difficult to understand. Studying a topic should be scheduled well in advance of the class in which it is supposed to be discussed. This allows for time to think about the assignment and formalize answers to the questions the instructor might ask. It also allows for time to prepare questions for the instructor about material not understood.

▼ PRACTICE 1   Drafting a Process Paragraph

Write a paragraph explaining, step by step, how one of the following activities is accomplished.

- ▼ fix a meal
- ▼ study for a test
- ▼ plant a garden
- ▼ purchase a car
- ▼ plan a party

Directional Process

There are two methods to develop a topic using process: directional and informational. **Directional process** explains how to do something: how to bake a cake, how to tune a car engine, or how to write a process essay. The intent, or goal, of directional process writing is to enable the readers to do something (to duplicate some process) after they have followed the directions. Recipes, assembly instructions, how-to books, and manuals are all examples of directional process writing. The following directional process paragraph explains, in part, how to plan for an inexpensive vacation.

Example

Setting a budget not only helps when planning a trip but can help to save money. Decide how much money is available, and plan the trip around places fitting the budget. Once the budget is set, look on the Internet for sites offering discounts on travel/ hotel packages. If suitable package deals aren't available, call hotels in the area. Inquire about seasonal discounts. Discounted tickets for events and places of interest usually are available for cities promoting tourism. Also, stop by travel agencies for brochures on the locations and other discounted packages.

Informational Process

Informational process explains how something was made, how an event occurred, or how something works: how a treaty between two or more countries was finalized, how the Panama Canal was built, or how an industrial laser is used in medical procedures. After reading informational process writing, readers should understand the process, but they usually do not repeat it. Duplication is not the intent of informational process. After all, you might understand how the Panama Canal was built, but you would never be able to duplicate its construction. Look at the following informational process paragraph that describes the process a patient suffering from GERD (gastroesophageal reflux disease) must undergo to determine if surgery is necessary.

Example

When the doctor suggests that an operation is necessary, a GERD sufferer may be referred to a gastroenterologist or gastrointestinal surgeon. The patient will undergo a series of upper gastrointestinal X-rays that involve swallowing a chalky substance called barium and watching the substance go down the esophagus into the stomach for diagnosis of a hiatal hernia that may demonstrate gastroesophageal reflux. The specialist may recommend endoscopy, wherein a small tube with a microscopic camera attached to the end is placed into the esophagus, helping the doctor visualize the damage done to the lining of the esophagus by gastric juices. If GERD is confirmed, the surgeon will help the patient make the decision whether or not to have the surgery.

Writing a Process Paragraph

A process paragraph introduces the process under discussion and outlines the steps in the process. Transitional expressions relate the steps in the process to one another to help connect ideas, so the steps do not seem merely like an uncoordinated list.

The Topic Sentence in a Process Paragraph

Directional and informational process paragraphs begin with a topic sentence that clearly states what the reader should be able to do or to understand after reading the steps of the process. The topic sentence also should point out why the process is important. Read the following topic sentence for an informational process paragraph.

> **Example**
>
> A series of dubious events led to the outbreak of the Spanish-American War.

The entire paragraph might read this way:

> A series of dubious events led to the outbreak of the Spanish-American War. Cubans had long attempted to overthrow Spanish rule in their country. The rebellion began in 1885 and lasted for many years. William Randolph Hearst, owner of the *New York Journal*, falsely reported on the war; his reporters made the conflict seem as if the Spanish were massacring the Cubans. Such propaganda caused a wave of anti-Spain feelings to sweep across America. In late February 1898, the American vessel *Maine*, sent to Cuba to protect American people and property, blew up in Havana harbor, killing more than 260 people. Consequently, Americans instantly assumed that the Spanish had blown up the *Maine* by means of a submarine. War frenzy broke out in the United States, and Americans wanted war more than ever. "To hell with Spain, remember the *Maine!*" was a popular chant shouted by war enthusiasts.

In the example above, the process that led to the Spanish-American War is as follows: the Cubans rebel against the Spanish, the *New York Journal* prints false reports of the treatment of Cuban rebels by the Spanish, the vessel *Maine* is sent to Havana, the *Maine* blows up, Americans think the Spanish are responsible. All of these steps eventually led to the war between Spain and the United States. The reason the writer thinks the topic is important is expressed in the word *dubious*. This attitude suggests that some of the events that led to the war were less than genuine. The writer uses words like *falsely, propaganda,* and *frenzy* to suggest that Americans were, in many ways, tricked into their anti-Spain attitude.

Organizing the Process Paragraph

Directional and informational process paragraphs are developed according to the order in which the steps of the process occur. Sticking to chronological order avoids confusion. For example, in describing how to save information to a floppy disk using a computer, you would not give the instructions as suggested in the list on the left; rather, you would follow the chronological order as listed on the right.

Wrong	Right
1. Click on the Save icon	1. Click on the File icon
2. Move cursor to down arrow	2. Move cursor to "Save As"
3. Click on "$3\frac{1}{2}$ Floppy (A:)"	3. Click on "Save As"
4. Move cursor to "Save As"	4. Open Menu by clicking on arrow
5. Open Menu by clicking on arrow	5. Click on "$3\frac{1}{2}$ Floppy (A:)"
6. Click on File icon	6. Click on the Save icon

PRACTICE 2   Organizing and Rewriting a Process Paragraph

Using the paragraph you wrote for Practice 1, go through the paragraph and make a numbered list of the steps in the process. Are they out of chronological order? Are any important steps missing? If so, rewrite the paragraph so that all relevant steps are included in the proper chronological order. If your paragraph for Practice 1 did not need to be rewritten, choose another of the topics from Practice 1, create a numbered list of relevant steps in the process, and write a paragraph following the correct chronological order for the steps.

Transitional Expressions: Connecting the Steps

Once you have the steps of your process in the correct order, you have to connect them so that they follow each other smoothly. Using transitional expressions will help you connect the steps of the process, and they will announce to the reader that a step is forthcoming. Of course, transitional expressions will also add rhythm to the paragraph, making it easier to read.

Transitional Expressions for Process			
afterwards	before	initially	to begin
as	begin by	later	until
as soon as	during	meanwhile	upon
at first	finally	next	when
at last	first, second	now	while
at this point	following	then	

Using the paragraph you wrote for Practice 1, add at least three appropriate transitional expressions. When you have finished, compare the two paragraphs. The paragraph containing the transitional expressions should be easier to understand and easier to read.

Moving from Paragraph to Essay

Now that you have studied and practiced the techniques to create effective process paragraphs, it is time to expand your ideas to a larger writing unit: the process essay. Using the prewriting and writing techniques you learned in Part 1 regarding developing the essay paragraphs and the process techniques you have just learned, you can write a process essay. This might be a good time to return to Part 1 and review the techniques for developing the full essay.

Creating the Introductory Paragraph

Because process writing uses chronological order to organize its development, writers sometimes think that they needn't be concerned about overall organization and focus. But a process essay is writing, and all writing has specific purpose. The thesis statement in a process essay should state the essay's overall purpose, the writer's attitude toward the topic, and the organizational structure.

The thesis for directional and informational process essays should blend naturally into the introductory paragraph. The following example of an introductory paragraph was written by a student for a directional process essay. You will see the full essay a bit later. Notice how the thesis statement announces the topic (*taking photographs using a digital camera*), the writer's combined attitude and controlling idea about the topic (*certain steps are necessary to make the process successful*), and the essay map containing the body paragraph subtopics (*how to take a picture, viewing the images taken, and downloading and saving the images to a computer*). The thesis statement in the example is underlined for identification purposes.

> **Example**
>
> Using a traditional film camera can be tricky and require a lot of technical know-how that takes years to learn. In addition, developing photographs requires an expensive and space cluttering darkroom filled with equipment and chemicals. Today, with the invention of the digital camera, much of this expertise, equipment, and space is no longer needed to take quality photographs. Anyone who owns a computer can produce photographs—and even send them via the Internet—relatively easily. But first, it's necessary to master the digital camera to shoot photographs. Within a few minutes, sharp, quality photographs can be a reality—and without the expense of film and developing. Taking photographs successfully using a digital camera depends on having a basic knowledge of how to take a picture, viewing the images taken, and downloading and saving the images to a computer.

This essay will continue by developing each of the subtopics in the body paragraphs as outlined in the essay map. Using the thesis statement with the essay map makes the content and organizational structure clear for both writer and reader.

PRACTICE 4   Writing a Thesis Statement for a Process Paragraph

Create a thesis statement with an attitude, a controlling idea, and a three-item essay map using the topic idea in the paragraph you wrote for Practice 3. Make certain that the three essay map items you choose are suitable for developing the topic as the controlling idea and attitude suggests. (See "The Attitude in the Thesis Statement" and "The Controlling Idea in the Thesis Statement" in Chapter 4 if you need to review this information.)

Creating the Body Paragraphs

For a paper on the topic of creating a successful photograph using a digital camera, the focus of the body paragraphs will be the topics listed in the thesis statement's essay map. The first body paragraph's topic will be "how to take a picture," the second body paragraph's topic will be "viewing images taken," and the third body paragraph's topic will be "downloading and saving the images to a computer." Remember, as you write about each of these topics, your focus should not be on film speed, types of cameras, or lighting equipment. Keep the focus on the attitude and the controlling idea: the steps necessary *to make taking digital photographs easier.*

Creating the Concluding Paragraph

The approach of the concluding paragraph should flow naturally from the essay's main topic. Because the essay's focus is the steps necessary to make taking digital photographs easier, an *evaluation* of the importance of the essay's subject seems appropriate. You might mention that photographic equipment and supplies such as scanners, portable wallets, and memory drives can help the digital photographer. You might remind the readers that they probably will put a lot of time and thought into the photographs they are taking, so care and patience during the shoot is critical. (Refer to Chapter 6 for other approaches for concluding paragraphs.)

Sample Directional Process Student Essay: USING A DIGITAL CAMERA SUCCESSFULLY

Jocilyn Jimenez

Photography is a popular activity for millions of people. But with today's automatic cameras that promise to do everything but ensure a smile on the subject's face, there comes a price. The photographs taken with these technological marvels don't always live up to the expectations of the amateur picture-taker. In this essay, "Using a Digital Camera Successfully," student writer Jocilyn Jimenez explains how to produce quality photographs using a digital camera. She uses many transitional expressions to help connect relevant ideas and keep the steps in the process in chronological order.

Vocabulary

Before starting to read, use a dictionary to look up the definitions of the following words appearing in the essay.

adept (5)	designated (4)	engaged (2)	enhance (5)
expertise (1)	initially (3)	port (4)	scrolling (3)
sufficient (2)			

Using a Digital Camera Successfully

1　　Using a traditional film camera can be tricky and require a lot of technical know-how that takes years to learn. In addition, developing photographs requires an expensive and space cluttering darkroom filled with equipment and chemicals. Today, with the invention of the digital camera, much of this expertise, equipment, and space is no longer needed to take quality photographs. Anyone who owns a computer can produce photographs—and even send them via the Internet—relatively easily. But first, it's necessary to master the digital camera to shoot photographs. Within a few minutes, sharp, quality photographs can be a reality—and without the expense of film and developing. **Taking photographs successfully using a digital camera depends on having a basic knowledge of how to take a picture, viewing the images taken, and downloading and saving the images to a computer.**

Thesis Statement with Essay Map →

Topic Sentence →

2　　Before a picture can be taken, the digital camera must be set properly. Digital cameras do not use film; instead, they use a "smart disk" to hold images. First, check to make certain that a smart disk is in the camera. Second, remove the LENS CAP. Next, turn the "ON/OFF" dial so it points at the "REC" dot, and press the "ON" button in the middle of the dial. Now, a picture can be taken. However, if there is not sufficient light, the flash can be engaged. Release the flash by pressing the "FLASH LEVER," usually located on either side of the lens barrel. Then, for a close-up, the ZOOM feature can be engaged. Usually the zoom is engaged by pressing a small button near the picture-taking button on the top of the camera. Now, point and shoot! It's that easy.

Topic Sentence →

3　　Images can be viewed right on the camera, so a decision can be made about whether or not to keep them. That's one of the exciting features of the digital camera—no wasted film, and no paying for prints that don't turn out well for whatever reason. Initially, set the on/off dial to "PLAY." The stored images will then be shown, starting with the first image taken and scrolling to the last. Second, scroll through the images by pressing the "+" or "-" buttons. To DELETE an Image, scroll until the image appears in the monitor window. Next, press the red "DELETE" button. A menu will appear asking whether or not the image is to be deleted. Press "OK" if you want to erase the image, and simply press the "DELETE" button a second time if you decide to keep the Image. Again, it's that easy.

Topic Sentence →

4　　Finally, saving the images is a simple matter of downloading them to a computer. Find the IMAGE TRANSFERRING CABLE, and plug it into the designated port on the digital camera. Then, connect the other end to the proper port on the computer. Next, set the camera "ON/OFF" button to "PLAY." The system is ready to transfer images. Remember to keep the LENS CAP *on*. The system will not download if the cap is off. Now, from the START menu, select PROGRAMS. Click on "DOWNLOAD," and then select where you want to save the images. Usually, saving images to a disk or ZIP or to a DOCUMENT folder on the desktop is sufficient. Finally, click "SAVE," and the download process will begin.

5　　Using the digital camera frequently, a photographer can create good but simple photographs. As the user becomes more adept, he or she can purchase many accessories to enhance the quality of the photographs. Programs that crop, frame, border, and add/delete background can be bought at almost any camera shop or on the Internet. Eventually, the user might want to buy a scanner, a portable memory drive, a creative filter system, a high performance transfer cable, a fisheye converter, and a portable digital wallet storage unit. While expensive, accessories can make photography a fun, creative, and rewarding activity. Lastly, while accessories can enhance the quality and ease of photographic development, time and patience during the shoot is critical. All the advanced technology in the world can't make up for a head out-of-frame or subjects with their eyes closed!

Process Technique Questions

1. How many steps are there in the process? List them below.

_____

_____

_____

2. Identify some of the transitional expressions the writer uses. How do they help organize the steps chronologically?

_____

_____

_____

_____

_____

3. Identify any steps that, in your opinion, were not clearly expressed or needed more explanation. Can you suggest any additional information that would make the process clearer and more understandable?

_____

_____

Critical Reading Questions

1. Which of the steps is explained in the most detail? Why do you think the writer chose to focus more on that step than on the others? Did this add or detract from the essay's effectiveness? Explain.

_____

_____

_____

_____

2. What is the main idea of the essay?

_____

_____

3. Does the information in the concluding paragraph make you want to run out and buy a digital camera, or does it make you leery of doing such a thing? Explain.

_____

_____

_____

Process Writing Exercises

1. Write a directional or informational process paragraph about a popular or unusual hobby. If directional, be certain to provide readers with steps to ensure their being able to duplicate the process. If informational, be certain that the steps in the process allow readers to understand how the process was completed.

2. Now, expand the paragraph you wrote for exercise 1, and write a full essay. Before writing, make a list of the steps in the hobby, and put them in chronological order. Be sure to add appropriate transitional expressions to help order the steps, create rhythm, and create sentence variety.

▼

Sample Informational Process Student Essay: HOW TO BE SUCCESSFUL AT KICKING THE SMOKING HABIT

Stephany K. Higgs

With the advent of so many advances in medical technology, the negative effects of smoking have been known for a long time. The depth and breadth of smoking's short- and long-term effects on the body, and even fetuses in the womb, has caused millions to quit the habit and prevented millions more from beginning the activity in the first place. Yet despite educational programs, the surgeon general's warning on each pack of cigarettes, and continual public service announcements in all the media, millions more find it next to impossible to kick the habit. In this essay, "How to Be Successful at Kicking the Smoking Habit," student writer Stephany K. Higgs outlines the steps necessary to stop smoking. Notice how she mixes both tangible activities that can help the smoker quit with the psychological motivations that must be understood to make the process of quitting effective.

Vocabulary

Before you begin reading, use a dictionary to look up the definitions for the following words appearing in the essay.

cessation (3)	cravings (2)	designated (4)	empowered (2)
induced (3)	resolve (1)	skepticism (3)	tenacity (1)

How to Be Successful at Kicking the Smoking Habit

Thesis Statement with Essay Map →

1   On New Year's Eve, millions of people resolve to quit smoking during the upcoming year. Unfortunately, many people fail before they even get started because smoking is both a physical and psychological addiction. Quitting will require commitment and tenacity. Quitting smoking can be done if smokers explore the reasons why they smoke, develop a plan with a method for stopping smoking, and obtain support from friends and family.

Topic Sentence → 2   People smoke for many reasons; therefore, it is important for smokers to identify the reasons why they smoke. Analyzing the origin of the habit is the first positive step toward kicking the habit. For most people, smoking is a learned behavior; consequently, smokers tend to come from families where one or more of their parents were smokers. The majority of them are anxious people who started smoking because it seemed to provide a temporary release from current or future distress and uncertainties. Some tobacco users started smoking to be cool and to fit in with the crowd; moreover, others started smoking because they enjoyed the taste of tobacco upon trying it out. While others did not necessarily enjoy the act of smoking, they felt addicted to the nicotine and needed to continue to satisfy their cravings. Now, with the origin of the habit exposed, the smoker is empowered with the knowledge of why he or she smokes and can seek out healthier alternatives to satisfy needs.

Topic Sentence → 3   Developing a plan with a method for cessation of smoking is the next important step. There are many products on the market today, available with or without prescription, which can be helpful to the smoker trying to quit. Smokers need to decide which method would be most effective for them; some methods are more costly than others although not necessarily more effective. Nicotine patches, gum, and tablets are some of the many aids available to the smoker. Therefore, discussing these aids with the smoker's physician, friends, family, and co-workers can be helpful in stopping the habit because many of them have knowledge, either directly or indirectly, about these products and how they have worked for themselves and/or friends and loved ones. Alternative methods such as hypnotism and sleep-induced behavior modification have been viewed with skepticism by the medical community and should be approached with caution and research by the smoker. Once smokers choose a method they believe will work best for them, it is important to make the commitment to stay with it. Additionally, smokers must realize there will be times when they will feel the method is not working. There will be times when they will fall off the quit-smoking-wagon and will need to climb back on again. If they expect this and have a plan to handle the climb back up, they can reach their goal.

Topic Sentence → 4   Receiving support from friends, family, and co-workers in the effort to quit smoking can be one of the deciding factors in whether or not a smoker will stop smoking and remain smoke free. Letting those closest to the smoker know that the smoker's intention is to quit smoking gives the smoker a support system. Finding someone who would also like to quit can be effective because the two can support each other by calling on one another when they feel weak in their effort to give up. Family members, friends, and co-workers should be sensitive to the ups and downs the smoker will experience by smoking only in designated areas until such time as the smoker feels strong enough to be around other smokers without joining them. Engaging the support of a former smoker can be helpful in getting smokers trying to quit over the rough spots.

5 On every package of cigarettes there is a warning by the Surgeon General: "Smoking Causes Lung Cancer, Heart Disease, Emphysema, and May Complicate Pregnancy." Health related illnesses are the number one reason most people would like to quit smoking. Beyond that, it is a smelly, messy, and expensive addiction. Sadly, it is one of the hardest addictions to break. However, with determination and support, quitting smoking can be done, and succeeding greatly increases the chance for continued good health.

Process Technique Questions

1. Although the essay is informational, how many steps does the writer focus on in the process?

2. The writer does not use many transitional expressions as illustrated in this chapter. Point out some places in the essay where transitional expressions could be used. How would they make the essay more effective?

Critical Reading Questions

1. Why does the writer focus on smokers' motivations for smoking? Wouldn't it be better to write a directional process essay so smokers could follow steps that would stop them from smoking? Explain.

2. The writer talks about a variety of "behavior modification" procedures and products that a smoker can use to help stop the habit. She also men-

tions consulting with a doctor and informing friends and family about the commitment to stop smoking. Why are these support mechanisms important?

_____

_____

_____

_____

_____

_____

_____

_____

_____

Process Writing Exercises

1. Write an informational process paragraph about a hard-to-break habit or addiction. It can be about a dangerous addiction, such as to heroin or alcohol, or a seemingly benign one, such as being addicted to watching soap operas or eating chocolate. Don't forget to create an attitude in the topic sentence that shows the importance of the process.

2. Now, write an informational essay about a habit or addiction. Expand your ideas by using one or more of the prewriting techniques you have studied. Remember, the intent of the informational process essay is to have the reader understand the process, not necessarily to be able to duplicate it or the results stemming from it.

▼
Sample Professional Essay: CAT BATHING AS MARTIAL ART

Bud Herron

Not much is known about Bud Herron; in fact, surfing the Internet yields no information at all about this humorist. "Cat Bathing as Martial Art" can be found at many humor sites on the Web, but it was originally published in the *Franklin Daily Journal* (Indiana) in 1984. This rendition was found at **lifestorywriting.com.** This very funny essay is a good example of an informational process essay. While the essay is satirical and very humorous, especially for cat owners who have ever tried the futile and dangerous activity of the title, it is also carefully organized according to the steps in the process.

Vocabulary

Before you start to read, use a dictionary to look up the definitions for the following words appearing in the essay.

berserk (3)	contrary (2)	enzyme (1)	flak (4)
folklore (2)	latherings (8)	nonchalantly (6)	saliva (1)

Cat Bathing as Martial Art

1   Some people say cats never have to be bathed. They say cats lick themselves clean. They say cats have a special enzyme of some sort in their saliva that works like new, improved Wisk—dislodging the dirt where it hides and whisking it away.

2   I've spent most of my life believing this folklore. Like most blind believers, I've been able to discount all the facts to the contrary: the kitty odors that lurk in the corners of the garage and dirt smudges that cling to the throw rug by the fireplace. The time comes, however, when a man must face reality, when he must look squarely in the face of massive public sentiment to the contrary and announce: "This cat smells like a port-a-potty on a hot day in Juarez." When that day arrives at your house, as it has at mine, I have some advice you might consider as you place your feline friend under your arm and head for the bathtub:

3 ▼ Know that although the cat has the advantage of quickness and lack of concern for human life, you have the advantage of strength. Capitalize on that advantage by selecting the battlefield. Don't try to bathe him in an open area where he can force you to chase him. Pick a very small bathroom. If your bathroom is more than four feet square, I recommend that you get in the tub with the cat and close the sliding-glass doors as if

you were about to take a shower. (A simple shower curtain will not do. A berserk cat can shred a three-ply rubber curtain quicker than a politician can shift positions.)

4 ▼ Know that a cat has claws and will not hesitate to remove all the skin from your body. Your advantage here is that you are smart and know how to dress to protect yourself. I recommend canvas overalls tucked into high-top construction boots, a pair of steel-mesh gloves, an army helmet, a hockey face mask, and a long-sleeved flak jacket.

5 ▼ Prepare everything in advance. There is no time to go out for a towel when you have a cat digging a hole in your flak jacket. Draw the water. Make sure the bottle of kitty shampoo is inside the glass enclosure. Make sure the towel can be reached, even if you are lying on your back in the water.

6 ▼ Use the element of surprise. Pick up your cat nonchalantly, as if to simply carry him to his supper dish. (Cats will not usually notice your strange attire. They have little or no interest in fashion as a rule. If he does notice your garb, calmly explain that you are taking part in a product testing experiment for J. C. Penney.)

7 ▼ Once you are inside the bathroom, speed is essential to survival. In a single liquid motion, shut the bathroom door, step into the tub enclosure, slide the glass door shut, dip the cat in the water, and squirt him with shampoo. You have begun one of the wildest 45 seconds of your life.

8 ▼ Cats have no handles. Add the fact that he now has soapy fur, and the problem is radically compounded. Do not expect to hold on to him for more than two or three seconds at a time. When you have him, however, you must remember to give him another squirt of shampoo and rub like crazy. He'll then spring free and fall back into the water, thereby rinsing himself off. (The national record for cats is three latherings, so don't expect too much.)

9 ▼ Next, the cat must be dried. Novice cat bathers always assume this part will be the most difficult, for humans generally are worn out at this point and the cat is just getting really determined. In fact, the drying is simple compared to what you have just been through. That's because by now the cat is semipermanently affixed to your right leg. You simply pop the drain plug with your foot, reach for your towel and wait. (Occasionally, however, the cat will end up clinging to the top of your army helmet. If this happens, the best thing you can do is to shake him loose and to encourage him toward your leg.) After all the water is drained from the tub, it is a simple matter to just reach down and dry the cat.

10 In a few days the cat will relax enough to be removed from your leg. He will usually have nothing to say for about three weeks and will spend a lot of time sitting with his back to you. He might even become psychoceramic and develop the fixed stare of a plaster figurine. You will be tempted to assume he is angry. This isn't usually the case. As a rule he is simply plotting ways to get through your defenses and injure you for life the next time you decide to give him a bath. But at least now he is clean.

Process Technique Questions

1. Is the essay intended to be directional or informational?

2. How many steps are explained?

_____

_____

_____

_____

_____

3. Identify any transitional expressions that are used. Do they help organize the information chronologically? Explain.

_____

_____

_____

_____

_____

4. Would some transitional expressions be effective? Which ones would you add, and where would you place them? Do the bullets take the place of transitional expressions?

_____

_____

_____

Critical Reading Questions

1. What process is being explained in the essay?

_____

_____

_____

2. Herron's humor is based largely on exaggeration (hyperbole). What examples in the essay do you find particularly effective and why?

_____

_____

_____

3. The title of the essay includes the phrase "Martial Art," but the activity is never mentioned in the text. How is bathing a cat like a martial art, and how do the owner and the cat resemble martial artists?

_____

_____

_____

Process Writing Exercises

1. Write an informational process paragraph describing an activity people do with pets. Make a list of the steps in the activity, and use transitional expressions to link them together.

2. Expand the ideas in the paragraph you wrote in exercise 1. Write an informational process essay about the owner-pet activity. Expand your original list of steps by using one or more of the prewriting techniques you have studied. Remember to connect the steps using transitional expressions to create rhythm, order steps chronologically, and add sentence variety.

More Topics for a Process Essay

Here are some possible topics for directional and informational essay writing assignments. Remember, your process essay should have a clearly defined purpose.

1. How to repair a machine or appliance (for example, photocopier, lamp, toaster, radio).

2. How to act on a first date in order to guarantee a second date.

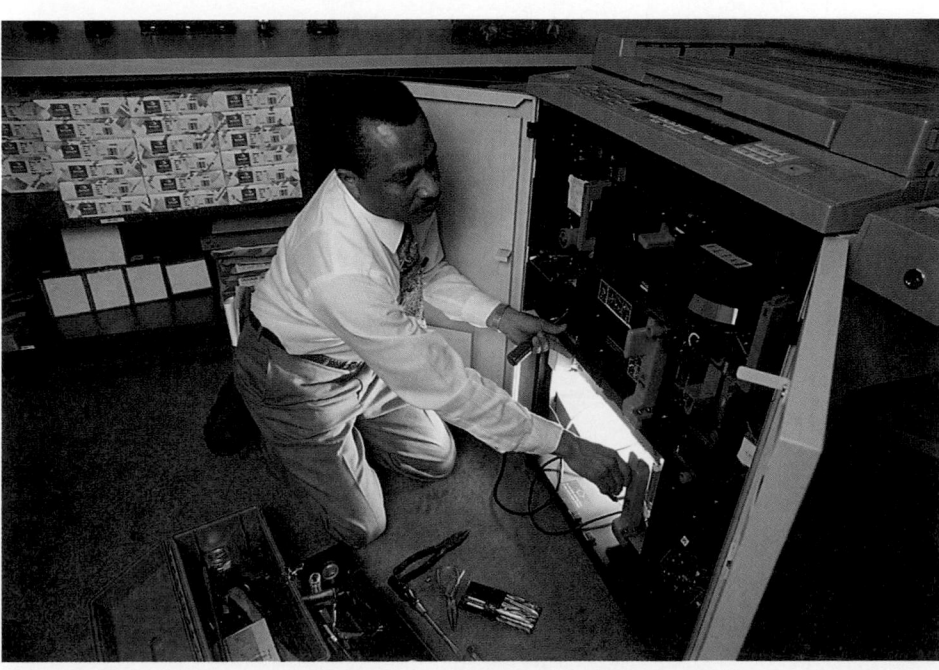

3. How to preserve a food (for example, pickles, peaches, tomatoes).
4. How a camera works.
5. How stars form (and/or die).
6. How a cure for a disease was discovered.
7. How a bill is processed in a legislature.
8. How to install computer hardware (for example, sound card, modem, Zip drive).
9. How to start a home-based business.
10. How to propose marriage.

☑ Writing Checklist for a Process Essay

❏ **1.** Choose a topic.

❏ **2.** Explore the topic using one or more of the prewriting techniques you have studied.

❏ **3.** Decide whether to write an informational or directional essay.

❏ **4.** Write a thesis statement. Remember to include an attitude and a controlling idea.

❏ **5.** Choose as many of the steps in the process as you think will adequately develop the process and make it either duplicatible (directional) or understandable (informational) for the reader.

❏ **6.** Include any tips or insights that will enable the reader to better comprehend the process you are describing.

❏ **7.** Write the essay, remembering to use transitional expressions to help the reader understand the order of the steps.

❏ **8.** Revise the first draft.

❏ **9.** Proofread the final draft.

❏ **10.** Print or type the essay and submit it.

CHAPTER REVIEW

▼ A process essay explains how something happened, how to do or make something, or how something works. Directional process essays explain how to do something or make something, and their purpose is to enable the reader to duplicate the process. Informational process essays explain how something was done or made, and their purpose is to have the reader understand the process but not duplicate it.

▼ In a process paragraph, the steps of the process are usually organized chronologically, and transitional expressions help keep the steps in sequence.

▼ In a process essay, the introductory paragraph introduces the process, outlines the main steps, and explains the importance of the process. The body paragraphs develop the main steps in sequence. In the concluding paragraph, an evaluation of the process is a possible approach.

Visit *The Write Start* Online!

For additional practice with the materials found in this chapter, visit our Website at

http://www.ablongman.com/checkett

The Website also features additional readings, quizzes, writing activities, and Internet links, as well as a bulletin board and interactive chat.

12 The Comparison or Contrast Essay

As your writing opportunities increase, often you will need to discuss an object, person, idea, event, or item not only in terms of its own features but also in terms of how it relates to another object, person, idea, event, or item. This type of writing can be challenging because it forces you to think about each item independently of the other and then to think about how the items relate to each other. Are they alike? Are they different? How? Why? Developing a topic in this fashion is called comparison or contrast.

Identifying Your Purpose

When using **comparison-contrast** to organize a paragraph or essay, you are looking for similarities and differences. When *comparing,* you are looking for similarities. When *contrasting,* you are looking for differences. For example, consider two computers. In comparing them, you might notice that the monitor screens both measure 14 inches, the housings are made of a high-impact plastic, the keyboards have all the same function keys, and the hard drives have the same information storage capacity. In contrasting them, however, you might notice that one has a black housing and the other has a blue one, one has a combination battery and CD-ROM port and the other does not, and one has a monitor and a CPU that stand separate from the keyboard while the other system has the monitor, CPU, and keyboard self-contained in one housing. By comparing and contrasting, then, you know that both units are computers, but that one is a traditional desktop model while the other is a laptop. Comparison and contrast, therefore, helps you understand one person, place, feeling, idea, event, or object in relation to another. Look at the following two examples.

Example Comparison Paragraph

The occupations of cosmetologist and nurse may seem very different, but they share many common attributes. For instance, the cosmetologist makes the client's appearance better by using the proper grooming techniques. The nurse uses the latest medical procedures when treating a patient. A cosmetologist's client often feels depressed or anxious about his or her appearance. By using the coloring products appropriate to the client's complexion and age, the cosmetologist can change her appearance dramatically, making the client feel good about herself once again. The nurse makes the patient feel better by administering the proper medications or exercise appropriate for the patient's problem and age group. Both the cosmetologist and the nurse make people in their care feel better about themselves.

Even though the occupations of cosmetologist and nurse do not seem very similar on the surface, points of comparison can be found. Of course, there must be a purpose to the comparison and, in the comparison above, the fact that both the cosmetologist and the nurse make their patients feel better is the important consideration.

Example Contrast Paragraph

In the novel *Runaway Jury*, by John Grisham, the character development is superb because the writer alludes to certain aspects of the characters' personalities throughout the development of the plot. One of the strong points of this novel is that the reader is being fed only enough information about the characters at crucial times; therefore, a desire is created within the reader to know each character more intimately and to know how they will relate to the rest of the story. In contrast, *The Testament*, also by John Grisham, has a glaring lack of character development from the very beginning of the story. There is some confusion in the first few chapters as to who the main characters are. Instead of revealing the nature of each personality throughout the book, the author gives bland, generic, and brief descriptions of them. There also is an overabundance of characters who truly are not necessary to the development and enrichment of the plot, so the desire to know the characters better and to see how the plot relates to them is not achieved.

Although both novels are written by the same author, and both novels involve lawyers and the law (John Grisham trademarks), the contrasts clearly are definable and important on several levels. First, if you are going to pay $24.95 for a novel, you certainly want its characters to be well developed and interesting. Secondly, on a technical level, you want to know that a writer you are considering investing time and money in is an accomplished artist who can bring his characters to life in a lively and compelling way that will hold your interest.

You might, at times, be called on to compare and contrast many people, places, events, or items. But most of the time you will be comparing or contrasting two items and, for the sake of simplicity, that is what you will learn how to do in this chapter.

Look at the following pairs of topics. Indicate whether it would be better to compare or contrast each pair by putting a check mark in the space provided.

	Compare	Contrast
1. Fire and ice	_____	_____
2. Alaska and Arizona	_____	_____
3. Capitalism and communism	_____	_____
4. Men and women	_____	_____
5. Soccer and rugby	_____	_____
6. Email and snail mail	_____	_____
7. Swimming in a lake and swimming in a pool	_____	_____
8. Canoeing and kayaking	_____	_____
9. Thin-crust and deep-pan pizza	_____	_____
10. Being married and being single	_____	_____

Writing a Comparison or Contrast Paragraph

When you write a paragraph about two items, your first task is to decide whether to compare or contrast them. Once that is done, you can select the appropriate supporting details, write an appropriate topic sentence, and decide how to organize the points in your paragraph.

Deciding to Compare or to Contrast and Selecting Supporting Details

Sometimes, it will be obvious to you whether to compare or contrast two items. At other times, the similarities and differences may not jump out at you. After you have chosen your pair of topics to develop, what is the best method to use to help you decide if you should compare or contrast the two items? How will you know if there are enough elements between the two items to make comparing or contrasting them worthwhile? Creating a chart like the one in the following example is an easy method that helps you make such decisions.

Compare and Contrast Chart
Two items:

Humungous University   TinyTown College

Similarities:

Great humanities departments   Exceptional fine arts

Faculty 90% PhDs	Faculty 85% PhDs
Computer friendly campus	Each student receives laptop
In-state campus near home	Out of state but only 100 miles away

Differences:

All traditional sports teams	"Club" sports and intramurals
Federal and state financial aid	Private and government aid
50,000 students	5,000 students
Student/faculty ratio 30:1	Student/faculty ratio 11:1
Many graduate degrees	M.A. & M.F.A. degrees only

Once you have filled in the similarities and differences of the two items, it should become obvious which approach will result in the better paragraph. You will also be able to use the items in your list as supporting details as you develop the paragraph. So, using the chart can make developing your paragraph much easier.

▼ **PRACTICE 2**   **Making a Compare and Contrast Chart**

Choose one of the topics from Practice 1 and complete a compare and contrast chart for it.

Compare and Contrast Chart

Two items:

_____   _____

Similarities:

_____   _____

_____   _____

_____   _____

_____   _____

Differences:

_____   _____

_____   _____

_____   _____

_____   _____

The Topic Sentence in a Comparison or Contrast Paragraph

The topic sentence in a comparison or contrast paragraph clearly states the two items being developed and why comparing or contrasting them is important. The following is an example of a topic sentence for a comparison or contrast paragraph.

> When choosing between ice hockey and roller hockey for a child's participation, cost is usually the deciding factor.

This topic sentence clearly states the two items for comparison: ice hockey and roller hockey. The important reason for discussing the topic is the cost factor, which also indicates that contrast, not comparison, will be the method of development.

▼ PRACTICE 3   Writing a Topic Sentence

Write a topic sentence for the subject you chose in Practice 1 and for which you completed a comparison and contrast chart in Practice 2.

Organizing a Comparison or Contrast Paragraph

Once you know whether you are comparing or contrasting and the supporting details you will use, you need to organize your thoughts and decide how to present them. There are two commonly used organizational plans for comparison and contrast paragraphs: block and point-by-point.

1. The *block method* presents all the information about one item first, then uses this information for comparison or contrast when presenting information about the second item.

2. The *point-by-point method* presents the information about both items together, creating an ongoing series of comparisons and contrasts.

In the following paragraph about ice hockey and roller hockey, the block method is used.

> ### Block Method Example
>
> When choosing between ice hockey and roller hockey for a child's participation, cost is usually the deciding factor. Playing roller hockey in small in-house leagues costs on average seventy-five dollars. If children show talent, they may play for a "select" tournament team, and the average cost will skyrocket to three hundred dollars. Equipment for roller hockey, although expensive, is necessary for protection against injury. Well-padded, durable skates can cost an average of two hundred dollars; helmets, on average, cost fifty dollars; and kneepads, girdle, and pants can cost one hundred and fifty dollars. This brings the total average cost of roller hockey to four hundred seventy-five dollars for an in-house league and seven hundred fifty dollars for a select tournament team. Ice hockey is considerably more expensive than roller hockey because more equipment is required. Playing ice hockey in an in-house league costs an average of three hundred fifty dollars, and playing for a select tournament team can

cost six hundred dollars. As with roller hockey equipment, ice hockey equipment is expensive. In addition, ice hockey requires shoulder pads while roller hockey does not. The pads can cost upwards of seventy-five dollars. Also, ice hockey requires a thicker, heavier stick that can cost ninety to one hundred dollars. Ice hockey skates have an average cost of three hundred dollars, which is one hundred dollars more than roller hockey skates. Helmets, kneepads, girdle, and pants can cost two hundred to three hundred fifty dollars. The total average cost for playing ice hockey in an in-house league is nine hundred to twelve hundred dollars.

Notice that the cost elements of roller hockey are discussed in the first half of the paragraph (without mention of ice hockey). Then the same elements in regard to ice hockey are discussed in the second half of the paragraph. But this time as each ice hockey item is mentioned, reference is made to the corresponding roller hockey item as well. In this way, the comparison between the elements is continually made. If this were not done, then the two halves of the paragraph would seem disconnected, and the contrast would not exist.

The block method can be diagrammed in this manner:

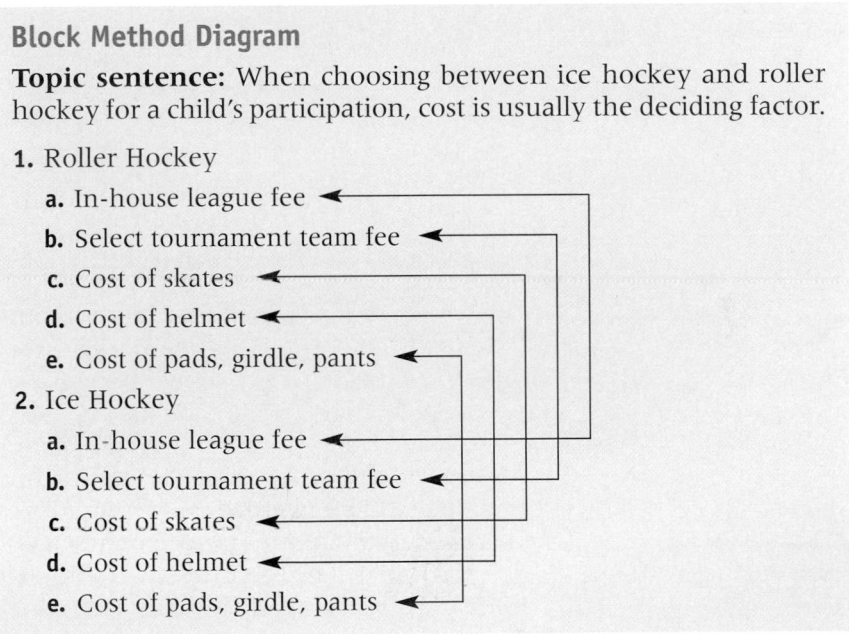

Block Method Diagram

Topic sentence: When choosing between ice hockey and roller hockey for a child's participation, cost is usually the deciding factor.

1. Roller Hockey
    a. In-house league fee
    b. Select tournament team fee
    c. Cost of skates
    d. Cost of helmet
    e. Cost of pads, girdle, pants

2. Ice Hockey
    a. In-house league fee
    b. Select tournament team fee
    c. Cost of skates
    d. Cost of helmet
    e. Cost of pads, girdle, pants

Remember, when using the block method, you discuss all the factors in the first item of comparison or contrast in the first part of the paragraph without mentioning the second item being compared or contrasted. Then, in the second half of the paragraph, you discuss each point regarding the second item in the comparison or contrast, remembering to make reference to each item that was mentioned in the first half of the paragraph. This will connect the two items so that the paragraph will not seem to be about two items that have nothing to do with one another.

In the point-by-point method, the similar point in regard to the second item in the comparison or contrast follows each point concerning the first item. The point-by-point method is diagrammed in this manner:

Point-by-Point Method Diagram

Topic sentence: When choosing between ice hockey or roller hockey for a child's participation, cost is usually the deciding factor.

First Point:	**a.**	Roller hockey in-league fee
	b.	Ice hockey in-league fee
Second Point:	**a.**	Roller hockey Select Tournament Team
	b.	Ice hockey Select Tournament Team
Third Point:	**a.**	Roller hockey skates
	b.	Ice hockey skates
Fourth Point:	**a.**	Roller hockey helmets
	b.	Ice hockey helmets
Fifth Point:	**a.**	Roller hockey pads, girdle, pants
	b.	Ice hockey pads, girdle, pants

For the point-by-point method, the paragraph contrasting ice hockey and roller hockey might be rewritten like this:

Point-by-Point Method Example

When choosing between ice hockey and roller hockey for a child's participation, cost is usually the deciding factor. When playing roller hockey in small in-house leagues, the average cost is seventy-five dollars. On the other hand, playing ice hockey in an in-house league costs an average of three hundred fifty dollars. If children show talent, they may play for a "select" tournament team, and the average roller hockey team cost will skyrocket to three hundred dollars. Whereas, on a select ice hockey tournament team, the costs can soar to six hundred dollars. Equipment for roller hockey, although expensive, is necessary for protection against injury. Well-padded, durable roller hockey skates can cost an average of two hundred dollars, while ice hockey skates have an average cost of three hundred dollars and up. In roller hockey, helmets, on average, cost fifty dollars. Similarly, ice hockey helmets cost about fifty to sixty dollars. Knee pads, girdle, and pants for roller hockey can cost one hundred fifty dollars. However, ice hockey knee pads, girdle, and pants can cost two hundred to three hundred fifty dollars. In addition, ice hockey requires shoulder pads while roller hockey does not. The pads can cost upwards of seventy-five dollars. Also, ice hockey requires a thicker, heavier stick than does roller hockey, and the stick can cost ninety to one hundred dollars. In conclusion, the average cost for playing in a roller hockey in-house league is four hundred seventy-five dollars and nine hundred to twelve hundred dollars for playing in an ice hockey in-house league. While the cost for playing for a roller hockey select tournament team can rise to seven hundred fifty dollars, playing for an ice hockey select team can be as much as fourteen hundred dollars.

▼ PRACTICE 4 | **Writing Block and Point-by-Point Method Paragraphs**

Using the topic sentence you wrote in Practice 3, write a comparison or contrast block method paragraph for the topic you have chosen. Then rewrite the paragraph using the point-by-point method.

Using Transitional Expressions to Connect Comparisons or Contrasts

Transitional expressions are important because they stress either comparison or contrast, depending on the type of paragraph you are writing. They also help keep the reader on track, because as we have seen, the organization of points in a comparison or contrast paragraph can be complex.

Transitional Expressions Showing Comparison

and	in addition
again	in the same way
also	like
as well as	likewise
both	neither
each	similarly
equally	similar to
furthermore	so
just as	the same
just like	too

Transitional Expressions Showing Contrast

although	on the contrary
but	on the other hand
despite	otherwise
different from	nevertheless
even though	still
except for	though
however	whereas
in contrast	while
instead	yet

▼ PRACTICE 5 | **Adding Transitional Expressions to a Comparison or Contrast Paragraph**

Add appropriate transitional expressions to one of the paragraphs you wrote for Practice 4. When you have finished, compare the two paragraphs. The paragraph with the transitional expressions should connect related ideas more effectively as well as add rhythm to the writing.

Moving from Paragraph to Essay

Now that you have studied and practiced the techniques to create effective comparison or contrast paragraphs, it is time to expand your ideas to a larger writing unit: the comparison or contrast essay. Using the techniques you learned in Part 1 regarding developing the essay paragraphs and the comparison or contrast techniques you have just learned enables you to write the comparison or contrast essay. This might be a good time to return to Part 1 and review the techniques for developing the full essay.

Creating the Introductory Paragraph

A comparison or contrast essay needs a clearly defined organization and a thesis statement to announce to the reader just how the subject will be developed. The thesis statement of the introductory paragraph should state the items to be compared or contrasted, the writer's attitude toward the topic, the controlling idea, and the organizational structure. By using an appropriate lead-in technique, the thesis should blend naturally into the rest of the introductory paragraph.

By using a variation of the compare and contrast chart you have already practiced to produce a comparison or contrast paragraph, you can extend and develop the ideas expressed in the chart to help you create the thesis statement for a comparison and contrast essay.

Comparison and Contrast Essay Chart

Two items:

1. _____ 2. _____

Attitude and controlling idea combined:

1. _____ (in relation to) 2. _____

Comparison and contrast points:

1. _____   _____

2. _____   _____

3. _____   _____

4. _____   _____

5. _____   _____

6. _____   _____

Thesis Statement:

_____

_____

_____

Once you have chosen your two items and have listed elements that are similar and different, choose whether you are going to compare or contrast the two topics. Next, decide on your attitude and controlling idea.

Then, choose the *three comparison or contrast points* from your list that you want to use in your essay. These will be the three subtopics for the essay map in your thesis statement.

Finally, write the thesis statement by following the elements you have listed in your chart.

Example
Two items:

Sequoia Medical School   Oceana Medical School

Attitude and controlling idea combined:

Sequoia Medical School *is better than* Oceana Medical School

Contrast points:

1. Faculty to student ratio

2. Tuition costs

3. Medical facilities

Thesis Statement:

Sequoia Medical School *is better than* Oceana Medical School

because of its faculty to student ratio, tuition costs,

and medical facilities.

Creating the Body Paragraphs

For an essay contrasting two medical schools, the focus of the body paragraphs will be the paragraph topics listed in the thesis statement's essay map. The first body paragraph's topic will be "faculty to student ratio"; the second body paragraph's topic will be "tuition costs"; the third body paragraph's topic will be "medical facilities." Remember, as you write about each of these topics, your focus should be that these are the reason *Sequoia Medical School is better than Oceana Medical School.* You can develop each of the body paragraphs using either the block method or the point-by-point method, but be consistent in the method you use within a single essay.

Creating the Concluding Paragraph

The approach of the concluding paragraph should flow naturally from the essay's main topic. Because the essay's focus is that the characteristics of one medical school makes it preferable to another, an *evaluation* of the main points seems appropriate. You might talk briefly about how the school's programs and features will help students gain acceptance to an area of medicine they want to specialize in, or how these elements will help them grow both as a person and as a professional. You might even mention if the school has professional connections to private companies that might offer employment possibilities in research. (Refer to Chapter 6 for other approaches for concluding paragraphs.)

PRACTICE 6   Writing a Comparison or Contrast Essay

Create a comparison or contrast essay chart for the topic you chose in Practice 4. After you have completed the chart, write your essay.

▼ Sample Comparison Student Essay: COMMERCIAL VS. RESIDENTIAL REAL ESTATE SALES

Nancy Smith

> Real estate sales is a popular and expanding job category. It may appear on the surface that selling commercial buildings and residential homes would be quite dissimilar. But in this essay, "Commercial vs. Residential Real Estate Sales," student writer and real estate agent Nancy Smith dispels the myth that commercial real estate sales is the more lucrative side of the business. While the essay is comparison, the writer does clarify an important difference. But by doing so, she in no way compromises the integrity of the essay's focus.

Vocabulary

Before you begin reading, use a dictionary to look up the definitions of the following words that appear in the essay.

applicant (1)	aspect (5)	commissions (4)
dwellings (3)	flexible (5)	flyers (2)
lack (4)	solicit (3)	striking (4)

Commercial vs. Residential Real Estate Sales

1   Thinking about a career in real estate? With the proper training and hard work, real estate can be a rewarding profession. Whether choosing commercial or residential sales, the decision can be easy when the applicant knows all the facts. **Commercial and residential real estate are very similar in the areas of marketing, client development, and income potential.**

Thesis Statement →

Topic Sentence → 2   **The marketing costs for commercial real estate are paid for by the real estate company; similarly, in residential real estate, costs are usually picked up by the real estate company as well.** Like residential real estate agents, commercial real estate agents send out thousands of flyers that advertise property for lease or sale. For example, both commercial and residential agents announce available properties by mailing advertising brochures to area residents and to other agents. Both commercial and residential agents can act alone or share commissions with other agents when a property is sold, rented, or leased.

Topic Sentence ———→ 3   Residential sales requires a lot of work to build up a good client base; likewise, commercial agents rely on repeat customers for fifty percent of their business. Commercial as well as residential agents also have to solicit business by "cold-calling" potential customers who may or may not be in the process of wanting to relocate. It might be surprising to find out that while businesses are looking for real estate for working space, many residential agents must provide the same characteristics for family dwellings. In families in which both parents work, "in home" office space is increasingly necessary.

Topic Sentence ———→ 4   While there are many similarities between the two sales positions, there are some striking differences. The commercial agent usually has to make fewer sales to achieve the same commissions as does the residential agent. However, because more families relocate at any given time than do businesses, the residential agent can make up in volume what the average residential commission lacks in amount.

5   With a healthy economy and more people becoming skilled in the areas employers desire, the job market for both commercial and residential real estate agents is booming. And do not overlook the "people skills" aspect of both sales environments. Selling real estate, whether commercial or residential, is as much art as it is science. With the addition of flexible work scheduling and improved benefits, most agents are finding the world of real estate a profitable, rewarding, and fun career.

Comparison Technique Questions

1. How many points of similarity does the author use? Identify them. Is the amount enough to be convincing? Explain.

   _____

   _____

2. Although this is a comparison essay, the writer identifies a contrasting point in the last body paragraph. Why does the author provide the apparent difference?

   _____

   _____

   _____

3. What organizational pattern does the writer use, point-by-point or block?

   _____

Critical Reading Questions

1. What is the main idea of the essay?

   _____

   _____

   _____

2. The real estate company does quite a bit to help each agent. But what personal attributes or "people skills" might an agent have to have to be successful?

_____

_____

3. Besides dedication, hard work, people skills, and industry support, what other condition must be present for a rewarding career as a real estate agent? Does this condition apply to other careers?

_____

_____

Comparison or Contrast Writing Exercises

1. Write a comparison or contrast paragraph about two jobs or two aspects of a job. Make a list of similarities and differences before deciding which paragraph to write.
2. Now, write a comparison or contrast essay following the comparison or contrast approach you used in the paragraph you wrote in exercise 1. Use facts rather than opinion to correct a misconception that most people might have about some aspect of the job. Use the block method to organize your essay.

▼
Sample Contrast Student Essay: TWO DIFFERENT NEIGHBORS

Tayde Cruz

The United States and Mexico have been neighbors for over two centuries, both countries are democratic in their political makeup, and they share some economic fortunes with the North American Free Trade Agreement (NAFTA). Yet, in this essay, "Two Different Neighbors," student writer Tayde Cruz states that the two countries are not very similar at all. Born and raised in Mexico, Cruz moved to the United States with her family right after graduating from high school. She develops the essay around subtopics that are of interest to persons her age. Cruz believes that the United States is a better place for a long-term stay rather than a short-term visit.

Vocabulary
Before beginning to read, use a dictionary to look up the following words that appear in the essay.

advantages (1)	festive (3)	millennium (2)
optimistic (5)	pyramids (2)	severe (5)

Two Different Neighbors

1   Living in the United States means living in a country where there can be a good future for just about anybody; however, the United States is not the best place to vacation if the vacationer longs for activities going on all day long, each day of the year. Mexico, on the other hand, doesn't necessarily have all the advantages of the United States when planning a future, but it has many advantages when it comes to planning a short-term vacation. In Mexico, activities begin early in the morning. For instance, there are breakfast places beside the hotel pool, so the visitor can combine swimming and pool activities with the first meal of the day. What a wake-up call! **Thesis Statement** → Mexico is a better vacation destination than the United States because of its historical sites, festive atmosphere, and low drinking age.

Topic Sentence → 2   The United States has many historical sites but, in contrast to Mexico, these places are very young. For example, the Statue of Liberty is not even a century old. Another place to visit in the United States is Philadelphia. Philadelphia is an important city to visit because of its connection to the colonies winning independence from England two hundred years ago. On the other hand, in Mexico, the pyramids found at Tenochtitlan are at least a millennium old, predating the Liberty Bell by over eight hundred years. Despite its current modern architecture, Mexico City's political importance goes back to the early 16th century when the Aztec Empire fell and colonial rule was instituted by the Spanish conquerors.

Topic Sentence → 3   Festivals occur in the United States, mostly on specific weekends several times during the year. New Year's Eve happens on one night. While the evening is long and full of excitement, it is over rather quickly for such a momentous event. Mardi Gras is another popular festive event. Although it lasts for four or five days, the party is localized to one city, New Orleans. And, in the United States, fireworks are reserved for one night only, the Fourth of July. In Mexico, there's no need for a specific reason to celebrate. In Mexico, festive atmospheres are found all year long in almost any location, particularly on the coast. Puerto Vallarto has become known worldwide for its year round partying. Fireworks are exploded all year in Mexico to celebrate, well . . . anything!

Topic Sentence ⟶ 4 In most states in America, the legal drinking age is 21 years of age. Young people can die for their country in the armed forces or vote for president, but they have to wait three years to have an alcoholic drink. All summer long and during spring break on college campuses throughout the United States, young people flock to Mexico because the legal drinking age is eighteen years of age. Cancun, Mazatlan, Tijuana, and Acapulco are just a few of the cities young Americans visit to drink without worry of arrest while they celebrate graduations, a break from schoolwork, and any other rite of passage they can think of.

5 Mexico, in general, might not be the greatest place to live. It has severe financial problems, and its government is not always reliable in taking care of its citizens; whereas, it is a wonderful place to visit if only for a weekend. Mexico is a great place to get away to and forget about work, school, or the ordinary world that we all have to put up with. Still, no matter how poor Mexico's economy might be, it always has a festive and optimistic outlook on life. That is the true beauty of Mexico—its people!

Contrast Technique Questions

1. What is the writer contrasting in the essay?

_____

2. What organizational pattern does the writer use, point-by-point or block?

_____

3. Which transitional expressions does the writer use to move you smoothly from idea to idea?

_____

_____

_____

_____

Critical Reading Questions

1. What is the main idea of the essay?

_____

_____

2. Does the writer use enough specific examples to develop and clarify the contrast? Explain.

_____

_____

_____

_____

_____

3. Although this is a contrast essay in regard to Mexico and the United States, what conclusion does the writer come to about the problems with the Mexican government and the Mexican economy and the Mexican people?

_____

_____

Comparison or Contrast Writing Exercises

1. Write a comparison or contrast paragraph about two places; they can be countries, states, regions, cities, or neighborhoods. Make a list of similarities and differences before deciding which paragraph to write.
2. Now, write a comparison or contrast essay following the approach you used in the paragraph in exercise 1. Use personal observation rather than facts when writing the essay. Use the point-by-point method to organize your essay.

Sample Professional Essay: LIGHT SKIN VERSUS DARK

Charisse Jones

The following essay, "Light Skin versus Dark," by Pulitzer Prize–winning *New York Times* journalist Charisse Jones, first appeared in *Glamour* magazine. In it, the author recounts a time during her high school years when she was first confronted with "colorism," a type of racism that she considers even more injurious because it comes from those of her own race. It is an unusual issue for whites because they are not confronted with this type of bias within their own race. In this regard, as you read the essay, try to decide what audience Jones is writing for, whites or blacks.

Vocabulary

Before you start reading, use a dictionary to look up the definitions of the following words that appear in the essay.

eradicated (13)	foil (13)	lexicon (4)
litany (10)	mantra (5)	notorious (6)
nuances (12)	reap (4)	smirking (2)
spectrum (8)	subtext (6)	synonymous (5)

[handwritten margin note: probably writing to an African-American audience, or also mixed or white audience]

Light Skin versus Dark

1   I'll never forget the day I was supposed to meet him. We had only spoken on the phone. But we got along so well, we couldn't wait to meet face-to-face. I took the bus from my high school to his for our blind date. While I nervously waited for him outside the school, one of his buddies came along, looked me over, and remarked that I was going to be a problem, because his friend didn't like dating anybody darker than himself.

2   When my mystery man—who was not especially good-looking—finally saw me, he took one look, uttered a hurried hello, then disappeared with his smirking friends. I had apparently been pronounced ugly on arrival and dismissed.

3   That happened nearly fifteen years ago. I'm thirty now, and the hurt and humiliation have long since faded. But the memory still lingers, reinforced in later years by other situations in which my skin color was judged by other African Americans—for example, at a cocktail party or a nightclub where light-skinned black women got all the attention.

4   A racist encounter hurts badly. But it does not equal the pain of "colorism"—being rejected by your own people because your skin is colored cocoa and not cream, ebony and not olive. On our scale of beauty, it is often the high yellows—in the lexicon of black America, those with light skin—whose looks reap the most attention. Traditionally, if someone was described that way, there was no need to say that person was good-looking. It was a given that light was lovely. It was those of us with plain brown eyes and darker skin hues who had to prove ourselves.

5   I was twelve, and in my first year of junior high school in San Francisco, when I discovered dark brown was not supposed to be beautiful. At that age, boys suddenly became important, and so did your looks. But by that time—the late 1970s—black kids no longer believed in that sixties mantra, "Black is beautiful." Light skin, green eyes, and long, wavy hair were once again synonymous with beauty.

6   Colorism—and its subtext of self-hatred—began during slavery on plantations where white masters often favored the lighter-skinned blacks, many of whom were their own children. But though it began with whites, black people have kept colorism alive. In the past, many black sororities, fraternities, and other social organizations have been notorious for accepting only light-skinned members. Yes, some blacks have criticized their lighter-skinned peers. But most often in our history, a light complexion had been a passport to special treatment by both whites *and* blacks.

7   Some social circles are still defined by hue. Some African Americans, dark and light, prefer light-skinned mates so they can have a "pretty baby." And skin-lightening creams still sell, though they are now advertised as good for making blemishes fade rather than for lightening whole complexions.

8   In my family, color was never discussed, even though our spectrum was broad—my brother was very light; my sister and I, much darker. But in junior high, I learned in a matter of weeks what had apparently been drummed into the heads of my black peers for most of their lives.

9   Realizing how crazy it all was, I became defiant, challenging friends when they made silly remarks. Still, there was no escaping the distinctions of color.

10   In my life, I have received a litany of twisted compliments from fellow blacks. "You're the prettiest dark-skinned girl I have ever seen" is one; "you're pretty for a dark girl" is another.

11   A light-complexioned girlfriend once remarked to me that dark-skinned people often don't take the time to groom themselves. As a journalist, I once interviewed a prominent black lawmaker who was light-skinned. He drew me into the shade of a tree while we talked because, he said, "I'm sure you don't want to get any darker."

12   Though some black people—like film-maker Spike Lee in his movie *School Daze*—have tried to provoke debate about colorism, it remains a painful topic many blacks would rather not confront. Yet there has been progress. In this age of Afrocentrism, many blacks revel in the nuances of the African American rainbow. Natural hairstyles and dreadlocks are in, and Theresa Randle, star of the hit film *Bad Boys*, is only one of several darker-skinned actresses noted for their beauty.

13   That gives me hope. People have told me that color biases among blacks run too deep ever to be eradicated. But I tell them that is the kind of attitude that allows colorism to persist. Meanwhile, I do what I can. When I notice that a friend dates only light-skinned women, I comment on it. If I hear that a movie follows the tired old scenario in which a light-skinned beauty is the love interest while a darker-skinned woman is the comic foil, the butt of "ugly" jokes, I don't go see it. Others can do the same.

14   There is only so much blacks can do about racism, because we need the cooperation of others to make it go away. But healing ourselves is within our control.   BLACK AUDIENCE

15   At least we can try. As a people we face enough pain without inflicting our own wounds. I believe any people that could survive slavery, that could disprove the lies that pronounced them less than human, can also teach its children that black is beautiful in all of its shades.

CALL TO ACTION

16   Loving ourselves should be an easy thing to do.

Comparison and Contrast Technique Questions

1. Is this a comparison or a contrast essay? Give examples.

More contrast (although there is some of both)

_____

_____

2. Is there a thesis statement that clearly states the topic to be discussed? If so, identify it. If not, state what you think is the thesis of the essay.

_____

_____

_____

3. The title suggests the pair of items being contrasted. What other subtopics are contrasted or compared in the essay?

_____

_____

Critical Reading Questions

1. How does the author distinguish between "colorism" and "racism"?

_____

_____

_____

2. The author believes that "colorism" is more harmful than "racism." Do you agree with her assessment? Explain.

_____

_____

_____

3. What examples in the essay point to the author writing for a black audience? What examples point to her writing for a white audience?

_____

_____

_____

_____

_____

Comparison or Contrast Writing Exercises

1. Write a comparison or contrast paragraph about a physical characteristic that can have a negative effect because it is not considered desirable or normal by society.

2. Now, write an essay comparing or contrasting two cultural attitudes about the physical characteristic you chose to write about in a paragraph in exercise 1. Make a list of the negative and positive aspects of how the culture views the physical characteristic before you begin writing. Choose whether the block or the point-by-point method is the best way to organize and present the information.

More Topics for a Comparison or Contrast Essay

Here are some possible topics for both comparison or contrast essay writing assignments. Remember, your comparison or contrast essay should have a clearly defined purpose.

Frederic Leighton, *Study of a Lady*   Pablo Picasso, *Head of a Woman*, 1939

1. Two pieces of art.
2. A famous person's public image versus his or her private image.
3. Two colleges.
4. Two bosses or co-workers.
5. Past attitudes about AIDS, lesbianism, or male homosexuality and attitudes today.
6. A falsely held belief or myth and the factual reality.
7. How people act in private versus public.
8. How opinions have changed concerning a political issue.
9. How people's thoughts about the future have changed.
10. Employment opportunities in two states, countries, or regions.

☑ Writing Checklist for a Comparison or Contrast Essay

❑ 1. Choose two things to compare or contrast.
❑ 2. Make a list of similarities and differences using one or more of the prewriting techniques you have studied, or use a comparison and contrast chart.
❑ 3. Choose whether you want to compare or contrast.
❑ 4. Use the comparison and contrast chart to help write the thesis statement.
❑ 5. Choose either the block or point-by-point method to organize and present your ideas.
❑ 6. Write the essay, using transitional expressions to connect related ideas, add rhythm, and add sentence variety.

❑ **7.** Revise the draft.

❑ **8.** Proofread the final essay.

❑ **9.** Print or type the essay and submit it.

CHAPTER REVIEW

▼ When you compare two or more items, you are looking for similarities. When you contrast them, you are looking for differences.

▼ When you write a comparison or contrast paragraph, you must first decide whether to compare or contrast the two items. In a comparison and contrast chart, you can list similarities and differences and so choose whether to compare or to contrast based on the strength of the details. The topic sentence of a comparison or contrast paragraph clearly states the items to be compared or contrasted and the controlling idea and attitude.

▼ There are two basic methods for organizing a comparison or contrast paragraph. In the block method, you present all the information about one item first, then use this information when you present information about the second item. In the point-by-point method, you present information about both items together, creating a series of comparisons or contrasts. Transitional expressions help make the organization of comparison and contrast paragraphs clear to the reader.

▼ In the introductory paragraph of a comparison or contrast essay, the thesis statement states the two items to be compared or contrasted, the controlling idea and attitude, and the subtopics that will be compared or contrasted. In the body paragraphs, either the block method or point-by-point method can be used to develop the subtopics. Finally, evaluation is a good approach to the concluding paragraph of a comparison or contrast essay because it allows you to express a judgment about the items you've been comparing or contrasting.

Visit *The Write Start* Online!

For additional practice with the materials found in this chapter, visit our Website at

http://www.ablongman.com/checkett

The Website also features additional readings, quizzes, writing activities, and Internet links, as well as a bulletin board and interactive chat.

13 The Definition Essay

As you write, you may use concepts, terms, and words that you think your reader may not understand. You might use a term such as *black hole* or *macroeconomics*. Concepts such as *domino theory* or *Jungian psychology* may be foreign to your reader, so you may need to explain them so your reader fully understands what you are trying to communicate. Read the following short paragraph.

> "Purple cows are purple cows because they are colored purple." The tautological reasoning embedded in the statement make its truthful wording obvious and unnecessary.

What is the paragraph trying to tell you? Is the meaning clear? Unless you know what *tautological* means, you probably will not understand the meaning of the paragraph. A better paragraph might look like this:

> "Purple cows are purple because they are colored purple." The statement contains all logical possibilities and, therefore, is always true. The statement, then, is a tautology, a needless repetition of the same, obvious concepts.

Defining the concept of *tautology* helps the reader understand why the statement regarding the purple cow is unnecessarily obvious and repetitive. The statement does not adequately explain why the cow is purple, just that it is—which is already obvious just by looking at it. A tautology, then, is considered circular reasoning.

Identifying Your Purpose

When we clearly explain the meaning of words, terms, and concepts, we are using **definition** as a method of communicating to the reader. There are two types of definition, simple and extended.

175

Simple Definition

Simple definitions are brief explanations such as those you might find in a dictionary. There are three types of simple definitions:

▼ **Synonym definition** defines a word by supplying another simpler word that means the same thing. For example, *conundrum* means *riddle* or *puzzle*, while *cacophony* means *noise*.

▼ **Class definition** defines a word by placing it in a broad category of similar things that readers will readily understand, and then providing a specific detail that makes the original term or word different from the others in the class. For example, a *convertible* is a *car* with *a top that goes up and down*. In this definition, *convertible* is the term being defined. It is put into *a class of similar things (cars)*, and then it is made different from other cars, such as sedans and coupes, because *it has a top that goes up and down*.

▼ **Definition by negation** begins by saying what a given word or term *is not* before saying what the word or term *actually is*. For example, a *bagel* just *isn't* a doughnut-shaped piece of bread that's deep-fried. A bagel is much more than that. It's actually *a unique type of bread that's boiled before it's baked*.

Definition is important because clear communication depends upon clear understanding. Precise language is essential if you are to understand what someone else means. One word can have multiple meanings, so it is essential that you define terms for your reader.

PRACTICE 1   Writing Simple Definitions

Write a synonym, class, and negation definition for one of the following words: freedom, rustic, malevolent, prude, shark, tomato, symbol, topography, simplicity.

_____

_____

_____

_____

_____

_____

_____

_____

_____

Extended Definition

At times, terms such as *black hole, macroeconomics, domino theory,* and *Jungian psychology* cannot be adequately defined using a simple definition. Instead, you may need to use a few sentences or an entire paragraph to define such terms so that they are understood clearly. This longer type of definition is called an **extended definition.** Extended definition can be accomplished by means of any one mode of development or any combination of the modes of development: description, narration, example, classification, process, comparison and contrast, and cause and effect.

Therefore, to help you define your term, you might

▼ describe some of its characteristics

▼ incorporate it into a story

▼ give some examples

▼ place it into a category

▼ explain its process (how it works)

▼ compare or contrast it to other things

▼ explain its causes or its effects

▼ **PRACTICE 2**   **Writing An Extended Definition**

Write an extended definition for the word you chose in Practice 1.

_____

_____

_____

_____

_____

_____

_____

Writing an Extended Definition Paragraph

In an extended definition paragraph, you may use just one of the modes listed above to develop your definition, or you may use as many modes in your paragraph as you find necessary. For example, if you were writing a simple definition for the term *soul music,* it might read as follows: music relating to or characteristic of African American culture. This definition, while informative, does not give the reader the full flavor of just how soul music represents a part of the American culture. An extended definition might expand on this idea:

> **Example**
>
> Soul music is a merging of gospel and blues, two African American musical styles. While blues praised the worldly desires of the flesh, gospel extolled the virtues of spirituality. This opposition of themes was melded into a wide-ranging and extremely diverse style, full of passions, pride, and optimism mixed with the historical emotion of pain and discrimination.

Developing a term or concept more fully allows readers to appreciate a broader set of ideas. It gives them a clearer understanding of the purpose and importance of the term or concept.

PRACTICE 3   **Writing An Extended Definition Paragraph**

Using one or more of the modes of development you have studied (description, example, compare or contrast, etc.), write an extended definition paragraph for a term from Practice 1 that you have not yet defined.

The Topic Sentence of an Extended Definition Paragraph

The topic sentence of an extended definition paragraph clearly states the term being defined, indicates the mode of development that will be used to define the term, and explains why defining the term is important. There are many reasons for supplying a reader with a definition and many types of terms you might need to define in your writing. Therefore, your topic sentence must clarify why you are defining a given term. For example, you may be defining

▼ a specialized term that is unfamiliar to most people, such as *quantum theory* or *eyelet cell transplant*

▼ an abstract term that can have a variety of meanings, such as *independence* or *responsibility*

▼ a concept that is often misunderstood, such as *free speech* or *Generation X*

▼ a new slang or cultural term, such as *extreme sports* or *anime*

Here is an example of a topic sentence for a definition paragraph about anabolic steroids:

> Anabolic steroids offer help in suppressing autoimmune diseases.

This topic sentence clearly states the term to be defined, *anabolic steroids*, and why it is important to define the term (because they offer help in fighting disease). It indicates the mode of development for defining the term, through examples of the types of diseases (autoimmune) they help to fight. The entire paragraph might read as follows:

> Anabolic steroids offer help in suppressing autoimmune diseases. Fortunately, modified steroids aid in Addison's disease by regulating fat, carbohydrate, and protein metabolism. To help overcome severe allergies and arthritis, adrenocorticotropic hormone is used as an anti-inflammatory to alleviate the symptoms. By taking prescription steroids, patients may enjoy life without having uncontrollable pains in joints as well as constant fatigue.

Using Transitional Expressions in Definition Paragraphs

Definition writing uses any and all modes of development, such as description, narration, example, classification, process, compare and contrast, and cause and effect. Therefore, you must decide how you are developing your definition as you write, and then you must use the appropriate transitional expressions to help connect related ideas and to add rhythm to your writing.

For example, the paragraph above regarding the use of anabolic steroids is defined primarily through example. If the writer used appropriate example transitional expressions, the paragraph might look like this:

> Anabolic steroids offer help in suppressing autoimmune diseases. **For example,** modified steroids aid in Addison's disease by **specifically** regulating fat, carbohydrate, and protein metabolism. To help overcome severe allergies and arthritis, **for instance,** adrenocorticotropic hormone is used as an anti-inflammatory to alleviate the symptoms. By taking prescription steroids, **as a case in point,** patients may enjoy life without having uncontrollable pains in joints as well as constant fatigue.

When the two paragraphs are compared, it is obvious that the one with the transitional expressions is easier to understand and easier to read because the examples are announced and the sentence variety adds rhythm to the writing.

After you have decided which mode of development to use for your definition essay, refer to the appropriate chapter in this textbook to find the list of transitional expressions for the mode you are using.

▼ **PRACTICE 4**   **Rewriting A Paragraph Using Transitional Expressions**

Rewrite the paragraph you created for Practice 3. First, find the chapter dealing with the mode of development that you used in the paragraph. Second, select and add the appropriate transitional expressions to connect related ideas and to add rhythm to the paragraph. Finally, compare the two paragraphs when you have finished. The paragraph with the transitional expressions should be easier to understand and to read.

Moving from Paragraph to Essay

Now that you have studied and practiced the techniques to create effective definition paragraphs, it is time to expand your ideas to a larger writing unit: the definition essay. Using the techniques you learned in Part 1 regarding developing the essay paragraphs and the definition techniques you have just learned enables you to write the definition essay. This might be a good time to return to Part 1 and review the techniques for developing the full essay.

Creating the Introductory Paragraph

Like all essays, the definition essay needs a clearly defined organization at the beginning to announce to the reader just how the subject will be developed. The thesis statement should state the item to be defined, the writer's attitude toward the topic, the controlling idea, and organizational structure. By using an appropriate lead-in technique, the thesis statement should blend naturally into the introductory paragraph.

For example, read the following introductory paragraph that would introduce the body paragraph regarding anabolic steroids you read earlier. The thesis statement is underlined for identification purposes.

> Many believe anabolic steroids were developed to create the perfect superhuman. Searching for the perfect body eventually spawned a new breed of athlete; these athletes found steroids gave them more muscles and bulk, allowing them to enhance their performances. As time passed, athletes, in an effort to become even bigger and stronger, abused steroids. Because of this abuse, steroids have a bad reputation with the general public. However, steroids, when used properly for the right reasons, provide excellent health benefits. <u>The medical use of steroids is beneficial because they help fight autoimmune diseases, facilitate muscular development in patients with arm and leg immobility, and aid in the regeneration of dysfunctional organs.</u>

Creating the Body Paragraphs

Notice that the first item in the essay map above speaks to steroids helping to fight autoimmune diseases. As has been mentioned already, this essay would use example as its mode, or method, of developing the topic in the body paragraphs. The first body paragraph's topic would be how steroids "help fight autoimmune diseases"; the second body paragraph's topic would be how steroids "facilitate muscular development in patients with arm and leg immobility"; the third body paragraph's topic would be how steroids "aid in the regeneration of dysfunctional organs." Remember, as you write about each of these topics, your focus should be that steroid use *is beneficial*. Your focus should not be on the *harmful effects of steroid abuse,* or on the *illegality* or the *cost* of steroids. Keep your focus on the *beneficial* aspects of steroid use.

However, the essay about steroids could just as easily be written as a process essay that specifies how steroids work effectively to aid in the fight against disease, limb, and organ disabilities. The writer has the responsibility to choose the mode that best develops the topic.

For example, in the following paragraph regarding the definition of a "perfect store," the writer could have chosen to develop the topic through example, by giving examples of characteristics that define a perfect store, such as friendly employees, fast service, and fair pricing. But the writer chose to use process to define the perfect store.

> While shopping in a perfect store, customers are generally sold products at an inexpensive price. Shoppers are typically offered items that are clearly marked with price tags on each separate package. This allows customers to choose rapidly and easily the product that gives them the best buy. There aren't any reasons to look for the price on the store shelf and then have to worry about whether or not the item matches the price tag. A perfect store not only honors its own sales coupons but also accepts other department store advertised prices and coupons. This gives the customers the convenience of shopping at one store instead of having to go to two or three. No matter what store shoppers patronize, these pricing policies offer them the opportunity to receive the best possible price.

Before deciding on which mode of development to use in the body paragraphs, you might try planning a paragraph using two or more modes. This technique can help you choose the mode that works best for the paragraph's topic. In other words, you might find that developing the topic *choosing a career* is clearer and more effective if you write it as an *example paragraph* rather than as a *compare or contrast paragraph.* In many definition essays, including the two sample student essays that follow, the writer uses a different mode (and sometimes combines modes) for each body paragraph.

▼ **PRACTICE 5**   **Rewrite A Definition Paragraph Using A New Mode**

Rewrite the paragraph you wrote in Practice 4 using a different mode of development. Don't forget to use the transitional expressions appropriate to your new mode of development choice.

Creating the Concluding Paragraph

The approach of the concluding paragraph should flow naturally from the essay's main topic. Because our essay's focus is the beneficial use of steroids, a *warning* would seem an appropriate choice. Since the lead-in mentioned how some athletes abuse steroids in their search for more power and strength, you might mention some of the adverse effects that misusing steroids can have, such as brain tumors, cancer, and loss of bone mass. (Refer to Chapter 6 for other approaches for concluding paragraphs.)

Sample Definition Student Essay: ORDER THROUGH DISCIPLINE

Heather Hanshew

> In this essay, "Order Through Discipline," student writer Heather Hanshew defines a concept that almost everyone thinks they understand. Generally, most people think of discipline as either self-control or a punishment to change another's behavior. The author, however, sees a much deeper and more substantial role that discipline plays in our lives. Pay close attention to the repetition of key nouns that keeps the reader focused on the basic concept of discipline while its definition is being expanded with more complex ideas.

Vocabulary
Before you start reading, use a dictionary to look up the definitions of the following words appearing in the essay.

accountable (4)	competent (4)	efficiency (1)	encompass (1)
exhibit (1)	factor (4)	insignificant (2)	mantra (5)
trivial (2)	unbearable (2)	vital (4)	

Order Through Discipline

1   Most individuals believe they exhibit discipline when punishing loved ones in order to change behavior. Others believe they demonstrate discipline when they awake a half hour early three times a week to exercise. While these are forms of discipline, they only encompass a small part of a larger,

Thesis Statement with Essay Map ⟶ more important concept. Discipline is developing knowledge in order to develop self-control, character, orderliness, and efficiency. In order to live a productive lifestyle, discipline should be used at home, at school, and at work.

Topic Sentence ⟶ 2   First, the process of achieving home discipline may seem small and insignificant, but practice is an important part of learning the skill. Simple household chores, such as vacuuming, doing the dishes, the laundry, and dusting, teach orderliness. Without orderliness, living space could become unbearable. Even simple activities such as going to bed and awakening on time teach discipline; by conditioning the body, self-control is exhibited. Another form of household discipline is caring for pets. Feeding and cleaning animals can be time-consuming and an irritation; however, the job needs to be done. The life of the pet depends upon household members demonstrating daily discipline by caring for pets in a consistent manner. This may seem trivial at first glance, but the best predictor of future performance is past behavior; consequently, what works or does not work at home can extend to school.

Topic Sentence ⟶ 3   The second category of discipline displayed occurs at school. School instills a considerable amount of discipline in youngsters. Practicing good behavior in the classroom and during other school activities teaches self-control. Good outward behavior is a sign of inner character. The organization skills necessary for doing homework and completing it on time reveals both orderliness and efficiency. Finally, attending school regularly shows that the student is disciplined enough to be at the right place at the right time. Good attendance affects good grades, and good grades are a sign of proper self-discipline. Not learning self-discipline at an early age can affect future success in the workplace.

Topic Sentence ⟶ 4   The last place discipline is shown is in the workplace. Obviously, work is critical for a family's well-being, so discipline at work is fundamental. A key factor in demonstrating discipline at work is the ability to be on time when completing projects and attending meetings: by doing so, a competent employee shows the self-control needed to organize time wisely. Being held accountable for specific actions and responsibilities at work takes orderliness, efficiency, and character. Teamwork is another vital element needed in the workplace. The character and discipline learned earlier in life at home and in school only can be beneficial in showing those skills needed on the job. Lastly, these characteristics become embedded in one's work ethic, and they are carried as personal attributes throughout life.

5   The knowledge obtained through discipline builds self-control, character, orderliness, and efficiency. Discipline builds life-long traits needed for long-term success. Without discipline, chaos can disrupt lives at home, at school, and at the workplace. Order through discipline should become a mantra in everyone's life, and the earlier the better.

Definition Technique Questions

1. How many modes of development does the writer use to help define the essay?

_____

_____

_____

2. Are transitional expressions used? How do they help the reader?

_____

_____

_____

_____

_____

3. What is the function of the last sentence in each body paragraph?

_____

_____

_____

_____

Critical Reading Questions

1. What is the main idea of the essay?

_____

_____

_____

2. How is the term _discipline_ expanded from traditional definitions?

_____

_____

_____

_____

3. The author mentions that certain activities may seem insignificant to achieving discipline, but that they are not. Explain, using examples.

_____

_____

_____

_____

Definition Writing Exercises

1. Write a definition paragraph about a skill that is necessary at home, at school, and at the workplace. In your topic sentence, remember to state your purpose for defining the concept. Use the prewriting techniques you have studied to develop the definition.
2. Now, write a definition essay using the term you defined in exercise 1. Continue to expand the term by using one or more of the prewriting techniques you have studied. Although you most likely will use one mode of development predominantly as you define the term, do not hesitate to use as many modes of development as you deem necessary.

▼

Sample Definition Student Essay: A SHRIMPER'S LIFE

Donna Morris

> In this essay, "A Shrimper's Life," student writer Donna Morris defines a job with which most people are not familiar. Most people love to eat shrimp, but there is little doubt that most people have little or no idea about how shrimp are caught and what the people are like who do the catching. Originally from Louisiana, the author plans to live in Florida, where she would like to start her own shrimping business on the Caribbean coast.

Vocabulary
Before you begin reading, use a dictionary to look up the definitions of the following words that appear in the essay.

definitely (2)	dwellers (1)	equity (1)	lurking (4)
marine (4)	pelagic (1)	octopi (4)	task (1)

A Shrimper's Life

1   Everyone knows what a shrimp is (at least they think they do), but few know what life is like for those taking on the task of bringing the shrimp from the ocean to the table. Shrimp come in a variety of sizes, ranging from those no bigger than an insect to monsters over eight inches long. While most shrimp inhabit shallow coastal waters, there are shrimp that live their lives swimming in the open ocean. Shrimp come in both freshwater and saltwater varieties. While the most common commercially harvested shrimp is the white shrimp, other varieties include the brown-grooved and pink-grooved shrimp. Except for the pelagic shrimp, all others are bottom dwellers feeding on smaller animals and plants; therefore, catching them involves quite a lot of work. Since demand for the small shellfish is high during a booming economy, the profits for successful shrimpers are equally high. Shrimping is a rewarding occupation because of the relatively short work season, low equity risk, and the fascinating marine life.

Thesis Statement with Essay Map →

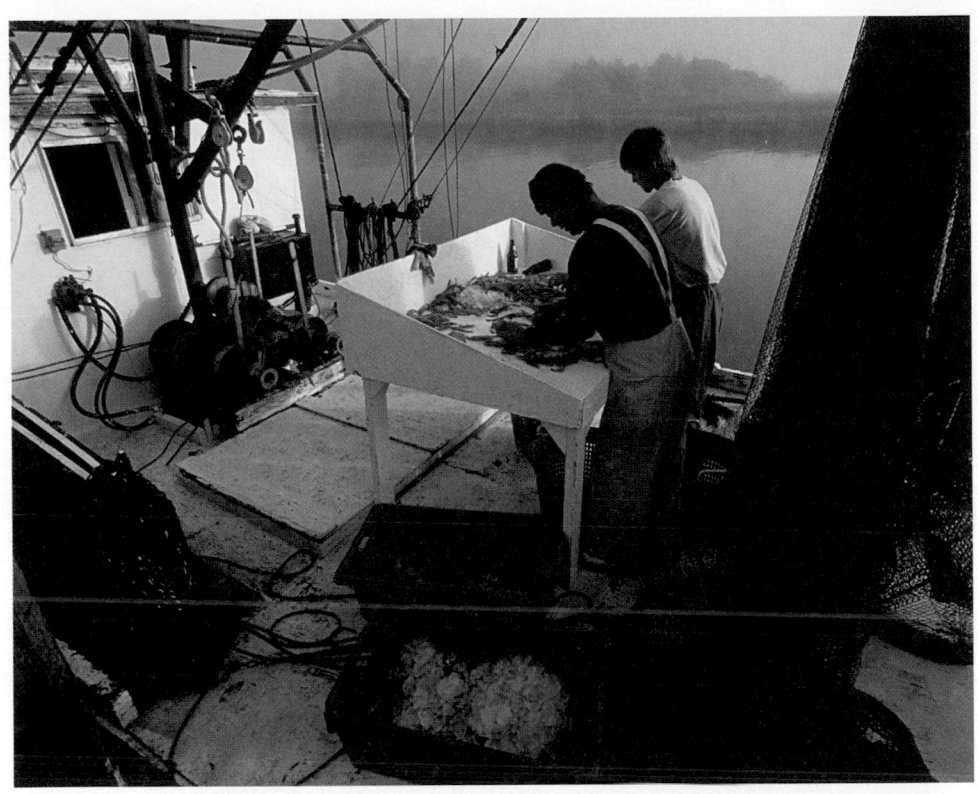

Topic Sentence ⟶ 2   Before leaving shore, the boats fuel up and take on board plenty of ice to keep the shrimp frozen. The workers take a trip to the grocery store and buy enough supplies for the two-week trip. Although two weeks sounds like a long time, shrimpers only work a few of these excursions each year. Ninety percent of their time is spent on shore planning for the next trip, tending to their shrimp nets, and making sure the shrimp boat is in tip-top shape. Even the shrimper's daytime hours are spent eating, sleeping, and getting ready for the harvesting. Shrimp boats travel during the day and fish at night because shrimp sleep during the day and hunt for food by moonlight. Yes, shrimpers are definitely night-owls.

Topic Sentence ⟶ 3   Expenses for shrimpers are relatively low compared to other fishermen. Commercial tuna and cod fishermen, for instance, have heavy expenses. Not only do they have to have larger boats to handle their loads, their nets have to be heavier and larger, they have to stay at sea for longer periods of time, and their crews have to be larger in number, meaning more money and bonuses have to be paid out after the harvesting profit is realized. Because of the high profit with shrimp, one catch usually pays for the year's fuel, groceries, and crew's salaries. Because of the smaller shrimp boat, shrimpers do not have high fuel bills, and maintenance is not high either.

Topic Sentence ⟶ 4   The best aspect of being a shrimper is the exotic marine life discovered in the shrimp nets. Because the shrimp nets are sent to the bottom of the ocean as they are dragged to harvest the shrimp, all residents lurking on the bottom are gathered into the nets as well. Sea cucumbers, hermit crabs, dogfish, and sea anemones are just a few of the unusual marine life that are pulled up in the shrimp nets. The shrimp are then picked out and buried in the ice to keep them as fresh as possible. Crabs, octopi, and stingrays, along with the other captives, are returned to their ocean home to live another day. A marine biologist would do well to work on a shrimp boat once in awhile.

5   As with any job, shrimping is not all fun and games. Sometimes the ocean can get pretty rough, and sometimes the catch can be pretty small.

Couples with small children will have to make some sacrifices if someone is to stay home with the kids. And those wanting the rigid schedule of a nine-to-five job would never get used to the odd hours that the shrimper must get used to. However, if some danger and excitement every so often isn't a problem, as well as some awesome sunsets at sea, then the shrimper's life can be an exciting alternative to the world of suits and cubicles.

Definition Technique Questions

1. What are the modes of development used in the essay?

_____

_____

_____

_____

_____

2. Point out an example of defining by negation.

_____

_____

_____

3. Identify an instance where comparison is used to define.

_____

4. How is *shrimp* defined in the introductory paragraph?

_____

_____

_____

_____

Critical Reading Questions

1. What is the main idea of the essay?

_____

_____

_____

2. What are the major conclusions reached by the author about the shrimping lifestyle?

_____

_____

_____

3. What are some of the downsides of shrimping?

_____

_____

_____

_____

_____

Definition Writing Exercises

1. Write a definition paragraph about an occupation that you think your audience does not know much about. Develop ideas by using the prewriting techniques you have studied.

2. Now, write a definition essay using the term you defined in exercise 1. Use a variety of modes of development in your essay to expand the definition. Also, try to define by negation in one of the body paragraphs where appropriate.

Sample Definition Professional Essay: A JERK

Sydney J. Harris

This essay, "A Jerk," by the late Sydney J. Harris, a syndicated columnist for the *Chicago Daily News* and the *Chicago Sun-Times*, appeared in his book *Last Things First*. Harris was famous for writing about every aspect of contemporary American life. His musings appeared daily in his column, "Strictly Personal." While this may not look like the type of essay you have been writing in college, it is an extended definition that also uses a variety of definition formats, such as class definition and simple definition.

Vocabulary
Before you begin reading, use a dictionary to look up the definitions of the following words that appear in the essay.

apt (3)	aroma (4)	coined (3)	cum laude (5)	egotist (6)
emanating (4)	extent (6)	fluffed (2)	inane (2)	insight (4)
persuasive (4)	shuddering (5)	subtle (4)	tactless (6)	utterly (6)

A Jerk

1   I don't know whether history repeats itself, but biography certainly does. The other day, Michael came in and asked me what a "jerk" was—the same question Carolyn put to me a dozen years ago.

2   At that time, I fluffed her off with some inane answer, such as "A jerk isn't a very nice person," but both of us knew it was an unsatisfactory reply. When she went to bed, I began trying to work up a suitable definition.

3   It is a marvelously apt word, of course. Until it was coined, not more than 25 years ago, there was really no single word in English to describe the kind of person who is a jerk—"boob" and "simp" were too old hat, and besides they really didn't fit, for they could be lovable, and a jerk never is.

4   Thinking it over, I decided that a jerk is basically a person without insight. He is not necessarily a fool or a dope, because some extremely clever persons can be jerks. In fact, it has little to do with intelligence as we commonly think of it; it is, rather, a kind of subtle but persuasive aroma emanating from the inner part of the personality.

5   I know a college president who can be described only as a jerk. He is not an unintelligent man, nor unlearned, nor even unschooled in the social amenities. Yet he is a jerk *cum laude*, because of a fatal flaw in his nature—he is totally incapable of looking into the mirror of his soul and shuddering at what he sees there.

6   A jerk, then, is a man (or woman) who is utterly unable to see himself as he appears to others. He has no grace, he is tactless without meaning to be, he is a bore even to his best friends, he is an egotist without charm. All of us are egotists to some extent, but most of us—unlike the jerk—are perfectly and horribly aware of it when we make asses of ourselves. The jerk never knows.

Definition Technique Questions

1. Identify the similar terms that Harris puts in the same class as *jerk*. How does he define *jerk* differently than the other terms in the class?

_____

_____

_____

2. Where in the essay does Harris give a simple definition for the term *jerk*?

_____

_____

3. Identify some examples where Harris defines *jerk* by negation.

_____

_____

_____

Critical Reading Questions

1. Harris begins the essay by relating a brief story about his daughter and son asking him to define *jerk*. How does this anecdote help introduce the topic?

_____

_____

_____

2. What is the main idea of the essay?

_____

3. The author says that the jerk is a person without insight. Why is this particularly dreadful?

_____

_____

_____

_____

Definition Writing Exercises

1. Write a definition paragraph defining a term used by a contemporary group or by society as a whole. For example, you might define a term used by a particular group, such as *dead-head*, or you might define a slang term such as *slacker* that is used by many groups, including national marketing agencies, in the larger society.
2. Now, write a definition essay using the same term you selected in exercise 1, but define it according to how your generation defines it. For example, Harris states that his generation defined *jerk* as a "boob" and a "simp." Today, "geek" and "nerd" are used rather than "boob" and "simp." For your essay, you might consider including other similar terms in the same class, and then clarify how other groups differ in how they define the term. You also might consider defining by negation in your essay.

More Topics for a Definition Essay

Here are some possible topics for extended definition essay writing assignments. Remember, your definition essay should have a clearly defined purpose.

1. Reality television programs
2. Pornography
3. Democracy
4. Heroism or cowardice
5. Talk show

6. Success or failure

7. A fanatic

8. Stand-up comedian

9. A new term from an extreme sport

10. The perfect sandwich (or pizza, dessert, barbecue, etc.)

☑ Writing Checklist for a Definition Essay

❏ 1. Choose a concept, term, or word to define.

❏ 2. Write simple definitions for the topic: synonym definition, class definition, and definition by negation. Consult a dictionary or other references if necessary.

❏ 3. Explore other definitions used by specific groups or by the society as a whole. Use one or more of the prewriting techniques you have studied.

❏ 4. Define your purpose by writing a thesis statement.

❏ 5. Choose which mode(s) of development you want to use to define the topic.

❏ 6. Draft the essay, remembering to use transitional expressions as needed.

❏ 7. Revise the first draft.

❏ 8. Proofread the final draft.

❏ 9. Print or type the essay and submit it.

CHAPTER REVIEW

▼ A definition clearly explains the meaning of words, terms, and concepts. Definitions can be simple, as a dictionary definition, or extended, in which a term is described at length.

▼ An extended definition paragraph uses one or more of the modes of development to describe its topic. The topic sentence states the term and explains why it is important and it is being defined. Transitional expressions help the reader follow as the topic is developed.

▼ In a definition essay, the thesis statement states the topic to be defined, the controlling idea or attitude toward the topic, and the main points that are going to be made. The thesis statement should suggest the mode or modes that will be used in the body paragraphs. In a definition essay, the body paragraphs often vary in mode, and sometimes modes are blended within a single body paragraph. The concluding paragraph's approach should flow from the content of the previous paragraphs.

Visit *The Write Start* Online!

For additional practice with the materials found in this chapter, visit our Website at

http://www.ablongman.com/checkett

The Website also features additional readings, quizzes, writing activities, and Internet links, as well as a bulletin board and interactive chat.

14 The Cause or Effect Essay

When attempting to persuade others about a belief or point of view you hold, often you try to convince them by pointing out special relationships that different things or events share. By doing this, you are using a powerful tool that focuses on a strong logical method of developing a topic: cause or effect. This mode of development analyzes **causal relationships,** the connection between cause and effect.

Identifying Your Purpose

Cause or effect development explains the reasons or results associated with some thing or event: *cause* analysis develops *why* something happens, and *effect* analysis explains *the results and consequences* stemming from causes. Causal relationships help us understand why things happen in the world around us, and the possible consequences that may result from actions or events.

For example, a writer might ask the question, "Why did President Clinton lie to the American public about the Monica Lewinsky affair?" as a way of finding out the possible causes of his action. (*Possible causes:* he didn't define his actions with Monica Lewinsky as "having sex"; he didn't want the First Lady, Hillary Rodham Clinton, to find out about his relationship with Lewinsky; he did not want to be embarrassed publicly in the press; he didn't want history to focus on this aspect of his presidency.) The writer also might ask, "What might happen because President Clinton lied to the American public?" as a way of figuring out the events that might occur as a result of the lying. (*Possible effects:* he might have been impeached for "high crimes and misdemeanors"; history books might focus on this aspect of his presidency rather than his successes with domestic and foreign affairs; Democratic candidates might find it difficult to get elected or re-elected to office.) As we now know, President Clinton was impeached. Although the impeachment did not succeed, his reputation took quite a few hits, and many believe his then vice president, Al Gore, lost the 2000 presidential election to George W. Bush because of the effects of President Clinton's activities. Another equally interesting but opposite "effect" was that his wife, Hillary Rodham Clinton, won election to the United States Senate and has subsequently written a best-selling book about her time as First Lady.

Writing a Cause or Effect Paragraph

Obviously, the search for cause or effect answers can be a complex undertaking. More than one explanation usually can be found, and often many of the answers are possible. This complexity can be helpful in achieving thorough development of an issue. Thoroughly developing your point of view can help you persuade your reader that your view of an issue has been both logically and reasonably stated. Look at the following two examples of paragraphs focusing on cause and effect.

Example Cause Paragraph

Obtaining money and managing money are common causes of stress, especially for those who have little. For students, and those hoping to attend college, securing funds is a top priority. Of course, there are grants, loans, and scholarships, but sometimes those resources are not enough. Getting a job or obtaining a loan doesn't ease any of the tension and, more likely, will cause even more stress. Knowing how to manage money is very important. A poor expenditure plan can cause shortfalls affecting payment of bills and tuition. Being in debt not only means needing money to pay bills, but extra money will be necessary to pay penalties and interest. Money isn't the root of all evil—poor planning is!

In the paragraph above, *obtaining money* and *money management* are the twin *causes* of stress. The link between the two causes is that once you do get the money, you must manage the funds properly or more troubles can occur.

Example Effect Paragraph

The possibility of health risks is extremely high for a prescription drug addict. Every medication that is taken has side effects, such as headache, nausea, and sleep problems. Constipation results from many potent prescription drugs. A high emotional and physical feeling followed by a corresponding low emotional and physical state are effects that often occur when prescription drugs are abused. The addict usually takes different types of drugs to counteract this emotional roller coaster. The effect of this new addiction is potential heart problems. Other effects stemming from prescription drug abuse are dental problems and poor immunity against diseases because prescribed drugs can remove essential vitamins and minerals from the body.

In the paragraph above, health risks, such as *headache, nausea, sleep deprivation, emotional highs and lows,* and *potential heart problems* are the effects of prescription drug abuse. The link between the effects is that new drugs to counteract one set of effects can lead to other negative effects.

Causal Chains

Whether you are focusing on cause or on effect, it is helpful, before you begin writing, to develop a **causal chain.** A causal chain demonstrates the series of events that can develop and help clarify the relationships that exist between events.

Cause and Effect Diagram 1

Causes		Effects
Too many unpaid bills	can lead to	increased physical tension.
Increased physical tension	can lead to	severe headaches.
Severe headaches	can lead to	nausea and loss of appetite.
Nausea and loss of appetite	can lead to	physical and mental fatigue.
Physical and mental fatigue	can lead to	health problems.

In the example above, notice how an effect can become a cause for the next effect. Things and events do not exist in a vacuum isolated from the other things and events around them. Yes, you can focus on cause, and you can focus on effect, but to be most persuasive, you should share with readers the special insights you have learned from the causal chain.

Another method for identifying causes and effects is to use the following diagram:

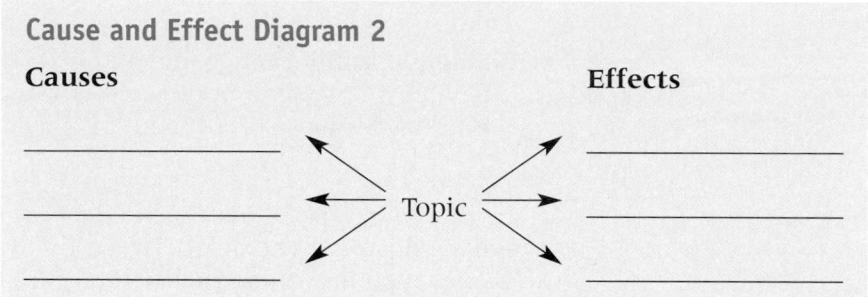

Cause and Effect Diagram 2

Causes   Effects

Topic

By filling in the spaces under Causes and Effects, you can separate the links in the causal chain. By doing so, you can decide which elements you want to be the focus of your essay.

Cause and Effect Example Diagram

Causes   Effects

sloppy bookkeeping   poor money   physical tension
being disorganized   management   loss of appetite
mental fatigue   health problems

Once readers know *why* something has happened (causes) and the consequences that might stem from the causes (effects), they are much more likely to be receptive to your conclusions about the topic. In other words, they understand your view of a topic, and understanding an issue is often half the battle to accepting the writer's ideas concerning the issue.

▼ **PRACTICE 1**   **Creating Causal Chains**

Create a causal chain for each of the topics on page 195. While you can make the chain as long as you want, try to have at least three causes and effects in the chain. Use both techniques illustrated in Diagrams 1 and 2 to develop your chain and then to separate the causes from the effects.

▼ road rage
▼ overbuilding houses
▼ ozone depletion

Problems to Avoid

When using cause and effect reasoning, do not confuse **chronological order** and **coincidence** with true cause and effect relationships. Do not assume that, because one event follows another in time, the first event causes the second to occur. No true causal relationship exists between two events just because one follows the other.

> ### Example
>
> Every time a black cat crosses my path, something bad happens to me.

Bad things indeed may happen to you, but the proverbial black cat as a cause of bad luck is a superstition that has no basis in reality. Your bad luck is probably due to your not being properly prepared for the events in your life or possibly just being at the wrong place at the wrong time—coincidence. Do not assume that, because two or more events occur around the same time, one causes the other and that a cause and effect relationship exists between them.

> ### Example
>
> After I attended a movie, several days later I came down with a cold. Someone in the theater must have been ill, and I must have caught it from them. Therefore, my going to the movies caused me to catch a cold.

Many people that you come in contact with each day may have colds. You could catch a cold from any one of them. Cause and effect is posited in the example, but there is no proof of a link. In this case, coincidence is just as likely a possibility.

PRACTICE 2   Identifying Chronological Order and Coincidence

Explain why the following events do not have a causal relationship, either because of *chronological order* or *coincidence*.

1. The successful field goal, passing through the uprights just as the final gun sounded, won the game by a score of 17 to 14.

_____

_____

_____

_____

_____

_____

2. I always get sick the day after Thanksgiving. I need to stop eating so much, and I guess I'll have to stop going on those brisk, long walks that my family always takes after dinner.

_____

_____

_____

_____

_____

_____

_____

_____

_____

The Topic Sentence in a Cause or Effect Paragraph

The topic sentence in a cause or effect paragraph clearly states the topic and why the topic's causes or effects are being developed. After choosing your subject, create your causal chain to identify the causes and effects stemming from the topic. When this step is completed, decide whether you are going to focus on causes or effects. The topic sentence will announce your purpose to the reader, and it will clarify the paragraph's development.

> **Examples**
>
> *Focus on Causes*
> Proper nutrition can lead to a long, healthful life. (This paragraph will develop *proper nutrition* as a cause of a *long, healthful life.*)
>
> *Focus on Effects*
> A long, healthful life can increase earnings potential. (This paragraph will develop *earnings potential* as an effect or result of a *long, healthful life.*)

▼
PRACTICE 3 **Developing a Paragraph About Causes**

This practice will help you develop a paragraph that focuses on causes.

1. Pick one of the following topics.

   a phobia (an unreasonable fear, such as fear of heights, spiders, open spaces, flying)

   looking for a new job

   a good relationship

2. List as many causes of your topic choice as you can think of.

a. _____

b. _____

c. _____

d. _____

e. _____

3. If any of the causes in your list are merely chronological or coincidental, draw a line through them.

4. Write a topic sentence that focuses on causes.

_____

_____

_____

_____

_____

5. Write a sentence for each of the causes in your list that is not merely chronological or coincidental.

_____

_____

_____

_____

_____

_____

_____

6. On a separate sheet of paper, rewrite your sentences into paragraph form.

▼
PRACTICE 4   **Developing a Paragraph About Effects**

This practice will help you develop a paragraph that focuses on effects.

1. Pick one of the following topics.
   having a child out of wedlock
   children watching too much television violence
   using a cell phone while driving

2. List as many effects of your topic choice as you can think of.

a. _____

b. _____

c. _____

d. _____

e. _____

3. If any of the effects in your list are merely chronological or coincidental, draw a line through them.

4. Write a topic sentence that focuses on effects.

_____

_____

_____

_____

5. Write a sentence for each of the effects in your list that is not merely chronological or coincidental.

_____

_____

_____

_____

_____

_____

6. On a separate sheet of paper, rewrite your sentences into paragraph form.

Using Transitional Expressions in Cause and Effect Writing

There are several transitional expressions you will find useful when writing about causes or effects.

Cause	Effect
because	as a consequence of
causes, caused by	as a result (of)
the reason	consequently
since	then
therefore	resulting in

| PRACTICE 5 | Adding Transitions to Cause and Effect Paragraphs |

Add appropriate transitional expressions to the cause paragraph you created for Practice 3 and the effect paragraph you created for Practice 4. When you have finished, compare the paragraphs pairs. The paragraphs containing the transitional expressions should be easier to read and understand.

Moving from Paragraph to Essay

Now that you have studied and practiced the techniques to create effective cause and effect paragraphs, it is time to expand your ideas to a larger writing unit: the cause or effect essay. Using the techniques you learned in Part 1 regarding developing the essay paragraphs and the cause or effect techniques you have just learned, you can create the cause or effect essay. This might be a good time to return to Part 1 and review the techniques for developing the full essay.

Creating the Introductory Paragraph

A cause or effect essay needs a clearly defined organization in the introductory paragraph to announce to the reader just how the subject will be developed. The thesis statement should indicate whether the essay will focus on cause or effect, the writer's attitude toward the topic, the controlling idea, and the organizational structure. By using an appropriate lead-in technique, the thesis should blend naturally into the rest of the introductory paragraph.

Using one of the causal chain techniques you have studied can help you identify causes and effects. You then can extend and develop the ideas expressed in the diagrams to create the thesis statement for a cause or effect essay.

Example Cause Thesis Statement
Sloppy bookkeeping, lack of organization, and mental fatigue can lead to poor money management.

Example Effect Thesis Statement
Poor money management can lead to physical tension, loss of appetite, and health problems.

Although both essays are concerned with poor money management, the focus of each essay is different: The first essay will focus on causes of poor money management, while the second essay will focus on the effects of poor money management.

Creating the Body Paragraphs

For an essay on the causes of poor money management, the focus of the body paragraphs will be the paragraph topics listed in the thesis statement's essay map. The first body paragraph's topic will be "sloppy bookkeeping," the second body paragraph's topic will be "lack of organization," and the third body paragraph's topic will be "mental fatigue." Remember, as you write about each of the topics, your focus should be that these are *causes for poor money management.* Your focus should not be on how reading the *Wall Street Journal* can help you be more successful in picking stocks or how reading *GQ* magazine can help you dress more like a businessperson. Keep your focus on the controlling idea or attitude: the three causes can lead to poor money management.

For an essay on the effects of poor money management, the focus of the body paragraphs will be the paragraph topics listed in the thesis statement's essay map. The first body paragraph's topic will be "physical tension," the second body paragraph's topic will be "loss of appetite," and the third body paragraph's topic will be "health problems." Remember, as you write about these topics, your focus should be that these are the negative effects caused by poor money management. Your focus should not be how poor money management can reduce the value of your stock portfolio or how it can cause your plans to buy a house to be put on hold. Keep your focus on the controlling idea: that poor money management can lead to health-related problems.

Creating the Concluding Paragraph

The approach of the concluding paragraph should flow naturally from the essay's main topic. Because the first essay's focus is the causes leading to poor money management, a *call to action* would seem an appropriate choice. You might suggest some actions business people can take to help correct sloppy bookkeeping practices. You might even suggest that they survey some book-keeping services that will handle their accounts for a reasonable fee. You might suggest that they take a workshop on enhancing organization skills, or that they enroll in a yoga or tai chi class to get rid of unwanted, destructive tension.

Because the second essay's focus is the effects caused by poor money management, a *warning* would seem an appropriate choice. You might warn the reader that there are other negative consequences that might come from poor money management: negative credit reports, relationship problems (with spouses, business partners, and friends), and short- or long-term business plans. Remember to keep the focus connected to the essay's idea of importance or attitude: the negative effects caused by poor money management. (Refer to Chapter 6 for other approaches for concluding paragraphs.)

▼ Sample Cause Student Essay: PROBLEMS IN PARENTING

Mark Collom

> Raising a family is a challenging endeavor no matter what the age or socioeconomic status of the parents. Literally thousands of books and articles have been written about parenting. In this essay, "Problems in Parenting," student writer Mark Collom, speaking from his own experiences as a parent, focuses on the rewarding but difficult aspects of raising children.

Vocabulary

Before you begin reading, use a dictionary to look up the definitions of the following words that appear in the essay.

abstract (1)	baton (5)	bestow (2)	commendable (1)
conversely (1)	depict (2)	endeavors (5)	enterprises (1)
extravagances (4)	intrinsic (5)	precedence (4)	pungent (2)

Problems in Parenting

1   Think for a moment or two, and recall the name of some commendable young man or woman. If the background of the admirable person were known, more often than not, they would be considered the product of a good mother and father. Conversely, all quickly can point to some delinquent character and assess that poor parenting was the cause of that person's problems. Good parenting might appear to be an easy skill, perhaps, even an art. But good parents are made, not born. Being a proper Mom and Dad is one of life's most challenging enterprises and one of its most rewarding, as well. **The abstract mixture of love, discipline, and sacrifice make good parenting a difficult task.**

Thesis Statement with Essay Map →

Topic Sentence → 2   **When the first newborn is proudly brought home from the hospital, life makes an almost complete change for the parents.** The new child, with helpless innocence, is the focus of all the love the parents can bestow. "Precious Moments" figurines are likely to depict parental love as a baby being cradled in the arms of the mother; however, the parent's love is also represented in many other not so pleasant events. Volumes of stained, pungent diapers in need of attention, equally offensive vomit upon Mother's newest blouse, and months of "yo-yo" nights of interrupted sleep are all taken in stride. Countless adversities are magically reduced by love into mere inconveniences.

Topic Sentence → 3   **Good parenting relies upon the conscience of the adults making decisions for the welfare of the youngsters.** Although limitations upon the children are easy to point out, usually such judgments also result in restrictions on the mother and father. With the children sprawled about the family-room floor, Mom and Dad opt for *Sabrina the Teenage Witch* and *Boy Meets World* because the movie on another station carries the "R" rating. Even though both grown-ups would prefer to watch the "other" movie, good parenting dictates the more suitable program. The weather may be stormy, and the bed warm and comfortable, but Mom and Dad will rise to get the kids ready so the family can make it to church on Sunday. Parental obligations confront the adults at every turn.

Topic Sentence → 4   **Yes, Mom does deserve the Caribbean cruise she's always wanted.** No, Dad's aged sedan is not a classic, yet he's not shopping for a new car. The

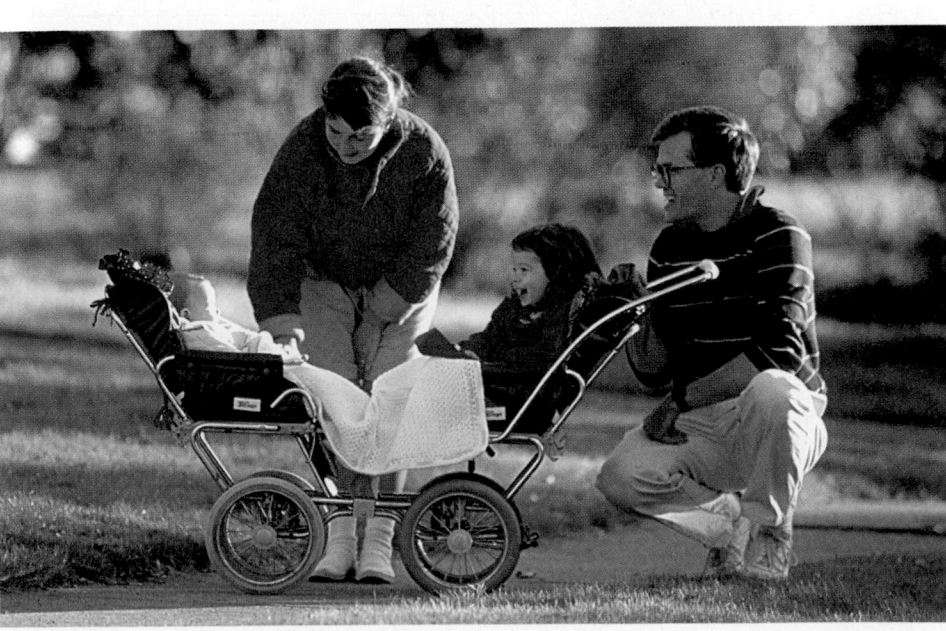

Caribbean will wait; the old Buick can make another winter or two, for children inhabit a home, and extravagances are not high on the parental agenda. Decisions are made with offspring in mind, for the parents realize years pass quickly and the young will soon be grown and gone. New bicycles on birthdays, hockey trips with the team, and Christmas trees buried in a mound of Santa's gifts all take precedence in the eyes of Mom and Dad. Soon enough, the two will cruise the southern seas.

5   Parenting is a swirl of all the emotions. It is pride in seeing a little pitcher strike out an opponent, yet sorrow when they cannot find the strike zone any longer, and the midget hurler walks in the winning run. It is a delight when a little child joyfully speeds to Daddy's arms after making a first successful twirl on new skates; however, a sadness overcomes the father when, years later, the teenager runs out the door to be with friends without even saying goodbye. With all the intrinsic difficulties, being a good parent is the most challenging of all endeavors. The role is also the most fulfilling; therefore, every generation will continue to accept the passing of the baton.

Cause Technique Questions

1. What causes does the writer focus on that make parenting difficult?

_____

_____

_____

_____

2. Does the writer use many transitional expressions? If not, which ones would be appropriate, and where would you place them?

_____

_____

_____

_____

3. Identify some of the specific sacrifices that parents often have to make.

_____

_____

_____

_____

Critical Reading Questions

1. What is the main idea of the essay?

_____

_____

2. What does the writer mean by "yo-yo" nights of interrupted sleep?

_____

_____

3. Point out some of the other "yo-yo" elements in the life of parents raising children. How do these examples support the "yo-yo" nights of interrupted sleep idea? Is there a deeper significance than just for the day-to-day routine?

_____

_____

_____

_____

Cause Writing Exercises

1. Write a paragraph about what causes a couple to be defined as "good parents." Before you begin writing, create a causal chain, and pick out at least three cause elements to use in your paragraph.
2. Write a cause essay based on the cause elements you used in exercise 1. For your essay, speak to some foreign students to get their opinions about what makes "good parents." Add their ideas to your essay.

▼
Sample Effect Student Essay: GIVING OUT

Yvonne Olsen

Most people would think that a person applying for a volunteer position would be doing so only because the effects of helping others would bring the charitable person a great measure of satisfaction and personal growth. In this essay, "Giving Out," just the opposite happens. Student writer Yvonne Olsen relates how a friend took a position for a somewhat selfish reason, but that some unforeseen, beneficial effects became a part of the total equation.

Vocabulary

Before you begin to read, use a dictionary to look up the definitions to the following words that appear in the essay.

anticipated (3)   discourteous (2)   eager (2)   energetic (4)

gourmet (2)   miraculously (5)   mumble (3)   volunteer (1)

interact (3)

Giving Out

1   Cindy left the interview feeling undecided about the job she had just gotten. She did not interview for a paying job; rather, she had sought a volunteer position at a local hospital. Cindy wanted to volunteer at the hospital because she wanted to see what the medical profession was all about. She was a good science student, so she thought going to medical school might be an option. She wasn't all that excited about getting up at 5:30 in the morning each day, and the thought of having to do a lot of work without pay wasn't high on her list, either. She thought it was going to be a long summer. Instead, the volunteer position turned out to be very rewarding mentally, socially, and educationally.

Thesis Statement with Essay Map →

Topic Sentence → 2   The first day at the hospital was a mental shock. Cindy was working on the full admit floor where the patients were very ill. Most of them had spent weeks in the hospital. Most were elderly, depressed, or bored. Some of them looked lifeless, for all hope of leaving the hospital had been delayed when a physician scheduled them for another set of tests or for another surgery. When Cindy saw that most of the patients were hooked to oxygen, she learned to appreciate her own good health. The first few times at the hospital were depressing for her, as well, but soon she began to focus on some positive aspects. A feeling of happiness ran through her mind when she got to take discharged patients out of the hospital to meet their families. These patients, seemingly in the depths of despair only days earlier, now were all smiles because they knew that soon they would be home. The patients were eager to see their families, and they would tell her about what they were going to do once they left the hospital. Of course, not all of the discharged patients were going home; some would be going to nursing homes or to other extended care facilities. Positive feelings rose in her chest when she was helping nurses run specimens to the lab, picking up prescriptions from the pharmacy, and serving patients their breakfast. When patients wanted a newspaper or fresh gourmet coffee, she would go to the lobby and return to smiling faces and outstretched hands. They often were grateful for such small things, while people on the outside of the hospital were often discourteous or accepted such favors without thanks. Cindy's self-esteem began to rise.

Topic Sentence → 3   Besides all of the mental benefits, there were also social benefits that she hadn't anticipated. Cindy had always been a bit shy, but being with so many patients and co-workers helped her to become more talkative. She talked to elderly patients about their families and illnesses. She listened to endless love stories of when they were her age. They liked the fact that there was someone to listen to their stories. Of course, not all of the patients were easy to talk to. The younger patients would not want to speak to anyone because they were angry at being stuck in a hospital away from friends and video games. Cindy could not understand all of her patients, particularly those who were heavily sedated and could only mumble. She learned that even if she could not understand the patient, she could pretend to just to make them feel important. At times, she would assure nervous patients that the tests or the surgeries were not as serious as they seemed. As it became easier to relate to the patients, it became easier to interact with her co-workers. Questions became easier to ask, and thoughts became easier to express. As the weeks went by, Cindy lost most of her shyness.

Topic Sentence ⟶ 4   Volunteering also turned out to be a great educational experience. After all, the hospital does have many nursing and medical students. She learned the structure of the hospital from the maintenance crew to the kitchen personnel to the neurosurgeons. She learned about the different medical tools that were used in the various departments. Cindy heard of many medical conditions that she never knew existed. Speaking to doctors and nurses helped her to see what their professions were like. Nurses worked hard to make the patients comfortable and assist the doctors in curing the patients. Volunteering taught her about good, energetic life and about weak, dying life. These educational experiences helped Cindy decide that a career in medicine was going to be her life's calling.

5   The volunteer position helped Cindy in many ways. Being around people less fortunate taught her to be grateful that her family and friends were healthy, which she used to take for granted. After her volunteer experience, she realized that illness could strike at any time. But most of all, she got a sense of how she wanted to direct her life. Cindy decided to go to medical school because she saw how a good physician could help a patient recover miraculously. Even though she was not paid for her services, Cindy felt that volunteering in the hospital earned her more than she could ever calculate.

Effect Technique Questions

1. What effects does the writer focus on that finally made Cindy's experience worthwhile?

_____

_____

_____

_____

_____

2. Did the writer use many transitional expressions? If not, which ones would be appropriate, and where would you place them?

_____

_____

Critical Reading Questions

1. How did Cindy's expectations differ from the reality she found at the hospital?

_____

_____

_____

_____

2. How does the title "Giving Out" provide additional meaning now that you have read the essay?

_____

_____

_____

_____

Effect Writing Exercises

1. Write a paragraph about the effects of a particular experience: a job, boot camp, attending college, moving away from home. Before starting to write, create a causal chain, and choose at least three effects to use in your paragraph.
2. Write an essay based on the topic and effect elements you used in exercise 1. Expand the list of effects by focusing on the initial expectations prior to the experience and how those expectations eventually changed.

▼

Sample Professional Essay: WHY ENGLISH-ONLY LAWS ARE USELESS

Rosa Rivera

There has been much written about making English the official language of the United States. Legislation has been introduced (but so far not passed) in Congress. Much of the debate for such a law is a reaction to the numbers of minority communities in the United States where languages other than English are commonly spoken. This essay, "Why English-Only Laws Are Useless," was written for the University of Rochester's *Campus Times* by Rosa Rivera when she was a senior. Rivera is a former president of the university's Spanish and Latin Students' Association.

Vocabulary
Before you begin reading, use a dictionary to look up the definitions of the following words that appear in the essay.

access (3)   electoral (3)   integral (4)
mandates (2)   medium (4)   repercussions (1)
resurgence (1)   unify (5)   invalidation (2)
crucial (3)

Why English-Only Laws Are Useless

1   The newest move to bash immigrants in the United States has arrived with the resurgence of the "English-only" movement. The type of legislation called for by this movement is sure to have negative repercussions for American society at large.

2   In 1996, the Supreme Court agreed to review a lower court's invalidation of Arizona's 1988 constitutional amendment making English the official language of that state. This law mandates that voting ballots be in English only and that English be the official language of all government functions and actions, including government documents. Government officials and employees are to conduct business in English only. Additionally, schools are not allowed to teach in any other language unless the class is specifically geared toward teaching a foreign language.

3   Legislation that would make English the official language of the United States would affect institutions that are crucial to all Americans: elections, government, and education. Citizens who cannot understand the English language would not be able to understand voter registration forms. They would not be able to vote in local or national elections, even though they have a constitutional right to participate in electoral politics. Government documents that are currently printed in several languages in addition to English would only be printed in English. That would mean that non-English-speaking people applying for housing, health care, welfare and other social services would no longer have access to these services. In addition, students who do not speak English would not be able to learn—their access to education would be cut off. Should government officials want to help the affected individuals by explaining application procedures or school policies, they would not be able to; according to the law, official business must be conducted in English. Should the proposed legislation be passed, government employees probably would not have the necessary language skills to assist people. There would probably be no hiring preferences given to those with knowledge of a foreign language and, therefore, no motivation to learn one.

4   Aside from my concern about the consequences that this proposed legislation might have on a large group, the whole issue strikes me as un-American. This country was founded by immigrants and now it is trying desperately to turn its back on them. Immigrants have it hard enough in this country without being forced to abandon their native language. Language is an integral part of culture; it is the medium through which the culture is passed on from generation to generation. The "English-only" movement (and others like it) is trying to create something in the United States that our rich history prevents: one unified culture.

5   Presidential candidate Bob Dole and others argue that making English the official language of the United States would unify the country. I disagree. Ethnic divisions and racism go a lot deeper than language.

Cause and Effect Technique Questions

1. Does this essay focus primarily on cause or effect? Identify some of the causes or effects depending upon which one you choose.

_____

_____

_____

_____

2. Give some examples of why Rivera titles her essay "Why English-Only Laws Are Useless."

_____

_____

_____

_____

3. Does the writer use many transitional expressions? If not, which ones would be appropriate, and where would you place them?

_____

_____

_____

_____

Critical Reading Questions

1. What is the main idea of the essay?

_____

_____

2. Why does Rivera list such specific services as housing, health care, welfare, and education? Why doesn't she simply say "English-only" laws would deny non-English-speaking individuals access to government?

_____

_____

_____

3. What does Rivera think an "English-only" law will create in the United States?

_____

_____

_____

_____

Cause and Effect Writing Exercises

1. Write either a cause or effect paragraph as to why a particular law or piece of legislation is unfair. Before starting to write, create a causal chain and choose at least three causes or effects to support your position.
2. Write either a cause or effect essay based on your position in exercise 1. State why you think the law or piece of legislation is unfair based either on causes or effects. Choose either position, not both.

More Topics for a Cause or Effect Essay

Here are some possible topics for cause or effect essays. Remember, cause or effect writing must have a purpose, so don't forget to create a thesis statement. Use the essay map to organize the topics for your body paragraphs.

Causes

1. The causes of drug abuse
2. The causes of the increasing high school dropout rate
3. The causes of test anxiety
4. The causes of high taxation
5. The causes of road rage or for being relaxed behind the wheel

6. The causes of divorce or for a long-lasting, happy marriage
7. The causes of spousal abuse or for diffusing tension in a relationship
8. The causes of a high teen pregnancy rate
9. The causes of low unemployment
10. The causes of high prison populations

Effects

1. The effects of a large corporation leaving a small town
2. The effects of pollution
3. The effects of a week's vacation
4. The effects of over-prescribing antibiotics
5. The effects of high speed limits
6. The effects of owning a pet
7. The effects of international trade agreements
8. The effects of reading a popular book or seeing a movie
9. The effects of a tornado
10. The effects of prejudice

☑ Writing Checklist for a Cause or Effect Essay

❏ 1. Choose a topic.
❏ 2. Create a causal chain to discover both causes and effects.
❏ 3. Decide whether to write a cause or an effect essay.
❏ 4. Choose an appropriate number of either causes or effects to fit the assignment.
❏ 5. Create a thesis statement.
❏ 6. Draft the essay. Don't forget to use transitional expressions.
❏ 7. Revise the first draft.
❏ 8. Proofread the final draft.
❏ 9. Print or type the essay and submit it.

CHAPTER REVIEW

▼ A cause or effect essay explains the reasons associated with some thing or event: cause analysis develops *why* something happens, and effect analysis explains *the results and consequences* stemming from the causes.

▼ Developing a causal chain is a prewriting activity that can help you focus on important causes and effects.

▼ While developing cause or effect writing, avoid seeing a causal relationship when either coincidence or simple chronology is at work.

▼ In a cause or effect paragraph, the topic sentence announces the topic and indicates whether causes or effects will be discussed. Transitional expressions help show cause and effect relationships.

▼ In a cause or effect essay, the thesis statement in the introductory paragraph indicates the topic, attitude, controlling idea, and the causes or effects that will be discussed in the remainder of the essay.

Visit *The Write Start* Online!

For additional practice with the materials found in this chapter, visit our Website at

http://www.ablongman.com/checkett

The Website also features additional readings, quizzes, writing activities, and Internet links, as well as a bulletin board and interactive chat.

15 The Persuasive Essay

When you try to convince someone else that your point of view or belief is correct, you are using **persuasion.** Persuasion is one of the most common types of writing in college. Persuasive writing attempts to convince the reader that a particular point of view is justifiable because of the evidence used to explain and support the topic. For your point of view to be persuasive, your writing must have a clearly stated position and specific support to make your opinion believable.

Identifying Your Purpose

Persuasive writing can be informal, formal, or semiformal. Think of informal persuasion as when you and your friends or family try to convince one another about the rightness of your opinions on issues ranging from which college basketball team should be number one to which fast food restaurant has the best pizza. Commercials on radio and television also are types of informal persuasion. So are public service ads for nonprofit organizations and most political advertisements.

Formal persuasion is usually called **argumentation.** This type of persuasion requires not only that you argue for your own beliefs, but also that you argue directly against someone else's beliefs. Argumentation uses evidence from primary and secondary sources (information often found in the library) that are cited using a formal documentation process (Modern Language Association or American Psychological Association, for example). Research papers, analytical essays, and certain business reports fall into this category. You will be introduced to the argument research essay in Chapter 16.

However, in this chapter, we are interested in semiformal persuasion—a type of persuasion that falls somewhere between the two mentioned above. Semiformal persuasion requires a bit more logical thought and organization than is needed around the kitchen table in informal arguing but not quite the rigid structure that is made necessary by the quotations and accompanying documentation of formal argumentation.

Writing a Persuasive Paragraph

In quizzes, papers, and exams, you will be required to argue for and against ideas. Therefore, learning the fundamentals of persuasive writing is one of the most important skills you can learn. Exhibit 15.1 shows a persuasive paragraph that tries to convince the reader that the author has a well-thought-out point of view.

**Exhibit 15.1
The Persuasion
Paragraph**

> Mandatory drug testing will help eliminate poor job performance. Workers will do better quality work to meet the standards of the company. The company will be more successful because of the quality of the product the workers will produce. Additionally, the workers' job performance will improve because of a better attitude. Mandatory drug testing also will reduce the number of job-related accidents; that, in turn, will enhance performance. A safe work environment promotes better performances as employees will feel safer and more secure as they do their jobs. Workers having more confidence in the employer, fellow employees, and the workplace will complete tasks more confidently and successfully.

In the paragraph above, the writer's conclusion, that "mandatory drug testing will help eliminate poor job performance," is supported by statements that suggest that mandatory drug testing will create a safer workplace and a safer employee. A safer atmosphere creates a better attitude on the part of the worker who, in turn, will perform better on the job. The ideas that support the conclusion are not outlandish or overblown; rather, they are reasonably expressed and developed in a convincing manner.

The Topic Sentence in a Persuasive Paragraph

In a persuasive paragraph, the topic sentence states the writer's conclusion or point of view about a particular topic. The writer's conclusion either can be for or against (pro or con) the idea concerning the topic. Therefore, the topic sentence is the key to a successful persuasive paragraph. The verbs used in a persuasive topic sentence are usually *should/should not* or *must/must not*.

Examples

The pending legislation on the right of citizens to carry concealed handguns should be defeated.

This paragraph will argue against (con) citizens having the right to carry concealed handguns.

Employers should provide day care for their employees.

This paragraph will argue for (pro) companies providing day care for the children of their employees.

> *Euthanasia should be legalized because of our constitutional rights of personal freedom.*
>
> This paragraph will argue for (pro) physician-assisted suicide.
>
> *Athletics should not receive more funding than academics.*
>
> This paragraph will argue against (con) sports receiving more money than academics.

▼ **PRACTICE 1**   **Writing Persuasive Topic Sentences**

For the ten topics listed below, write either a pro (for) topic sentence or a con (against) topic sentence. Try to write five pro sentences and five con sentences.

1. Topic: Selling cigarettes to teens under eighteen years of age

_____

_____

_____

2. Topic: Regulation of sexually explicit material on the Internet

_____

_____

_____

3. Topic: Organized prayer in public schools

_____

_____

_____

4. Topic: Lower speed limits on federal highways

_____

_____

_____

5. Topic: Military draft for eighteen-year-old males and females

_____

_____

6. Topic: Adoption of children by gay and lesbian couples

_____

_____

_____

7. Topic: Safety inspections for automobiles

_____

_____

_____

8. Topic: Elimination of athletic scholarships

_____

_____

9. Topic: Increasing the income tax

_____

_____

10. Topic: Legalization of marijuana

_____

_____

_____

The Pro and Con List

Once you have decided on a topic, it is vital that you know the major argument points on both sides of the issue, whether or not you know which side you are going to take. First, list as many points for each side that you can think of in a pro and con list, as shown in Exhibit 15.2.

**Exhibit 15.2
The Pro and Con List**

Topic: Nuclear Energy

Pro (For) List	_Con (Against) List_
Cheaper fuel costs	Radioactive waste
Less dependence on foreign oil	Unemployment in fossil-fuel industries
Creates high tech jobs	Environmental pollution
Saves natural resources	Nuclear power plant accidents
Ensures strong nuclear arsenal	Nuclear weapons proliferation

Once you have listed as many points as you can think of, consider the points on both sides of the argument, and choose the side you wish to argue for. Decide which points you will use in your paragraph to support your topic.

▼ **PRACTICE 2**   **Creating Pro and Con Lists**

Create a pro and con list for each of the following topics. Think of as many items for each list as you can.

1. Topic: Teaching sex education in mixed-gender classes

Pro	Con
_____	_____
_____	_____
_____	_____
_____	_____
_____	_____

2. Topic: Gays serving in the military

Pro	Con
_____	_____
_____	_____
_____	_____
_____	_____
_____	_____

3. Topic: Smoking in public places

Pro	Con
_____	_____
_____	_____
_____	_____
_____	_____
_____	_____

4. Topic: Foreign language requirements in high school and college

Pro	Con
_____	_____
_____	_____
_____	_____
_____	_____
_____	_____
_____	_____

5. Topic: Affirmative action in employment

Pro	Con
_____	_____
_____	_____
_____	_____
_____	_____
_____	_____

Techniques to Support the Argument

To persuade the reader that a particular position is convincing, writers use a variety of support techniques in the persuasive paragraph: answering the opposition, referring to an authority, predicting consequences, stating facts, and providing examples. While you probably will never use all of them in one paragraph, you will use them when you write persuasively.

Answering the Opposition

At times, the best way to persuade your reader is to respond directly to an opponent's point. This also shows your reader that you are aware of your opponent's side of the issue, not just your own.

Referring to an Authority

An authority is a person or a group that is considered an expert on the subject under discussion and will give an unbiased but knowledgeable opinion.

Predicting Consequences

Predicting consequences can strengthen an argument and persuade your reader to agree with your point of view and disagree with your opponent's.

Stating Facts

Facts are those things that actually exist or have existed, such as people, places, things, and events. A *fact* differs from an *opinion* in a quite significant way. An opinion is how we think about, or interpret, facts. For instance, it is a *fact* that in 1978 the U.S. Congress removed our currency from the gold standard (the dollar amount of paper money and coins in circulation could not exceed the dollar amount of gold stored at Fort Knox in Kentucky). That fact cannot be argued. However, whether or not you think it was a good idea to remove the gold standard is your *opinion*, and that can be argued. Whether your *opinion* or your opponent's *opinion* is the more persuasive, the *fact* remains that the gold standard was removed in 1978.

Providing Examples

Good examples can develop an idea quickly and clearly and help convince your reader of your point of view. Examples also are used to clarify, illustrate, or make concrete a general idea about the subject. Therefore, be certain that your examples support your position or convincingly argue against your opponent's.

▼ PRACTICE 3	Drafting Pro and Con Paragraphs

Select one of the pro and con lists you created in Practice 2. Write a sentence for each of the pro items you listed, and write a sentence for each of the con items you listed. Next, write a topic sentence for the group of pro sentences, and write a topic sentence for the group of con sentences. Finally, rewrite your sentences into standard paragraph form. These are your rough drafts for your persuasive paragraphs on both sides of an issue.

Logical Fallacies

When choosing the supportive evidence that proves your point, keep in mind that some ideas will sound good at first but might have flaws on closer inspection. Some support information might be irrelevant, misleading, over-simplified, unfair, or lead to erroneous conclusions. These proofs actually prove nothing, and they can destroy an otherwise good argument.

It is very important that you recognize statements that exhibit false logic. These statements are known as *logical fallacies.* If readers catch you using logical fallacies as proof, they will think you are a poor arguer, or that you are an unethical arguer because you are purposely trying to be deceptive.

Although there are many logical fallacies, a few of the more common ones are listed below.

▼ **Ad hominem** (Latin: "to the man") arguments attack the person's character rather than the person's ideas. Example (politics): *My opponent is an avowed atheist; therefore, he cannot lead this country out of the economic disaster we find ourselves in.* While many voters may not like the fact that a particular candidate does not believe in God, such a spiritual position probably has little if anything to do with the candidate's ability to handle economic problems. The ad hominem argument shifts the focus away from the argument and to the person.

▼ **Bandwagon** arguments suggest that because everyone else is doing something, so should you. Example (advertising): *Millions of people are using ampheta-cal to lose weight. So what are you waiting for?* Even if the claim were true, an amphetamine-based product that overstimulates the central nervous system may be medically dangerous. The bandwagon argument tries to persuade you to be like everyone else.

▼ **Either-or** arguments state that there are only two ways of dealing with a problem. Example (law): *Abortions should either be permitted in all situations or be illegal under any circumstances.* This argument does not allow for alternative choices, such as allowing abortions when the mother's life is in danger or the pregnancy is due to rape, or disallowing abortions when one of the parents is willing to raise the child or adoptive parents are available. The either-or argument does not allow for compromise.

▼ **Hasty generalization** arguments jump to conclusions using too little evidence. Example (education): *Inner-city students don't do well on standardized tests because they don't study enough.* Inner city students may study as much as students in the suburbs or rural locales. Standardized tests often are biased against inner-city students because of the language and examples used in developing questions. Also, how is "inner-city" being defined? What population must a city have to qualify for the study? Do the inner-city students come from various ethnic groups or a particular ethnic group? What are the boundaries of the "inner city" as opposed to the "outer city"? Has such a distinction been made, and if so, what is the rationale for making the distinction? The hasty generalization argument often jumps to a conclusion based on too few examples or unfairly designed definitions.

▼ **Non sequitur** (Latin: "it does not follow") arguments have a conclusion that does not follow from the evidence. Example (business): *Women should not own businesses because they don't play golf as well as men.* While it may be true that some business is conducted on golf courses, the vast majority of successful business transactions have nothing whatsoever to do with the game of golf. In fact, most businessmen and businesswomen don't play golf at all. The non sequitur argument is not an argument at all. In fact, the evidence does not provide for a logical, reasonable conclusion.

▼ **Red herring** arguments create false issues that lead the reader away from the real argument. (The term *red herring* comes from the practice of English dog trainers dragging a sack of dead herring across the scent of a fox in an attempt to distract the dogs.) Example (sports): *Our football team is not playing well because the owners never come to the games.* The real reason for the team not playing well probably has little to do with owners attending or not attending games. Poor coaching, play calling, player selection, and conditioning are more likely to be the reasons for the team's poor play. The red herring argument makes use of misleading information to divert the reader's attention from the real issue.

▼ **PRACTICE 4**   **Identifying Logical Fallacies**

Write the name of the logical fallacy in the space provided after each of the argument statements listed below.

1. It's not safe to swim in the ocean because there have been several shark attacks over the past few years in Australia and South Africa.

_____

2. Are we going to increase the number of mounted police in the park, or are we going to abandon it to the homeless, to the drug dealers, and to robbers and rapists?

_____

3. I'm sure Raoul's parents are wealthy because he drives a new car to school.

_____

4. Mom, I need a Palm Pilot because all the kids at school have them.

_____

5. She would not make a good governor because her husband has never been involved in politics, his business takes him out of town a lot, and he wasn't even born in this country.

_____

6. My opponent doesn't support handgun legislation because he is a coward interested more in his own safety than the well-being of defenseless women and children.

_____

 Organization Patterns

Once you have made your pro and con list and have chosen the types of evidence you want to use to support your topic, you will need to organize your paragraph for an effective presentation. There is no defined pattern that a writer has to use when writing persuasively. However, there are several patterns that will logically organize your points into a convincing persuasive paragraph.

Pattern 1: Arguing Only Your Own Points

In the first organizational pattern, you use only support points that argue for your point of view. Therefore, you use only pro list items if you are arguing for a point of view, or you use only con list items if you are arguing against a point of view.

Example: Arguing Only Your Own Points

Nuclear energy should not be more widely used because of radioactive waste disposal problems and the possibility of a nuclear reactor accident. One of the problems with nuclear energy is waste management. Radioactive waste can remain dangerous for thousands of years; therefore, disposal sites must meet rigid safety standards to keep the public safe. Sites must be deep in the ground to shield the public from possible radiation exposure, and they must be immune to earthquake damage. Such sites are hard to find and expensive to maintain. In addition to the waste disposal problem, nuclear accidents pose a real danger to people living near nuclear reactors. In 1986, in the Ukrainian town of Chernobyl, a nuclear reactor accident put thousands at risk of radioactive poisoning. A radiation cloud spread over northern Europe and Great Britain. Thirty-one Soviet citizens died, and over 100,000 had to be evacuated from surrounding areas. The risks involved in the long-term control and management of such a volatile substance as radioactive materials makes it a very risky proposition. Until more trustworthy safeguards can be developed in both the use and disposal of radioactive substances, we should not increase our use of nuclear energy.

Pattern 2: Arguing Against Your Opposition's Points

Another way to organize a persuasive paragraph is to state only your opposition's support points (either pro or con) and then argue against them.

Example: Arguing Against the Opposition

Despite the possible benefits to society, nuclear energy should not be more widely used as a fuel source. Many scientists and researchers claim nuclear energy is desirable as an energy source because it creates enormous amounts of power from small resources. While this may be true, other costs outweigh the purely monetary. In 1986, in the Ukrainian town of Chernobyl, a nuclear reactor accident killed 31 Soviet citizens and caused 100,000 people to be evacuated. A radioactive cloud covered much of northern Europe and Great Britain. Military leaders in Washington, D.C., state that a nuclear energy industry will also ensure a continuous source of radioactive material necessary to maintain our nuclear weapons arsenal for the defense of the nation. However, every year there are reports of nuclear byproducts missing from government inventories. Enemies of the United States could use this material to build nuclear weapons with which to threaten us. Also, unfriendly nations could steal the technology for nuclear reactors that could be used to produce materials for making nuclear weapons. The potential for disaster far outweighs the potential benefits coming from the nuclear energy industry. Nuclear energy is not a safe or practical energy source.

Pattern 3: Alternating Your Points with Arguing Against the Opposition

The third pattern of organization is alternating use of support points for your side of the argument and listing your opponent's points and arguing against them. Note that this is a hybrid or mixing of patterns 1 and 2.

Example: Alternating Your Points with Arguing Against the Opposition

Despite the possible benefits to society, nuclear energy should not be more widely used as a fuel source. One of the problems with nuclear energy is waste management. Radioactive waste can remain dangerous for thousands of years; therefore, safe deposit sites must meet rigid safety standards to keep the public safe. Sites must be deep in the ground to shield the public from possible radiation exposure, and the sites must be immune to earthquake damage. Many scientists and researchers claim nuclear energy is desirable as an energy source because it creates enormous amounts of power from small resources. While this may be true, other costs outweigh the purely monetary. In 1986, in the Ukrainian town of Chernobyl, a nuclear reactor accident killed 31 Soviet citizens and caused 100,000 people to be evacuated. A radioactive cloud covered much of northern Europe and Great Britain. Nuclear weapons proliferation is another problem if nuclear energy production is increased. Every year there are reports of nuclear byproducts missing from government inventories. Enemies of the United States could use this material to build nuclear weapons

Nuclear Energy

with which to threaten our security. Economists like to say that increasing the nuclear energy industry will create more high-tech jobs, but the same industry will cause widespread unemployment in traditional fossil-fuel industries like coal, oil, and gas. The potential for both disaster and a negative impact on the economy should convince lawmakers to not increase our use of nuclear energy as a fuel source.

Once you have chosen an organization pattern for your paragraph, select several points from the appropriate list or lists and write sentences for each. Arrange the sentences according to the organization pattern you have chosen.

PRACTICE 5 — Using the Organizational Patterns of Persuasion

Using the rough draft persuasive paragraph you created in Practice 3, rewrite the paragraph three times, using the three organizational patterns you have just studied.

Using Transitional Expressions in the Persuasive Paragraph

Transitional expressions are useful for connecting related ideas and adding rhythm to a paragraph so that it reads more smoothly. Although transitional expressions can be used anywhere they are appropriate, writers often use them to signal the types of evidence they are using in persuasive paragraphs.

Example: Alternating Your Points with Arguing Against the Opposition

Despite the possible benefits to society, nuclear energy should not be more widely used as a fuel source. One of the problems with nuclear energy is waste management. Radioactive waste can remain dangerous for thousands of years; therefore, safe deposit sites must meet rigid safety standards to keep the public safe. Sites must be deep in the ground to shield the public from possible radiation exposure, and the sites must be immune to earthquake damage. Many scientists and researchers claim nuclear energy is desirable as an energy source because it creates enormous amounts of power from small resources. While this may be true, other costs outweigh the purely monetary. In 1986, in the Ukrainian town of Chernobyl, a nuclear reactor accident killed 31 Soviet citizens and caused 100,000 people to be evacuated. A radioactive cloud covered much of northern Europe and Great Britain. Nuclear weapons proliferation is another problem if nuclear energy production is increased. Every year there are reports of nuclear byproducts missing from government invento-ries. Enemies of the United States could use this material to build nuclear weapons with which to threaten our security. Economists like to say that increasing the nuclear energy industry will create more high-tech jobs, but the same industry will cause widespread unemployment in traditional fossil-fuel industries like coal, oil, and gas. The potential for both disaster and a negative impact on the economy should convince lawmakers to not increase our use of nuclear energy as a fuel source.

Transitional Expressions for Persuasive Writing

Answering the Opposition and Referring to Authority	Predicting Consequences and Stating Conclusions	Facts and Examples
according to	consequently	another, next
although	in conclusion	because, since
nevertheless	therefore	finally, last
of course	thus	first, second
on the other hand		for
others may say		

Go back and read the paragraph example in Exhibit 15.1. Then, read that same paragraph as illustrated below with transitional expressions included. The transitional expressions are in boldface for identification purposes.

Mandatory drug testing will help eliminate poor job performance. **Consequently,** workers will do quality work to meet the standards of the company. The company, **therefore,** will be more successful because of the quality of the product the workers will produce. **Next,** the workers' job performance will increase **because** of a better attitude. Mandatory drug testing also will reduce the number of job-related accidents; that, **of course,** will enhance performance. **Thus,** a safe work environment promotes better performances as employees will feel safer and more secure as they perform their jobs. **Lastly,** workers having more confidence in the employer, fellow employees, and the workplace will complete tasks more confidently and successfully.

PRACTICE 6   Rewriting Paragraphs Using Transitional Expressions

Using appropriate transitional expressions, rewrite the three persuasive paragraphs you wrote for Practice 5. After you have finished, compare the two sets of paragraphs. The ones exhibiting the transitional expressions should be easier to understand and easier to read.

Moving from Paragraph to Essay

Now that you have studied and practiced the techniques to create effective persuasion paragraphs, it is time to expand your ideas to a larger writing unit: the persuasive essay. Using the techniques you learned in Part 1 regarding developing the essay paragraphs and the persuasion techniques you have just learned, you can write a persuasive essay. This might be a good time to return to Part 1 and review the techniques for developing the full essay.

Creating the Introductory Paragraph

Like all essays, the persuasive essay needs a clearly defined organization and a thesis statement to announce to the reader just how the subject will be developed. The thesis statement should state the topic, the writer's attitude toward the topic, the controlling idea, and the organizational structure. By using an appropriate lead-in technique, the thesis statement should blend naturally into the rest of the introductory paragraph.

Using the Pro and Con Lists to Create the Thesis Statement for a Pro Essay

Before writing an essay about students working while in college (reprinted below), one student created pro and con lists. After examining both lists, he chose the pro position and constructed a thesis statement with an essay map consisting of three of the five items on the pro side of the list. Notice that the pro and con lists, when used as the basis for the essay map, act both as an organizational tool and a working outline. The pro and con lists and thesis are illustrated below.

Topic: Working While in College

Pro	*Con*
1. Compels the students to pursue education more seriously.	1. Working would have a negative impact on the students' grade point average.
2. Working teaches the students responsibility.	2. Parents created the students, so parents ought to pay for college.
3. Working removes the financial burden from parents.	3. Going to college teaches the students to be responsible.
4. Working causes the students to appreciate college.	4. Working takes away from study time.
5. Working gives the student extra money for living expenses and extracurricular activities.	5. Working would make the student tire easily at college.

Using the numbers 1, 2, and 3 in the Pro list, the writer constructed the following thesis statement.

Thesis Statement: Students should work their way through college because doing so compels the students to pursue education more seriously, teaches the students responsibility, and removes the financial burden from parents.

The topic of the essay is "students working while attending college," and the writer's combined attitude and controlling idea is "students should work while attending college" (pro) as opposed to a paper that might argue "students should not work while attending college" (con). Notice that the essay map in this thesis statement comes as a series at the end of the sentence. The three items in the series will be the topics of the first, second, and third body paragraphs, respectively.

Creating the Body Paragraphs

In the sample student essay on working while in college, the three items in the essay map form the basis of the three body paragraphs: students will pursue education more seriously, learn responsibility, and ease the parents' financial burden. In writing the body paragraphs, you can use only one of the organization patterns for a persuasive paragraph, or you can mix them as appropriate.

Creating the Concluding Paragraph

As in all types of essays, the concluding paragraph should grow out of the introductory and body paragraphs. All of the approaches to the concluding paragraph work well in persuasive essays. For example, *evaluation* is a good approach, especially if you have chosen the pattern in which you answer the opposition or use a mix of arguing your own points and answering the opposition. With evaluation, you can emphasize the strength of your position and the weakness of the opposition's position. If you have chosen simply to argue for your own position, you might take the *prediction* approach to the concluding paragraph, indicating the future benefits if your point of view prevails. If you have chosen to argue primarily against the opposition, *warning* would be a good technique to use. You can indicate the dire consequences that may come to pass if your opposition's point of view prevails. Finally, a *call to action* in the concluding paragraph works well to persuade the reader to join you in working to see that your point of view is adopted.

Sample Student Essay: WORKING PAYS OFF

Randy Raterman

In this essay, "Working Pays Off," student writer Randy Raterman favors students working while in college. Notice how well the author develops each topic in the body paragraphs. His attention to detail makes the reader feel that he has thought about the issues thoroughly, and that he probably worked during his college career.

Vocabulary

Before you begin reading, use a dictionary to look up the following words that appear in the essay.

altered (1) compels (1) convey (3) diligently (2)
excel (2) excursions (2) fathom (5) imposes (1)
paraphernalia (3) perseverance (3) shebang (4) tedious (2)

Working Pays Off

1   Many students have argumentative perspectives toward working their way through college. Some students feel working would have a negative impact on the grade point average. As far as being responsible, numerous students believe going to lectures every day, taking notes, and cramming for

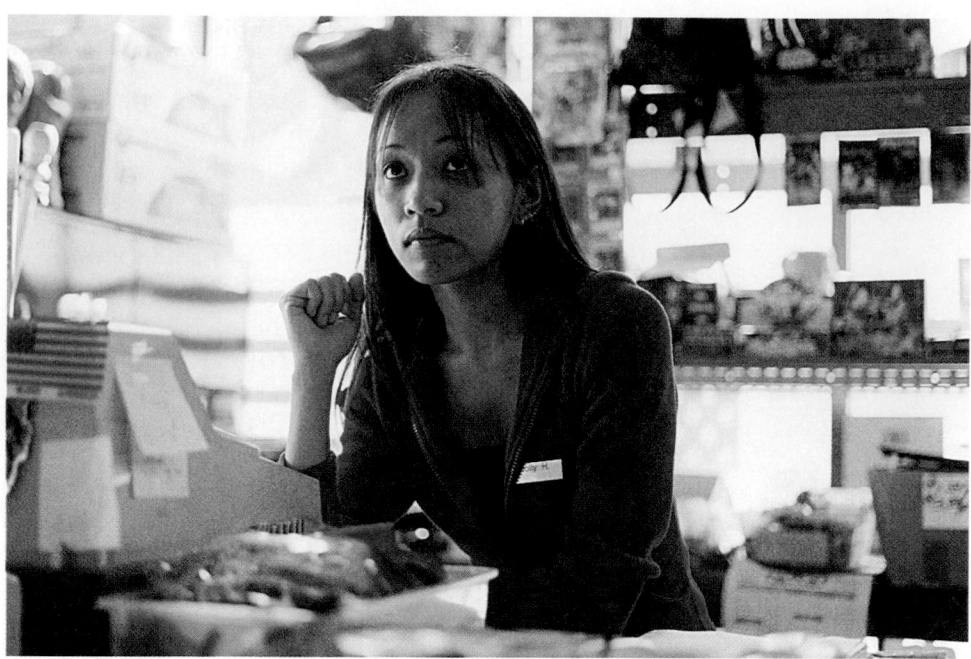

exams imposes enough responsibility in itself; additionally, others feel the parents ought to pay for college because it was Mom and Dad who created them. Somehow, the attitude of students not working needs to be altered so that the students better appreciate college education. **Students should work their way through college because doing so compels the students to pursue education more seriously, teaches the students responsibility, and removes the financial burden from parents.**

Thesis Statement with Essay Map ⟶

Topic Sentence ⟶ 2   **Many working class students experience firsthand what it's like to have backbreaking, monotonous jobs with no particular ladder to climb.** The main goals of these individuals are to do everything humanly possible to excel in college, graduate, and quit their dead-end, tedious, everyday jobs. Consequently, several students argue grade points averages would be substantially lower if they had to work. Being concerned about a lower G.P.A. is a good point, but one having no leg to stand on. True, the extra load of working along with going to school robs time from social activities and family excursions; however, working students labor diligently on scholastics knowing failure leads nowhere and climbs no ladders. Unemployed students never experience the level of gratification gained by employed students with high G.P.A.'s. Yes, employment may consume a little of the students' study time; although time can be regained by reevaluating priorities, numerous students will continue searching for excuses not to work. While nobody will ever proclaim working their way through college was easy, the experience is truly rewarding and compels the student to be responsible.

Topic Sentence ⟶ 3   **Being a responsible adult is another admirable trait hard work leaves ingrained in your personality.** Numerous unemployed students lack perseverance and have carefree attitudes originating from parents paying the bills for tuition, books, and other paraphernalia. A majority of the jobless who are enrolled for classes only fear being kicked off of their parents' insurance or losing various funds provided by Uncle Sam if they flunk out. Nevertheless, employed students convey to others, after having finished the process, that paying for college teaches responsibility. True, nonworking students attending classes and achieving good grades show signs of a responsible nature, but the high magnitude of responsibility is much more prevalent in working students. Many employed students maintain a high G.P.A. along with raising a family. Children add an enormous amount of additional responsibility to a student's daily grind. Yes, working can make anyone tire easily, but the hard work, long hours, and high level of responsibility are extremely gratifying when college is completed and the students can quit their dead-end, fatiguing, tedious jobs.

Topic Sentence ⟶ 4   The employed students also can be proud of keeping their financial burden off their parents, or at least of keeping monetary setback to a minimum. Many loving parents go to their wits end trying to support their offspring though college. While mortgaging the family residence, working two and three jobs, and depleting life savings, parents become overwhelmed by the cost of education. Stress, due to insufficient funds for the children's education, can sometimes cause major difficulties between the parents. There have even been divorces caused by such financial problems. The responsible, working students pay their own way through school or at least pay a significant portion of the tuition, easing the stress and monetary problems of the parents. Proud parents of children working their way through college will have enough funds to help out and enough to help with their own retirement. In the future, this can be a blessing to both parents and children. Unfortunately, a few students believe that since their parents brought them into the world, the parents owe them everything. After all, they didn't ask to be born! Such attitudes may stem from a lack of responsibility during the development stage when they were young. Although it is true that the parents did bring the children into the world, they should not pay for the whole shebang; no, such thinking on the part of the children is not socially or morally acceptable.

5   Many working students simultaneously envy and despise the nonworking student. Although most students wish they were born with a silver spoon in their mouths, few ever are; as a result, many college goers are employed and do work their way through college. Working also provides students with money for living expenses and extracurricular activities, so going to a movie theater is not a financial dilemma. Nevertheless, students working their way through college can be proud of scholastic accomplishments while carrying high levels of responsibility from day to day. The enormous level of gratification and satisfaction students experience while working their way through college is one which nonworking students will never fathom.

Persuasion Technique Questions

1. What organization pattern does the writer use?

_____

_____

_____

_____

2. Can you think of any pro points the author could have considered that might have made his argument even stronger?

_____

_____

_____

3. The writer uses many transitional expressions. Pick out one or two in each body paragraph, and explain how it helps make the writer's position more believable.

_____

_____

_____

_____

Critical Reading Questions

1. What is the main idea of the essay?

_____

_____

_____

2. Does the writer use mostly opinion, or does he use mostly facts? Point out sentences that support your answer.

_____

_____

_____

_____

3. How convincing is the support evidence? Does the writer make any claims that seem too extreme or opinionated? Point out examples.

_____

_____

_____

_____

Persuasive Writing Exercises

1. Write a persuasive paragraph either for or against parents supporting their adult children who come back home to live, perhaps because of a divorce or sudden unemployment. Before writing, create a pro and con list to discover points of view of both children and the parents.
2. Now, write a persuasive essay by expanding the ideas you created in exercise 1. Don't forget to use transitional expression to order your ideas logically and to create rhythm within the essay.

Creating the Introductory Paragraph and Thesis Statement for a Con Essay

Before writing an essay about mixed-gender training in the military (reprinted below), one student created pro and con lists. After examining both lists, he chose the con position and constructed a thesis statement with an essay map consisting of three of the four items in his con list. Notice that the pro and con lists, when used as the basis for the essay map, act both as an organizational tool and a working outline. The pro and con lists and thesis are illustrated below.

Topic: Men and Women Training Together in the Military

Pro	*Con*
1. Men and women have to work together at some point, so let them train together.	1. There would be more sexual harassment cases.
2. If you separate by sex, then why not by race and religion. It's the same concept.	2. It would increase complaints of favoritism.
3. Good manners and behavior are a part of military custom whether women are around or not.	3. Men would be concentrating on whether they might say or do something offensive to women rather than concentrating on duties.
4. There would still be complaints of being separate but not equal.	4. Mixed-sex units would cause less unit cohesion.

Using numbers 1, 2, and 4 in the Con list, the writer constructed the following thesis statement.

Thesis Statement: Training men and women in same-sex units would lead to a breakdown in unit cohesion, more complaints of sexual harassment, and increased complaints of favoritism.

The first, second, and third body paragraphs, then, will develop the topics of a breakdown in unit cohesion, more sexual harassment complaints, and increased favoritism.

▼
Sample Student Essay: GUYS AND GALS

Bryan Kemper

In his essay "Guys and Gals," student writer Bryan Kemper, a military veteran, explains why he is against men and women training together in the same military units. Kemper is neither against women being in the military, nor is he against women receiving equal training. His conclusion is that, if they were trained separately, both men and women would be better trained and, therefore, the military's effectiveness would be increased.

Vocabulary

Before you begin reading, use a dictionary to look up the following words that appear in the essay.

cohesion (1)	comply (1)	designated (3)
favoritism (3)	harassment (1)	integration (1)
preferential (1)	reprimanded (4)	stereotypes (4)

Guys and Gals

1   The integration of women and men has become an increasing problem in the American military. There are concerns about women being sexually harassed in the workplace, and concerns about men receiving preferential treatment. Other issues include women having easier standards to comply with, and men having to attend time-consuming sensitivity training. Both men and women should receive the same opportunities and fair treatment. **Training men and women in same-sex units would lead to more complaints of sexual harassment, a breakdown in unit cohesion, and increased complaints of favoritism.** [*Thesis Statement with Essay Map*]

2   [*Topic Sentence*] **Sexual harassment is a problem that will not go away, and the problem will not get any better as long as men and women are being trained together.** Some advocates of same-sex training units believe that men and women will have to work together at some point in their military careers. Because the military is about discipline and teamwork, men and women should be trained together so they will learn to get along with each other. However, when there are men and women working together, there is the potential for sexual harassment to occur. Training in two separate units can insure that men and women are given equal amounts of quality training. Separate male and female units would also afford women the opportunity to prove their abilities to perform the same duties as any male unit in the military after the proper amount of training, without the added pressure of performing in front of their male counterparts before they are ready.

3   [*Topic Sentence*] **Under the current system, women are not allowed the same opportunities for duty assignments as men.** The different job assignments allowed for women, especially in combat units, are very limited. Separation of male and female units would not lessen the opportunity of duty assignments for women; separate units would increase women's opportunity for different duty positions made available. Female training units should be specially designated for the performance of certain combat duty assignments; moreover, units should be set aside to perform exactly the same duties as a male unit. Women should be given the same training as men, using the same standards. Because of equal opportunity for separate male and female units, there would be no complaints of favoritism or preferential treatment. Separate units would be more beneficial for women and men alike; in the end, each unit would be more cohesive, and the military, as a whole, would become more effective in succeeding in its missions.

4   [*Topic Sentence*] **Women and men are not judged by the same standard in today's military; consequently, there are complaints that women receive preferential treatment.** Often men are reprimanded for incidents involving sexual harassment or misconduct; the man's side of the story often is not taken into consideration. Men are given more opportunity for job promotion or advancement than women, and there are more men in leadership positions. Because of gender

stereotypes, women are excused from performing required duties. Favoritism can be argued for either side. If trained separately, men and women would be evaluated among their peers based solely on merit and job performance. If evaluated with peers of the same sex, neither men nor women would receive favoritism according to their gender.

5   Men and women are still going to have to work together in the military. Not all units and job assignments should be separate, but there are many combat units where they should be segregated. If there are separate units for men and women, they still should be trained to work together; however, the units should be kept separate as much as possible. Perhaps a block of training hours could be set aside every week for just such a purpose. But, for the most part, men and women should be trained in separate units for real equal opportunity employment conditions to exist.

Persuasion Technique Questions

1. What organizational pattern does the writer use?

_____

_____

_____

_____

2. Does the writer use mostly opinion or mostly facts? Point out sentences that support your answer.

_____

_____

_____

3. Did the writer use many transitional expressions? If not, which ones would be appropriate, and where would you place them?

_____

_____

_____

Critical Reading Questions

1. What is the main idea of the essay?

_____

_____

2. How convincing is the support evidence? Does Kemper make any claims that seem too extreme or opinionated? Point out examples.

_____

_____

_____

3. What techniques does the writer use in the concluding paragraph? How does it support the writer's point of view put forward in the body paragraphs?

_____

_____

Persuasive Writing Exercises

1. Write a persuasive paragraph either for or against women participating with men in a traditionally all-male sport, such as wrestling, baseball, football, ice hockey, soccer, or basketball. You can use facts, opinions, or a combination of both to support your thesis.

2. Write a persuasive essay about a behavior that in the past was considered unacceptable for women but today is considered permissible, such as women asking men out on a date, women working as mechanics or race car drivers, or single women having or adopting children to raise on their own. Before writing your essay, make a pro and con list that reflects both sides of the issue. Choose which side you wish to defend, and then write your essay using transitional devices to connect your ideas.

▼

Sample Professional Essay: LAST RITES FOR THE INDIAN DEAD

Suzan Shown Harjo

This essay, "Last Rites for the Indian Dead," was written by Suzan Shown Harjo, a Native American of Cheyenne descent, and it first appeared in the _Los Angeles Times_. In her essay, Harjo identifies a problem that affects Native Americans, but she also argues that the issue poses an ethical conflict for all Americans.

Vocabulary

Before you begin reading, use a dictionary to look up the definitions for the following words that appear in the essay.

abhorrent (7)	archaeological (2)	cranial (3)	curation (11)
decapitated (3)	desecration (8)	exhumed (3)	funerary (15)
macabre (10)	mastodons (6)	pseudo- (4)	relic (7)
rummaging (8)	strewn (8)		

Last Rites for the Indian Dead

1   What if museums, universities, and government agencies could put your dead relatives on display or keep them in boxes to be cut up and otherwise studied? What if you believed that the spirits of the dead could not rest until their human remains were placed in a sacred area?

2   The ordinary American would say there ought to be a law—and there is, for ordinary Americans. The problem for American Indians is that there are too many laws of the kind that make us the archaeological property of the United States and too few of the kind that protect us from such insults.

3   Some of my own Cheyenne relatives' skulls are in the Smithsonian Institution today, along with those of at least 4,500 other Indian people who were violated in the 1800s by the U.S. Army for an "Indian Cranial Study." It wasn't enough that these unarmed Cheyenne people were mowed down by the cavalry at the infamous Sand Creek massacre; many were decapitated and their heads shipped to Washington as freight. (The Army Medical Museum's collection is now in the Smithsonian.) Some had been exhumed only hours after being buried. Imagine their grieving families' reaction on finding their loved ones disinterred and headless.

4   Some targets of the Army's study were killed in noncombat situations and beheaded immediately. The officer's account of the decapitation of the Apache chief Mangas Coloradas in 1863 shows the pseudoscientific nature of the exercise. "I weighed the brain and measured the skull," the good doctor wrote, "and found that while the skull was smaller, the brain was larger than that of Daniel Webster."

5   These journal accounts exist in excruciating detail, yet missing are any records of overall comparisons, conclusions, or final reports of the Army study. Since it is unlike the Army not to leave a paper trail, one must wonder about the motive for its collection.

6   The total Indian body count in the Smithsonian collection is more than 19,000, and it is not the largest in the country. It is not inconceivable that the 1.5 million of us living today are outnumbered by our dead stored in museums, educational institutions, federal agencies, state historical societies, and private collections. The Indian people are further dehumanized by being exhibited alongside the mastodons and dinosaurs and other extinct creatures.

7   Where we have buried our dead in peace, more often than not the sites have been desecrated. For more than 200 years, relic hunting has been a popular pursuit. Lately, the market in Indian artifacts has brought this abhorrent activity to a fever pitch in some areas. And when scavengers come upon Indian burial sites, everything found becomes fair game, including sacred burial offerings, teeth, and skeletal remains.

8   One unusually well-publicized example of Indian grave desecration occurred two years ago in a western Kentucky field known as Slack Farm, the site of an Indian village five centuries ago. Ten men—one with a business card stating "Have Shovel, Will Travel"—paid the landowner $10,000 to lease digging rights between planting seasons. They dug extensively on the 40-acre farm, rummaging through an estimated 650 graves, collecting burial tools, tools, and ceremonial items. Skeletons were strewn about like litter.

9   What motivates people to do something like this? Financial gain is the first answer. Indian relic-collecting has become a multimillion-dollar industry. The price tag on a bead necklace can easily top $1,000; rare pieces fetch tens of thousands.

10   And it is not just collectors of the macabre who pay for skeletal remains. Scientists say that these deceased Indians are needed for research that some-

day could benefit the health and welfare of living Indians. But just how many dead Indians must they examine? Nineteen thousand?

11   There is doubt as to whether permanent curation of our dead really benefits Indians. Dr. Emery A. Johnson, former assistant surgeon general, recently observed, "I am not aware of any current medical diagnostic or treatment procedure that has been derived from research on such skeletal remains. Nor am I aware of any during the 34 years that I have been involved in American Indian . . . health care."

12   Indian remains are still being collected for racial biological studies. While the intentions may be honorable, the ethics of using human remains this way without the full consent of relatives must be questioned.

13   Some relief for Indian people has come on the state level. Almost half of the states, including California, have passed laws protecting Indian burial sites and restricting the sale of Indian bones, burial offerings, and other sacred items. Representative Charles E. Bennett (D–Fla.) and Sen. John McCain (R–Ariz.) have introduced bills that are a good start in invoking the federal government's protections. However, no legislation has attacked the problem head-on by imposing stiff penalties at the marketplace, or by changing laws that make dead Indians the nation's property.

14   Some universities—notably Stanford, Nebraska, Minnesota, and Seattle— have returned, or agreed to return, Indian human remains; it is fitting that institutions of higher education should lead the way.

15   Congress is now deciding what to do with the government's extensive collections of Indian human remains and associated funerary objects. The secretary of the Smithsonian, Robert McAdams, has been valiantly attempting to apply modern ethics to yesterday's excesses. This week, he announced that the Smithsonian would conduct an inventory and return all Indian skeletal remains that could be identified with specific tribes or living kin.

16   But there remains a reluctance generally among collectors of Indian remains to take action of a scope that would have a quantitative impact and a healing quality. If they will not act on their own—and it is highly unlikely that they will—then Congress must act.

17   The country must recognize that the bodies of dead American Indian people are not artifacts to be bought and sold as collectors' items. It is not appropriate to store tens of thousands of our ancestors for possible future research. They are our family. They deserve to be returned to their sacred burial grounds and given a chance to rest.

18   The plunder of our people's graves has gone on too long. Let us rebury our dead and remove this shameful past from America's future.

Persuasion Technique Questions

1. Does Harjo use mostly opinion or mostly facts in the essay? Point out some examples.

_____

_____

_____

_____

_____

_____

_____

_____

_____

_____

2. Is the evidence that Harjo uses effective in convincing you that her ideas should be taken seriously by Congress and by average Americans? Explain.

_____

_____

_____

_____

_____

3. Did the writer use many transitional expressions? If not, which ones would be appropriate, and where would you place them?

_____

_____

_____

_____

_____

Critical Reading Questions

1. What kind of conclusion does Harjo use to end the essay? Why is this an effective choice?

_____

_____

_____

_____

_____

2. Harjo clearly points out that desecrating Indian graves is a problem. But what is the ethical issue she raises that confronts the entire nation?

_____

_____

_____

_____

_____

_____

_____

_____

Persuasive Writing Exercises

1. Write a persuasive paragraph either in support of or against the United States government having made reparation payment to the families of Japanese-Americans whose homes, possessions, and businesses were confiscated and who were interred in American concentrated camps during World War II.

2. Write a persuasive essay either for or against the United States government making reparation payments to the families of African-Americans who were held as slaves up until the end of the Civil War. To complete the assignment, you may have to consult an encyclopedia or do some research at the library or on the Internet.

More Topics for a Persuasive Essay

Here are possible topics for persuasive essay writing assignments. Remember, your essay should have a clearly defined purpose. Pick either a pro or a con position for your essay.

1. Organized prayer in public schools should (not) be allowed.
2. Parents on welfare should (not) be required to work.
3. Controversial organizations (Communist Party, Ku Klux Klan) should (not) be allowed to advertise in campus publications.
4. Two years of studying a foreign language should (not) be required in high school.
5. Parents should (not) be held legally responsible for their minor children's actions.
6. Affirmative action should (not) be implemented for college enrollment.
7. The legal drinking age should (not) be 18 years of age.
8. Marijuana should (not) be legalized for medical purposes.
9. English should (not) be legally designated as the official language of the United States.
10. Single adults should (not) be allowed to adopt children.

☑ Writing Checklist for a Persuasive Essay

- ❑ **1.** Choose an issue.
- ❑ **2.** Make a pro and con list to explore both sides of the issue.
- ❑ **3.** Choose a side to argue.
- ❑ **4.** Create a thesis statement.
- ❑ **5.** Choose an organizational pattern for the body paragraphs.
- ❑ **6.** Draft the essay using transitional expressions to connect related ideas.
- ❑ **7.** Make sure you support your point of view with sound evidence.
- ❑ **8.** Check for logical fallacies.
- ❑ **9.** Revise the first draft.
- ❑ **10.** Proofread the final draft.
- ❑ **11.** Print or type the essay and submit it.

CHAPTER REVIEW

▼ A persuasive essay attempts to convince the reader that a particular point of view is correct. Persuasive writing can be informal, semiformal, or formal (also called argumentation).

▼ In a persuasive paragraph, the topic sentence states the writer's point of view about a topic—pro or con. In developing such a paragraph, it's useful first to list the pros and cons about the topic. The pro and con list can help you adopt a position and choose supporting points for the paragraph.

▼ Techniques to support an argument include answering the opposition, referring to an authority, predicting consequences, using facts, and using examples. Transitional expressions help signal which technique is being used.

▼ A persuasive paragraph has three basic patterns of organization: arguing only your own points, arguing against your opposition's points, and alternating arguing your own points and arguing against the opposition.

▼ When you write a persuasive essay, you can use the pro and con list to develop your controlling attitude (pro or con) and to select the items for the essay map, and consequently, the body paragraphs.

▼ The four approaches to the concluding paragraph—evaluation, warning, prediction, and call to action—can all be used effectively in a persuasive essay.

Visit *The Write Start* Online!

For additional practice with the materials found in this chapter, visit our Website at

http://www.ablongman.com/checkett

The Website also features additional readings, quizzes, writing activities, and Internet links, as well as a bulletin board and interactive chat.

Special Writing Situations

As you progress in your academic life, you will encounter three special writing situations on numerous occasions: **the research paper, timed in-class writing, and literary analysis.** Although all writing relies on the principles and skills you have developed in your basic writing classes, these three special writing situations call for additional approaches and techniques if you are to complete them successfully.

The Research Paper

You will be required to write research papers in many of your classes. Research papers give you the opportunity to dig deeply into a topic. You will find information about the topic through many sources in the library and on the Internet. In your essay, you will document your sources. More times than not, you will argue against a point of view that you have discovered by offering your own conclusions on the subject. You will use the source material you have found to support your conclusions.

Timed In-Class Writing

One of the most common types of writing you will encounter in college is the in-class essay exam. Because you will have a limited amount of time to answer, there is an added dimension to this type of writing experience: time pressure. To be successful, you must have a method to organize your thoughts quickly in order to effectively construct a developed essay in a short amount of time.

Literary Analysis

Many classes, not just English, will require you to interpret and analyze literature: novels, short stories, drama, and poetry. Sociology, political science, history, and many other courses use literature to study various cultures, events, and famous people. Literary analysis often takes a persuasive approach, meaning you will have to take a position about some aspect of the work and defend it by using your interpretation of what certain aspects of the work mean to you.

In the following three chapters, you will be introduced to the elements and techniques that will enable you to write successfully in these three areas of your college work.

16 The Research Paper

The research paper is an extended essay. Because you will be using documented sources to support, clarify, and exemplify your observations and
conclusions, the research paper is generally longer than other types of essays,
normally from seven to 20 pages. The work involved in writing a research
paper is considerable, so you should allow yourself as much time as you
need—usually a month or more—to research, write, and proofread the paper.

The research paper writing process can be divided into distinct steps:

1. Select a topic that you know you can find information about in the
   library or on the Internet.
2. Limit the topic by stating the paper's purpose.
3. Research the topic and take notes.
4. Outline your paper.
5. Select the quotations and citations you have on your note cards and
   printouts that you will use to support your stated purpose.
6. Arrange the quotations and citations in the order in which they will be
   used in your paper.
7. Write the paper.
8. Document the paper using the appropriate format.
9. Proofread the paper for grammatical, spelling, and documentation format
   errors.
10. Revise the paper for submission by making the necessary changes you
    found while proofreading.

Following these basic steps can save you a lot of time and energy as you
make your way through the research process. For a thorough understanding
of the research writing process, you should read the detailed explanations that
follow.

Select a Topic

It is of vital importance that the subject you choose to write about can be
researched. Generally speaking, this means that the subject must have books,
articles, and critical essays written about it. If it does not, then you will not be
able to find sources written by others that agree with your point of view to
use as support for your conclusions.

A lack of source material is not usually a problem when you are doing research about famous people, places, and events of the past. However, when writing about current people, places, and events, you must be careful that there is enough information from which to draw your support material.

Before you do anything else, go to the library and make certain that there are enough books, articles, and critical essays about your topic to make continuing the process worthwhile. If you can find a minimum of ten to 20 books, articles, and critical essays about your topic, you should be able to find enough material to support your views. If you cannot, you should probably select another topic.

Limit the Topic

Research papers, like all writing, must have a clearly defined purpose. Use the techniques you studied in Chapter 4 regarding constructing a thesis statement to clearly define the parameters of your paper's approach.

The thesis statement with essay map will automatically limit your paper to the stated subtopics, and it will clearly define your attitude toward the topic and the paper's organization. Using the thesis statement with essay map also will help you bring into focus those specific areas (the essay map subtopics) for which you will collect your support material. This will save you a lot of time and effort because you only will use 5 to 10 percent of all the material you find. The more focused the research, the less time you will waste.

Before finalizing your thesis statement, however, you might want to do some research and reading to gain a clear perspective on your final subtopics.

Research the Topic and Take Notes

To find information in a library regarding your topic, you can use the following sources to focus your research: the general online catalog, *The Reader's Guide to Periodical Literature, The Bibliographic Index,* and the specific indexes for such disciplines as the humanities and the social sciences. Your library, in all probability, uses *NewsBank,* which you can use to access over a thousand newspapers for information, or it may subscribe to other computerized databases of periodicals and journals. Most libraries also have source information on microfilm, microfiche, and CD-ROM.

You also can use a variety of encyclopedias to find information regarding your topic. Many instructors will not allow you to use information from encyclopedias in your formal research paper, but they are good sources in which to find general background information that can lead you to other sources and ideas.

You can search for information on the Internet by doing a simple *key word search.* Ask the reference librarian for assistance if you are not familiar with this process.

As you gather information related to your stated purpose, you need to save citations and quotations to use in your paper. You can use index cards or computer printouts for keeping such information. It is best to use a separate index card for each citation or quotation.

Outline the Paper

Follow whatever outlining method you are comfortable with or that your instructor has required. Some instructors require you to submit an outline, and some do not. There are *essay map outlines, sentence outlines, paragraph outlines,* and *topic outlines.* Your instructor will explain which one he or she wants you to use. Whichever outline you use, begin fleshing out your ideas in the order that your outline suggests, and incorporate your support materials where appropriate.

Select the Researched Support Material

Before you use any support material in your paper, you must decide whether or not it will actually support your points and conclusions. To do this, ask a series of questions about the material:

▼ Does the material support your attitude toward the topic as stated in the thesis statement?

▼ How current is the information? This may not be important if you are dealing with an historical subject, such as the Spanish Inquisition or World War II. However, if you are writing about a new medical procedure such as Lasik eye surgery or a new photographic technique such as a CCD (charged coupled device), information that is only a few years old may be out of date.

▼ Does the information come from an objective or biased source? The best sources for gathering information are those that are not published or written by people having a particular political, social, or monetary reason for publishing the information. In other words, if they have a lot to gain personally by persuading people with the information, then the material might be too biased to be convincing. On the other hand, if you use material from persons or groups who do not stand to gain personally by convincing others to support their position, then the information is usually more objective. Using support material that is objective usually is considered more convincing.

▼ What kind of material should you look for to support your ideas and conclusions? The most convincing evidence to support your claims are appeals to reason, not emotion. To persuade the reader that a particular position is convincing, use the following support evidence: *answering the opposition, referring to an authority, predicting consequences, stating facts,* and *providing examples.* See Chapter 15 for information regarding these types of evidence.

Arrange the Quotations

With the outline completed, you should arrange your index cards and computer printouts in the order in which you will use them in the paper. You can identify their placement in the paper by marking them with numbers or letters corresponding to those of your outline sections.

Write the Paper

Remember to include your thesis statement in the introductory paragraph, and develop your subtopics in the body paragraphs. The research paper, because of its length, has more body paragraphs than the short essay model you have been studying in this textbook. In addition, the thesis statement with essay map may be too short for this type of paper. You can use several sentences or short paragraphs to introduce the paper's overall topic and the topics of the body paragraphs.

Finish the essay by using one of the techniques you have studied for concluding paragraphs. See Chapters 4, 5, and 6 to review the basic elements of the introductory, body, and concluding paragraphs.

As you write your paper, try to use transitional expressions you have studied in this textbook to connect related ideas, add sentence variety, and create rhythm within the paper.

Document the Paper

When using the work of others in your paper, you must tell the reader from what source you quoted or cited the material. The borrowed information must be cited within the text of the paper and at the end of the paper in the Works Cited section.

Use the Appropriate Format

Different disciplines use different documentation formats. For example, in the humanities (English, speech, communication, theater, foreign language, and art), the Modern Language Association (MLA) is commonly used; whereas in the sciences (biology, botany, psychology, nursing, and chemistry), the American Psychological Association (APA) documentation format is commonly used.

Because this is a textbook for an English course, the MLA documentation format will be explained later in this chapter. You will also see examples of documentation in a student-written research paper, as well as a research paper written by a professional writer.

Avoid Plagiarism

Beware of plagiarism. It can cause your paper to receive a failing grade, and it can cause you other academic problems, such as suspension or expulsion from school. **Plagiarism** occurs when you use someone else's ideas as if they were your own and do not give the other person credit. Plagiarism also includes buying a paper or letting someone else substantially write or edit your work for you.

Plagiarism can arise because of poor note taking. Misquoting or inaccurately summarizing or paraphrasing can also cast suspicion on the integrity of your writing. When you take notes for a quotation or citation, be certain you copy the information carefully. If you put someone else's idea into your own words by summarizing or paraphrasing, you are still required to document the information. Failure to do so is considered plagiarism.

Plagiarism is the worst kind of academic dishonesty because it degrades our ability to trust that others are writing honestly and with integrity about their own thoughts and ideas and about the thoughts and observations of others.

Proofread the Paper

Submitting a paper that is substantially free of errors will create a positive impression in your instructor's mind. A paper free of misspelled words, grammatical errors, and documentation errors tells the reader that the writer cares about the writing and the reader's experience in reading it.

Conversely, a paper full of errors reflects poorly on the writer and the assignment. Errors reduce the pleasure of the reading experience, sidetrack the reader's attention from the paper's purpose, and create the impression that the writer is either careless, uneducated, or both.

Proofreading is the process of eliminating mechanical and content errors. *Mechanical errors* encompass misspelled words (including typos), punctuation, capitalization, and spacing. *Content errors* include incorrect facts or inaccurate or misleading information that makes the expressed ideas difficult or confusing to understand. It is the writer's responsibility, with minor assistance from others, such as tutors and writing lab staff, to find and correct both types of errors. Generally, proofreading is more effective if you do it at least twice: once for content errors and again for mechanical errors.

Prepare the Paper for Submission

Instructors often have their own preferences, but there are some standard guidelines for preparing research papers for submission. Needless to say, a research paper should not be handwritten. It should be prepared on a computer or word processor using the following guidelines.

▼ Use bright, white, unlined computer paper. Do not use gray or colored paper.

▼ Use 20- or 25-lb. paper. This paper weight is substantial enough to resist creases and tears.

▼ Use black ink.

▼ Set margins at 1 to $1\frac{1}{2}$ inches.

▼ Double space. Your instructor has to read many papers, and double spacing makes them easier to read. In addition, the double spacing leaves room for the instructor's comments.

▼ Anchor the pages with a staple in the upper left corner of the paper.

▼ Look through the paper. If it is not professional in appearance, make the necessary changes before submitting the paper to your instructor.

▼ Hand the paper in flat, not folded.

The Modern Language Association (MLA) Documentation Format

This section illustrates just a few of the many entry examples for documenting citations from sources such as books, periodicals, and electronic media. You can find complete guides to documenting in a variety of formats in any bookstore, library, or on the Internet.

When documenting sources from which you have used information, you must cite the material in two places in your research paper: within the narrative of the paper and at the end in the Works Cited section.

Citing Within the Paper

MLA uses a parenthetical documentation method to cite sources when they are quoted or paraphrased. When citing a source, the borrowed material is followed by parentheses ( ) containing the last name of the author, a space, and then the page number where the information can be found. If the quotation is introduced with a statement containing the author's name, the name is not repeated in the parentheses. Two examples follow.

parenthetical citation

> "There is no truth to the rumor that the chemical formula tested by the company did not answer the problem that had surfaced," stated Dr. Angela Washington (28).
>
> A prominent chemist stated, "There is no truth to the rumor that the chemical formula tested by the company did not answer the problem that had surfaced" (Washington 28).

To find the full citation information, the reader can consult the entry for "Washington" in the Works Cited list at the end of the paper.

Some points to remember regarding citations in the text:

▼ Use only the last name of the author in the parentheses. If you quote from two different people having the same last name, include the initial of the first name to distinguish between the two authors.

▼ Do not use a comma to separate the author's name from the page number.

▼ Place the parentheses immediately after the quotation. If it is at the end of a sentence, place it before the period.

▼ Parentheses usually do not follow citations taken from the Internet because these sources rarely have page numbers, and MLA suggests mentioning the author's name in the text, or frame (frames will be discussed later in this chapter). If you do not place the author's name in the frame, or a page number is available, then you do place this information in parentheses. Do not place the URL (online address) after the quotation. MLA considers URLs too long and cumbersome for inclusion in the text. They appear only in entries in the Works Cited section.

▼ If a quotation is taken from an article that appears only on one page of a magazine or journal, it is not necessary to duplicate the page number in the parentheses following the quotation.

In-Text and Block Citations

If your quotation is short, no more than three or four typed lines, provide an **in-text citation.** An in-text citation incorporates the material into the text. Place quotation marks around the quoted material. Be certain that your finished sentence is grammatically correct.

> **In-Text Citation**
>
> According to a well-documented theory, "the most likely reason the dinosaurs became extinct was a large meteor struck the earth throwing up enough dust to block out sunlight for months" (Smith 74). The theory has been supported by evidence from around the world. A thin layer of iridium has been found at the K-T boundary in Europe, North and South America, Asia, and Africa.

If your quotation is five or more typed lines, separate it from the text by using a **block citation.** Indent the entire quotation ten spaces from the left margin. Leave the right margin alone. Do not put quotation marks at the beginning and end of the quoted material as you do for an in-text quotation. Be certain to follow the quotation with the parenthetical citation.

Block Method Citation

A child's performance in school has a lot to with his home environment. According to Dr. Gerald Gaines, an expert in elementary education issues,

> However well-meaning advocates of testing and standards are, the current plan does not factor in the changing composition of American families and how these changes have affected a child attending school today. Children coming through the schoolhouse doors may have just left a home that would have been largely unrecognizable thirty years ago. The phenomenal increase in single-parent families, poverty level income families, and families in which child abuse occurs on a regular basis has changed how these children face their day in school. (143)

The government needs to take a closer look at how welfare money and services are interfacing with the educational models that have been poor predictors as to how children will fare in their formative educational years.

Framing the Quotation

You should never put a quotation into your writing without introducing it to the reader. You can introduce the quotation by stating the name of the person you are quoting, his or her title, or expertise. You can even offer a brief comment on the quotation's content. This information is called a **frame,** and it can be placed before the quotation, after the quotation, or in the middle of the quotation.

In a *front frame,* the punctuation (a comma or colon) is placed after the final word of the frame but always before the opening quotation mark.

The Front Frame

Company spokesperson Ashonti Mekela said, "Marketing expertise can guarantee good sales over a short period of time even though the product has no real perceived value to the consumer" (12).

In the *end frame*, the punctuation (comma) is placed after the final word of the quotation and is always *before* the closing quotation mark.

> **The End Frame**
>
> "Marketing expertise can guarantee good sales over a short period of time even though the product has no real perceived value to the consumer," said company spokesperson Ashonti Mekela (12).

In the *middle frame*, the first punctuation (comma) is placed after the last word in the first part of the quotation but always *before* the first closing quotation mark, while the second punctuation (comma) is placed after the last word of the frame but always *before* the second opening quotation mark.

> **Middle Frame**
>
> "Marketing expertise," according to company spokesperson Ashonti Mekela, "can guarantee good sales over a short period of time even though the product has no real perceived value for the consumer" (12).

Try not to use the same framing style repeatedly. Like all other characteristics of good writing, variety shows maturity of content and style.

Citing at the End of the Paper—The Works Cited Section

As stated earlier, when you use someone else's information, you must cite the information in two places in your paper. You have just studied the first place, in the text of the paper using a parenthetical citation. The second place you must cite the borrowed information is at the end of the paper in the **Works Cited** section. The parenthetical citation in the text of your paper indicates to the reader where in the Works Cited section the full citation information can be found.

The Works Cited section lists only those works that you cited in your paper. Do not list any sources that you did not quote from or paraphrase. When constructing your Works Cited list, adhere to the following criteria:

▼ Entries in the list appear alphabetically according to the author's last name.

▼ Entries are not numbered.

▼ Entries without an author appear alphabetically by the first word in the title.

▼ The first line of an entry extends to the left margin. Subsequent lines of the entry are indented five spaces.

▼ Double-space the entries.

See the Works Cited pages of the student and professional research papers at the end of this chapter for examples of how this section should be set up.

Examples of Works Cited Entries

Use the following models to guide you as you construct your Works Cited section.

Books
Book by One Author

Rodriquez, Mario. <u>The Middle Child</u>. New York: Century, 1999.

The author's last name is placed first, followed by the first name. Titles of books are underlined. The city where the publishing company is located comes next, followed by a full colon and then the name of the publishing company. A comma follows the name of the publisher, and the publication date follows the comma.

Book by Two or More Authors

Han, Yichuan, and Mel Simons. <u>The Black Hole: Galaxy-Eater</u>. London:

Yorkshire, 2000.

The first author's name appears as it did for the Book by One Author entry, but all subsequent authors' names appear first name first, followed by the last name.

Book by Unknown Author

<u>Growing Flowers in an Apartment</u>. Phoenix: Piaget, 1998.

If the author is not known, the title of the book comes first.

Periodicals

Periodicals are publications that come out on a regular basis: daily, weekly, monthly, quarterly, semiannually, and annually. They include journals, magazines, and newspapers. Journal, magazine, and newspaper article entries use the following order:

1. Author(s)
2. Article's title
3. Name of the periodical
4. Series number, if available
5. Volume number (usually for journals)
6. Issue number, if available
7. Publication date
8. Page numbers of the entire article

Article with One Author

Washington, Pervis. "The Black Experience." <u>Personal Life Digest</u> 16

(1999): 31–47.

Titles of articles are enclosed by quotation marks. The publication in which they appear is underlined. The series or volume number is followed by the publication date in parentheses to separate it from the series or volume number (to avoid confusion). Use a full colon after the date of publication, followed by the page numbers for the entire article.

Article with Unknown Author

"Computers and You." <u>Computer Journal</u> 4 (Winter 2000): 118–24.

If the author is not known, the title of the article comes first.

Article in a Weekly Magazine

Bigtree, Watasha. "Climate for Change in the Industrial Regions in
the United States." Social Issues 10 Sept. 2000: 13–36.

"10 Sept." is the indicator that this is a weekly periodical.

Article in a Monthly Magazine

Miller, Judy. "Attention to Detail in the Boardroom: Planning for an
Effective Meeting." Female Executive Jan. 1999: 57–62.

"Jan." is the indicator that this is a monthly periodical.

Article in a Newspaper with Numbered Sections

Edwards, Connie. "Parenting in the Millennium." Globe-Sentinel
8 Aug. 2000, sec. 7: 3.

The first number after "sec." is the section, followed by the specific page
number.

Article in a Newspaper with Lettered Sections

Achiba, Kwazi. "Using Filers in Astrophotography." Daily Gazette
3 May 1999: C2.

"C" is the section heading, followed by the specific page number—in this
entry, "2."

Electronic Sources: Internet and CD-ROM

Entries for Internet sources look just like entries for periodicals with one
major exception: the Universal Resource Locator (URL—the online address).
The URL always follows the information in the entry. MLA style is to enclose
URLs in angle brackets, as shown in the examples that follow. The URL
should not be underlined, nor should it be a different color from the rest of
the text. However, when you type a URL using a computer, most programs
automatically change the address to a hyperlink. If your printer has a color
cartridge, the address will print in blue and will be underlined. If your printer
has a black ink cartridge, the URL will print in black and will be underlined.
Most instructors are used to seeing these URLs in student papers. Unless your
instructor tells you to do otherwise, leave it alone. Or you can ask what format your instructor prefers.

Online Journal Article

Bahamma, Rahal. "Some New Thoughts about Pi." Math-Mavin
3 (2000). 4 Sept. 2000 <http://www.mathmavin.org/journals.html>.

Online Magazine Article

Sahad, Ahmad. "Genetic Mutations in Genome Sequences." Genome
Feb. 1999. 15 Mar. 2003 <http://www.genseqpro.com/1999/html>.

When there are two dates in the source, the first date indicates when the
information was placed online. It is followed by a period. The second date
indicates when you accessed the information. It is not followed by a period.

Article on CD-ROM

Mirinakov, Mikail. "Political Reformation in Former Russian Satellite

Countries." Soviet Daily Citizen 21 Oct. 2000: 7. Soviet Daily

Citizen Ondisc. CD-ROM. Infoquest. Dec. 2000.

CD-ROMs, like other electronic sources, do not always have complete publication information. In such cases, provide the information that is available.

▼
Sample Student Research Paper with Documentation: SIX-YEAR-OLD HARASSERS?

Jennifer Staggs

> This research paper, "Six-Year-Old Harassers," by student writer Jennifer Staggs, argues against an idea that six-year-old children cannot be held responsible for acts defined as sexual harassment, and that school districts may be exempt from being sued over adolescent sexual misconduct. Staggs uses material from a variety of secondary sources to support her conclusions, and she documents it using the MLA format. Although paragraph numbers appear in the margins of the research paper that follows, these are provided for reference purposes within this text only and are not a standard element in the MLA format. In the paper itself, the pages would have running heads, and the Works Cited Section would begin on a new page.

Jennifer Staggs

English 102.01

Professor Checkett

January 5, 2000

Six-Year-Old Harassers?

1   The words "sexual harassment" may give individuals mental pictures of one adult harassing another in the corporate world or even in the military. However, in George F. Will's article, "Six-Year-Old Harassers?" printed in Newsweek magazine, sexual harassment is now affecting school-aged children. Will claims normal adolescent behavior should not provoke lawsuits and disrupt school districts from receiving federal aid funds. Furthermore, he points out the Supreme Court's poor interpretation of a 1972 law sending school districts across the nation into "defensive silliness" due to the lawsuit between a fifth-grader named LaShonda and a Georgia school district. Since the lawsuit became publicized, other children,

including a six-year-old boy, have been suspended for kissing girls on the cheek or for other "normal" adolescent behaviors. Although Will's point sounds reasonable, he does not use substantial evidence to back his claim that school districts should not be held responsible, and he does not state any of the effects that so-called "normal" adolescent behavior or "sexual harassment" has on the accused or the victim.

2   G. F., the fellow fifth-grade boy accused of sexually harassing LaShonda, continued harassing LaShonda and other students for five months. His sexual misbehavior included sexually explicit language, groping, and other crudities; however, Will justified G. F.'s actions by stating that G. F. "was no more vulgar than many fifth-grade boys occasionally are" (88). George Will believes others are overreacting to typical adolescent behavior. Because accusing a young boy of sexual harassment is very serious, we must first understand what normal adolescent sexual behavior is before dismissing the behavior as typical. William N. Friedrich, a pediatrician, stated in an article:

> Sexual intrusiveness has captured considerable concern of late, particularly with our increasing awareness that preteens can behave in sexually coercive ways with other children. . . . More normative manifestations of this behavioral domain could include the mutual touching of another child's sex parts, self-stimulating behaviors, and exhibitionism. Sexual knowledge is a child's basic understanding of sexual acts and varies with the child's age. (10)

Although G. F.'s behavior may seem normal to Will, the fifth-grader's excessive sexual bullying continued for a long five months, evoking anxiety in a young girl offended by this behavior.

3   Another problem related to sexual harassment in schools is that school districts are being held responsible. In the 1994 case of LaShonda and her Georgia school district, she had the right to hold the school liable due to a 1972 federal law prohibiting any form of sexual discrimination in any educational program receiving federal funds. LaShonda is seeking $500,000 from her school district, which only received $679,000 in federal aid in the 1992–93 school year. George Will blames the Supreme Court for misinterpreting the law and allowing such a lawsuit that may diminish funding for schools.

However, in an interview with Caroline Konieczka, an elementary school teacher for twenty years, she stated, "Students must feel safe in the classroom. School is a place of learning, and teachers must do what is in the best interest of their students. If a child comes to a teacher for help, the teachers must take certain steps necessary to help that child." Mrs. Konieczka feels five months is too long for any type of misbehavior to go on, and the school district and parents should be held responsible for such negligence. Most parents want their children to feel safe and secure in school. After all, school is a home away from home for children.

4   Today, teachers have a lot more responsibility than the teachers of yesterday. Not only do they teach children how to read, write, and do arithmetic, they fill the roles of parent, sociologist, and psychologist, all the while expected to create a safe learning environment. Parents and communities expect teachers to mold children into healthy, happy, functional learners. Teachers are expected to keep up with new learning techniques, keep order in the classroom, and develop personal relationships with students to better monitor each child's learning style. "Handling sexual harassment is just one more task confronting today's teachers. And lest elementary teachers think they are exempt, this episode [the LaShonda/Georgia case] makes it clear that sexual harassment presents a challenge to teachers at all grade levels," declares Tish Raff, an elementary school assistant principal (1). Because parents are not as accessible during the day due to work schedules and more mothers entering the workplace, teachers have difficulty making contact with a child's parents to discuss matters like sexual harassment or any other type of behavior. Therefore, more responsibility is put on educators' shoulders to monitor and interpret questionable or abnormal adolescent behavior. And teachers may not pick up on certain type of behaviors. Who should be held responsible then? According to a study by the American Psychological Association, "It is estimated that four out of five students report that they have been the target of sexual harassment, but only seven per cent told a teacher what happened" (Finks 122). Programs should be set up in all schools to stress communication between the teacher, parent, and student. Children should be able to communicate with teachers, so they can respond properly.

5   In recent years, it has been a school's responsibility to conduct sex education in the classroom; however, a change is due. Parents should be heavily involved in the process. Not only is sex education very important, children are catapulted into an adult subject that may make them feel insecure about themselves and others of the opposite sex. Moms and dads with school-aged children need to be sensitive in addressing the subject of sex and should address what is being taught in the classroom. "Children may show excessive modesty or anxiety at displays of affection between parents or other individuals. Alternatively, children may be very curious and open regarding sexual matters, including interest in the opposite sex and interest in more mature television shows or videos," states pediatrician and mother-of-two Dr. Naomi Neufeld, Director of UCLA's Kidshape Program (12). Therefore, a parent's involvement and sensitivity in the sex education of their child is remarkably important. The mother and father may then instruct the child on appropriate behavior between two individuals of the opposite sex and validate the material being taught in the classroom.

6   As George Will suggests, school districts may be protected from sexual harassment lawsuits under the Individuals With Disabilities Education Act of 1994. The 1994 Act limits disciplinary actions against students with "behavior-disorder disabilities," even if the child was not diagnosed before committing any crime or unacceptable behavior. Consequently, most children who behave badly from time to time may end up with the label "disabled." It is understandable that a school district would not want to be held liable for sexual harassment in the classroom and jeopardize losing federal funding, but to pass the buck to children by insisting they have a disability is not solving the problem. A better solution is for the school district to accept responsibility, move in, and prevent such bad behavior from escalating in the future. Assistant Superintendent Beverly Lydiard has developed a program that stresses communication where "teachers are trained in an intervention technique which uses a letter from the victim to the harasser as a communication document, rather than as an accusation." She also says, "If the problem behavior does not change, the situation is then handled more traditionally." This intervention technique allows the

victim to express their feelings on paper rather than the potentially intimidating circumstance of a face-to-face confrontation, and the harasser can read the letter to better understand and reflect on how the victim is feeling. The harasser may then write an apology to the victim. Cases of harassment have dwindled since this process has been instituted.

7   In his article, George Will challenges the victims of sexual harassment. He claims if every adolescent claimed their grades suffered and were unable to concentrate, schools across the nation could be held accountable. The evidence Will uses is the 1994 study by the American Association of University Women. The study indicated that 81% of the students report having experienced some form of sexual harassment during their school years. Yet, he attacks the study by saying it was "hysteria mongering" conducted by "victimization feminists." There is a major flaw in his article's thesis; he is notably insensitive toward victims. Victims of any sexual harassment encounter can undergo extreme amounts of stress and anxiety. Just like LaShonda, many adolescents should not have had to endure harassment or bullying that can affect the quality of life. It clearly states in *The Merck Manual* [a well-respected manual that provides information on the diagnosis and therapy for a wide array of medical and psychological afflictions] that anxiety makes "decision-making difficult, and concentration is burdensome" (Berkow et al. 1499). Anxiety can create many other side-effects including sleeplessness, depression, irritability, fearfulness, and vomiting. It is crucial to keep in mind that anxiety does not just fade away. Victims like LaShonda may take a long time to heal, and it is possible that their outlook on sex and the opposite sex can be damaged forever.

8   If LaShonda had never filed suit against her school district, she, as well as others, would probably still be easy targets of sexual harassment. Since the lawsuit, schools across the nation have increased awareness of improper behavior. Hopefully, parents also will become more involved with the sex education of their children to promote open communication with school faculty to intervene in such situations before any lasting damage is done. Again, normal adolescent behavior should be expected and allowed, but the

difference between normal and abnormal should be explored and understood. Children are sacred. The nation must use the law to protect them from harm and to promote positive self-esteem.

Works Cited

Berkow, Robert, et al. The Merck Manual. 13th ed. West Point: Merck Sharp & Dome, 1973.

Finks, Rosie. "Sexual Harassment: Myths and Realities." American Psychological Association 4 Apr. 1996: 2. 1 Dec. 1999 <http://www.apa.org/pubinfo/harass.html>.

Friedrich, William N. "Normative Behavior in Children." Pediatrics 9 (1991): 5–7.

Konieczka, Caroline. Personal Interview. 10 Nov. 1999.

Lydiard, Beverly. "Intervention." Prevention Oct. 1996: 2.

Neufeld, Naomi. "Sex Education." Redbook Aug. 1997: 11–15.

Raff, Tish. "Sexual Harassment: A Guide for Faculty, Staff, and Students." University of Tennessee 5 Sept. 1996: 1–2. 1 Dec. 1999 <http://www.cs.utk.edu/~bartley/ut/sexualHarass.html>.

Will, George F. "Six-Year-Old Harassers?" Newsweek 7 June 1999: 88.

Research Paper Technique Questions

1. What is the main idea of the essay?

_____

_____

_____

_____

_____

_____

_____

2. Do you agree more with Staggs or with George Will? Explain.

_____

_____

_____

_____

3. In the essay's second paragraph, there is a block quotation containing [. . .] markings. What does this indicate has happened to the original quotation?

_____

_____

_____

_____

_____

4. In paragraph 6, the writer did not include the author's name or a page number in a parenthetical reference marker at the end of the quotation beginning "Teachers are trained [. . .]." Is this proper MLA formatting?

_____

_____

_____

_____

_____

_____

▼

Sample Professional Research Paper with Documentation: THE ECSTASY OF WAR

Barbara Ehrenreich

This research paper, "The Ecstasy of War," by professional writer, social critic, and lecturer Barbara Ehrenreich was taken from her book *Blood Rites: Origins and History of the Passions of War* (1997). In the paper, she analyzes the psychology of war and argues that the "aggressive instinct" is prominent in men. She further concludes that it generates a mental zone during war in which "men enter an alternative realm of human experience, as far removed from daily life as those things which we call 'sacred.'"

The Ecstasy of War

So elemental is the human need to endow the shedding of blood with some great and even sublime significance that it renders the intellect almost entirely helpless. (Van Creveld 166).

—Van Creveld

1   Different wars have led to different theories of why men fight them. The Napoleonic Wars, which bore along with them the rationalist spirit of the French Revolution, inspired the Prussian officer Carl von Clausewitz to propose that war itself is an entirely rational undertaking, unsullied by human emotion. War, in his famous aphorism, is merely a "continuation of policy . . . by other means," with policy itself supposedly resulting from the same kind of clearheaded deliberation one might apply to a game of chess. Nation-states were the leading actors on the stage of history, and war was simply one of the many ways they advanced their interests against those of other nation-states. If you could accept the existence of this new superperson, the nation, a battle was no more disturbing and irrational than, say, a difficult trade negotiation—except perhaps to those who lay dying on the battlefield.

2   World War I, coming a century after Napoleon's sweep through Europe and northern Africa, led to an opposite assessment of the human impulse of war. World War I was hard to construe as in any way "rational," especially to that generation of European intellectuals, including Sigmund Freud, who survived to ponder the unprecedented harvest of dead bodies. History textbooks tell us that the "Great War" grew out of the conflict between "competing imperialist states," but this Clausewitzian interpretation has little to do with the actual series of accidents, blunders, and miscommunications that impelled the nations of Europe to war in the summer of 1914.[1] At first swept up in the excitement of the war, unable for weeks to work or think of anything else, Freud was eventually led to conclude that there is some dark flaw in the human psyche, a perverse desire to destroy, countering Eros and the will to live (Stromberg 82).

3   So these are, in crude summary, the theories of war which modern wars have left us with: That war is a means, however risky, by which men seek to advance their collective interests and improve their lives. Or, alternatively, that war stems from subrational drives not unlike those that lead individuals to commit violent crimes. In our own time, most people seem to hold both views at once, avowing that war is a gainful enterprise, intended to meet the material needs of the groups engaged in it, and, at the same time, that it fulfills deep and

"irrational" psychological needs. There is no question about the first part of this proposition—that wars are designed, at least ostensibly, to secure necessaries like land or oil or "geopolitical advantage." The mystery lies in the peculiar psychological grip war exerts on us.

4   In the 1960s and '70s, the debate on the psychology of war centered on the notion of an "aggressive instinct," peculiar to all humans or only to human males. This is not the place to summarize that debate, with its endless examples of animal behavior and clashes over their applicability to human affairs. Here I would simply point out that, whether or not there is an aggressive instinct, there are reasons to reject it as the major wellspring of war.

5   Although it is true that aggressive impulses, up to and including murderous rage, can easily take over in the heat of actual battle, even this statement must be qualified to take account of different weaponry and modes of fighting. Hand-to-hand combat may indeed call forth and even require the emotions of rage and aggression, if only to mobilize the body for bursts of muscular activity. In the case of action-at-a-distance weapons, however, like guns and bows and arrows, emotionality of any sort can be a distinct disadvantage. Coolness, and the ability to keep aiming and firing steadfastly in the face of enemy fire, prevails. Hence, according to the distinguished American military historian Robert L. O'Connell, the change in the ideal warrior personality wrought by the advent of guns in the fifteenth and sixteenth centuries, from "ferocious aggressiveness" to "passive disdain" (119). So there is no personality type—"hot-tempered," "macho," or whatever—consistently and universally associated with warfare.

6   Furthermore, fighting itself is only one component of the enterprise we know as war. Wars are not barroom brawls writ large, or domestic violence that has been somehow extended to strangers. In war, fighting takes place within battles—along with much anxious waiting, of course—but wars do not begin with battles and are often not decided by them either. Most of war consists of *preparation* for battle—training, the organization of supplies, marching and other forms of transport—activities which are hard to account for by innate promptings of any kind. There is no plausible instinct, for example, that impels a man to leave his home, cut his hair short, and drill for hours in tight formation. As anthropologists Clifton B. Kroeber and Bernard L. Fontana point out, "it is a large step from what may be biologically innate leanings toward individual aggression to ritualized, socially sanctioned, institutionalized group warfare" (166).

7   War, in other words, is too complex and collective an activity to be accounted for by a single warlike instinct lurking within the individual psyche. Instinct may, or may not, inspire a man to bayonet the first enemy he encounters in battle. But instinct does not mobilize supply lines, manufacture rifles, issue uniforms, or move an army of thousands from point A on the map to B. These are "complicated, orchestrated, highly organized" activities, as social theorist Robin Fox writes, undertaken not by individuals but by entities on the scale of nations and dynasties (15). "The hypothesis of a killer instinct," according to a commentator summarizing a recent conference on the anthropology of war, is "not so much wrong as irrelevant" (McCauley 2).

8   In fact, throughout history, individual men have gone to near-suicidal lengths to avoid participating in wars—a fact that proponents of a warlike instinct tend to slight. Men have fled their homelands, served lengthy prison terms, hacked off limbs, shot off feet or index fingers, feigned illness or insanity, or, if they could afford to, paid surrogates to fight in their stead. "Some draw their teeth, some blind themselves, and others maim themselves, on their way to us" (Mitchell 42), the governor of Egypt complained of his peasant recruits in the early nineteenth century. So unreliable was the rank and file of the eighteenth-century Prussian army that military manuals forbade camping near a woods or forest: The troops would simply melt away into the trees (Delbrück 303).

9   Proponents of a warlike instinct must also reckon with the fact that even when men have been assembled, willingly or unwillingly, for the purpose of war, fighting is not something that seems to come "naturally" to them. In fact, surprisingly, even in the thick of battle, few men can bring themselves to shoot directly at individual enemies.[2] The difference between an ordinary man or boy and a reliable killer, as any drill sergeant could attest, is profound. A transformation is required: The man or boy leaves his former self behind and becomes something entirely different, perhaps even taking a new name. In small-scale, traditional societies, the change was usually accomplished through ritual drumming, dancing, fasting, and sexual abstinence—all of which serve to lift a man out of his mundane existence and into a new, warriorlike mode of being, denoted by special body paint, masks, and head-dresses.

10   As if to emphasize the discontinuity between the warrior and the ordinary human being, many cultures require the would-be fighting man to leave his human-nests behind and assume a new form as an animal.[3] The young Scandinavian had to become a bear before he could become an elite warrior, going "berserk" (the word means, "dressed in a bear hide"), biting and chasing

people. The Irish hero Cuchulain transformed himself into a monster in preparation for battle: "He became horrible, many-shaped, strange and unrecognizable," with one eye sucked into his skull and the other popping out of the side of the face (Davidson 84). Apparently this transformation was a familiar and meaningful one, because similarly distorted faces turn up frequently in Celtic art.

11   Often the transformation is helped along with drugs or social pressure of various kinds. Tahitian warriors were browbeaten into fighting by functionaries called Rauti, or "exhorters," who ran around the battlefield urging their comrades to mimic "the devouring wild dog" (Keeley 146). The ancient Greek hoplites drank enough wine, apparently, to be quite tipsy when they went into battle (Hanson 126); Aztecs drank pulque; Chinese troops at the time of Sun Tzu got into the mood by drinking wine and watching "gyrating sword dancers" perform (Griffith in Sun Tzu 37). Almost any drug or intoxicant has served, in one setting or another, to facilitate the transformation of man into warrior. Yanomamo Indians of the Amazon ingest a hallucinogen before battle; the ancient Scythians smoked hemp, while a neighboring tribe drank something called "hauma," which is believed to have induced a frenzy of aggression (Rolle 94–95). So if there is a destructive instinct that impels man to war, it is a weak one, and often requires a great deal of help.

12   In seventeenth-century Europe, the transformation of man into soldier took on a new form, more concerted and disciplined, and far less pleasant, than wine. New recruits and even seasoned veterans were endlessly drilled, hour after hour, until each man began to feel himself part of a single, giant fighting machine. The drill was only partially inspired by the technology of firearms. It's easy enough to teach a man to shoot a gun; the problem is to make him willing to get into situations where guns are being shot and to remain there long enough to do some shooting of his own. So modern military training aims at a transformation parallel to that achieved by "primitives" with war drums and paint: In the fanatical routines of boot camp, a man leaves behind his former identity and is reborn as a creature of the military—an automaton and also, ideally, a willing killer of other men.

13   This is not to suggest that killing is foreign to human nature or, more narrowly, to the male personality. Men (and women) have again and again proved themselves capable of killing impulsively and with gusto. But there is a huge difference between a war and an ordinary fight. War not only departs from the normal; it inverts all that is moral and right: In war one <u>should</u> kill, <u>should</u>

steal, <u>should</u> burn cities and farms, should perhaps even rape matrons and little girls. Whether or not such activities are "natural" or at some level instinctual, most men undertake them only by entering what appears to be an "altered state"—induced by drugs or lengthy drilling, and denoted by face paint or khakis.

14   The point of such transformative rituals is not only to put men "in the mood." Returning warriors may go through equally challenging rituals before they can celebrate victory or reenter the community—covering their heads in apparent shame, for example; vomiting repeatedly; abstaining from sex (Keeley 144). Among the Maori, returning warriors could not participate in the victory celebration until they had gone through a whaka-hoa ritual, designed to make them "common" again: The hearts of slain enemies were roasted, after which offerings were made to the war god Tu, and the rest was eaten by priests, who shouted spells to remove "the blood curse" and enable warriors to reenter their ordinary lives (Sagan 18). Among the Taulipang Indians of South America, victorious warriors "sat on ants, flogged one another with whips, and passed a cord covered with poisonous ants, through their mouth and nose" (Métraux 397). Such painful and shocking postwar rites impress on the warrior that war is much more than a "continuation of policy . . . by other means." In war men enter an alternative realm of human experience, as far removed from daily life as those things which we call "sacred."

Works Cited

Davidson, Hilda Ellis. *Myths and Symbols in Pagan Europe: Early Scandinavian and Celtic Religions.* Syracuse, NY: Syracuse UP, 1988.

Delbrück, Hans. *History of the Art of War, vol. 4. The Dawn of Modern Warfare.* Lincoln: U of Nebraska P, 1985.

Dumézil, Georges. *Destiny of the Warrior.* Chicago: U of Chicago P, 1969.

Fox, Robin. "Fatal Attraction: War and Human Nature." *The National Interest* (Winter 1992/93): 11–20.

Grossman, Lt. Col. Dave. *On Killing: The Psychological Cost of Learning to Kill in War and Society.* Boston: Little, Brown, 1995.

Hanson, Victor Davis. *The Western Way of War: Infantry Battle in Classical Greece.* New York: Knopf, 1989.

Keeley, Lawrence H. *War Before Civilization: The Myth of the Peaceful Savage.* New York: Oxford UP, 1996.

Kroeber, Clifton B., and Bernard L. Fontana. *Massacre on the Gila: An Account of the Last Major Battle Between American Indians, with Reflections on the Origin of War.* Tucson: U of Arizona P, 1986.

McCauley, Clark. "Conference Overview." *The Anthropology of War*. Ed. Jonathan Haas. Cambridge: Cambridge UP, 1990. 1–25.

Métraux, Alfred. "Warfare, Cannibalism, and Human Trophies." *Handbook of South American Indians*, vol. 5. Ed. Julian H. Steward. New York: Cooper Square, 1963. 383–409.

Mitchell, Timothy. *Colonizing Egypt*. Berkeley: U of California P, 1991.

O'Connell, Robert L. *Of Arms and Men: A History of War, Weapons, and Aggression*. New York: Oxford UP, 1989.

Rolle, Renate. *The World of the Scythians*. Berkeley: U of California P, 1989.

Sagan, Eli. *Cannibalism: Human Aggression and Cultural Form*. New York: Harper and Row, 1974.

Stoessinger, John G. *Why Nations Go to War*. New York: St. Martin's, 1993.

Stromberg, Roland. *Redemption by War: The Intellectuals and 1914*. Lawrence: U of Kansas P, 1982.

Sun Tzu. *The Art of War*. Trans. Samuel B. Griffith. London: Oxford UP, 1971.

Van Creveld, Martin. *The Transformation of War*. New York: Free Press, 1991.

Notes

[1]See, for example, Stoessinger, *Why Nations Go to War*, 14–20.

[2]See Grossman, *On Killing*.

[3]In the mythologies of the Indo-European tradition, Dumézil relates, thanks "either to a gift of metamorphosis, or to a monstrous heredity, the eminent warrior possesses a veritable animal nature" (140).

Research Paper Technique Questions

1. What do you think is Ehrenreich's purpose in writing the essay? Point out a passage in the essay that supports your answer.

_____

_____

_____

_____

_____

_____

2. What other information in the essay caused you to take the position you did in Question 1?

_____

_____

_____

_____

3. In the parenthetical reference marker following the quotation in paragraph 5, the author's name is not included along with the page number. Is this proper MLA formatting?

_____

_____

_____

4. In paragraph 1, Ehrenreich quotes the famous Prussian military officer Clausewitz's conclusion that wars are brought about in a rational, non-emotional way. Explain why you agree or disagree with Clausewitz's statement.

_____

_____

_____

CHAPTER REVIEW

▼ A research paper is an extended essay that uses documented sources to support, clarify, and exemplify your observations and conclusions.

▼ There are ten steps in writing a research paper: (1) Select a topic that you know you can find information about in the library or on the Internet. (2) Limit the topic by stating the paper's purpose. (3) Research the topic and take notes. (4) Outline your paper. (5) Select the quotations and citations that you will use to support your stated purpose. (6) Arrange the quotations and citations in the order they will be used. (7) Write the paper. (8) Document the citations using the appropriate format. (9) Proofread the paper for grammatical, spelling, and documentation format errors. (10) Prepare the paper for submission by making the necessary changes you found while proofreading.

▼ The documentation format used in a research paper depends on the subject area of the paper. Two frequently used formats are the Modern Language Association format and the American Psychological Association format.

Visit *The Write Start* Online!

For additional practice with the materials found in this chapter, visit our Website at

http://www.ablongman.com/checkett

The Website also features additional readings, quizzes, writing activities, and Internet links, as well as a bulletin board and interactive chat.

17

The Essay Exam

☆ look over
next week — in-class essay

It's one thing to write an essay when you have time to plan your approach and organization, do research, write a rough draft, and seek the advice and counsel of teachers and tutors. It is quite another when you have to write an in-class essay, most often without benefit of notes but with the added pressure of a very short time in which to accomplish the task.

Time and Grade

How you prepare quickly to answer a prompt for an essay exam rests largely on three elements: (1) the exam's time frame; (2) whether the exam comprises one essay question, multiple short-answer essay questions, or a mix of essay and other types of questions; (3) how much grading weight has been given to the various parts of the exam.

A one-hour exam might include true-or-false questions, fill-in-the-blank questions, one or more short essay questions, or one long essay question. It is important to know how much the test is worth as part of the semester grade, and it is also important to know how much each part of the test is worth. How much time and effort you spend on any one part of an exam ultimately depends on the value of each section of the test.

For instance, suppose the exam period is one hour. The exam consists of a single essay prompt and some true or false questions, and the essay is worth 75 points out of 100 for the entire exam. You should certainly spend 30–45 minutes out of the hour on it, with 10–15 minutes given to the other questions. Or, if you have 90 minutes to answer three short-answer essay questions, then you would want to give 30 minutes to each question because they surely will be given equal weight when graded by the instructor.

It goes without saying that you should always try to do your best on any exam. But you should take into account time frames and weight of grade when you allot the time necessary to finish an essay exam or the essay portion of an exam with a variety of questions.

Key Terms in Essay Questions

Essay questions are *prompts*. The prompt either identifies one topic or a list from which you can choose one or more topics to write about. After receiving the prompt, never begin writing immediately. Take a few minutes to make a plan. Before making a plan, however, you need to be certain what the prompt is asking you to do. Understanding the key terms of the prompt will go a long way in helping you figure out how to respond. Study the following steps.

1. Read the prompt several times to identify the key terms in the prompt. These key terms will often tell you the approach (the kind of response) the instructor is looking for.

   ▼ *analyze/explain*: explain how a process works and why the process is important.

   ▼ *argue/discuss*: take a stand or have a definite point of view supported by evidence (such as facts, statistics, examples, and quotations from experts).

   ▼ *cause/effect*: if cause, identify the reasons for something occurring; if effect, identify the results of something occurring. Some questions will want you to explain both the causes and effects.

   ▼ *classify*: divide the topic idea into categories and relate why the categories are important.

   ▼ *compare/contrast*: if comparison, discuss how two or more items are similar; if contrast, discuss how two or more items are different from one another.

   ▼ *define*: write an extended definition in which you choose examples to illustrate the concept's meaning.

   ▼ *evaluate*: discuss the pros and cons of an issue, and make a judgment.

   ▼ *illustrate:* give specific examples of a general topic.

   ▼ *narrate:* describe something that happened.

   ▼ *summarize*: briefly present the main ideas from a list of many ideas, some major and some minor.

2. Once you have the topic and the approach identified, select those specific ideas that will support your thesis concerning the topic. Because you have studied the thesis statement with essay map in this book, we suggest using it to organize your response. The essay map is a multiple-item series that identifies the subtopics you will use to explain your response to the overall topic. The essay map allows you to state your conclusion and organizational approach to a topic quickly and clearly. It is an outline in sentence form.

3. Use each of your essay map items (we suggest two or three) as the topic of each corresponding body paragraph in which you will develop your ideas concerning the overall topic.

4. Try to save a few minutes to check your essay for sentence fragments (incomplete ideas) and spelling errors. Neatly write in corrections.

Prompts with Thesis Statement and Essay Map Examples

Following are examples of prompts that could be asked in a variety of college courses. Also provided are possible thesis statements that are mini-outlines for the essay to be written.

Sociology

Prompt:	Explain the meaning of "class stratification" in relation to education and employment.
Key term: meaning.	The approach is to define the term by showing how it relates to two aspects of society.
Possible thesis:	<u>Class stratification negatively affects poor people by making it more difficult for them to go to college and to get meaningful employment.</u>

History

Prompt:	Analyze the reasons for the rise of Germany's militarism prior to World War II.
Key term: analyze.	The approach will be to explain how the events after World War I led to the rise of Hitler and his military forces.
Possible thesis:	<u>The stringent terms placed on Germany by the Treaty of Versailles, coupled with the world-wide economic depression, led to the rise of Hitler's military machine prior to World War II.</u>

Business

Prompt:	Discuss the causes of the 1982 economic stagnation in the United States.
Key term: causes.	The approach will be to identify and discuss those economic policies and events that led to the economic downturn.
Possible thesis:	<u>High interest rates, soaring fuel costs, and high unemployment led to the 1982 economic crisis in America.</u>

Art

Prompt:	Summarize the history of Modern Art from the mid-19th century until the present using three specific "schools" as your reference points.
Key term: summarize.	The approach will be to divide Modern Art into three parts and briefly explain why each of three "schools" represents modern artistic evolution.
Possible thesis:	<u>The history of modern art can be traced to the elements of three schools of painting: Impressionism, Surrealism, and Cubism.</u>

Criminology

Prompt:	Defend the position that the insanity defense should be abolished.
Key term: defend (argue).	The approach will be to use evidence to support the idea that the insanity defense should be eliminated.

Possible thesis:	The insanity defense should be abolished because "insanity" is a legal term not a psychological one, incarceration in a mental institution is not punishment, and parole boards do not have control over when the "prisoner/patient" is released.

Literature

Prompt:	Compare two symbols in Frost's poems "Stopping by Woods on a Snowy Evening" and "Desert Places."
Key term: compare.	The approach is to choose two symbols in each poem and discuss their similarities.
Possible thesis:	The snow and the woods in Frost's poems "Stopping by Woods on a Snowy Evening"and "Desert Places" represent loneliness.

Remember, before you can write about a topic, you must understand the question's focus regarding the topic. Identify the key term in the prompt, and then write your thesis.

PRACTICE   Writing Timed Essays

Your skill and confidence in taking essay exams will increase the more you practice timed essay writing. Over the next few weeks, practice by writing essays for the following prompts. Be certain to use only the amount of time stated in each prompt.

1. *The prompt:* In any discussion, the participants must define terms to avoid misunderstanding and confusion. Pick one of the following terms and write an essay clarifying what you mean when you use it in a specific context: freedom, conservative, maturity, intelligence, liberal, beauty, success, independent, wealth.

   Time: 15 minutes.

   Grade value: 25% of exam.

   Key term: _____

2. *The prompt:* Scientists have been cloning sheep, mice, and other animals for a number of years. Now, however, scientists are exploring cloning a human. Write an essay in which you evaluate the pros and cons of cloning a human.

   Time: 30 minutes.

   Grade value: 50% of exam.

   Key term: _____

3. *The prompt:* Although a few young people from poor backgrounds find success in movies such as *Good Will Hunting* and *Finding Forester*, poor economic environments cause many young people to fail in school and in their personal lives. Write an essay about poverty's devastating effects on young people.

Time: 60 minutes

Grade value: 100% of exam.

Key term: _____

4. *The prompt:* Imagine you live next to a small, beautiful park. The park consists of a pond, a walking trail, a gazebo, and stands of shade trees and flowering shrubs. You find out that there is a plan being put before the city council to build a mega-store and parking lot where the park is located. The mega-store will mean 200 full- and part-time jobs and tens of thousands of tax dollars for the community. Write an essay in which you contrast the value of the new mega-store versus that of the park for the people of the community.

Time: 2 hours

Grade value: 25% of total semester grade.

Key term: _____

Introductory and Concluding Techniques

While you may not be able to quote statistics or famous people in the introduction or conclusion of your exam essay (unless the exam is open-book or one for which you can bring prepared notes), you can construct a good introduction and conclusion. Refer to Chapter 4, "The Introductory Paragraph, and Chapter 6," "The Concluding Paragraph," to review the techniques for effectively introducing your thesis and for giving your essay a sense of completeness. Try to memorize the various types of techniques; often, the prompt will suggest an idea that will help you create a few interesting lead-in sentences in the introductory paragraph and a relevant concluding remark.

CHAPTER REVIEW

▼ Writing an essay exam always involves the added pressure of limited time, and usually involves the added challenge of relying on your memory for ideas and facts. It's a good idea to pace yourself on an essay exam, allowing time in proportion to the essay question's value in the exam or semester grade.

▼ Essay questions are prompts, and they contain key terms that indicate the approach that you should take in your answer.

▼ Use an essay map to plan your essay before writing it.

Visit *The Write Start* Online!

For additional practice with the materials found in this chapter, visit our Website at

http://www.ablongman.com/checkett

The Website also features additional readings, quizzes, writing activities, and Internet links, as well as a bulletin board and interactive chat.

CHAPTER

18 Literary Criticism

Criticism has various meanings. In academic work, it refers to the act of making judgments, evaluations, or interpretations of original creations in the world of art, music, literature, philosophy, or the various social sciences. Such judgments may be favorable, unfavorable, or neutral. A critical essay or term paper contains the student's evaluation or interpretation of some aspect of another person's work.

But what of the audience that will read your critical papers? You may be asking yourself, what can my interpretations of an artistic or literary work do for other people? We can approach this question by pursuing another question: What do *you* look for when you read a review of a movie, play, or book? Do you want to know why a certain character behaved in a certain way? Did the plot puzzle you? Do you want to confirm your own ideas about a work by seeking the knowledgeable opinion of someone else? These are all reasons we read movie reviews and other criticism. As a writer of criticism, you should approach these very same questions when you critique another's work.

What are the demands placed upon a critical writer? First, the writer must have firsthand knowledge of the work. Also, the writer must be perceptive, sensitive, and analytical. The writer must also support his or her opinions by directly referring to specific passages or characteristics of the work to support the points made in the criticism.

In college, much of the criticism you write is literary criticism. When you write literary criticism, you should try to satisfy the demands that you as a reader make on other critics. The first step in the process is a careful reading of the poem, story, novel, play, or essay. But how do you go about this? What is it that you should look for in a literary work that will lead you to conclusions about the work itself?

The Elements of Literary Analysis

When reporters construct a story, they answer six questions about the events: who, what, where, when, why, and how. When analyzing literature, the critical writer takes the same approach. Only in literature, different labels are used when you analyze the events of the poem, short story, novel, or play: character (who), plot (what), setting (where), time (when), theme (why), and technique (how).

273

The Questions	The Areas	The Issues
Who?	Character	The function, traits, and credibility of the people in the work.
What?	Plot	The series of related actions involving a problem that builds to a crisis and is resolved.
Where?	Setting	The physical location and general environs, including social, political, and other conditions affecting the characters.
When?	Time	The time structure of the work and the period it is set in.
Why?	Theme	The central or controlling idea that is conveyed mainly through the characters and plot.
How?	Technique	The author's use of language devices to make an effect.

By asking these questions of a literary work and by searching for satisfying answers, you should be better able to analyze and understand it. You should then be better able to communicate your judgments about the work to your reader.

Character: Who?

How Do Writers Develop a Character?
There are two basic ways that writers develop their characters:

▼ In the *expository method,* the narrator tells us about the characters.

▼ In the *dramatic method,* the characters reveal themselves through their own words, thoughts, and actions.

What Is the Result of the Characterization?
The characters can be thought of in terms of the way they are characterized:

▼ **Static characters** remain essentially unchanged throughout the work.

▼ **Developing characters** undergo some significant change or changes.

▼ **Round characters** are presented as complicated, multidimensional individuals.

▼ **Flat characters** are portrayed as representative, incomplete, or not complex—as types rather than individuals.

What Is the Character's Function?
Characters usually function in one of three ways:

▼ **Central characters** have a great impact on the story, and the story revolves around these characters. For example, in Herman Melville's classic novel about whaling and personal obsession, *Moby Dick,* central character

Captain Ahab is obsessed with hunting down and killing the great white whale that bit off his leg in a previous encounter, even to the point where he endangers the ship and crew. Another central character is Ishmael, a naive sailor and the narrator of the story, who is the spiritual opposite of Ahab.

▼ **Supporting characters** add to the overall understanding of the story. As Ahab's first officer, Starbuck must continually balance his loyalty to his captain and his loyalty to the crew and to the ship's owners. He must explain Ahab's actions to the crew to keep them from mutiny, and he must remind Ahab that the ship's owners expect their whaling contract to be fulfilled, and that the ship and its crew are not there to help Ahab seek revenge against Moby Dick.

▼ **Background characters** add to the overall description and reality of the story. The seamen, as they go about their ship's chores, represent the delights and fears and the knowledge and ignorance of all people who are at the mercy of an unfair and maniacal authority. The crew, because of their dress, activities, language, and interactions with each other, help flesh out the story and give it authenticity.

Does the Character Change?

Most central characters in a literary work change as a result of their experiences. For example, in Stephan Crane's novel *The Red Badge of Courage*, set during the Civil War, Henry Fleming goes off to war as a young man full of bravado, commits an act of cowardice, and then, by facing his fears, redeems himself through discovering his own courage.

But some central characters do not change. In stark contrast to Henry Fleming, Captain Ahab, in *Moby Dick*, does not change at all from the first time we meet him until the last we see him as he disappears beneath the sea, lashed to the great white whale's body by the rope of his own harpoon.

Look for a change, determine whether and how and why it takes place—or does not—and you will gain more insight into the character.

What Is Your Overall Impression of the Character?

After you have answered the questions above, you are ready to run a tally. What does it all add up to? Is the character admirable or not? Or, more crudely put, is the character a good guy or a bad guy? Sometimes the answer is simple. For example, Fagin in *Oliver Twist* is a villain because he trains young boys to steal and rob, while Antony in *Julius Caesar* is a hero because his actions are motivated by his desire to have Rome governed by moral and responsible leadership.

More often than not, central characters are somewhere in between, not pictured as all good or all evil. Trying to arrive at some conclusion about them, therefore, forces you to analyze them in some depth.

How Credible Is the Character?

When you evaluate whether a character is credible or believable, look at the following:

▼ *Motivation.* Does the character have believable motives for his or her actions?

▼ *Consistency.* Are the characters consistent? Generally, we should be able to anticipate how a character will respond in certain situations based on previous actions. Jim, in Joseph Conrad's *Lord Jim*, dreams of being a hero, yet he fails to act heroically time after time when presented with situations in which bravery is called for.

▼ *Individuality.* A character must be handled reasonably. Although consistency is important, if a character behaves too consistently, he or she may lack the complexity necessary for growth. Individual idiosyncrasies must be allowed for if the characters are to represent mankind with all its frailties and aberrations. There is a need in most central characters for a certain complexity for depth of meaning and reader interest. Therefore, the inept Willie Loman, in Arthur Miller's *Death of a Salesman,* can be both a loving husband and father and a womanizer and poor role model for his sons.

Plot: What?

The plot consists of a series of related actions. The events build to a climax, and then the problems developed as the plot unfolds come to a resolution. The events of the plot can occur in the following manner:

▼ The events in **chronological plots** are portrayed in natural time sequence.

▼ In **inverted plots**, the events are portrayed out of sequence.

▼ In some plots, a **flashback** is used to interrupt the chronological sequence so that a past event can be introduced.

The Basic Elements of the Plot

A plot has several basic elements: exposition, complication, rising action, climax, falling action, and resolution. Usually they occur in that order.

▼ **Exposition** introduces you to the universe of the work and to the characters and their interrelationships. It allows you to discover where you are, who the people are, and what kind of social, physical, and cultural surroundings they live in. It also can inform you about the narrator's point of view.

▼ **Complication** closely follows the exposition because readers require some problem or conflict to stimulate interest.

▼ **Rising action** occurs because of the conflicts arising from the complication. Increased emotional effect is created when additional events or ramifications happen.

▼ **Climax** is the point at which the protagonists learn a truth that forever changes them. In Sophocles' play *Oedipus,* the married King and Queen of Thebes, Oedipus and Jocasta, learn that they are mother and son and that Oedipus killed Jocasta's first husband, Laius (Oedipus' father).

▼ **Falling action** are those events that happen after the climax. Normally, there is a lessening of tension, and the actions are less dramatic.

▼ **Resolution** (often called *denouement*) occurs when the complications are resolved, but not necessarily in a satisfactory way when compared to the traditional legal, ethical, or moral values of society.

When evaluating a plot or piece of a plot you should also consider foreshadowing, reliance on chance, unity, and the plausibility of the ending.

▼ **Foreshadowing** is a device to prepare readers for what is to follow. It may take the form of a strange remark ("Beware the Ides of March" in *Julius Caesar*), a prophecy, or some other foreboding image.

▼ **Reliance on chance** occurs when the lives of the characters are manipulated by chance occurrences or by probable happenings. Generally, chance is fine in the exposition to make things more complicated, but you should be wary of chance in the resolution of a work because the author may be using it to create an easy way out of a complicated plot.

▼ **Unity** is achieved when all the events in the plot contribute to the development of the plot. Are they necessary? For example, are the sex scenes in much of today's popular literature really necessary for plot development, or are they thrown in to titillate the reader? Is it soul or sale that the author is interested in?

▼ **Plausibility of the ending** is achieved when the resolution is both logical, growing naturally out of the plot, and satisfying, concluding logically from the issues raised in the work. You should be particularly wary of happy endings created by chance or by sudden character transformations (for example, a hardened criminal suddenly wants to become a priest).

Setting: Where?

Setting consists of both spatial (house, community, region, country) and cultural qualities (social, moral, economic, political, psychological). The setting can create an atmosphere, playing on our feelings about certain locations. Poe's settings in "The Fall of the House of Usher" and "The Cask of Amontillado" greatly add to the suspense and to the mood of gloom, melancholy, and apprehension in those stories.

The setting can also serve as a force in conflict with human desires and endeavors. In James Dickey's *Deliverance*, the central characters battle the river as much as they battle human antagonists. In Ernest Hemingway's *The Old Man and the Sea*, Santiago fights nature's creatures (sharks) as well as himself.

Setting also includes the human environment apart from the physical. We are shaped by the religious, social, moral, and political worlds in which we live. We must consider these aspects of life when we critique how characters act and respond to their world.

Time: When?

In what period of time does the work take place? What is the significance of its being set at that time? What difference would it make if the work were set in another time?

How does the author handle the passage of time in the work? Does the plot follow a natural, chronological time sequence, or does the author use flashbacks or inverted plot elements? For example, Kurt Vonnegut Jr. uses flashbacks in *Slaughterhouse Five*. What are the advantages or disadvantages of each method?

Theme: Why?

The question "Why?" as it applies to literary analysis of theme commits you to examine the ideas, particularly the central idea, in a work to determine what statement it makes about life in general or about a specific facet of life. Every work, no matter how slight, contains some basic observation about the nature of people, the freedom of the individual, the opportunity for happiness, the role of society, the importance of love, the discovery of self, the existence of evil, or some other important subject.

The theme grows out of the ending or, more specifically, out of how the complications are resolved. Often, at this point, either the action exemplifies the central idea, or a favorably presented character expresses it. But there are other ways to support and express opinions about a theme. Almost everything in a work, all those elements we have talked about so far, should point to and contribute to the theme.

Questions to Determine Theme

In some works, thematic ideas are not stated by characters or suggested in titles. Here are some questions you should ask of the work to determine theme.

▼ What happens to the central character or characters? Why?

▼ Was what happened the characters' own fault or due to forces beyond their control? If the action was a character's own fault, what weakness did it reveal?

▼ If the character overcame a difficulty, what new realization or trait did the resolution require?

▼ Did the other characters have similar problems? What do their actions reveal?

▼ If the central character's problem cannot be attributed to human weakness, what was it caused by?

▼ Can this problem be overcome? If so, how? If not, how can human beings cope with it?

▼ Are people or things (animals, etc.) portrayed as good or evil or indifferent?

▼ Do the characters find happiness? If not, why not? If so, why? How?

▼ Is nature favorable or unfavorable, hospitable or inhospitable? Why?

▼ Does the work make any statement about ethical, religious, economic, social, or political matters?

▼ Does the work provide any insight into psychological problems about sex, love, death, guilt, alienation, chance happenings, or other issues?

Generally, a theme should not be a moral, a commandment, or a directive about how to live or what to do. Rather, it is a statement about life and people—an observation, a pronouncement, a verdict.

Of all the elements in a literary work, the theme is the most difficult to perceive. The difficulty in uncovering the theme stems from the work's presentation of specifics: certain characters in certain places at certain times engaged in certain actions. On the other hand, the theme is an abstraction, a generalization. Consequently, you need to consider all the elements in a work to arrive at the theme. Once you have established the theme after considering all the elements, you can then discuss the theme in relation to each element independent of the other elements.

Problems to Avoid

When discussing theme, you should avoid two problems:

1. Unless it is a specific instruction in the assignment, do not discuss how the work affected you personally. Although it is natural to identify with characters and situations, you should detach yourself when writing critically. Suppress your personal grievances and preferences and respond to

the work on its own merits, objectively and intellectually. Focus on the work, not on your own emotional reaction to it.

2. Do not assume that you know what the author intended the work to mean—even if you have read his or her comments about it. You should not ignore an author's comments, but you should realize that the comments are not the only possibilities. For instance, the author could be untruthful, might not remember all the thematic values, or might not realize some of the unconscious networks of ideas connected in the work. Criticize the work based on the elements of literary analysis you are studying in this chapter.

Technique: How?

No work can be adequately discussed without an analysis of how the writer crafted it. In literary analysis this usually involves *point of view, language devices,* and *word selection.*

Point of View

Point of view refers to the type of narrator. Who tells the story?

▼ A *first-person observer* is a narrator involved in the story from the sidelines who speaks as "I." This first-person narrator tells the story from his or her perspective. The information you get is limited by what the narrator can know or surmise. Therefore, it is not necessarily true or accurate.

▼ A *first-person participant* is a narrator involved in the action who speaks as "I." This narrator relates the story as if it is just occurring, although flashbacks can be used to give new information or perspectives to episodes of the plot. This narrator is also one of the characters in the story. The events of the story, therefore, are filtered through the eyes of the narrator and are, consequently, open to inaccuracies and misperceptions.

▼ A *third-person narrator* relates the story in the third person and does not speak as "I" or appear as a character. Sometimes the third-person narrator comments on the thoughts of the characters and passes judgment. Sometimes this narrator simply records the action without commentary. The information from this narrator is considered accurate and truthful.

Language Devices

Writers often attempt to clarify and explain ideas through the use of special language devices. These language constructions also make the story, its characters, and its themes more interesting and compelling. For example, writers frequently make use of symbols. A **symbol** is an object that has taken on abstract meaning and value. The most effective symbols are a natural part of the story. In *The Old Man and the Sea*, for instance, the sharks are both natural inhabitants of the setting and representatives of the natural forces around us with which we must cope.

Concepts can also be symbols. The "Catch-22" rule in the novel of the same name is a rule that comes to represent the stupid workings of bureaucracy and the frustration of trying to cope logically and reasonably with entities that have top-heavy administrations, such as those found in the military and the corporate world. A writer can use a symbol to communicate the theme or central idea of the work.

Another language device is **metaphor,** a statement in which one thing is used to explain another. In a metaphor, a description is offered in the form of an equation as if one thing *is* another, even though we know it actually is not. "Smith is a lion among men." Metaphors state an imaginary identity. They claim that fictions are, in a symbolic way, unusual truths. We know Smith is not a lion, but the metaphor suggests that he shares many lion-like qualities: he is powerful, loud, aggressive like a predator, and he is king of the jungle.

A **simile,** like a metaphor, creates a relationship between two entities. With a simile, however, the relationship is not as forceful. Whereas the metaphor infers that one thing *is* another, the simile states that one thing is "like" or "as" another thing. For example, a simile would state that "Smith is *like* a lion among men." Or "Smith is gentle *as* a lamb."

In **personification,** animals, objects, or even ideas are given human emotions or characteristics. For example, "The hyenas *cheated* the vultures out of a meal," or "The sled *rested* in the basement after a long day on the snowy hill," or "Love *danced* in their eyes."

A **paradox** is a statement that appears self-contradictory on first reading, but after a closer reading, the statement actually makes sense. For instance, a parent, just before spanking a child, might say, "This is going to hurt me worse than it will you." The parent means that punishing the child will cause the parent emotional pain.

An **oxymoron** is a form of paradox. An oxymoron occurs when two words are used side by side to create a startling or unusual effect. "Jumbo shrimp," "deafening silence," and "sweet sorrow" are examples of oxymorons.

Word Selection

The words that writers choose and how those words are put together influence the reader's perception of the meaning that the writer is trying to portray. Words and combinations of words can have *denotative* and *connotative* meaning.

Denotative language is the use of words in their accepted, dictionary-defined sense. For example, the heart is an organ in the body that acts as a pump in circulating blood throughout the body. On the other hand, **connotative** language is the use of words that have (or develop) associations and implications apart from their explicit sense. Thus, the heart represents love ("She has given her heart to her partner"), empathy ("He has a lot of heart"), or courage ("She has the heart of a lion"—this is also a metaphor).

Abstract language is the use of words that refer to ideas or concepts that cannot be perceived through the senses: "He wears his heart on his sleeve" (*heart* is used to indicate an emotional state).

Concrete language is the use of specific words to portray the unique complex nature of the real world: "The hot asphalt sent waves of volcanic steam into the teeming, sweating crowd jostling shoulder to shoulder under the sweltering heat of the noonday sun" (a passage to support the idea that the city can be a difficult place in which to live).

Irony can be either *verbal* or *situational*. It creates a reality the opposite from what appears true. *Verbal irony* occurs when someone says something but means the opposite, such as when someone does something less than intelligently and is told, "Way to go, Einstein!" *Situational irony* occurs when something that happens creates a reality that is the opposite of what is expected. For example, Oedipus kills Laius, but Oedipus does not know that Laius is his father. In killing him, Oedipus unknowingly fulfills a prophecy that he would someday kill his father.

The Thesis Statement in Literary Analysis

When called upon to write a literary analysis, you will need a central idea that focuses on a topic and states your opinion about some aspect of the topic. The thesis statement will focus your thoughts about the topic.

The thesis statement should exhibit five properties:

1. Author
2. Genre
3. Title
4. Topic
5. Evaluation of topic

Examples

In Robert Frost's poem "Design," white represents death/life.
(1) (2) (3) (4) (5)

In John Updike's short story "A&P," Sammy's actions at the end are not realistic based on the exposition.
(1) (2) (3) (4) (5)

In Shirley Jackson's short story "The Lottery," the conclusion is foreshadowed by three earlier events.
(1) (2) (3) (4) (5)

In Hemingway's short story "Soldier's Home," the title is ironic.
(1) (2) (3) (4) (5)

Your thesis can also display a sixth element, the essay map that you have studied elsewhere in this text (some texts also call this a *forecasting thesis*), because the elements of the thesis statement are the body paragraph topics that support and explain the overall topic.

If an essay map were included in each of the thesis statements above, each would become a forecasting thesis and might be rewritten as follows.

Examples

In Robert Frost's poem "Design," the **white spider, moth, and flower** represent a cycle of life/death.

In John Updike's short story "A&P," Sammy's actions at the end of the story are not realistic based on his **character, the setting, and the atmosphere** as offered in the exposition.

In Shirley Jackson's short story "The Lottery," the conclusion is foreshadowed by the condition of the **lottery items and rituals, the crowd's nervousness, and the boys' actions.**

In Ernest Hemingway's short story "Soldier's Home," Harold's relationships with his **parents, other soldiers, and females** cause the title to be ironic.

> The following is an analysis of the Robert Frost poem "After Apple-Picking," from his book of poems *North of Boston* (1914). The paper focuses on the central metaphor of the poem (apple-picking) that the poet has created to carry the theme. The paper also cites from outside sources and uses the MLA documentation format (see Chapter 16).

After Apple-Picking
Robert Frost

My long two-pointed ladder's sticking through a tree
Toward heaven still,
And there's a barrel that I didn't fill
Beside it, and there may be two or three
5 Apples I didn't pick upon some bough.
But I am done with apple-picking now.
Essence of winter sleep is on the night,
The scent of apples: I am drowsing off.
I cannot rub the strangeness from my sight
10 I got from looking through a pane of glass
I skimmed this morning from the drinking trough
And held against the world of hoary grass.
It melted, and I let it fall and break.
But I was well
15 Upon my way to sleep before it fell,
And I could tell
What form my dreaming was about to take.
Magnified apples appear and disappear,
Stem end and blossom end,
20 And every fleck of russet showing clear.
My instep arch not only keeps the ache
It keeps the pressure of a ladder-round.
I feel the ladder sway as the boughs bend.
And I keep hearing from the cellar bin
25 The rumbling sound
Of load on load of apples coming in.
For I have had too much
Of apple-picking: I am overtired
Of the great harvest I myself desired.
30 There were ten thousand thousand fruit to touch,
Cherish in hand, lift down, and not let fall.
For all
That struck the earth,
No matter if not bruised or spiked with stubble,
35 Went surely to the cider-apple heap
As of no worth.
One can see what will trouble
This sleep of mine, whatever sleep it is.
Were he not gone,
40 The woodchuck could say whether it's like his
Long sleep, as I describe its coming on,
Or just some human sleep.

John Smith

Literature 302

Professor Jones

June 1, 2004

To Pick or Not To Pick—That Is the Question

1   In Robert Frost's poem "After Apple-Picking," the analogy between a person's life and the seasons is well paralleled. The metaphor is quite simply stated: as apple-picking takes place in late fall, when the harvest of life is over and the prospect that awaits is winter, is the season of snow and ice a coming of death or merely a temporary dormancy?

2   Apple-picking becomes, then, the central metaphor of a particular activity within the larger construct of life. The problem proffered is whether to attach to the "After" of the title a finality (death) or a shorter cessation that has at its core a continuation. That latter thesis seems to have more support within the conventions of the poem.

3   On the surface, the poem's description of the activity is told in a straightforward fashion. A farmer has just finished harvesting the crop of apples in his orchard, and the toughness of the job has made him enormously tired. One can empathize with the farmer because he has obviously taken great care to tend the trees through the spring and summer and has worked very long hours in harvesting the crop. But his excitement is tempered by the aching in his arches from standing long hours on the ladder picking the apples and from the realization that he won't be able to harvest all of the apples. Many of them lay bruised and battered on the ground and are destined for the "cider-apple heap" (35). On the surface of it, this might be interpreted as human endeavors often end up negatively.

4   But, on further inquiry, the loss of some apples should be expected. To make too much of this scene is to bring to it too much of the ideal and not enough of the real. Frost's realism would be undermined if one expected no loss during the process. Even the tiredness of the farmer should be expected. After all, according to Alvan Ryan,

> Few of Frost's protagonists are passive victims, nor do they escape into a romantic dream-world; we see them at a moment of crisis confronting the existential situation in

all its ironic reality. And they have the integrity that comes with the awareness, however dim, that more than circumstances is involved in their trials. Somehow they have chosen, and would not have it otherwise. (136)

All around the farmer autumn is setting in and making ready for the long winter. The woodchuck is hibernating in its burrow, and the leaves are falling off the trees as they go dormant. Even the farmer lies on his bed wearied from his toil. It would seem obvious, then, that winter, commingled with these other details, becomes death. However, other interpretations come to the fore upon closer examination.

5   In the first two lines, the "two-pointed ladder's sticking through a tree / Toward heaven still" (1–2) could readily be seen as an affirmation of something joyously attained after hard work is finished. Heaven, after all, has an aspect of death necessary for its attainment, but it also is a symbol of rebirth because of the infinitely wonderful life bestowed on its entrants. Additionally, the woodchuck is only hibernating—he will awaken from his "death" in the spring to resume life. Both the ladder pointing skyward and the woodchuck represent the potential for a reawakening to occur in the spring. The cycle is not at all interrupted; rather, it is a process that unfolds naturally, albeit haltingly, on an annual basis.

6   The farmer, to be sure, is apprehensive, frustrated, and somewhat overwhelmed. But considering the Puritan work ethic endemic in the eastern United States (and one Frost was particularly aware of and did not altogether share), this should not be unexpected. As Lawrance Thompson observes,

> Most of the Puritans were more bold than talented in their attempts to prove that art is concerned with directing the individual to apprehension; that art is therefore a means to knowledge and truth . . . Robert Frost's poetic theory, quite at odds with Puritan aesthetics, is nevertheless colored by his Yankee heritage of Puritan teaching. His own belief in poetry as "a clarification of life" seems to have close relation to the Puritan ideal "provided they could be inspired with flexible vitality." (32)

7   The frustration and weariness sets in because of the emotional let-down occurring when the farmer realizes that the original goal of picking the "ten thousand thousand fruit" (30) was not possible—that no matter how good and noble our intentions, the fruit of our life's work will often be bruised and apportioned to the apple-cider pile (34–35). With this realization comes a certain resignation that, coupled with weariness, the daily toil seems not worth all the effort. This, again, is a quite natural feeling produced by circumstance.

8   But the farmer says "I am done with apple-picking now" (6). It is important to note that the line ends with the word "now," not "forever." Again, there is the hint, the suggestion, that the farmer's mental and spiritual predicament is only a temporary state. The resolution comes to the farmer in the form of an evolutionary triumvirate of thought: to rest from the work, to judge his performance, and to eventually accept his conclusion.

9   Thankfully, Frost does not lead us to a prettily wrapped conclusion. His observations of humans and their world are depicted in terms that solidify humanity's cyclical relationship with nature in both positive and negative terms. Each symbol works, making the metaphorical insights move toward a rendering that both pleases and disturbs in its tenuous fragility.

[next page]

Works Cited

Ryan, Alvan S. "Frost and Emerson: Voice and Vision." Critical Essays on Robert Frost. Ed. Phillip Gerber. Boston: G. K. Hall, 1982. 124–37.

Thompson, Lawrance. "Robert Frost's Theory of Poetry." Robert Frost: A Collection of Critical Essays. Ed. James Cox. Englewood Cliffs: Prentice-Hall, 1962. 16–35.

Sample Literary Analysis of a Novel: *SULA* BY TONI MORRISON

> The following is an analysis of Nobel Laureate Toni Morrison's 1973 novel *Sula*. The essay focuses on the difficulties that young black women have in transitioning into adulthood, considering that their chance is slim of meeting a black man who is ready and able to establish and carry on a mature relationship.

Black Woman's Burden

1   Toni Morrison's novel Sula (1973) concerns the lifelong relationship between two black women, Sula and Nel. Growing up in a poor, black neighborhood, Sula and Nel develop a relationship of shared dreams and secret desires. But their beautiful bond suffers when Sula leaves to conquer the unknown cities of America while Nel settles down as wife and mother. When Sula returns, she has changed to the extent that she is a virtual stranger, repelling everyone, including Nel.

2   A brief sketch of the males presented in the novel is necessary to indicate the overwhelmingly negative effect that males have on the evolution of black females in Toni Morrison's world.

Shadrack: A World War I soldier who went to fight for his country and returned insane. He symbolizes, through the town's establishment of a National Suicide Day, the eventual destruction of community, as portrayed by Shadrack leading townspeople to a tunnel that collapses, killing them.

Plum: A junkie. He is not only a negative role model representative of the lack of potential husbands for black women, but he is killed by his mother so that he won't destroy her life. In this instance, the male is shown to be a negative force through his own choices (drugs) and through the destruction of the black male by the female (out of self-preservation). The irony is as obvious as it is terrible. Throughout the novel, Morrison lets the reader know that this emasculation is as complex for the male as the maturation process is for the female.

Chicken Little: The male child who symbolizes the male potential. He dies "accidentally" at the hand of Sula as Nel watches, as a silent co-conspirator of sorts. Considering Sula's promiscuity in later life and Nel's unfulfilled married life later on, this event is fraught with self-destructive overtones.

White, Irish boys: They torment the black children on the way home from school. Sula attempts to overcome their brutishness, but she only ends up cutting off the tip of her finger in a futile gesture of defiance.

Wiley: Nel's father, a cook on a ship. His absence sets up a matriarchal family situation.

Jude: Nel's husband, who has an adulterous affair with Sula. This is double commentary on the role of black men and the capriciousness of female relationships without acceptable and complementary relationships with black men.

Ajax: Sula's husband, who leaves her because he feels that she is becoming too possessive.

3   It becomes obvious that the absence of black role models in reference to the possibility of future stable relationships between black women and black men (i.e., marriages) is accidental, self-induced, and both societal and self-imposed by black males. This is, then, a very complex situation that black females find themselves in, and it is understandably difficult for them to complete the initiation process into complete, mature, defined adulthood. As Jane Bakerman comments, "Both the Peace and Wright families are essentially fatherless; thus, the girls learn their most important lessons from their mothers, and in each case, the mother fails her daughter" (549). The problem, then, becomes the quintessential "vicious circle." The mother, unable to form a good, long-lasting union with a mature male, hasn't the ability to be a comprehensive role model for her daughters. Bakerman continues, "Though the initiations of Sula Peace and Nel Wright also fail . . . it is still made clear that Sula and Nel are undervalued and that their families legislate toward the initiation failure, [sic] both girls make specific decisions and choices which also contribute" (548). But it must be remembered that Sula and Nel have mothers and grandmothers whose actions are based predominantly on a lack of support by males. They are forced to do what black females, left economically disadvantaged in a hostile society, can only do given their meager environment.

4   The main thrust of the novel falls on Sula and Nel. Their friendship is ultimately destroyed because of their inability to become "whole" women, just as this eluded their mothers and grandmothers. Their initiation left them incomplete. As this drew them together, it eventually tore them apart. Toni Morrison comments, "that there was a little bit of both in each of those two women, and that if they had been one person, I suppose they would have been a rather marvelous person. But each one lacked something the other one had" (Stepto 476). Sula represents "freedom," and Nel represents "constraint." But neither fulfills these designations. Morrison continues, "[Sula] is a woman who's an adventurer, who breaks rules . . . . Not a law-abiding woman. Nel knows and believes in all the laws of that community . . . . But there's a fatal flaw in all of that, you know, in both of those things. Nel does not make that "leap"—she doesn't know about herself" (476). But, ultimately, neither does Sula.

5   Sula is as incomplete as Nel. She not only loses Ajax, but because of her seduction of Nel's husband, she loses Nel as well. Their symbiotic relationship is never consummated later in life as it should be for old friends. As Carolyn Jones observes,

> During their childhood and adolescence, Nel provides Sula with restraint, and Sula offers Nel courage [the freedom and constraint paradigm]. More important, they offer each other a kind of security that neither finds in her own family . . . . Sula is cut off from the only relationship that gives her life meaning . . . [and] Nel too is rendered incomplete when her friendship with Sula dissolves. (621)

Of course, their adult relationship really never had a chance because the adolescent one was never wholly formed. This is shown starkly by Sula's affair with Nel's husband and Sula and Nel's failure to accept responsibility in the death of Chicken Little. Sula feels guilt, but that is not necessarily the same thing. The bitter irony is evident from the start in the foreshadowing elicited by their last names. Sula never achieves "peace," and Nel cannot find the "wright" relationship with either a man or her community that will take the place of the part of her that never developed.

6   Sula and Nel are inexorably linked like Siamese twins—destined never to be whole—whether together or apart.

Works Cited

Bakerman, Jane. "Failure of Love: Female Initiation in the Novels of Toni Morrison." American Literature 52 (1981): 541–63.

Jones, Carolyn. "Toni Morrison's Narratives of Community." African American Review 27 (1993): 615–26.

Stepto, Robert. "Intimate Things in Place: An Interview with Toni Morrison." Massachusetts Review 18 (1977): 473–89.

▼ **PRACTICE 1** Writing Literary Criticism of a Poem

Write an essay about the following poem in which you analyze these symbols and how they relate to the theme: the red wheelbarrow, rainwater, white chickens.

The Red Wheelbarrow
William Carlos Williams

so much depends
upon

a red wheel
barrow

5   glazed with rain
water

beside the white
chickens.

▼ **PRACTICE 2** Writing Literary Criticism of a Short Story

Write an essay explaining how the birth and death images in the following story, "Love," by Jesse Stuart, support a specific theme.

Vocabulary
Before you begin reading, look up the definitions for the following words that appear in the story.

incubate (11)	limber (10)	loamy (7)	mattock (16)
poised (9)	riddled (10)	spud (16)	stubble (1)
wilted (1)	windlass (18)		

Love

1   Yesterday when the bright sun blazed down on the wilted corn my father and I walked around the edge of the new ground to plan a fence. The cows kept coming through the chestnut oaks on the cliff and running over the young corn. They bit off the tips of the corn and trampled down the stubble.

2   My father walked in the cornbalk. Bob, our Collie, walked in front of my father. We heard a ground squirrel whistle down over the bluff among the dead treetops at the clearing's edge. "Whoop, take him, Bob," said my father. He lifted up a young stalk of corn, with wilted dried roots, where the ground squirrel had dug it up for the sweet grain of corn left on its tender roots. This has been a dry spring and the corn has kept well in the earth where the grain has sprouted. The ground squirrels love this corn. They dig up rows of it and eat the sweet grains. The young corn stalks are killed and we have to replant the corn.

3   I could see my father keep sicking Bob after the ground squirrel. He jumped over the corn rows. He started to run toward the ground squirrel. I, too, started running toward the clearing's edge where Bob was jumping and barking. The dust flew in tiny swirls behind our feet. There was a big cloud of dust behind us.

4   "It's a big bull blacksnake," said my father. "Kill him, Bob! Kill him, Bob!"

5   Bob was jumping and snapping at the snake so as to make it strike and throw itself off guard. Bob has killed twenty-eight copperheads this spring. He knows how to kill a snake. He doesn't rush to do it. He takes his time and does the job well.

6   "Let's don't kill the snake," I said. "A blacksnake is a harmless snake. It kills poison snakes. It kills the copperhead. It catches more mice from the fields than a cat."

7   I could see the snake didn't want to fight the dog. The snake wanted to get away. Bob wouldn't let it. I wondered why it was crawling toward a heap of black loamy earth at the bench of the hill. I wondered why it had come from the chestnut oak sprouts and the matted greenbriars on the cliff. I looked as the snake lifted its pretty head in response to one of Bob's jumps. "It's not a bull blacksnake," I said. "It's a she-snake. Look at the white on her throat."

8   "A snake is an enemy to me," my father snapped. "I hate a snake. Kill it, Bob. Go in there and get that snake and quit playing with it!"

9   Bob obeyed my father. I hated to see him take this snake by the throat. She was so beautifully poised in the sunlight. Bob grabbed the white patch on her throat. He cracked her long body like an ox whip in the wind. He cracked it against the wind only. The blood spurted from her fine-curved throat. Something hit against my legs like pellets. Bob threw the snake down. I looked to see what had struck my legs. It was snake eggs. Bob had slung them from her body. She was going to the sand heap to lay her eggs, where the sun is the setting hen that warms them and hatches them.

10   Bob grabbed her body there on the earth where the red blood was running down on the gray-piled loam. Her body was still writhing in pain. She acted like a green-weed held over a new-ground fire. Bob slung her viciously many times. He cracked her limp body against the wind. She was now limber as a shoestring in the wind. Bob

threw her riddled body back on the sand. She quivered like a leaf in the lazy wind, then her riddled body lay perfectly still. The blood covered the loamy earth around the snake.

11   "Look at the eggs, won't you?" said my father. We counted thirty-seven eggs. I picked an egg up and held it in my hand. Only a minute ago there was life in it. It was an immature seed. It would not hatch. Mother sun could not incubate it on the warm earth. The egg I held in my hand was almost the size of a quail's egg. The shell on it was thin and tough and the egg appeared under the surface to be a watery egg.

12   "Well, Bob, I guess you see now why this snake couldn't fight," I said. "It is life. Stronger devour the weaker even among human beings. Dog kills snake. Snake kills birds. Birds kill the butterflies. Man conquers all. Man, too, kills for sport."

13   Bob was panting. He walked ahead of us back to the house. His tongue was out of his mouth. He was tired. He was hot under his shaggy coat of hair. His tongue nearly touched the dry dirt and white flecks of foam dripped from it. We walked toward the house. Neither my father nor I spoke. I still thought of the dead snake. The sun was going down over the chestnut ridge. A lark was singing. It was late for a lark to sing. The red evening clouds floated above the pine trees on our pasture hill. My father stood beside the path. His black hair was moved by the wind. His face was red in the blue wind of day. His eyes looked toward the sinking sun.

14   "And my father hates a snake," I thought.

15   I thought about the agony women know of giving birth. I thought about how they will fight to save their children. Then, I thought of the snake. I thought it was silly of me to think such thoughts.

16   This morning my father and I got up with the chickens. He says one has to get up with the chickens to do a day's work. We got the posthole digger, ax, spud, measuring pole and the mattock. We started for the clearing's edge. Bob didn't go along.

17   The dew was on the corn. My father walked behind with the posthole digger across his shoulder. I walked in front. The wind was blowing. It was a good morning wind to breathe and a wind that makes one feel like he can get under the edge of a hill and heave the whole hill upside down.

18   I walked out the corn row where we had come yesterday afternoon. I looked in front of me. I saw something. I saw it move. It was moving like a huge black rope winds around a windlass. "Steady," I says to my father. "Here is the bull blacksnake." He took one step up beside me and stood. His eyes grew wide apart.

19   "What do you know about this," he said.

20   "You have seen the bull blacksnake now," I said. "Take a good look at him! He is lying beside his dead mate. He has come to her. He, perhaps, was on her trail yesterday."

21   The male snake had trailed her to her doom. He had come in the night, under the roof of stars, as the moon shed rays of light on the quivering clouds of green. He had found his lover dead. He was coiled beside her, and she was dead.

22   The bull blacksnake lifted his head and followed us as we walked around the dead snake. He would have fought us to his death. He would have fought Bob to his death. "Take a stick," said my father, "and throw him over the hill so Bob won't find him. Did you ever see anything to beat that? I've heard they'd do that. But this is my first time to see it." I took a stick and threw him over the bank into the dewy sprouts on the cliff.

CHAPTER REVIEW

▼ A work of criticism involves interpreting and evaluating someone else's work. Literary criticism involves analyzing a poem, story, novel, play, or essay.

▼ When analyzing a work of literature, you must consider the characters (who), plot (what), setting (where), time (when), theme (why), and technique (how).

▼ The thesis statement of a literary analysis essay should include the author, genre, title, topic, and evaluation of topic.

A FINAL WORD

We hope your experiences using this text have convinced you that it is essential for you to develop the skills necessary to construct a claim and support it through evidence from both primary and secondary sources. Expository writing, in all its various modes as demonstrated in this text, is an essential form of communication in many areas of your life. Whether you are presenting a report to your boss at work or a literary analysis to your professor at college, clear and concise communication is important. In the end, the clarity and coherence of your written communications will bear directly on how others think of you. We hope you will always remember that learning is a lifelong endeavor, and that learning, to be truly useful, requires a dialogue.

Visit *The Write Start* Online!

For additional practice with the materials found in this chapter, visit our Website at

http://www.ablongman.com/checkett

The Website also features additional readings, quizzes, writing activities, and Internet links, as well as a bulletin board and interactive chat.

The Writer's Resources

GRAMMAR

Nouns

Nouns are words that stand for people, places, or things. They can be *singular* or *plural*.

Nouns		
	Singular	**Plural**
Person	man	men
	woman	women
	child	children
Place	cave	caves
	beach	beaches
	forest	forests
	yard	yards
	mountain	mountains
Thing	ring	rings
	computer	computers
	discussion	discussions
	truth	truths
	sport	sports
	idea	ideas
	vacation	vacations
	conversation	conversations

To form the plural of most nouns, you simply add an *-s* or *-es* to the end of the word. However, there are some exceptions:

1. Nouns ending in *-f* or *-ve* form the plural by adding *-ves*:

half	halves
shelf	shelves

2. Hyphenated nouns (nouns that are formed by joining several short words with hyphens) form plurals by adding *-s* or *-es* to the main word in the phrase:

mother-in-law	mothers-in-law
sergeant-at-arms	sergeants-at-arms

3. Some nouns form plurals in other ways, such as by changing the spelling of the plural form. These are sometimes called irregular forms of plural nouns:

foot	feet
child	children
criterion	criteria
woman	women
man	men

4. Other nouns do not change at all when forming the plural. These exceptions must simply be memorized:

fish	fish
deer	deer
shrimp	shrimp

Nouns can also be classified as *proper* or *common*. *Proper nouns* are the specific names or titles of people, places, or things, and they are capitalized. *Common nouns* are general terms for people, places, or things, and they are not capitalized.

Common Nouns	**Proper Nouns**
singer	Sheryl Crow
beach	Corona Del Mar
magazine	*Time*
student	Julianne

▼ **PRACTICE 1   Finding Nouns**

Underline the nouns (not pronouns) in the following sentences. (*Note:* Sentences for the Writer's Resources exercises are based on the professional and student essays used in the text.)

Example: The <u>family</u> travels to the <u>mountains</u> every <u>weekend</u>.

1. I was twelve, and in my first year of junior high school.

2. I discovered black was not supposed to be beautiful.

3. At that age, boys suddenly became important.

4. But by that time, black kids no longer believed in that sixties mantra, "Black is beautiful."

5. Light skin, green eyes, and long, wavy hair were once again synonymous with beauty.

6. Colorism—and its subtext of self-hatred—began during slavery on plantations.

READ
All About It . . .

To read the full essay from which these sentences are excerpted, see page 169.

7. Some social circles are still defined by hue.

8. Some African Americans, dark and light, prefer light skinned mates, so they can have a "pretty baby."

9. In my family, color was never discussed, even though our spectrum was broad—my brother was very light; my sister and I much darker.

10. But in junior high, I learned in a matter of weeks what had apparently been drummed into the heads of my black peers for most of their lives. (Jones, "Light Skin versus Dark")

▼ PRACTICE 2   Singular and Plural Nouns

In the following paragraph from student essay "Two Different Neighbors" by Ms. Cruz, find and correct the errors in singular and plural noun use.

Example: Living in the United States means living in a ~~countries~~ **country** where there
can be a good ~~futures~~ **future** for just about anybody.

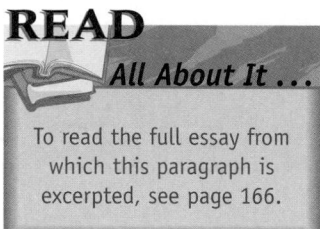

READ
All About It . . .

To read the full essay from which this paragraph is excerpted, see page 166.

However, the United States is not the best places to vacation if you are look-ing for a place with activity going on all days long, each day of the years. Mexico, on the other hands, doesn't necessarily have all the advantage when it comes to planning a short-term vacations. In Mexico, one can be active from the moment when one awakes. For instance, there are breakfast place beside the hotel pool, so the visitor can combine swimmings and pool activity with the first meal of the days. What a wake-up calls!

▼ PRACTICE 3   Correcting Errors in Noun Use

Find and correct the errors in noun use (singular/plural, common/proper nouns) in the following paragraphs by Ms. Cruz ("Two Different Neighbors").

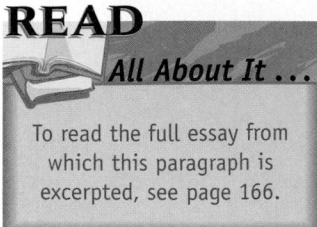

READ
All About It . . .

To read the full essay from which this paragraph is excerpted, see page 166.

The united states has many historic sites but, in contrast to mexico, these place are very young. For example, the statue of liberty is not even a centuries old. Another places to visit in the united states is Philadelphia. Philadelphia is an important cities to visit because of its connection to the colonie's winning independence from england two hundred year ago. On the other hand, in mexico the Pyramids found at tenochitlan are at least a millennium old, predating the liberty bell by over eight hundred years. Despite its current modern architectures, mexico city's political importance goes back to the early 16th Century when the aztec empire fell, and colonial rule was instituted by the Spanish conqueror.

Pronouns

A **pronoun** is a word that takes the place of, or refers to, a noun. The noun that the pronoun refers to is known as the antecedent of the pronoun.

> ### Example
> Fariba said that she did not understand the question. (The pronoun is *she*, and *Fariba* is its antecedent.)

Pronouns can be divided into several categories. The most common categories are *personal pronouns, relative pronouns, demonstrative pronouns, indefinite pronouns*, and *reflexive pronouns*.

Personal Pronouns

Personal pronouns refer to a specific person or thing (*I/me, you, he/him, she/her, it, we/us, they/them*). Personal pronouns are divided into three forms, depending on how they are used in a sentence. These forms are **subjective** (pronoun used as a subject), **objective** (pronoun used as an object), or **possessive** (pronoun used to indicates possession/ownership).

Subjective Pronouns

	Singular	Plural
1st person	I	we
2nd person	you	you
3rd person	he, she, it	they

Objective Pronouns

	Singular	Plural
1st person	me	us
2nd person	you	you
3rd person	him, her, it	them

Possessive Pronouns

	Singular	Plural
1st person	my (mine)	our (ours)
2nd person	your (yours)	your (yours)
3rd person	his (his)	their (theirs) its
	her (hers)	
	its (its)	

The following examples demonstrate the uses of these three types of personal pronouns:

> I frequently listen to music when I drive. (Subjective pronoun; the pronoun is used as a subject)
>
> They enjoy decorating their home. (Subjective pronoun)
>
> Dave is starting to annoy you. (Objective pronoun; the pronoun is the object of the sentence)
>
> He gave the same gift to him. (Objective pronoun)
>
> That is my sweater. (Possessive pronoun; the pronoun shows ownership or possession)
>
> He borrowed her keys. (Possessive pronoun)

PRACTICE 4　　Using Personal Pronouns

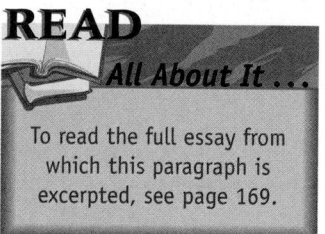

READ
All About It . . .

To read the full essay from which this paragraph is excerpted, see page 169.

In the following paragraph, underline subjective pronouns once, objective pronouns twice, and possessive pronouns three times. Some sentences may contain more than one type.

A racist encounter hurts badly. But it does not equal the pain of "colorism"—being rejected by your own people because your skin is colored cocoa and not cream, ebony and not olive. On our scale of beauty, it is often the high yellows—in the lexicon of black America, those with light skin—whose looks reap the most attention. Traditionally, if someone was described that way, there was no need to say that person was good-looking. It was a given that light was lovely. It was those of us with plain brown eyes and darker skin hues who had to prove ourselves. (Jones, "Light Skin versus Dark")

Pronoun-Antecedent Agreement

Pronouns take the place of other nouns or pronouns. The word or words to which a pronoun refers is the *antecedent*. It is important that pronouns agree with their antecedents. For example, the singular antecedent *everyone* must be used with the singular pronouns *he* or *she*.

The following examples illustrate sentences in which pronouns agree with the antecedent.

> If *someone* works late at night, *he* or *she* may not be able to concentrate in class the next morning.
>
> Or
>
> When *Adam* works late at night, *he* is not able to concentrate in class the next morning.
>
> *Each ticket holder* stood in line waiting for *his or her* refund.
>
> *Many* were angry that *their* efforts had not been rewarded.

▼ **PRACTICE 5** **Using Correct Pronoun-Antecedent Agreement**

In the sentences below, underline the antecedent and fill in the correct pronoun.

1. Louisa referred to a social crisis in _____ sociology project.

2. Anyone can learn to paint if _____ has effective instruction and patience.

3. Each baseball player gave _____ best effort in the tournament.

4. Elena and Marguerita gave _____ suggestions to Hoda.

5. She grows peppers and squash; _____ taste best fresh from the garden.

6. The graphic art students turned in _____ portfolios.

7. Someone left _____ towels all over the locker room.

8. The managers want us to attend _____ budget meeting next week.

9. The average consumer wants the best price, but _____ may not shop carefully enough to find one.

10. The faculty of the college argued over _____ grading policies all year.

Relative Pronouns

Relative pronouns introduce a qualifying or explanatory clause.

Relative Pronouns	
who	Used as a subject in reference to people
whom	Used as an object in reference to people
which	Used as a subject in reference to things
that	Used as a subject in reference to things
whoever	Used as a subject in reference to an uncertain number of people
whichever	Used as a subject in reference to an uncertain number of things

The following examples illustrate the use of relative pronouns:

Who made the phone call? (*Who* is used as the subject)

The phone call was made by whom? (*Whom* is used as the object)

Which movie shall we watch tonight? (*Which* is used as a subject referring to things)

I don't like that! (*That* is used as the object referring to a thing)

Demonstrative Pronouns

Demonstrative pronouns point out or specify certain people, places, or things.

Demonstrative Pronouns

Singular	Plural
this	these
that	those

Indefinite Pronouns

Indefinite pronouns refer to general or indeterminate people, places, or things.

Indefinite Pronouns

These pronouns do not refer to specific people, places, or things.

Singular

each	another	anybody	neither
everybody	somebody	anyone	nobody
everyone	someone	anything	no one
everything	something	either	nothing

Singular or plural

all	more	none
any	most	some

Plural

both	few	many	several

Reflexive Pronouns

Reflexive pronouns are formed by adding *-self* or *-selves* to certain pronouns. They are used to indicate action performed to or on the antecedent.

Reflexive Pronouns

	Singular	Plural
1st person	myself	ourselves
2nd person	yourself	yourselves
3rd person	himself	themselves
	herself	
	itself	

The following sentences illustrate the use of the reflexive pronoun:

> We gave *ourselves* a party to celebrate the end of the school year.
> Vinh found *himself* in an impossible situation.

The reflexive pronoun form can also be used to intensify meaning. This is called an *intensifier*.

> The instructor *herself* found the concepts confusing.
> Raoul *himself* had made the engine.

PRACTICE 6 Using Correct Pronoun-Antecedent Agreement

Fill in the blanks with the correct pronouns. Underline the antecedent of each pronoun.

Example: All <u>students</u> must do _____**their**_____ assigned reading before class.

1. Dr. Brenda Izen washed _____ car on a rainy afternoon.

2. Janet and Wayne are remodeling _____ basement.

3. The bankers and the insurance agents met today; _____ discussed many problems facing the elderly.

4. The highway looks slick because _____ is covered with a layer of black ice.

5. Everyone should be responsible for _____ behavior.

6. Anyone failing the test today must do well on _____ test at mid term.

7. Each lawyer presented _____ argument.

8. Have Ramona and Luis paid for _____ concert tickets?

9. Most of the exercises in this book have _____ specific objectives.

10. Each child left _____ home early for school.

PRACTICE 7 Using Pronouns Correctly

Correct the following paragraph for pronoun use. The first pronoun has been done for you; the correct answer is in parentheses. Some sentences are correct.

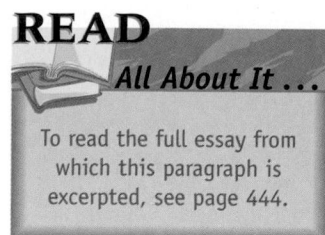

READ
All About It . . .

To read the full essay from which this paragraph is excerpted, see page 444.

        myself
I didn't disappoint ~~himself~~. I reveled in killing, maiming, bloodletting, and gutting. Never did you have the slightest thought regarding carrying capacity, overbrowsing, population dynamics, or any other game-management concept. The arguments that hunters advanced in defense of his sport were alien to me. I hunted in order to kill: you did not kill in order to have "the hunting experience." (Ruggeri, "Why I Don't Hunt")

▼ **PRACTICE 8**   **Using Pronouns Correctly**

Edit the following paragraph for pronoun usage. The first incorrect pronoun has been done for you. Some may be correct.

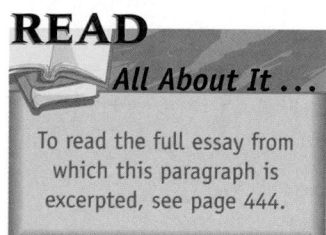

READ
All About It . . .

To read the full essay from which this paragraph is excerpted, see page 444.

         I
Why don't I hunt? ~~He~~ could allude to the fruits of exhaustive research into the ecological and biological consequences of hunting, and to the collective insight of biologists, ecologists, and naturalists which challenge the prevailing wildlife-management dogma. Yet, fundamentally, the answer can be expressed in simple moral terms: Hunting is wrong, and should be acknowledged to be so not only by these that espouse the strict precepts of the animal-rights credo, but by those who hold a common sense of decency, respect, and justice. When he have exposed the specious reasoning of the hunters' apologists and stripped its sport of its counterfeit legitimacy, the naked brutality of hunting defines itself: killing for the fun of it. (Ruggeri, "Why I Don't Hunt")

Verbs

A **verb** is a word indicating action, feeling, or being. Verbs can be divided into three classes: **action verbs, linking verbs,** and **helping verbs.** Additionally, the form of the verbs can indicate the time of the action: **present, past,** or **future** (also known as **tense**). Each of these tenses has many forms that we use every day. The most commonly used tenses are *simple present* and *simple past*.

Present Tense

Verbs in the Simple Present Tense
Sample verb: dance

	Singular	**Plural**
1st person	(I) dance	(we) dance
2nd person	(you) dance	(you) dance
3rd person	(he, she, it) dances	(they) dance

Use an -s or -es ending on the verb when the subject is *he, she,* or *it,* or the equivalent.

Past Tenses for Regular Verbs

Regular verbs are those verbs that form the past tense by adding -ed or -d. The simple past tense is used to refer to an action that began and ended at one time period in the past.

Simple Past Tense of Regular Verbs
Sample verb: dance

	Singular	**Plural**
1st person	(I) danced	(we) danced
2nd person	(you) danced	(you) danced
3rd person	(he, she, it) danced	(they) danced

▼ PRACTICE 9   Using the Present and Past Tense of Regular Verbs

Use each of the following regular verbs in a sentence, using the present tense. Then, change the sentence to the past tense. The first sentences are done for you.

1. (dance)   present tense: She dances every day for exercise.

present tense: She danced every day for exercise.

2. (walk)   present tense: _____

past tense: _____

3. (bake)   present tense: _____

past tense: _____

4. (talk)   present tense: _____

past tense: _____

5. (shop)   present tense: _____

                        past tense: _____

6. (follow)   present tense: _____

                        past tense: _____

7. (trip)   present tense: _____

                        past tense: _____

8. (travel)   present tense: _____

                        past tense: _____

9. (evaluate) present tense: _____

                        past tense: _____

10. (predict) present tense: _____

                        past tense: _____

Past Tenses for Irregular Verbs

Many irregular verbs (more than 100 in English) do not form the past tense by adding *-ed* or *-d.* Some verbs do not change forms at all. Some verbs form the past tense by changing the spelling of the entire word (these are called *stem-changing verbs*). The following is a list of the most commonly used irregular verbs.

The **past participle** is the form of the verb used with the "perfect" tenses (the verb tense requiring *has/have* showing ongoing action from past up to or including the present, as in the following sentence: He *has gone* to the store, but he will be back soon).

An Alphabetical List of Irregular Verbs

Simple Form	Simple Past	Past Participle
arise	arose	arisen
be	was, were	been
bear	bore	borne/born
beat	beat	beaten/beat
become	became	become
begin	began	begun
bend	bent	bent
bet	bet	bet
bid	bid	bid
bind	bound	bound
bite	bit	bitten
bleed	bled	bled
blow	blew	blown

Simple Form	Simple Past	Past Participle
break	broke	broken
breed	bred	bred
bring	brought	brought
broadcast	broadcast	broadcast
build	built	built
burst	burst	burst
buy	bought	bought
cast	cast	cast
catch	caught	caught
choose	chose	chosen
cling	clung	clung
come	came	come
cost	cost	cost
creep	crept	crept
cut	cut	cut
deal	dealt	dealt
dig	dug	dug
do	did	done
draw	drew	drawn
eat	ate	eaten
fall	fell	fallen
feed	fed	fed
feel	felt	felt
fight	fought	fought
find	found	found
fit	fit	fit
flee	fled	fled
fling	flung	flung
fly	flew	flown
forbid	forbade	forbidden
forecast	forecast	forecast
forget	forgot	forgotten
forgive	forgave	forgiven
forsake	forsook	forsaken
freeze	froze	frozen
get	got	gotten
give	gave	given
go	went	gone
grind	ground	ground
grow	grew	grown
hang	hung	hung
have	had	had
hear	heard	heard

(continued)

Simple Form	Simple Past	Past Participle
hide	hid	hidden
hit	hit	hit
hold	held	held
hurt	hurt	hurt
keep	kept	kept
know	knew	known
lay	laid	laid
lead	led	led
leave	left	left
lend	lent	lent
let	let	let
lie	lay	lain
light	lit/lighted	lit/lighted
lose	lost	lost
make	made	made
mean	meant	meant
meet	met	met
mislay	mislaid	mislaid
mistake	mistook	mistaken
pay	paid	paid
put	put	put
quit	quit	quit
read	read	read
rid	rid	rid
ride	rode	ridden
ring	rang	rung
rise	rose	risen
run	ran	run
say	said	said
see	saw	seen
seek	sought	sought
sell	sold	sold
send	sent	sent
set	set	set
shake	shook	shaken
shed	shed	shed
shine	shone/shined	shone/shined
shoot	shot	shot
show	showed	shown/showed
shrink	shrank/shrunk	shrunk
shut	shut	shut
sing	sang	sung
sit	sat	sat

Simple Form	Simple Past	Past Participle
sleep	slept	slept
slide	slid	slid
slit	slit	slit
speak	spoke	spoken
speed	sped/speeded	sped/speeded
spend	spent	spent
spin	spun	spun
spit	spit/spat	spit/spat
split	split	split
spread	spread	spread
spring	sprang/sprung	sprung
stand	stood	stood
steal	stole	stolen
stick	stuck	stuck
sting	stung	stung
stink	stank/stunk	stunk
strive	strove	striven
strike	struck	struck/stricken
string	strung	strung
swear	swore	sworn
sweep	swept	swept
swim	swam	swum
swing	swung	swung
take	took	taken
teach	taught	taught
tear	tore	torn
tell	told	told
think	thought	thought
throw	threw	thrown
thrust	thrust	thrust
understand	understood	understood
undertake	undertook	undertaken
upset	upset	upset
wake	woke/waked	woken/waked
wear	wore	worn
weave	wove	woven
weep	wept	wept
win	won	won
wind	wound	wound
withdraw	withdrew	withdrawn
wring	wrung	wrung
write	wrote	written

(continued)

The following are some differences in verb forms between American English and British English.

American	British
bet-bet-bet	*bet-bet-bet or bet-betted-betted*
fit-fit-fit	*fit-fitted-fitted*
get-got-gotten	*get-got-got*
quit-quit-quit	*quit-quitted-quitted*

American: *burn, dream, kneel, lean, leap, learn, smell, spell, spill, spoil* are usually regular: *burned, dreamed, kneeled, leaned, leaped,* etc.

British: simple past and past participle forms of these verbs can be regular but more commonly end with *-t: burnt, dreamt, knelt, leant, leapt, learnt, smelt, spelt, spilt, spoilt.*

Source: Betty S. Azar, *Understanding and Using English Grammar,* 2nd ed. (Englewood Cliffs, NJ: Prentice Hall Regents), 18–19. Used with permission.

Some irregular verbs do not follow the stem changing pattern.

Irregular Verbs That Do Not Change Their Form
(All end in *-t* or *-d.*)

Present Form	Past Form	Past Participle
bet	bet	bet
cost	cost	cost
cut	cut	cut
fit	fit	fit
hit	hit	hit
hurt	hurt	hurt
quit	quit	quit
spread	spread	spread

Because the verb *be* is used so often as a helping verb, as a linking verb, and to form verb tenses, it is useful to see how irregular the form is.

To be (infinitive form)

	Present Tense		Past Tense	
	Singular	*Plural*	*Singular*	*Plural*
1st person	I am	we are	I was	we were
2nd person	you are	you are	you were	you were
3rd person	he, she, it is	they are	he, she, it was	they were

PRACTICE 10   Using the Past Tense of Irregular Verbs

Supply the correct form of the past tense of the irregular verbs in the following sentences: The first one has been done for you:

1. (go) All winter we _____went_____ to the nearby resort to ski.

2. (be) They _____ alone for hours before they joined the rest of the group.

3. (win) The members of the band _____ the competition, even though their uniforms had burned in a fire.

4. (lie) The homework _____ on the kitchen counter instead of the teachers desk.

5. (be) Why _____ you absent for more than a month?

6. (withdraw) He _____ the funds necessary for the remodeling project.

7. (weave) The woman _____ the basket in a pattern passed down from generation to generation.

8. (string) He had the raquet _____ before the tournament.

9. (throw) Shelley _____ the first pitch, terrifying the batter.

10. (shrink) The new blouse _____ the first time she washed it.

Progressive Tenses and the Present Participle

The verb *be* is used to form the progressive tenses. To form the present progressive, past progressive, and future progressive tenses, combine the appropriate form of *be* + a verb + *–ing*.

Present Progressive	Past Progressive	Future Progressive
I am talking	I was talking	I will be talking
They are dancing	They were dancing	They will be dancing

▼ **PRACTICE 11**   **Choosing the Correct Verb Form**

READ
All About It . . .

To read the full essay from which this paragraph is excerpted, see page 399.

Supply the missing past tense or present participle in the following paragraphs.

Example: For her recital, the soprano _____sang_____ (sing) a variety of arias.

Since the days of early cinema, Latin men _____ (portray)

some of the most virile, passionate, and forbidden characters on the screen.

With their swarthy good looks and smoldering eyes, these "Latin lovers"

_____ (cause) female moviegoers to swoon for decades. But

unlike his blond counterpart, the Latin lover was generally not

_____ (cast) in the leading role. He _____ (play) the rogue to the Anglo gentleman. He _____ (be), however, suave and more than able to captivate even the strongest screen siren. Early screen actors such as Rudolph Valentino, Ramon Novarro, and Gilbert Roland invariably _____ (set) the stage for today's Latino film roles.

While the Latin lover stereotype seems like a whimsical characterization that only _____ (to exist) on the big screen decades ago, its effects _____ (seep) into the American psyche, _____ (force) Latinos, especially those in the film industry, into a smothering, tight mold. Although no stereotype should _____ (to be, deem) acceptable, some argue that the Latin lover image is just a step above the other stereotypes today's Latin actors have to play—drug runners, gang members, and crime lords. ("The Don Juan Syndrome" by Chapa)

▼ **PRACTICE 12   Correcting Verb Errors**

Correct the errors in verb forms in the following paragraph. The first sentence has been done for you.

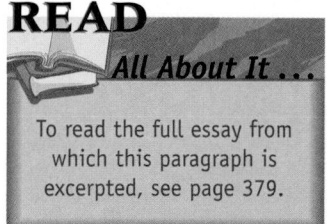

READ
All About It . . .

To read the full essay from which this paragraph is excerpted, see page 379.

         was
Joy Luck ~~is~~ an idea my mother remembered from the days of her first mar-
                                             came
riage in Kweilin, before the Japanese ~~come~~. That's why I think of the Joy Luck as her Kweilin story. It is the story she would always tell me when she is bored, when there was nothing to do, when every bowl had been washed and the Formica table had been wiped down twice, when my father sit reading the newspaper and smoking one Pall Mall cigarette after another, a warning not to disturb him. This is when my mother would take out a box of old ski sweaters sent to us by unseen relatives from Vancouver. She would snip the bottom of a sweater and pull out a kinky thread of yarn, anchoring it to a piece of cardboard. And as she begin to roll with one sweeping rhythm, she

will start her story. Over the years, she tell me the same story, except for the ending, which grow darker, casting long shadows into her life, and eventually into mine. (Tan, "The Joy Luck Club")

Complex Verb Forms

In addition to simple forms, there are more complex verb forms. The following chart illustrates the most commonly used verb tenses. Each tense expresses a specific time or duration. Students for whom English is a foreign language need to practice the use of each tense in spoken and written English.

Common Verb Tenses

Sample verb: talk

Tense	First Person Singular	Sample Sentence
present	I talk	I like to talk in a group.
present progressive	I am talking	I am talking on the phone now!
present perfect	I have talked	I have talked about this often.
present perfect progressive	I have been talking	I have been talking since dawn!
past	I talked	I talked to him last night.
past progressive	I was talking	I was talking about my car.
past perfect	I had talked	I had talked before I decided.
past perfect progressive	I had been talking	I had been talking before they sang.
future	I will talk	I will talk to you tomorrow.
future progressive	I will be talking	I will be talking all morning tomorrow.
future perfect	I will have talked	I will have talked enough by then.
future perfect progressive	I will have been talking	I will have been talking for three hours by the time the meeting is over.

The present perfect and past perfect tenses are formed by combining the appropriate form of the verb *have* with the **past participle** form of a verb. The past participle form of a verb usually ends with *-d, -ed,* or *-en.*

Present Perfect Tense

has or *have* + past participle of the main verb

Singular	**Plural**
He has talked	They have talked

Past Perfect Tense

had + past participle of the main verb

Singular	**Plural**
He had talked	They had talked

The **present perfect tense** is used to describe an action that started in the past and continues to the present time. It can also be used to describe an action that has recently taken place or an action for which the exact past time is indefinite.

Julia *has played* with the symphony for five years.

This sentence means that Julia began playing with the orchestra five years ago and is still playing with the symphony today.

Asim *has traveled* to Pakistan several times recently.

This sentence indicates no specific time for the travel mentioned. If a specific time is mentioned, the simple past would be used.

Asim *traveled* to Pakistan last December.

The **past perfect tense** is used to describe an action that occurred in the past before another point in time in the past or before another past activity.

Julia *had played* with the symphony for five years before she retired.

This sentence means that Julia played in the symphony for five years, and then she retired. All of this activity took place in the past.

▼ **PRACTICE 13**   **Using the Present Perfect and Past Perfect Tenses**

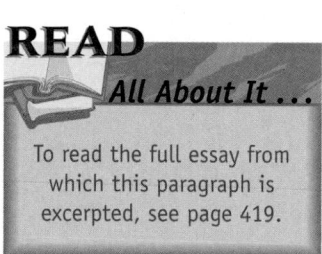

READ
All About It . . .

To read the full essay from which this paragraph is excerpted, see page 419.

Change the verb tenses from present to past, changing perfect tenses as needed. The first sentence has been done for you.

                               took   **had**

A volatile inner-city drama ~~is taking~~ place in New York where blacks ~~have~~ **been**

~~been~~ boycotting Korean groceries for four months. The recent attack on three

Vietnamese men by a group of blacks who mistook them for Koreans

has brought this long-simmering tension between two minority groups to the

world's attention. Korean newspapers from San Francisco to Seoul have been

running front-page stories. Non-Asian commentators around the country,

whose knowledge of Korea may not be much more than images from the Ko-

rean war and the ridiculous television series *M.A.S.H.*, are making all sorts of

comments. (Kang, "A Battle of Cultures")

Passive Voice

Most writing is done in the **active voice** for direct, concise expression. The **passive voice** is chosen when the actor of the sentence is not important or when the writer wishes to avoid naming the subject.

In the passive voice, the object of an active verb becomes the subject of a passive verb. The form of the verb becomes *be + past participle*.

		S	V	O	O
Active:		Carol	tells	the story.	
			S	V	O
Passive:		The story	was told	by Carol.	

The Active Voice Compared to the Passive Voice

In the *active voice,* the subject of the sentence does the acting (action verb/ transitive verb).

In the *passive voice,* the subject is acted upon.

> The students finished the project. (subject = *students*; active verb – *finished*)
> The project was finished by the students. (subject = *project* [acted upon by students]; passive verb = *was finished*)

The following list shows the conversion of the active to the passive voice for the important verb tenses:

	Active	**Passive**
present	Carol tells the story.	The story is told by Carol.
present progressive	Carol is telling the story.	The story is being told by Carol.
present perfect	Carol has told the story.	The story has been told by Carol.
past	Carol told the story.	The story was told by Carol.
past progressive	Carol was telling the story.	The story was being told by Carol.
past perfect	Carol had told the story.	The story had been told by Carol.
future	Carol will tell the story.	The story will be told by Carol.
future progressive	Carol will be telling the story.	The story is going to be told by Carol. (*going to* is often used instead of *will*)
future perfect	Carol will have told the story.	The story will have been told by Carol.

PRACTICE 14   Using the Active Voice

The following sentences are written in passive voice. Rewrite each in active voice.

1. The house was destroyed by the earthquake.

_____

2. The garden was planted by my mother.

_____

3. Creative recipes were developed by the chefs.

_____

4. Our mortgage payment was increased by the bank.

_____

5. The cake was devoured by the children.

_____

▼
PRACTICE 15   Using the Passive Voice

The following sentences are written in active voice. Rewrite each in passive voice.

1. The fire almost destroyed Yellowstone National Park.

_____

2. The insurance company did not raise their rates.

_____

3. Tiger Woods broke the tournament record.

_____

4. The thief mugged his grandfather in the park.

_____

5. The new skiers finally mastered the bunny slope.

_____

▼
PRACTICE 16   Using Correct Verb Forms and Tenses

Change the verb tense in the following paragraph from present to past. Next, underline all the verbs in the paragraph. The first sentence has been done for you.

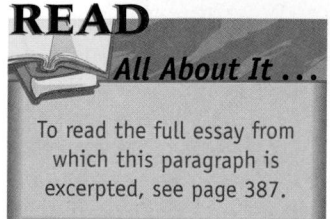

READ *All About It . . .*

To read the full essay from which this paragraph is excerpted, see page 387.

On December 8, 1941, the day after the Japanese attack on Pearl Harbor in

barricaded
Hawaii, my grandfather <u>barricades</u> himself with his family—my grandmother,

my teenage mother, her two sisters and two brothers—inside of his home in

La'ie, a sugar plantation village on Oahu's North Shore. This is my maternal

grandfather, a man most villagers call by his last name, Kubota. It could mean either "Wayside Field" or else "Broken Dreams," depending on which ideograms he uses. Kubota runs La'ie's general store, and one night, after a long day of bad news on the radio, some locals come by, pound on the front door, and make threats. One is said to brandish a machete. They are angry and shocked, as the whole nation is in the aftermath of the surprise attack. Kubota is one of the few Japanese Americans in the village and president of the local Japanese language school. He has become a target for their rage and suspicion. (Hongo, "Kubota")

PRACTICE 17   Using Correct Verb Forms and Tenses

In the following paragraph, supply the correct form or tense of the verbs in the spaces provided. The first sentence has been done for you. Be careful to use the perfect tenses when appropriate.

READ
All About It . . .

To read the full essay from which this paragraph is excerpted, see page 387.

He was a *kibei,* a Japanese American born in Hawaii (a U.S. territory then, so he _____**was**_____ (be) thus a citizen) but who was subsequently _____**sent**_____ (send) back by his father for formal education in Hiroshima, Japan, their home province. *Kibei* is _____ (write) with two ideograms in Japanese: one is the word for "return" and the other is the word for "rice." Poetically, it _____ (mean) one who returns from America, _____ (know) as the Land of Rice in Japanese (by contrast, Chinese immigrants _____ (call) their new home Mountain of Gold).

Kubota _____ (be, graduate) from a Japanese high school and then _____ (come) back to Hawaii as a teenager. He _____ (speak) English—and a Hawaiian creole version of it at that—with a Japanese accent. But he _____ (be) well liked and good at numbers, scrupulous and hard working like so many immigrants and children of immigrants. (Hongo, "Kubota")

Subject-Verb Agreement

Subjects and verbs should agree in number. Thus, singular subjects require verbs with singular endings, and plural subjects require verbs with plural endings. The following sentences illustrate correct subject-verb agreement.

> The *woman* (singular subject) *takes* (singular verb form) a cab.
> The *men* (plural subject) *take* (plural verb form) a cab.

▼
PRACTICE 18   **Using Correct Subject-Verb Agreement**

In the following sentences, choose the correct form of the verb in the parentheses.

First, underline each subject and decide whether it is singular or plural.

Next, underline the verb form that correctly agrees with the subject. The tense must also be accurate.

Example: He always (carry, <u>carries</u>) a credit card in his wallet.

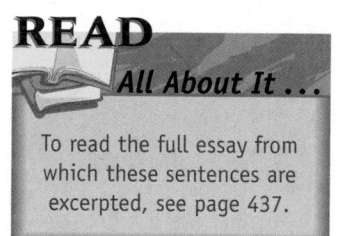

READ
All About It . . .

To read the full essay from which these sentences are excerpted, see page 437.

1. One of the fundamental features of our legal system (is, are) that we (is, are) presumed innocent of any wrongdoing unless and until the government (prove, proves) otherwise.

2. Random drug testing of student athletes (turn, turns) this presumption on its head, telling students that we (assume, assumes) they are using drugs until they (prove, proves) to the contrary with a urine sample.

3. The overwhelming majority of student athletes in Ridgefield Park, and throughout New Jersey, (is, are) law abiding citizens, and there (is, are) no basis in law or logic to presume otherwise or to treat them worse than accused criminals.

4. An equally cherished constitutional command (is, are) the rule that government officials may not (search, searches) us without an adequate reason.

5. Thus, for example, even though we (know, knows) there is a drug problem in our society, we do not (allow, allows) the police to randomly stop us on the street to see if we are carrying drugs.

6. The constitutional prohibition against "unreasonable" searches also (embody, embodies) the principle that merely belonging to a certain group is not a sufficient reason for a search, even if many members of that group (is, are) suspected of illegal activity.

7. Thus, for example, even if it were true that most men with long hair (was, were) drug users, the police would not be free to stop all long-haired men and search them for drugs.

8. Unfortunately, many school officials concerned about drug use by students (seem, seems) willing to ignore these principles.

9. There is no doubt that the concern (is, are) well placed, and it (is, are) one we share.

10. Drug use (is, are) a scourge on our society, exacting a terrible toll in lost lives. ("Just Say No to Drug Testing" by Rocah)

Compound Subject-Verb Agreement

Some sentences contain a compound subject. A **compound subject** is formed by two or more simple subjects joined with a coordinating conjunction. The verb form *must agree in number with the subject.* If the coordinating conjunction is *and,* the verb is usually plural.

> Fredric and Elise *are* working together on the project.

However, if the compound subject is thought of as a unit, a singular verb is used.

> Macaroni and cheese *is* a favorite dish for children.

If the compound subject is preceded by a singular term such as *each* or *every,* the verb is singular.

> After the storm, *every* person, plant, and animal *was* drenched.

If the compound subject is connected with the correlative conjunctions *either/or, neither/nor, not only/but also,* the verb must agree with the following rules:
If both subjects are singular, the verb is singular.

> Either Fredric or Elise *is* going to turn in the project to the boss.

If both subjects are plural, the verb is plural.

> Neither the violins nor the cellos *need* to rehearse their parts with the conductor.

If one subject is singular and the other is plural, the verb agrees with the subject closest to the verb.

> Either my sisters or my friend *is* going to help plan the reception.

▼
PRACTICE 19   **Using Correct Compound Subject-Verb Agreement**

In each sentence, underline the verb that agrees with the compound subject.

Example: During the summer, parents and children (<u>look</u>, looks) forward to vacations.

1. The top of the slalom course and the bottom (appear, appears) far apart.

2. Every mountain and ocean (is, are) indicated on the new map.

3. The sea lion and her cub (stands, stand) on the dock near Fisherman's Wharf.

4. Each gymnast and coach (congratulate, congratulates) the winner of the competition.

5. The costume on the mannequin and the one on my child (fit, fits) differently.

6. Each towel, sheet, and pillow case (turns, turn) pale in the bleach-filled water.

7. Members of the anniversary party or the guests (is, are) in the pictures in the album.

8. Either exhaustion or procrastination (delay, delays) my progress.

9. Neither a calculator nor a dictionary (was, were) available in the bookstore.

10. My sisters or my mother (are, is) going to join me for a vacation.

▼
PRACTICE 20   **Editing to Correct Subject-Verb Agreement**

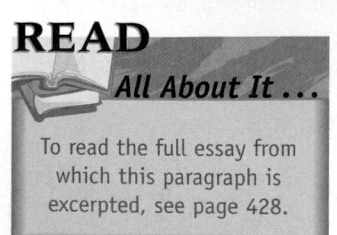

READ
All About It . . .

To read the full essay from which this paragraph is excerpted, see page 428.

Edit the following paragraph for subject-verb agreement. The first sentence has been done for you. Some sentences may be correct.

       know   **are**
We ~~knows~~ we have friends; at least I know my friends ~~is~~ with me, if not

always, at least most of the time. And most of the time I needs them, and

they me. We reaches over the phone lines for that word of comfort, the encouragement we needs to go on when our own store of willpower have

become depleted. (Franco, "A Magic Circle of Friends")

PRACTICE 21   Editing to Correct Subject-Verb Agreement

Edit the following paragraph for subject-verb agreement. The first verb has
been done for you.

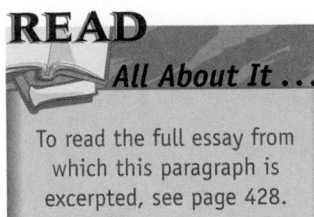

READ
All About It . . .

To read the full essay from
which this paragraph is
excerpted, see page 428.

                                                         have

We will do it instead at a slower pace, because, along the way, we ~~has~~
learned lessons both small and big: for example, that the world are in no
hurry to be changed and that we will has a better shot at it after a good
night's sleep. We may not complete our plans by tomorrow, or even by the
end of the week, because the details of our lives may interferes, such as a
child home from college, or a neighbor's emergency. (Franco, "A Magic Circle
of Friends")

▼ PRACTICE 22   Editing to Correct Subject-Verb Agreement

Edit the following passage for subject-verb agreement. The first sentence has
been done for you.

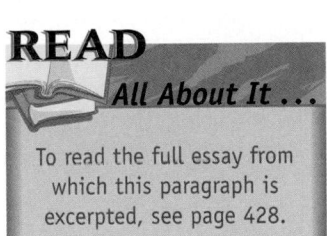

READ
All About It . . .

To read the full essay from
which this paragraph is
excerpted, see page 428.

                                  call

They ~~calls~~ us "late bloomers," they call us "returnees." We is sought by
schools, thanks to the sheer numbers we represent, not to mention the life
experience and the common sense that even the least bright among us bring
to the classroom. We feels flattered and surprised, and our ego is bolstered
by the realization that we is indeed quite capable. . . .

    We may just be beginning to feel a few arthritic pangs in our toes and
fingers, but with our hair neatly streaked and some expensive dental work,
we knows we still look good. We know we are still strong, smart, vital and,
most especially, ready to work. This time around we will makes a big difference. We knows, because for sure, we already was different. (Franco, "A Magic
Circle of Friends")

Adjectives and Adverbs [ESL]

Adjectives

An **adjective** is a word that modifies (or describes) a noun or pronoun. Although adjectives usually come before the nouns they describe, they can also follow the noun (in the predicate of the sentence).

> The *glistening* ocean sparkled in the sunset.
> The coffee tasted *hot*.

Adjectives can be *objective* (describing nouns with sensory details) or *subjective* (describing concepts, feelings, or ideas in more general terms that are open to personal interpretation). Both are useful in good writing and enhance meaning, especially in combination.

Objective Adjectives	Subjective Adjectives
glowing	beautiful
crashing	harsh
stabbing	painful
twisted	ugly
strident	persistent
tender	loving

Adverbs

An **adverb** is a word that modifies (describes) a verb, an adjective, or another adverb. Often adverbs end in *-ly*. Another test to identify an adverb is if it answers one of the questions *where, how,* or *when*. Adverbs describe the action of a passage; in some cases they refer to other adverbs to intensify meaning. As with adjectives, the careful use of effective adverbs can improve the style.

> Lisa stormed *angrily* up the stairs. (modifies the verb)
> He was *very* cold. (modifies the adjective)
> The guests were *too* early to dinner. (modifies the adverb)

Commonly Used Adverbs

happily	harshly	quietly	sadly	rudely
softly	perfectly	poorly	politely	slowly
sadly	loudly	quickly	carefully	very

Comparative and Superlative Forms

Comparative and **superlative** forms are used to compare more than two people or things; this forms a comparison in a matter of degree: as in tall/taller (**comparative**)/tallest(**superlative**); complex/more complex (**comparative**)/ most complex (**superlative**).

To Form Comparatives

Add *–er* to single-syllable adjectives and adverbs: big/bigger

Add the word *more* to adjectives and adverbs with more than one syllable: happily/more happily

To Form Superlatives

Add *-est* to adjectives and adverbs of one syllable: short/shortest

Add the word *most* before adjectives and adverbs that have two or more syllables: pleasant/most pleasant

*Exception: With two-syllable adjectives ending in *-y,* change the *y* to *i* and add *-est*: silly/silliest

---

PRACTICE 23   Using Adjectives and Adverbs

In the blanks provided, write an appropriate adjective or adverb from the lists of adjectives and adverbs above. Use some superlative forms when possible. The first answer has been done for you.

1. It was a _____**beautiful**_____ night. The colors of the sunset burned in the west as the sun slowly descended.

2. The _____ limbs of the tree grew up harshly into the winter sky.

3. The view from the bridge was the most _____ view she had ever seen!

4. The wound was very _____ to the touch.

5. The _____ bellow of the car's horn blared in front of the house.

6. The _____ player on the basketball team was also the most clumsy.

7. Demands of course work often interfere with _____ made plans.

8. The cacophony of sound from the orchestra room was the most _____ sounds the principal had heard all day.

9. His evaluation was the _____ the employees had ever received.

10. The cartoon characters encouraged the _____ behavior among the watching children.

▼
PRACTICE 24   Writing a Paragraph with Adjectives and Adverbs

Construct a descriptive paragraph of 5 to 8 sentences, using at least one adjective and one adverb in each sentence.

_____

_____

_____

_____

_____

_____

_____

_____

Sentence Basics

An understanding of the basic sentence is essential when writing and revising. The **basic sentence** is composed of a *subject* and a *verb*; the sentence must have "sufficient meaning." In other words, it must make sense! (When a sentence is combined with another sentence or clause, it is called an **independent clause.**)

In the following sections, elements within the basic sentence (**clauses** and **phrases**), as well as additional grammatical concepts (**conjunctions, interjections,** and **articles**) will be defined.

Clauses and Phrases

Independent and Dependent Clauses

A **clause** is a group of related words containing both a subject and a verb. Clauses can be *independent* or *dependent*. An **independent clause** can stand alone as a complete sentence. A **dependent clause** (or subordinate clause) begins with a subordinating conjunction or relative pronoun and cannot stand alone as a sentence.

> We went shopping during the holidays. *independent clause* (subject = *we*; verb = *went*)
>
> although we went shopping during the holidays. *dependent clause* (subordinate conjunction = *although*; subject = *we*; verb = *went*)
>
> Carl and Louisa were often late to class. *independent clause* (subject = *Carl and Louisa*; verb = *were*)
>
> because Carl and Louisa were often late to class. *dependent clause* (subordinate conjunction = *because*; subject = *Carl and Louisa*; verb = *were*)

Restrictive and Nonrestrictive Clauses

Some clauses can be *restrictive* or *nonrestrictive*. **Restrictive clauses** are essential to identify nouns or to complete the meaning. These clauses simply follow the nouns or ideas they are modifying. No commas are used to offset restrictive clauses.

> In the line, the young woman *who was wearing a red bandana and hoop earrings* needed a ticket. (This relative clause is essential to identify which woman needed a ticket.)

Most clauses beginning with *that* are restrictive clauses and are not set off with commas.

> Where is the report *that he left on the desk this morning?*

Nonrestrictive clauses are not essential to complete the meaning of the sentence. You can remove them from the sentence, and the basic meaning of the sentence will remain clear. Because they are nonessential, these clauses are always offset by commas.

> Linda and Burt, *who just returned from Alaska,* would go on another vacation tomorrow. (This relative clause is not essential because it just adds interesting details to the sentence; without it, the meaning of the sentence is still clear.)
>
> The cockatiels, *which were chirping loudly to the music of the nearby television,* should live for up to twenty years. (This clause is nonessential, supplying interesting details but not essential information.)

Combining Clauses

Often, clauses are combined using **conjunctions**. Independent clauses are combined using a comma and the following **coordinating conjunctions.**

Coordinating Conjunctions

for	and	nor	but
or	yet	so	

Example

The parents speak, *but* the children refuse to listen.

Independent clauses may also be joined with a semicolon (*The parents speak; the children refuse to listen*) or with a semicolon and an **adverbial conjunction**. These conjunctions may also serve as transition words.

Common Adverbial Conjunctions

accordingly	hence	nonetheless
additionally	however	now
also	incidentally	otherwise
anyway	indeed	similarly
besides	likewise	still
certainly	meanwhile	then
consequently	moreover	thereafter
finally	nevertheless	thus
furthermore	next	undoubtedly

Example

The team practiced in the morning; *furthermore,* they practiced again in the evening.

Dependent clauses are joined to independent clauses with the addition of a **subordinate conjunction.**

Common Subordinate Conjunctions

after	even though	when
although	if (as if)	whenever
as	since	wherever
because	though	whether
before	unless	while
during	until	

Example

The ship returned to port *because its propeller was broken.*

When a dependent clause precedes an independent clause, a comma follows the dependent clause.

Because its propeller was broken, the ship returned to port.

▼ **PRACTICE 25** | **Combining Clauses**

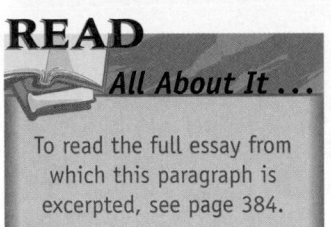

READ
All About It . . .

To read the full essay from which this paragraph is excerpted, see page 384.

Combine the following groups of sentences, using the correct conjunctions and the correct punctuation. Underline the conjunctions you choose to use.

Example: 1.1 My little girl is singing herself to sleep upstairs.
1.2 Her voice mingles with the sounds of the birds.
1.3 The birds are outside.
1.4 The birds are in the old maple trees.

My little girl is singing herself to sleep upstairs, <u>and</u> her voice mingles

with the sounds of the birds outside in the old maple trees.

2.1 My daughter is two.

2.2 I am nearly fifty.

2.3 I am very taken with her.

_____

_____

3.1 She came along late in my life.

3.2 She was unexpected.

3.3 She is a gift.

3.4 The gift is startling.

_____

_____

4.1 My wife and I laughed watching her.

4.2 We heard behind us a low guttural curse.

4.3 Then we heard an unpleasant voice.

4.4 The voice was raised in a guttural war whoop.

_____

_____

5.1 I turned to see a fat man in a bathing suit.

5.2 He covered his mouth.

5.3 He prepared to make the Indian war cry again.

_____

_____

6.1 He was middle aged.

6.2 He was younger than I was.

6.3 He had three little children lined up next to him.

6.4 They were grinning foolishly.

_____

_____

7.1 My wife suggested we leave the beach.

7.2 I agreed.

_____

_____

8.1 His beach behavior might have been socially unacceptable to more civilized whites.

8.2 His basic view of Indians is expressed daily in our small town.

8.3 These views are frequently on the editorial pages of the county newspaper.

_____

_____

9.1 It doesn't matter to them.

9.2 We were here first.

9.3 The United States Supreme Court has ruled in our favor.

_____

_____

10.1 It matters that we have something that they want.

10.2 They hate us for it.

Fragments, Comma Splices, and Run-on Sentences

Fragments, comma splices, and run-on sentences are the most common errors when combining independent and dependent clauses.

Fragments

Fragments are dependent clauses or phrases punctuated as if they are complete sentences.

> Because the propeller was broken.
> Running up the stairs.

To correct a fragment, attach the dependent clause to an independent clause or add a subject or verb to the phrase.

> Because the propeller was broken, the ship returned to port.
> She tripped as she was running up the stairs.

Comma Splices

A **comma splice** occurs when a comma is used instead of a semicolon to combine independent clauses.

Comma Splice
Brian studies the cello, David studies the piano.

Corrected Versions
Brian studies the cello, and David studies the piano.
Brian studies the cello; David studies the piano.

Run-on Sentences

A **run-on sentence** (or fused sentence) occurs when a sentence contains two or more independent clauses with nothing joining them together.

Run-on Sentence
Brian plays the cello David plays the piano.

Corrected Versions
Brian plays the cello; David plays the piano.
Brian plays the cello, and David plays the piano.

Phrases

A **phrase** is a group of related words without a subject, verb, or both subject and verb. Phrases are used in sentences to complete thoughts or add descriptive detail. To avoid problems with ambiguous meaning or errors in punctuation, phrases must be placed near the noun, verb, or other part of speech to which the phrase refers.

Several types of phrases are used as modifiers in sentences: **appositives, prepositional phrases, participial phrases, gerund phrases, infinitive phrases,** and **absolute phrases.**

Appositives

Appositives are words or phrases that rename the preceding words or phrases. **Appositives** are often identified as *noun phrases.*

> My friend *Mary* loves to cook with chocolate. (appositive as single word)
>
> Mary, *a chocolate lover,* shops carefully for the best chocolate in town. (appositive as a phrase)
>
> The novel *The Grapes of Wrath* is often studied in college English classes.

The punctuation of appositive words and phrases follows the rules for restrictive and nonrestrictive clauses.

Prepositional Phrases

A **prepositional phrase** contains a **preposition** (for example, *in, on, over, before, after*) and its object.

> He waited *for the train.*
> The cat prefers to stay *in the house.*
> They enjoy going out *for pizza after the football games.*

Participial Phrases

A **participial phrase** is a group of words consisting of a **participle** and its completing words. All verbs have present participle and past participle forms.

> *Staring at the blank computer screen,* Martin found himself unable to finish his essay. (present participle form)
>
> *Interrupted by the demands of his hungry two-year-old,* he could not finish reading the paper. (past participle form)
>
> *Walking down the hall,* she was hit by the door as it flew open at the end of class.
>
> *Bewildered by the question,* the student could not finish the test.

Gerund Phrases

A **gerund** is the *-ing* form of a verb that functions as a noun in a sentence. A **gerund phrase** includes a gerund and its completing words.

> *Dancing* is her favorite activity. (*Dancing* functions as the subject of the sentence.)
>
> *Writing a collection of poems* remains Sophia's secret hobby. (The gerund phrase functions as the subject of the sentence.)
>
> Employees will not be paid without *completing the weekly projects*. (The gerund phrase functions as the object of the preposition *without*.)

In some cases, the possessive form of a noun or pronoun precedes a gerund.

> The parents were not thrilled with their *son's tattooing a snake on his arm*.
>
> *Her dancing in the moonlight* amazed the children.

Infinitive Phrases

An **infinitive phrase** is a group of words consisting of *to* plus a verb and its completing words. An infinitive phrase can function as a noun, adjective, or adverb.

> *To read* is the best way to study grammar. (The infinitive phrase functions as a noun, the subject of the sentence.)
>
> Disneyland is one of the best places *to visit while on vacation*. (The infinitive phrase functions as an adjective and modifies the noun *places*.)
>
> Her daughter was too nervous *to play the piano in front of an audience*. (The infinitive phrase functions as an adverb, modifying the adjective *nervous*.)

Absolute Phrases

An **absolute phrase** consists of a noun or pronoun and a **participle** plus any other completing words. Absolute phrases modify the entire sentence and cannot be punctuated as a complete sentence.

> *Their project nearly completed,* the painters began to clean their equipment. (The past participle *completed* is used in the phrase.)
>
> The violinist, *her arms and shoulders aching with pain,* practiced long hours every night. (The present participle *aching* is used in this verb phrase.)

▼ PRACTICE 26   Identifying Clauses and Phrases

In the blank to the side of each group of words, write *IC* if the group of words is an independent clause, *DC* if the group of words is a dependent clause, and *P* if the group of words is a phrase. If the group of words is a phrase, identify the type of phrase.

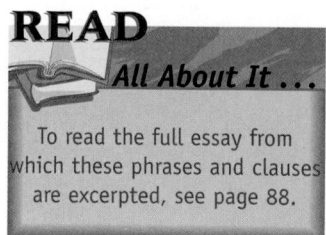

READ
All About It ...

To read the full essay from which these phrases and clauses are excerpted, see page 88.

Example: ___P (prepositional)___ Under the floor

1. _____ From the center of downtown Tucson

2. _____ the ground sloping gently away to Main Street.

3. _____ Here lies the section of the city

4. _____ known as El Hoyo.

5. _____ In no sense it is a hole

6. _____ as its name would imply.

7. _____ Its inhabitants are Chicanos

8. _____ who raise hell on Saturday night

9. _____ listening to Padre Estanislao

10. _____ on Sunday morning. (Suarez, "El Hoyo").

PRACTICE 27   Identifying Clauses and Phrases

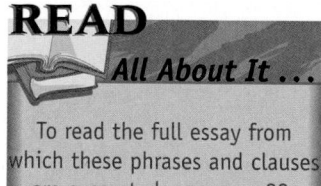

READ
All About It ...

To read the full essay from which these phrases and clauses are excerpted, see page 88.

In the blank to the side of each group of words, write *IC* if the group of words is an independent clause, *DC* if the group of words is a dependent clause, and *P* if the group of words is a phrase. If the group of words is a phrase, identify the type of phrase.

1. _____ In other respects

2. _____ living in El Hoyo has its advantages.

3. _____ If one is born with a weakness for acquiring bills

4. _____ El Hoyo is where the collectors are less likely to find you.

5. _____ When Teofila Malacara's house burned to the ground

6. _____ with all her belongings

7. _____ a benevolent gentleman carried through the gesture

8. _____ that made tolerable her burden.

9. _____ He made a list of 500 names

10. _____ soliciting from each a dollar.

Misplaced and Dangling Modifiers

Misplaced modifying phrases modify the wrong word in a sentence or are placed so that it is not clear which word is being described.

> Incorrect: The courier delivered the material to the vice president *in the red envelope*.
>
> Correct: The courier delivered the material *in the red envelope* to the vice president.

Dangling modifiers do not seem to modify anything in the sentence, or they may appear to describe a word in a way that makes no logical sense. Dangling modifiers usually occur at the beginning of a sentence. To correct the sentence, add the correct subject or verb to the phrase, or restructure the sentence for accurate meaning.

> Incorrect: *After painting the house*, the furniture was rearranged.
>
> Correct: *After painting the house*, we rearranged the furniture.

▼ PRACTICE 28   Correcting Misplaced or Dangling Modifiers

The sentences below have misplaced or dangling modifying phrases. Underline the misplaced or dangling phrase in each sentence and rewrite the sentence so that the meaning is clear and accurate.

Example: David fed the birds <u>in his robe and slippers</u>.

> In his robe and slippers, David fed the birds.

1. The storekeeper did not sell the book to the customer with the cover missing.

_____

_____

_____

2. Walking down the hall, the VCR cart nearly pushed her into the wall.

_____

_____

_____

3. The mail carrier delivered the package to the woman wrapped in holiday wrapping paper.

_____

_____

_____

4. To lift the exercise equipment up the stairs, a great deal of strength is required.

_____

_____

_____

5. After losing her job, her parents encouraged her to move back home with them.

_____

_____

_____

6. Singing in the basement, the dog began to whine, and the cat dashed up the stairs.

_____

_____

_____

7. The teacher gave the class a lecture with only five students.

_____

_____

_____

8. The salesman answered the angry customer's accusations smiling.

_____

_____

_____

9. Driving past the house, the signs of a forbidden party were suddenly obvious.

_____

_____

_____

10. Testing the samples, the lab suddenly filled with smoke.

_____

_____

_____

Prepositions ESL

A **preposition** connects a noun or pronoun to the rest of the sentence, often showing location or time.

Common Prepositions

about	before	despite	of	to
above	behind	down	off	toward(s)
across	below	during	on	under
after	beneath	for	out	until
against	beside	from	over	up
along	besides	in	since	upon
among	between	into	through	with
around	beyond	like	throughout	within
at	by	near	till	without

             S   **V**

(a) The student studies *in the **library.***

                       PREP **O of PREP**
                                (NOUN)

        S   **V**

(b) We enjoyed the party *at your **house.***

                     PREP   **O of PREP**
                             (NOUN)

(c) We went **to the zoo in the afternoon.**

           (place)   (time)

(d) **In the afternoon,** we went to the zoo.

An important element of English sentences is the prepositional phrase. It consists of a preposition (**PREP**) and its object (**O of PREP**). The object of a preposition is a noun or pronoun.

In (a): *in the library* is a prepositional phrase.

In (c): In most English sentences, place comes before time.

In (d): Sometimes a prepositional phrase comes at the beginning of a sentence.

PRACTICE 29   Identifying Prepositional Phrases

Find the subjects (S), verbs (V), objects (O), and prepositional phrases (PP) in the following sentences.

S   **V**   **O**   **PP**

Example: Jack put the letter in the mailbox.

1. The children walked to school.

2. Beethoven wrote nine symphonies.

3. Mary did her homework at the library.

4. Bells originated in Asia.

5. Chinese printers created the first paper money in the world.

6. He wrote poetry until the day he died.

7. He waited for the train.

8. The cat prefers to stay under the bed.

9. They enjoy going out for ice cream after the t-ball games.

10. Because of the stress, he was unable to sleep.

Preposition Combinations   ESL

The following list of preposition combinations is important for ESL students to study and practice, because these phrases can be unusual and idiomatic.

Prepositional Combinations with Adverbs and Verbs

A	
be absent from	apply to, for
accuse of	approve of
be accustomed to	argue with, about
be acquainted with	arrive in, at
be addicted to	*be* associated with
be afraid of	*be* aware of
agree with	
be angry at, with	**B** believe in
be annoyed with	blame for
apologize for	*be* blessed with
	be bored with

C *be* capable of
    care about, for
be cluttered with
be committed to
    compare to, with
    complain about
be composed of
be concerned about
be connected to
    consist of
be content with
    contribute to
be convinced of
be coordinated with
    count (up)on
    cover with
be crowded with

D decide (up)on
be dedicated to
    depend (up)on
be devoted to
be disappointed in, with
be discriminated against
    distinguish from
be divorced from
be done with
    dream of, about
be dressed in

E *be* engaged to
be envious of
be equipped with
    escape from
    excel in
be excited about
    excuse for
be exposed to

F *be* faithful to
be familiar with
    feel like
    fight for
be filled with
be finished with

be fond of
    forget about
    forgive for
be friendly to, with
be furnished with

G *be* grateful to, for
be guilty of

H hide from
    hope for

I *be* innocent of
    insist (up)on
be interested in
be involved in

J *be* jealous of

K *be* known for

L *be* limited to
    look forward to

M *be* made of, from
be married to

O object to
be opposed to

P participate in
be patient with
be polite to
    pray for
be prepared for
    prevent from
    prohibit from
    protect from
be proud of
    provide with
be provided with

R recover from
be related to
be relevant to
    rely (up)on
be remembered for
    rescue from
    respond to
be responsible for

(continued)

S	*be* satisfied with			*be* terrified of
	be scared of			thank for
	stare at			*be* tired of, from
	stop from		U	*be* upset with
	subscribe to			*be* used to
	substitute for			
	succeed in		V	vote for
T	take advantage of		W	*be* worried about
	take care of			

PRACTICE 30   Using Preposition Combinations

Fill in the blanks with the correct preposition combination. The verb has been indicated. Supply the correct form of the verb *to be* (if necessary) and the preposition. The first one has been done for you.

1. Denise could not (decide) __**decide upon**__ her classes for next semester.

2. Midwesterners must (be prepared) _____ severe storms.

3. She (be scared) _____ driving in a thunderstorm.

4. Students must (be responsible) _____ preparing for class.

5. Katherine could not (be content) _____ her new life in retirement.

6. Many students continue to (be discriminated) _____ in college admission policies.

7. Don't (hide) _____ the truth!

8. The neighbors (be known) _____ their outrageous parties.

9. You must not (forget) _____ the exams next week.

10. The young man was found (guilty) _____ breaking and entering.

PRACTICE 31   Combining Sentences

Combine the following groups of sentences, using a variety of sentence patterns studied above: coordination, subordination, insertion of phrases. Avoid repetition and misplaced/dangling modifiers. Double-check for correct punctuation. The first group of sentences has been done for you.

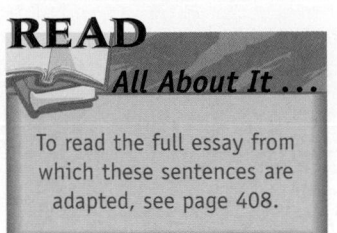

READ
All About It ...

To read the full essay from which these sentences are adapted, see page 408.

1.1 Americans can be divided into three groups.

1.2 One group is smokers.

1.3 One group is non-smokers.

1.4 One group is that expanding pack of us who have quit.

Answer: **Americans can be divided into three groups—smokers,**

nonsmokers, and that expanding pack of us who have quit.

2.1 Those who have never smoked don't know what they're missing.

2.2 Former smokers, ex-smokers, and reformed smokers can never forget.

_____

_____

3.1 We are veterans of a personal war.

3.2 We are linked by that watershed experience.

3.3 The experience is of ceasing to smoke.

3.4 The experience is also the temptation to have just one more cigarette.

_____

_____

4.1 Smoking is being restricted.

4.2 The restriction is in restaurants around the country.

4.3 Smoking will be banned in almost all indoor public places in New York.

4.4 This will take effect next month.

4.5 It is vital that everyone understand the different emotional states.

4.6 These emotional states can be caused by cessation of smoking.

_____

_____

5.1 I have observed four of these emotional states.

5.2 In the interest of science I have classified them.

5.3 One category is the zealot.

5.4 One category is the evangelist.

5.5 Another is the elect.

5.6 Last is the serene.

Articles ESL

An **article** is a type of word that introduces a noun and indicates whether it is specific or countable. The most frequently used articles are *a, an,* and *the.*

Using Articles: Generic Nouns

Ø means no article is used.

Singular Count Noun (a) *A banana* is yellow.*

A speaker uses generic nouns to make generalizations. A generic noun represents a whole class of things; it is not a specific, real, concrete thing but rather a symbol of a whole group.

Plural Count Noun (b) Ø *Bananas* are yellow.

In (a) and (b): The speaker is talking about any banana, all bananas, bananas in general. In (c): The speaker is talking about any and all fruit, fruit in general.

Noncount Noun (c) Ø *Fruit* is good for you.

Notice that no article (Ø) is used to make generalizations with plural count nouns and noncount nouns, as in (b) and (c).

Using *A* or *Some:* Indefinite Nouns

Singular Count Noun (d) I ate *a banana.*

Indefinite nouns are actual things (not symbols), but they are not specifically identified.

*Usually **a** or **an** is used with a *singular generic count noun:*
 A window is made of glass.
 A doctor heals sick people.
 Parents must give *a child* love.
 A box has six sides.
 An apple can be red, green, or yellow.

The is sometimes used with a singular generic count noun (not a plural generic count noun, not a generic noncount noun). Generic ***the*** is commonly used with, in particular:
 1. Species of animals
  The whale is the largest mammal on earth.
  The elephant is the largest land mammal.
 2. Inventions
  Who invented the *telephone? the wheel? the refrigerator? the airplane?*
  The computer will play an increasingly large role in all our lives.
 3. Musical instruments
  I'd like to learn to play *the piano.*
  Do you play *the guitar?*

Plural Count Noun   (e) I ate *some* *bananas*.

In (d): The speaker is not referring to "this banana" or "that banana" or "the banana you gave me." The speaker is simply saying that she or he ate one banana. The listener does not know nor need to know which specific banana was eaten; it was simply one banana out of that whole group of things in this world called bananas.

Noncount Noun   (f) I ate *some* *fruit*.

In (e) and (f): *Some* is often used with indefinite plural count nouns and indefinite noncount nouns. In addition to *some*, a speaker might use *two, a few, several, a lot of* with plural count nouns, or *a little, a lot of* with noncount nouns.

Using *The:* Definite Nouns

Singular Count Noun   (g) Thank you for *the* *banana*.

A noun is definite when both the speaker and the listener are thinking about the same specific thing.

Plural Count Noun   (h) Thank you for *the* *bananas*.

In (g): The speaker uses *the* because the listener knows which specific banana the speaker is talking about, i.e., that particular banana that the listener gave to the speaker.

Noncount Noun   (i) Thank you for *the* *fruit*.

Notice that *the* is used with both singular and plural count nouns and with noncount nouns.

General Guidelines for Article Usage

(a) *The* *sun* is bright today.
Please hand this book to *the* *teacher*.
Please open *the* *door*.
Jack is in *the* *kitchen*.

GUIDELINE: Use *the* when you know or assume that your listener is familiar with and thinking about the same specific thing or person you are talking about.

(b) Yesterday I saw *some dogs*.
The dogs were chasing *a cat*.
The cat was chasing *a mouse*.
The mouse ran into *a hole*.
The hole was very small.

GUIDELINE: Use *the* for the second mention of an indefinite noun.*
In (b): First mention = *some dogs, a cat, a mouse, a hole*. Second mention = *the dogs, the cat, the mouse, the hole*.

(c) Incorrect: *The apples* are my favorite fruit.
Correct: *Apples* are my favorite fruit.

GUIDELINE: Do not use *the* with a plural count noun (e.g., apples) or a noncount noun (e.g., gold) when you are making a generalization.

*__*The__* is not used for the second mention of a generic noun. Compare:
   1. What color is *a banana* (generic noun)? *A banana* (generic noun) is yellow.
   2. Tom offered me *a banana* (indefinite noun) or an apple. I chose *the banana* (definite noun).

(d) Incorrect: *The gold* is a metal.
Correct: *Gold* is a metal.

(e) Incorrect: I drove *car*.
Correct: I drove *a car*.
I drove *the car*.
I drove *that car*.
I drove *his car*.

GUIDELINE: Do not use a singular count noun (e.g., *car*) without:
1. an article (*a/an* or *the*); or
2. *this/that*; or
3. a possessive pronoun.

Source: The material on prepositions and articles was adapted from Betty S. Azar, *Understanding and Using English Grammar* (Englewood Cliffs, NJ: Prentice Hall Regents). Used with permission.

▼ **PRACTICE 32** **Using Articles**

In the following dialogues, try to decide whether the speakers would probably use *a/an* or *the*.

1. A: I have _____ idea. Let's go on _____ picnic Saturday.

B: Okay.

2. A: Did you have fun at _____ picnic yesterday?

B: Sure did. And you?

3. A: You'd better have _____ good reason for being late!

B: I do.

4. A: Did you think _____ reason Jack gave for being late was believable?

B: Not really.

5. A: Where's my blue shirt?

B: It's in _____ washing machine. You'll have to wear _____ different shirt.

6. A: I wish we had _____ washing machine.

B: So do I. It would make it a lot easier to do our laundry.

7. A: What happened to your bicycle? _____ front wheel is bent.

B: I ran into _____ parked car when I swerved to avoid _____ big pothole in the street.

A: Did you damage _____ car?

B: A little.

A: What did you do?

B: I left _____ note for _____ owner of _____ car.

A: What did you write on _____ note?

B: My name and address. I also wrote _____ apology.

8. A: Can you repair my car for me?

B: What's wrong with it?

A: _____ radiator has _____ leak, and one of _____ windshield wipers doesn't work.

B: Can you show me where _____ leak is?

9. A: Have you seen my boots?

B: They're in _____ closet in _____ front hallway.

PRACTICE 33   Using Articles

Complete the sentences with *a/an, the,* or Ø (Ø means no article).

1. _____ beef is a kind of _____ meat.

2. _____ beef we had for dinner last night was excellent.

3. Jack is wearing _____ straw hat today.

4. Jack likes to wear _____ hats.

5. _____ hat is _____ article of clothing.

6. _____ hats are _____ articles of clothing.

7. _____ brown hat on that hook over there belongs to Mark.

8. Everyone has _____ problems in _____ life.

9. My grandfather had _____ long life.

10. That book is about _____ life of Helen Keller.

11. Tommy wants to be _____ engineer when he grows up.

12. The Brooklyn Bridge was designed by _____ engineer.

13. John Roebling is _____ name of _____ engineer who designed the Brooklyn Bridge. He died in 1869 from _____ infection. He died before _____ bridge was completed.

14. _____ people wear _____ jewelry to make themselves more attractive.

15. _____ jewelry Diana is wearing today is beautiful.

16. Mary is wearing _____ beautiful ring today. It is made of _____ gold and _____ rubies. _____ gold in her ring was mined in Canada. _____ rubies came from Burma.

17. One of the first things you need to do when you move to _____ new city is to find _____ place to live. Most _____ newspapers carry _____ advertisements (called "want ads") for _____ apartments that are for rent. If you find an ad for a furnished apartment, _____ apartment will probably contain _____ stove and _____ refrigerator. It will also probably have _____ furniture such as _____ beds, _____ tables, _____ chairs, and maybe _____ sofa.

18. My wife and I have recently moved to this city. Since we're going to be here for only _____ short time, we're renting _____ furnished apartment. We decided that we didn't want to bring our own furniture with us. _____ apartment is in _____ good location, but that's about the only good thing I can say about it. Only one burner on _____ stove works. _____ refrigerator is noisy, and _____ refrigerator door won't stay closed unless we tape it shut. _____ bed sags in the middle and creaks. All of the rest of _____ furniture is old and decrepit too. Nevertheless, we're still enjoying living in this city. We may have to look for _____ another apartment, however.

Fill in the blanks in the following paragraph with the appropriate article or Ø.

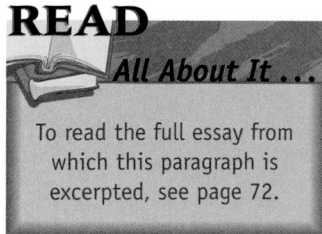

READ
All About It . . .

To read the full essay from which this paragraph is excerpted, see page 72.

Fisherman's Wharf offers the visitor _____ wide array of fascinating attractions. _____ fishing fleet docks along _____ Jefferson Street promenade. _____ early morning stroll along "Fish Alley" will allow you to see fishermen at work. Jefferson Street has _____ host of _____ specialty shops and _____ entertainment for _____ entire family. _____ Wharf has its share of museums, but they are _____ bit out of _____ ordinary. There's

_____ wax museum, _____ Ripley's Believe It or Not! Museum, and _____ museum in _____ guise of _____ medieval dungeon. If you're not too claustrophobic, you can visit _____ Pier 45 and tour _____ USS *Pampanito,* _____ retired WWII submarine. Also, you might want to visit Ghirardelli Square and pick _____ souvenir or two from _____ many specialty shops located there. Finally, before you leave _____ Wharf, make certain you take with you _____ loaf or two of San Francisco's famous sourdough bread. You'll probably want to visit Fisherman's Wharf several times before your vacation is over. (from "San Fransisco or Bust!")

Interjections

Interjections are words that express intense or sudden feelings or reactions. These words are often expressed forcefully, as in *Help!* or *Watch Out!* and are followed by exclamation points if they are the entire sentence. If the words are attached to a sentence, they are followed by a comma.

These expressions, however, are rarely used in formal expository writing. They are most often used in narrative or creative writing in which there is realistic dialogue.

> ### Examples
> *Wait!* You forgot your receipt!
> *Well,* now what should I do?

CAPITALIZATION AND NUMBERS

Capitalization

1. Capitalize proper nouns: for example, the names of specific people, places, and products. Capitalize proper adjectives (formed from proper nouns).

> Fredric Chopin
> Sacramento, California
> Fords
> German class

2. Capitalize the days of the week, names of months and holidays, and the titles of "works" such as books, movies, art work, poems, and songs, etc.

> Saturday, August 28
> Friday the 13th
> Christmas holiday
> *The Painted House*

3. Capitalize the first word of every sentence.

> The dog, cat, and birds all began to bark, growl, and chirp at once.

PRACTICE 1   Correcting Capitalization Errors

In the following paragraph from the essay "Why Blame TV," by John Leonard, correct the errors in capitalization. The first sentence has been done for you.

   A
actually, watching television, unless it's **C**cspan, is usually more interesting

C
than the proceedings of congress. Or what we read in hysterical books like

jerry mander's *four arguments for the elimination of television*. Or george

gilder's *life after television*, or marie winn's *the plug-in drugs* or neal

postman's *amusing ourselves to death* or bill mckibben's *the age of missing

information*. Or what we'll hear at panel discussions on censorship, where

right-wingers worry about sex and left-wingers worry about violence. Or just

lolling around an academic deepthink-tank, trading mantras like "violence profiles" (george gerbner), "processed culture" (Richard hoggart), "nacolep-

tic joys" (michael sorkin), and "glass teat" (harlan Ellison).

Numbers

1. Numbers (instead of words) should be used for dates, street addresses, page numbers, and time stated in terms of a.m. and p.m. (but words are used with the phrase "o'clock").

> August 29, 1998
> 321 Walnut St.
> page 34
> 12:00 a.m. (twelve o'clock)

2. Use numbers for figures above 100 (although some authorities tell us to spell out numbers that can be expressed in one or two words).

> 1,000 pages to be completed
> twenty-four hours
> $15.99 per ticket
> $20,000 (or twenty thousand dollars)

3. Use numbers in a short passage in which several numbers are used.

> On the initial placement test, Julia scored 75, Celia scored 60, and Luis scored 85.

4. Never begin a sentence with a number.

> 25 students filled the course. (Incorrect)
> Twenty-five students filled the course. (Correct)

> **PRACTICE 2**   **Correcting Number Errors**

Correct the mistakes in numbers in the following sentences. The first one has been done for you.

1. In the egg eating contest at the local bar, Fredric ate ~~sixteen~~ [16], Sarah ate ~~twenty~~ [20], but John could only eat ~~twelve~~ [12] before he gagged and ran off stage.

2. 100 guests visited the Washington Monument last year.

3. The marathon dancers had been on the floor for 24 hours.

4. She bought 4 Cornish game hens for the elegant dinner party.

5. The new house was built at three hundred West Nineteenth Street.

6. Tickets for the performance of <u>The Lion King</u> cost sixty-five dollars each.

7. Pauline picked up thirty four tour tickets, even though there were 50 tourists in her group.

8. At 1 p.m. the exam began; the students fled the building at two twenty.

9. 70 employees walked out when the strike vote was passed unanimously.

10. The poem "After Apple-Picking" begins with an unusual image: "My long two-pointed ladder's sticking through a tree/Toward heaven still" (Frost cited in Checkett, two hundred and forty six).

PUNCTUATION AND OTHER RULES OF STYLE

End Punctuation

The end of a complete sentence is signaled by using a **period.** However, sentences can also end with an **exclamation mark (!)** or, when the sentence is a question, a **question mark (?).** (See page 354 for more information on question marks.)

> **Examples:**
> A complete sentence must have a subject and a verb.
> Don't forget to lock the house when you leave!
> When are you coming back?

PRACTICE 1   Using Correct End Punctuation

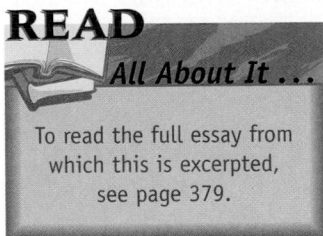

READ
All About It . . .

To read the full essay from which this is excerpted, see page 379.

In the following sentences from "The Joy Luck Club" by Amy Tan, select the correct end punctuation. The first one has been done for you.

1. "I thought up the Joy Luck on a summer night that was so hot even the moths fainted to the ground, their wings were so heavy with the damp heat __.__

2. Every place was so crowded there was no room for fresh air _____

3. My idea was to have a gathering of four women, one for each corner of my mah jong table _____

4. Each week one of us would host a party to raise money and to raise our spirits _____

5. What fine food we treated ourselves to with our meager allowances _____

6. Once we started to play, nobody could speak except to say "*Pung* _____" or "*Chr* _____" when taking a tile _____

7. We had to play with seriousness and think of nothing else but adding to our happiness through winning _____

8. What was worse, we asked among ourselves, to sit and wait for our own deaths with proper somber faces _____ Or to choose our own happiness _____

9. So we decided to hold parties and pretend each week had become the new
   year _____

10. And each week, we could hope to be lucky _____ That hope was our
    only joy _____ And that's how we came to call our little parties Joy Luck
    _____

Commas

As indicated earlier (see "Clauses and Phrases" on page 322), **commas** are an essential component of punctuation. To summarize, commas are used to join two **independent clauses** (in combination with a coordinating conjunction), after an initial **dependent clause,** and after an **introductory phrase** or other **sentence modifiers**. Additionally, commas are used to set apart other sentence **interrupters** such as **nonrestrictrive modifiers.**

Interrupters

Sentences may be interrupted by **nonrestrictive clauses**, **phrases**, or **appositives** that clarify or provide additional meaning. These clauses and phrases are usually set off with commas because they provide additional detail or description, yet they are not essential to the meaning of the sentence and can be removed, leaving the basic idea intact. **Restrictive modifiers,** in contrast, are essential to the meaning of the sentence and are not set off by commas.

> The dog *that was barking all night* annoyed the neighbors. (restrictive)
>
> The red Toyota, *by the way,* is mine. (nonrestrictive)

▼ PRACTICE 2   Punctuating Nonrestrictive Modifiers

Punctuate the phrases or clauses in the following sentences correctly, putting commas only around nonessential phrases and clauses. If a sentence is correct, write "C." The first one has been done for you.

1. The football players, who looked impressive in their new uniforms, marched in the homecoming parade.

2. The technical building which had been built in 1960 was now in need of renovation.

3. Emeralds that are artificially created appear brighter than natural emeralds.

4. The mortgage which was a large part of their budget was due to be paid off in one more year.

5. The committee that I have been requested to join meets twice a week.

6. The gift basket we received for Christmas included gifts for the entire family.

7. The snowstorm descending from the northern states threatened to cancel the first week of spring semester.

8. Professor Wilson gave the test to her new group of students who refused to read homework assignments.

9. We avoided only the speakers who presented outdated information.

10. The investments that were successful the previous year were less successful in the new year.

PRACTICE 3	Using Commas Correctly

READ
All About It . . .

To read the full essay from which these sentences were adapted, see "Why We Crave Horror Movies" by Stephen King on page 434.

Combine the following groups of sentences into one sentence each, using a variety of phrases and clauses, and using commas correctly.

1.1 I think that we're all mentally ill.

1.2 Those of us outside the asylums only hide it a little better.

1.3 We may not hide it all that much better, after all.

_____

_____

_____

_____

2.1 We pay four or five bucks.

2.2 We seat ourselves at tenth-row center in a theater.

2.3 The theater is showing a movie.

2.4 The movie is a horror movie.

2.5 This is daring the nightmare.

_____

_____

_____

_____

3.1 We also go to reestablish our feelings.

3.2 The feelings are of essential normality.

3.3 The horror movie is innately conservative.

3.4 It is even reactionary.

_____

_____

_____

_____

4.1 We are all insane.

4.2 Sanity becomes a matter of degree.

_____

_____

_____

_____

5.1 The potential lyncher is in almost all of us.

5.2 This excludes saints.

5.3 The saints are past and present.

5.4 Most saints have been crazy in their own ways.

5.5 This occurs every now and then.

5.6 The potential lyncher has to be let loose.

5.7 He must scream and roll around in the grass.

This sentence may need the judicious use of semicolons as well as commas!

_____

_____

_____

_____

Semicolons

As indicated earlier (see "Clauses and Phrases" on page 322), writers can combine simple sentences or independent clauses to create compound sentences by using a **semicolon (;).** A semicolon is not a substitute for a comma and is not used with a coordinating conjunction. The semicolon joins two complete sentences; additionally (as in this sentence) it can combine one independent clause with a second independent clause introduced with an adverbial conjunction. The semicolon is used sparingly and only to connect very closely related ideas. The semicolon can add sentence variety to your writing but should not be overused. The following sentences illustrate the correct use of the semicolon:

> ### Semicolon to Combine Two Sentences or Two Independent Clauses:
>
> The anaconda is the world's largest snake; it can grow to 30 feet or more in length. ("size" is the relating idea)
>
> The nurse measured the patient's blood pressure; she also took a blood sample. ("blood" is the relating idea)
>
> ### Semicolon to Combine Two Sentences (Independent Clauses), The Second of Which Is Introduced by an Adverbial Conjunction and a Comma.
>
> The team practiced in the morning; <u>furthermore</u>, they practiced again in the evening.
>
> Aunt Louisa stopped at the baker; <u>meanwhile</u>, her niece waited in the car.

Colons

To add sentence variety and to emphasize particular information, you can use a **colon (:).** Use a colon to introduce a list, when telling time, in the salutation of a business letter, and to separate titles of a book. See the following examples of the correct use of a colon.

1. Use a colon after an independent clause to introduce a list.

> **Example:** Preparing a soufflé requires four ingredients: milk, eggs, butter, and cheese.
>
> The pharmacy technician ordered popular items sold most often: asprin, gauze, bandages, and antacid.
>
> Making chocolate chip cookies can be a sensory delight: the smooth combination of butter, eggs, and sugar; the light, fluffy addition of flour; and, finally, the sinful addition of dark, bittersweet chocolate chips.
>
> (*Notice the use of the semicolon to separate the topics of the list, when those topics include items separated by commas.)
>
> *Note:* Do not use a colon before a list if the list immediately follows a verb or a preposition.
>
> *Improper use*
>
> The most popular condiments are: catsup, mustard, and mayonnaise. (omit the colon after the verb)

2. Use a colon when telling time.

> **Example:** The train arrives at 4:15 p.m.
>
> My 2:30 p.m. doctor's appointment was changed to 5:00 p.m.

3. Use a colon for the salutation of a business letter.

> **Example:** Dear Mrs. Howard:
>
> To whom it may concern:
>
> Sirs:

4. Use a colon to separate the titles and subtitles of a book:

> **Example:** *Accounting in Context: A Business Handbook*
>
> *Writing Made Easy: A Plain Language Rhetoric*
>
> *Washington: The First Leader of the Nation*

PRACTICE 4   Using Commas, Semicolons, and Colons

In the following sentences add a colon and/or semicolon or comma when appropriate:

Example: The teacher taught using a variety of methods: lecturing, using an overhead projector, and facilitating cooperative group projects.

1. The surgeon dressed in a green surgical gown she wore a protective cap covering her hair.

2. The falling leaves covered the ground consequently the golfers had a difficult time finding their golf balls.

3. The submarine dove to a depth of 300 fathoms it hovered silently at that depth for two hours.

4. Jerry enjoyed many activities while vacationing boating, fishing, and hiking.

5. Sheila hit the ball however she was thrown out at first base.

6. The offices workers ate lunch in a variety of places out by the lake in the cafeteria or at the nearby park.

7. The crew chief made out the weekly shift schedule subsequently she hired several new workers.

8. The two falcons found a tree gathered twigs and built a nest.

9. Joseph prefers to stay home and watch TV his wife longs to go out dancing.

10. The man's hidden career dreams were baseball-related to pitch a no hitter and hit a home run in the World Series.

Apostrophes

The **apostrophe** is used to indicate contractions or possession/ownership.

1. Some words can be combined, usually in informal writing, by using an apostrophe. This is a contraction.

> *Isn't* this strange? (is + not)
> We *couldn't* drive any farther. (could + not)

2. Add an apostrophe plus "*s*" to a noun to indicate possession.

> *Anna's* papers were left in the office.

3. To a plural noun ending in "*s*," add only an apostrophe to indicate possession.

> *Parents'* advice often is ignored.

4. For some words, an apostrophe plus "*s*" should be added to a singular word ending in *s*. This is most often true for a proper name.

> *Tom Billings's* recipe book

5. An apostrophe plus "*s*" can be used to form the plurals of figures, letters, and words being treated as words in isolation. (It is also acceptable to leave out this apostrophe.)

> Many students are not satisfied with *C's*.
> He scored *98's* on both tests.
> Don't use so many *"okay's"* when you speak.

Quotation Marks

1. Use quotation marks to set apart words that are quoted or the spoken words in dialogue.

> My mother wrote, "We will be travelling in our mobile home."
> Jung said, "I need to change my grammar text."

2. Periods and commas are placed inside the quotation marks, whereas semicolons and colons are placed outside the quotation marks. If the quoted material is a question, place the question mark inside the quotation marks. However, if the quoted material is part of a longer sentence that asks a question, put the question mark outside the quotation marks.

> "Do the bats fly at night?" he asked.
> Did I hear you say, "The bats fly at night"?
> He politely remarked, "I would like tea"; however, his wife asked for coffee.
> In the short story "Hills Like White Elephants," the male character makes several references to a "simple operation" as a solution to an inconvenient pregnancy.

3. Use quotation marks to set apart titles of essays, magazine articles, short stories, short poems, songs, and chapter headings that you refer to in your writing.

> The class discussed "The House on Mango Street" for two days.
> "Music of the Night" is her favorite song in *Phantom of the Opera*.
> The poem "Fire and Ice" by Frost illustrates two types of anger and destruction.
> "Letter from a Birmingham Jail" is an essay that effectively illustrates argumentation.

4. Quotation marks or italics can be used to set apart a word, phrase, or letter being discussed.

> Do not follow the conjunction *although* with a comma.
> Descriptive words such as "brilliant," "glowing," and "illuminating" support the dominant impression of "light."

5. Uncommon names or nicknames and words used in irony or sarcasm should be surrounded by quotation marks.

> James "Melon Ball" McCarthy prefers to shave his head.
> His crime of adultery almost made him "public enemy number one."

6. Single quotation marks should be used to indicate a quotation within a quotation.

> Tasha said, "My favorite song is 'Layla' performed by Eric Clapton."

Parentheses

1. Parentheses are used to set off specific details giving additional information, explanations, or qualifications of the main idea in a sentence. This would include words, dates, or statements.

> Many students name famous athletes as heroes (Sammy Sosa, Mark McGwire, and Maurice Green, for example).
> *Tom Sawyer* (1876) is one of Mark Twain's most enduring works.

2. The period for the sentence is placed outside the parenthesis when the enclosed information occurs at the end of the sentence and is not a complete sentence itself. If the enclosed information is a complete sentence, the period is placed inside the parenthesis.

> Many students name famous athletes as heroes (for example, Sammy Sosa).
> Many students name famous athletes as heroes. (One example is Sammy Sosa.)

Brackets

1. Brackets are used in quoted material to set apart editorial explanations.

> "The tenor sang 'Angel of Music' [original version sung by Michael Crawford] for his encore."

2. Brackets are also used to indicate editorial corrections to quoted material. The word "sic" (which means "thus") placed in brackets next to an error in quoted material means that the mistake appeared in the original text and that it is not the writer's error.

> The dean wrote, "All faculty must teach sumer [sic] school."

Dashes

1. The **dash** is used to set apart parenthetical information that needs more emphasis than would be indicated by parentheses.

> Irina's new teacher—a dynamic sociology teacher—helped her to understand American society.

2. Use a dash before a statement that expands on or summarizes the preceding statement (this could also include ironic or humorous comments).

> He studied for the exam for two days—then fell asleep before he finished!

Hyphens

1. **Hyphens** are used to form compound adjectives before a noun.

> a well-written play
> a forty-year-old woman

2. Do not use a hyphen after an adverb that ends in -*ly*.

> a quickly changed opinion
> a beautifully designed home

3. Check the dictionary for compound words that always require a hyphen.

> compound numbers (twenty-five, fifty-six)
> good-for-nothing
> father-in-law, mother-in-law
> president-elect

4. Some words with prefixes use a hyphen; check your dictionary if you are unsure.

> ex-husband
> non-English-speaking

5. Use a hyphen at the end of a line if you have to break a word into syllables. Do not divide a one-syllable word.

> Do not forget to review dependent clauses and subordinate conjunctions.

Underlining and Italics

1. The titles of books, magazines, journals, movies, works of art, television programs, CDs, plays, ships, airplanes, and trains should be either underlined or formatted in *italic* type. Underlining is equivalent to or a symbol for italics.

> The Sun Also Rises
> *Good Housekeeping*
> The New York Times
> *The Last Supper*
> Tapestry
> *Buffy the Vampire Slayer*
> H.M.S. Queen Mary

2. There are some exceptions to this rule. For example, the Bible, titles of legal documents (including the U.S. Constitution), and the title of your own essay on your title page would not be underlined or italicized.

▼
PRACTICE 5 | **Using Correct Punctuation and Capitalization**

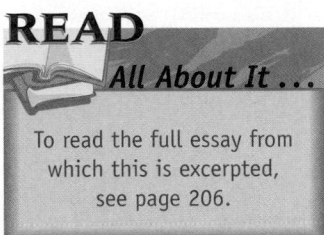

READ
All About It . . .

To read the full essay from which this is excerpted, see page 206.

Add the correct capitalization and punctuation, including correct comma usage and periods, to the following paragraphs. The first sentence has been done for you.

T
the newest move to bash immigrants in the united states has arrived with
U   S

E
the resurgence of the english-only movement. the type of legislation called

for by this movement is sure to have negative repercussions for american so-

ciety at large.

In nineteen ninety six the supreme court agreed to review a lower courts

invalidation of arizonas nineteen eighty eight constitutional amendment

making english the official language of that state this law mandates that

voting ballots be in english only and that english be the official language of

all government functions and actions including government documents

government officials and employees are to conduct business in english only

additionally schools are not allowed to teach in any other language unless

the class is specifically geared toward teaching a foreign language. (Rivera,

"Why English-Only Laws Are Useless")

PRACTICE 6 Using Correct Punctuation and Capitalization

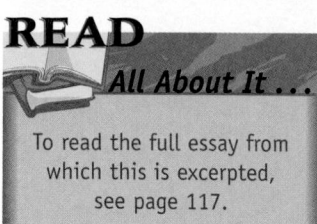

READ
All About It . . .

To read the full essay from which this is excerpted, see page 117.

Add the correct capitalization and punctuation to the following paragraphs.

blind from birth i have never had the opportunity to see myself and have been completely dependent on the image i create in the eye of the observer to date it has not been narcissistic

there are those who assume that since I cant see I obviously cannot hear very often people will converse with me at the top of their lungs enunciating each word very carefully conversely people will also often whisper assuming that since my eyes don't work my ears dont either

for example when I go to the airport and ask the ticket agent for assistance to the plane he or she will invariably pick up the phone call a ground hostess and whisper hi, jane weve got a seventy six here I have concluded that the word blind is not used for one of two reasons either they fear that if the dread word is spoken the ticket agents retina will immediately detach or they are reluctant to inform me of my condition of which I may not have been previously aware (Krents, "Darkness at Noon)

PRACTICE 7 Punctuating a "Works Cited" List Correctly

Using the following information, make a correct "Works Cited" page for the following sources. Use correct punctuation according to MLA format. Be sure to rearrange the entries in alphabetical order.

Lawrence Thompson (author)
Robert Frost's Theory of Poetry (title of essay)
Robert Frost: A Collection of Critical Essays (title of work)
James Cox (editor)
Prentice-Hall (publisher)
Englewood Cliffs (place of publication)
1962
16–35 (pages)

Alvan S. Ryan (author)
Frost and Emerson: Voice and Vision (title of article)
Phillip Gerber (editor)
Critical Essays on Robert Frost (title of work)

Boston (place of publication)

1982

124–37 (pages)

Jane Bakerman (author)

American Literature 52 (title of work and volume)

Failure of Love: Female Initiation in the Novels of Toni Morrison (title of essay)

1981 (date)

541–63 (pages)

_____

_____

_____

_____

_____

_____

_____

_____

_____

WORDS AND MEANING

Commonly Misspelled Words ESL

The following is a list of words that are frequently spelled incorrectly.

across	grammar	possible
address	height	prefer
answer	illegal	prejudice
argument	immediately	privilege
athlete	important	probably
beginning	integration	psychology
behavior	intelligent	pursue
calendar	interest	reference
career	interfere	rhythm
conscience	jewelry	ridiculous
crowded	judgment	separate
definite	knowledge	similar
describe	maintain	since
desperate	mathematics	speech
different	meant	strength
disappoint	necessary	success
disapprove	nervous	surprise
doesn't	occasion	taught
eighth	opinion	temperature
environment	optimist	thought
embarrass	particular	thorough
exaggerate	perform	tired
familiar	perhaps	until
finally	personnel	weight
government	possess	written

Words That Sound Alike ESL

Words aural/oral	Definition	Example
aural (adj.)	having to do with hearing	The doctor said that he needs testing for *aural* skills.
oral (adj.)	having to do with speech/the mouth	He had to give an *oral* presentation.

Words	Definition	Example
buy/by		
buy (verb)	to purchase	They *buy* shoes whenever there is a sale.
by (prep.)	past; near; not later than	The dog sits *by* the door.
capital/capitol		
capital (adj.)	fatal; major	The class debated *capital* punishment. The college is making *capital* improvements.
capital (noun)	money; seat of government	He invested his *capital* in the stock market. Sacramento is the *capital* of California.
capitol (noun)	a legislative building	The *capitol* building in Washington, D.C., is often visited by tourists.
complement/compliment		
complement (noun)	something that adds to or completes	The drapery is a *complement* to the furniture.
complement (verb)	to add to or complete	The drapery *complements* the furniture.
compliment (noun)	praise or admiration	He rarely gives *compliments*.
compliment (verb)	to express praise or admiration	He rarely *compliments* anyone.
passed/past		
passed (verb)	moved ahead	The Jeep *passed* the car on the highway.
past (noun)	time before present	The *past* haunted him.
past (prep.)	beyond	The boys ran *past* the graveyard.
past (adj.)	not current	The storms were dangerous this *past year*.
plain/plane		
plain (adj.)	clear; ordinary	The letter lay on the table in *plain* sight.

(continued)

Words	Definition	Example
plain (noun)	flat land with few trees	Early settlers lived in sod homes on *plains*.
plane (noun)	flat/level surface; aircraft; degree of development	As part of her geometry assignment, she was told to plot a line through a *plane*. He was afraid of *planes*. They talk on different *planes*.

presence/presents

presence (noun)	being present; a person's way of behavior	Her *presence* calmed the child. The president has a hypnotic *presence*.
presents (noun)	gifts	Tamiko received piles of *presents* on her birthday.

principal/principle

principal (adj.)	main; most important	The *principal* idea is truth. The *principal* violinist led the orchestra.
principal (noun)	head administrator of a public school; amount of money	The *principal* is rarely popular. The *principal* earns interest in the account.
principle (noun)	a basic truth, assumption	The *principle* of truth is crucial.

rain/reign/rein

rain (noun)	water falling to earth from clouds	The *rain* ended the drought.
rain (verb)	to rain	It *rained* all morning.
reign (noun)	time during which a royal person rules	The *reign* of Queen Elizabeth II of England has been controversial.
reign (verb)	to rule	The Queen *reigned* for many years.
rein (noun)	a strap attached to the bridle used by a rider to control a horse	The young rider grabbed the *reins* in fear.
rein (verb)	to pull on the reins	He *reined* in the horse forcefully.

Words	Definition	Example
sight/site/cite		
sight (noun)	ability to see; a view	Her *sight* was excellent. The pep assembly was a confusing *sight*.
site (noun)	a location	They visited the *site* of their new home.
cite (verb)	to quote as an expert in research	Always *cite* any outside sources used in your writing.
to/too/two		
to (prep.)	toward a given direction	The students ran *to* class.
too (adverb)	very; also	The sale was *too* tempting. My friend bought a dress and shoes, *too*.
two (adj.)	the number 2	He needs *two* cups of coffee in the morning.
waist/waste		
waist (noun)	the middle of the body and the part of clothing that covers this area	The *waist* of the suit fit too snugly.
waste (verb)	careless use	Don't *waste* your time in class.
waste (noun)	objects/concepts that are discarded	Often, *waste* can be recycled.
weather/whether		
weather (noun)	conditions of the atmosphere	The *weather* in the Midwest changes hourly.
whether (conj.)	if this were the case	He does not know *whether* or not he will pass.
whole/hole		
whole (adj.)	all; complete	She read the *whole* novel in one day.
hole (noun)	an opening	The mouse came through the *hole* in the wall.
write/right/rite		
write (verb)	to convey ideas using words	The students will *write* several essays.

(continued)

Words	Definition	Example
right (adj.)	correct; conforming to morality, justice, or law	She enjoys being *right*! We all know the *right* thing to do.
right (noun)	the location on the right-hand side; conservative political position	The president's agenda is shifting to the *right*.
rite (noun)	ritual; repeated ceremonial action	Getting a driver's license at age sixteen is a *rite* of passage for teenagers in our society.

Contractions That Sound Like Other Words ESL

Contraction	Definition	Example
it's/its		
it's	contraction: *it is*	*It's* going to rain.
its	belonging to it	*Its* wings were broken.
they're/their/there		
they're	contraction: *they are*	*They're* ready for any adventure.
their	belonging to them	*Their* pets run their home.
there	at that place	The library is over *there*, not here.
we're/were/where		
we're	contraction: *we are*	*We're* going to the beach for vacation.
were	past tense of *are*	We *were* ready for a week.
where	in which location	*Where* is the map?
who's/whose		
who's	contraction: *who is*	*Who's* going to the party?
whose	belonging to whom	*Whose* socks are on the sofa?
you're/your		
you're	contraction: *you are*	*You're* in the way.
your	belonging to you	*Your* gift is in the mail.

Words That Sound or Look Almost Alike [ESL]

Words	Definition	Example
accept/except		
accept (verb)	to acknowledge as true; to receive	She *accepted* his explanation. They *accepted* the wedding gifts.
except (prep.)	other than	All of the assignments *except* one were easy.
advice/advise		
advice (noun)	suggestions about solutions to a problem	He never listens to *advice*.
advise (verb)	to make suggestions; to give advice	The counselor *advise*s the confused freshmen.
affect/effect		
affect (verb)	to influence	The weather will *affect* your mood.
effect (noun)	end product; result	The *effect* of the accident was obvious for years.
breath/breathe		
breath (noun)	air inhaled or exhaled	The swimmer held his *breath*.
breathe (verb)	to exhale or inhale	The cat *breathes* silently.
choose/chose		
choose (verb)	to pick or select (present tense)	They could not *choose* a restaurant.
chose (verb)	picked or selected (past tense)	They *chose* to order pizza.
conscience/conscious		
conscience (noun)	thought process acknowledging right and wrong	He has no *conscience*.
conscious (adj.)	aware of existence; capable of thinking	The students were not *conscious* after lunch.
council/consul/counsel		
council (noun)	group that meets/plans/governs	The city *council* meets each month.

(continued)

Words	Definition	Example
consul (noun)	government official in foreign service	The German *consul* met with the president.
counsel (verb)	to advise	The department chair *counseled* the frustrated student.

desert/dessert

desert (noun)	dry, barren land	The sunsets on the *desert* are spectacular.
desert (verb)	to leave alone; abandon	His friends *deserted* him.
dessert (noun)	last dish of a meal, often sweet	They decided to avoid sweet, fattening *desserts*.

diner/dinner

diner (noun)	a narrow type of restaurant with counters and booths; a person who is eating	At the *diner*, they have an old juke box. The *diners* enjoy listening to oldies from the juke box.
dinner (noun)	the large, important meal at mid-day or evening	The fried chicken is for *dinner*.

emigrate/immigrate

emigrate (verb)	to leave a country	They *emigrated* from China.
immigrate (verb)	to enter a new country	Lila *immigrated* to the United Kingdom.

farther/further

farther (adv.)	greater distance (physically)	The sprinter ran *farther* than he had to.
further (adv.)	greater distance (mentally)	Most arguments can be *further* developed.
further (verb)	to advance an ideal or goal	The protesters *further* the cause of equality.

loose/lose

loose (adj.)	not tight	*Loose* fitting clothing has been in style recently.
lose (verb)	to misplace or be unable to find; to fail to win	I always *lose* my earrings. He *lost* the tennis match.

Words	Definition	Example
personal/personnel		
personal (adj.)	pertaining to the individual	*Personal* information should remain confidential.
personnel (noun)	employees	*Personnel* should be aware of their benefits.
quiet/quit/quite		
quiet (adj.)	without noise; peaceful	The class is too *quiet.*
quit (verb)	to stop; to give up	The employee *quit* suddenly.
quite (adv.)	definitely	You were *quite* right.
special/especially		
special (adj.)	unique	Their anniversary was a *special* event.
especially (adv.)	even more; very	Final exams can be *especially* difficult.
than/then		
than (conj.)	word to make comparison	Sale prices are better *than* original prices.
then (adv.)	at that time	First they studied; *then* they took the exam.
thorough/though/thought		
thorough (adj.)	detailed, complete, accurate	Social attitudes changed after several *thorough* studies were made.
though (conj.)	despite	*Though* the trees are changing colors, the temperature is warm.
through/threw		
through (prep.)	in one side and out the other	The ball crashed *through* the window.
threw (verb)	past tense of *throw*	The president *threw* the first pitch.

PRACTICE 1   Frequently Confused Words

Fill in the blanks of the following sentences with the correct word.

1. He was not telling her the _____ (hole, whole) story about the _____ (hole, whole) in the bay window.

2. Please _____ (rite/write/right) the _____ (write/rite/right) information in the insurance report.

3. The doctor will _____ (sight/cite/site) statistics to his patients about the necessity of protecting their _____ (site/sight/cite).

4. The boys want _____ (to, too, two) see _____ (to, too, two) movies tonight and hope you want to see them, _____ (to, too, two).

5. The school _____ (principal, principle) would never ask a teacher to betray her most basic _____ (principle, principal).

6. Do not _____ (except, accept) excuses from the students, _____ (accept, except) for me!

7. During his _____ (rain, reign, rein), the King would never appear in public in the _____ (rain, reign, rein).

8. Do not _____ (waist, waste) my time by boasting about the effect of the new equipment on the size of the model's _____ (waist, waste).

9. _____ (weather, whether) or not we attend the party depends on the _____ (whether, weather).

10. The swimmer cannot _____ (breath, breathe) under water; therefore, he takes several deep _____ (breaths, breathes) before he dives.

PRACTICE 2   Frequently Confused Words

Edit the following paragraph for correct word choice. Circle the errors, then write the correct words in the spaces provided.

Buy the time they reached the state capital, the students were very restless from the long bus ride. They jumped off of the bus quickly and formed a line in front of the tour guide. The tour guide greeted the fifth graders and complemented them on there exceptable behavior. She quickly gulped down an aspirin as she guided her charges up the steps to the state senate chambers. The students whispered and shuffled their feet as they past the halls where the lawmakers were working. They admired the portraits of famous governors, and stared up into the domed ceilings. After the tour was over, they ran down the plane cement steps and gathered, laughing and shouting,

in the park to eat lunch.

_____   _____

_____   _____

_____   _____

_____

Confusing Verbs That Sound Alike ESL

The verbs *lie/lay, rise/raise,* and *sit/set* are often confused. In order to under-stand how to use them correctly, it is important to understand the difference between *reflexive verbs,* which *do not* take an object (the verb needs no noun to complete the meaning of the sentence), and *transitive verbs,* which *do* take an object. *Lie, rise,* and *sit* are reflexive; *lay, raise,* and *set* are transitive.

Reflexive Verbs: Lie, Rise, Sit

	Present Tense	Present Participle	Past Tense	Past Participle
lie (to rest or recline)	lie	lying	lay	has/have lain
rise (to move upward)	rise	rising	rose	has/have risen
sit (to move body into sitting position)	sit	sitting	sat	has/have sat

The family dog loves *to lie* by the front door.

Let the bread dough *rise* on the warm kitchen counter.

She *sits* in front of a computer for eight hours every day.

Reflexive verbs are often followed by a prepositional phrase, not a stand-alone noun.

Transitive Verbs: Lay, Raise, Set

	Present Tense	Present Participle	Past Tense	Past Participle
lay (to put an object down)	lay	laying	laid	has/have laid
raise (to lift or move something up)	raise	raising	raised	has/have raised
set (to carefully place something)	set	setting	set	has/have set

> She *lay* the flowers carefully on the table.
> Please *raise* the window shades.
> He *set* the chair by the window.
>
> The object (underlined) is necessary to complete the meaning of these sentences.

PRACTICE 3   Lie/Lay, Rise/Raise, Sit/Set

Write your own sentences using each of the verbs listed below.

1. Lie

_____

_____

_____

2. Lay

_____

_____

_____

3. Rise

_____

_____

_____

4. Raise

_____

_____

_____

5. Sit

_____

_____

_____

6. Set

_____

_____

_____

Two- and Three-Word Verb Phrases [ESL]

Two-word and three-word verb phrases are often difficult for nonnative speakers of English. Many of them are idiomatic expressions, and they need to be studied or memorized.

Phrasal Verbs (Two-Word and Three-Word Verbs)

The term *phrasal verb* refers to a verb and preposition that together have a special meaning. For example, **put + off** means "postpone." Some phrasal verbs consist of three parts. For example, **put + up + with** means "tolerate." Phrasal verbs are also called *two-word verbs* or *three-word verbs*.

A phrasal verb may be either *separable* or *nonseparable*.

Separable Phrasal Verbs

(a) I **handed** *my paper* **in** yesterday. (b) I **handed in** *my paper* yesterday.	With a separable phrasal verb, a noun may come either between the verb and the preposition or after the preposition, as in (a) and (b).
(c) I **handed it in** yesterday. (Incorrect: I handed in it yesterday.)	A pronoun comes between the verb and the preposition if the phrasal verb is separable, as in (c).

Nonseparable Phrasal Verbs

(d) I **ran into** an old friend yesterday. (e) I **ran into** her yesterday. (Incorrect: I ran an old friend into.) (Incorrect: I ran her into yesterday.)	With a nonseparable phrasal verb, a noun or pronoun must follow the preposition, as in (d) and (e).

Phrasal verbs are especially common in informal English. Following is a list of common phrasal verbs and their usual meanings. The phrasal verbs marked with an asterisk (*) are nonseparable.

A	ask out	*ask someone to go on a date*
B	bring about, bring on...........	*cause*
	bring up	*(1) rear children; (2) mention or introduce a topic*

C call back .... *return a telephone call*

call in .... *ask to come to an official place for a specific purpose*

call off .... *cancel*

*call on .... (1) *ask to speak in class;* (2) *visit*

call up .... *call on the telephone*

*catch up (with) .... *reach the same position or level*

*check in, check into .... *register at a hotel*

*check into .... *investigate*

check out .... (1) *take a book from the library;* (2) *investigate*

*check out (of) .... *leave a hotel*

cheer up .... *make (someone) feel happier*

clean up .... *make clean and orderly*

*come across .... *meet by chance*

cross out .... *draw a line through*

cut out .... *stop an annoying activity*

D do over .... *do again*

*drop by, drop in (on) .... *visit informally*

drop off .... *leave something/someone at a place*

drop out (of) .... *stop going to school, to a class, to a club, etc.*

F figure out .... *find the answer by reasoning*

fill out .... *write the completions of a questionnaire or official form*

find out .... *discover information*

G *get along (with) .... *exist satisfactorily*

get back (from) .... (1) *return from a place;* (2) *receive again*

*get in, get into .... (1) *enter a car;* (2) *arrive*

*get off .... *leave an airplane, a bus, a train, a subway, a bicycle*

*get on .... *enter an airplane, a bus, a train, a subway, a bicycle*

*get out of .... (1) *leave a car;* (2) *avoid work or an unpleasant activity*

*get over .... *recover from an illness*

*get through .... *finish*

*get up .... *arise from bed, a chair*

give back .... *return an item to someone*

give up .... *stop trying*

*go over .... *review or check carefully*

*grow up (in) .... *become an adult*

---

*Indicates a nonseparable phrasal verb.

H	hand in	*submit an assignment*
	hang up	(1) *conclude a telephone conversation;* (2) *put clothes on a hanger or a hook*
	have on	*wear*
K	keep out (of)	*not enter*
	*keep up (with)	*stay at the same position or level*
	kick out (of)	*force (someone) to leave*
L	*look after	*take care of*
	*look into	*investigate*
	*look out (for)	*be careful*
	look over	*review or check carefully*
	look up	*look for information in a reference book*
M	make up	(1) *invent;* (2) *do past work*
N	name after, name for	*give a baby the name of someone else*
P	*pass away	*die*
	pass out	(1) *distribute;* (2) *lose consciousness*
	pick out	*select*
	pick up	(1) *go to get someone (e.g., in a car);* (2) *take in one's hand*
	point out	*call attention to*
	put away	*remove to a proper place*
	put back	*return to original place*
	put off	*postpone*
	put on	*put clothes on one's body*
	put out	*extinguish a cigarette or cigar*
	*put up with	*tolerate*
R	*run into, *run across	*meet by chance*
	*run out (of)	*finish a supply of something*
S	*show up	*appear, come*
	shut off	*stop a machine, light, faucet*
T	*take after	*resemble*
	take off	(1) *remove clothing;* (2) *leave on a trip*
	take out	(1) *take someone on a date;* (2) *remove*
	take over	*take control*
	take up	*begin a new activity or topic*
	tear down	*demolish; reduce to nothing*

*Indicates a nonseparable phrasal verb.

tear up	*tear into many little pieces*
think over	*consider carefully*
throw away, throw out	*discard; get rid of*
throw up	*vomit; regurgitate food*
try on	*put on clothing to see if it fits*
turn down	*decrease volume or intensity*
turn in	*(1) submit an assignment;*
	(2) go to bed
turn off	*stop a machine, light, faucet*
turn on	*begin a machine, light, faucet*
turn out	*extinguish a light*
turn up	*increase volume or intensity; arrive*

Source: The material on verb phrases is from Betty S. Azar, *Understanding and Using English Grammar* (Englewood Cliffs, NJ: Prentice Hall Regents). Used with permission.

▼ PRACTICE 4   Phrasal Verbs

Select from the following list of phrasal verbs and complete the following sentences.

call in	figure out
pick out	put up (with)
get back (from)	pick up
look up	takes after
keep out (of)	turn in

1. Please _____ the toys after you are finished playing.

2. _____ the edge of the canyon!

3. The students will _____ their assignments at the beginning of class.

4. The young man examined all of the flowers as he tried to _____ a corsage for his date.

5. _____ the poison ivy!

6. I cannot _____ the answer to this problem!

7. The child _____ his father in looks but after his mother in personality.

8. While you are on vacation, please try not to _____ to the office too often.

9. The teacher would no longer _____ the rudeness of the students.

10. If you are unsure about your project, _____ your topic on the online database at the library.

Additional Readings

Beyond the College Essay

All the student essays in this text demonstrate the five-paragraph mode of essay development. While this essay format is useful in teaching developing writers the elements of effective essay writing for an academic setting, other formats are used by more advanced writing students and professional writers.

There's an old saying that "form follows function." This means that the format that the writing takes is created to best suit the ideas the author is trying to get across to the reader. For instance, while paragraphs in college essays usually have at least four or five sentences, some paragraphs in professional essays may consist of a single sentence. Perhaps the writer wished to emphasize a particular idea or image by presenting it in a stand-alone sentence. This focuses the reader's attention on the idea or image without the distraction of other ideas and images in other sentences in a longer paragraph. Also, when advanced writing students and professional writers take on an assignment, the professor or editor, respectively, might give the writers specific instructions or guidelines that the writer must follow in order to complete the assignment. So, as you read the professional essays in the Additional Readings section, be aware that their formats are designed specifically to present particular ideas or assignments in the most effective manner.

DESCRIPTION

HAVE YOU EVER MET AN ASIAN MAN YOU THOUGHT WAS SEXY?

Eric Kim

> In this essay, the writer talks about stereotypes, an oversimplified opinion or conception based on conventional characteristics (for example, Asians are good at math; blondes are dumb). Think of some stereotypes that you might hold. Keep them in mind as you read the essay.

Vocabulary

Before you begin reading, look up the definitions of the following words that appear in the essay. The number in parentheses after each word refers to the paragraph number of the essay.

affront (3)	asexual (2)	caricatures (7)
chauvinist (4)	diatribes (5)	nonentity (6)
retrospect (2)	shun (4)	spewing (7)
waylaid (7)		

Have You Ever Met an Asian Man You Thought Was Sexy?

1   "Yo, Bruce Lee! Hey, whatzaah happening?" That's what a group of teenage guys shouted at me a couple of years ago as I walked down the street with a friend. They followed that up with a series of yelps and shrieks that I took to be their attempts at kung fu sounds. As I was about to turn and

respond, my friend quickly pointed out that it would be better, and safer, to ignore these guys.

2   In retrospect, though, I wonder if rising above it was the best response. Sometimes I don't believe I can change people's stereotypes about Asians without confronting them. At least Bruce Lee, the late martial arts expert, is at the macho end of the spectrum, along with the stereotype of the greedy, wealthy businessmen who are invading America. At the other end of the spectrum, Asian men in America are seen as geeks—short, nerdy, passive, and somewhat asexual "Orientals."

3   As a six-foot, 180-pound, Korean American guy, I always hated that people would assume I was a wimpy bookworm who couldn't play sports. It pleased me to see how upset non-Asians would get after a few Asian friends and I whipped them in a game of full-court basketball. Before we hit the court, the other guys would snicker and assume we'd be easy to beat. Afterward, they'd act as if being outdone in sports by an Asian was an affront to their masculinity.

4   It's different for Asian women, who are usually stereotyped as exotic, passive, sensual, the ultimate chauvinist fantasy. The reality of these stereotypes is played out on the street: Look around and you'll see an Asian woman with a Caucasian man a lot sooner than you'll see a white woman with an Asian date. Even Asian women sometimes shun Asian men as being either too wimpy or too dominating. I was born and grew up in Seoul, South Korea, and went to an international high school there. The student body was about 80 percent Asian and 20 percent Caucasian. I think being in the majority gave me a certain social confidence. I never thought twice about dating or flirting with non-Asian girls. If I felt nervous or awkward, it was because I was shy, not because I wasn't white.

5   When I started college in the United States, I promised myself that I'd meet people of all races, since most of my friends in Seoul had been Asian. Yet when I arrived here, for the first time in my life I felt like a minority. For the first time in my life, I was told to "go back home" and had to listen to strangers on the bus give me their diatribes on Vietnam and Korea. Feeling I was a minority affected how I approached other people.

6   Even though there were a lot of attractive non-Asian women at school, I hesitated to approach them, because I imagined that they were only interested in Caucasian guys. I assumed that non-Asian women bought the Asian stereotypes and saw me as a nonentity. It wasn't that I kept trying and getting shot down; I simply assumed they would never consider me. The frustrating mix of my own pride and the fear of getting rejected always managed to keep me from approaching a non-Asian woman I was attracted to.

7   My girlfriend now is Asian American. There are many things I love about her, and it strengthens our relationship that we have a cultural bond. Relationships are about trust, vulnerability, and a willingness to open up. That can be hard for an Asian man to achieve with a non-Asian woman; though he may find her attractive, his emotions may be blocked by fear, waylaid by the caricatures of Asian men as paranoid deli owners, Confucius-spewing detectives, or kung fu fighters with fists of fury.

8   These images say little about what it means to be a twenty-four-year-old Asian man. These images don't reflect our athleticism, our love of rap, or our possible addiction to ESPN. Because of these images, Asian men are rarely seen for what we are—and so we may look at a non-Asian woman with interest, then tuck that interest away.

9   It's not easy to confess that I know many women don't find me attractive. But for me, the very process of facing down Asian stereotypes makes them less meaningful. Most of all, I try to keep a sense of humor about it. After all, when my friends and I whip some unsuspecting non-Asians on the basketball court, *they* are the ones who are victims of the stereotypes, not us.

Descriptive Technique Questions

1. Identify paragraphs in which the writer uses objective description and those in which he uses subjective description.

_____

_____

_____

2. How does the author describe the Asian male when perceived as the antithesis of Bruce Lee?

_____

_____

_____

3. How does the writer describe the stereotypical Asian female?

_____

_____

_____

Critical Reading Questions

1. What is the main idea of the essay?

_____

_____

_____

2. What does the author mean in the last paragraph when he says _"they_ [non-Asians] are the ones who are victims of the stereotypes, not us"?

_____

_____

_____

3. According to the author, what are the negative consequences of stereotyping?

_____

_____

_____

Descriptive Writing Opportunities

1. At the beginning of the essay, Kim recounts something a group of teenagers shouted at him. Write a paragraph describing a variety of people by the stereotypical things they say or believe.

2. Inspect another's outward appearance, clothing, and physical features. Write an essay about how others might describe that person in stereotypical terms.

▼
THE JOY LUCK CLUB

Amy Tan

> The following is an excerpt from Amy Tan's novel *The Joy Luck Club*. In the excerpt, Tan describes how the club started, surrounded by the devastation and atrocities committed by the Japanese when they invaded Kweilin, China, in the 1930s.

Vocabulary

Before you begin reading, look up the definitions of the following words that appear in the essay. The number in parentheses after each word refers to the paragraph number of the essay.

ingots (13)   kinky (3)   meager (14)

prolong (19)   rickshaw (8)   scurried (9)

shabby (5)

The Joy Luck Club

1   My mother started the San Francisco version of the Joy Luck Club in 1949, two years before I was born. This was the year my mother and father left China with one stiff leather trunk filled only with fancy silk dresses. There was no time to pack anything else, my mother had explained to my father after they boarded the boat. Still his hands swam frantically between the slippery silks, looking for his cotton shirts and wool pants.

2   When they arrived in San Francisco, my father made her hide those shiny clothes. She wore the same brown-checked Chinese dress until the Refugee Welcome Society gave her two hand-me-down dresses, all too large in sizes for American women. The society was composed of a group of white-haired American missionary ladies from the First Chinese Baptist Church. And because of their gifts, my parents could not refuse their invitation to join the church. Nor could they ignore the old ladies' practical advice to improve their English through Bible study class on Wednesday nights and, later, through choir practice on Saturday mornings. This was how my parents met the Hsus, the Jongs, and the St. Clairs. My mother could sense that the women of these families also had unspeakable tragedies they had left behind in China and hopes they couldn't begin to express in their fragile English. Or at least, my mother recognized the numbness in these women's faces. And she saw how quickly their eyes moved when she told them her idea for the Joy Luck Club.

3   Joy Luck was an idea my mother remembered from the days of her first marriage in Kweilin, before the Japanese came. That's why I think of Joy Luck as her Kweilin story. It was the story she would always tell me when she was bored, when there was nothing to do, when every bowl had been washed and the Formica table had been wiped down twice, when my father sat reading the newspaper and smoking one Pall Mall cigarette after another, a warning not to disturb him. This is when my mother would take out a box of old ski sweaters sent to us by unseen relatives from Vancouver. She would snip the bottom of a sweater and pull out a kinky thread of yarn, anchoring it to a piece of cardboard. And as she began to roll with one sweeping rhythm, she would start her story. Over the years, she told me the same story, except for the ending, which grew darker, casting long shadows into her life, and eventually into mine.

4   "I dreamed about Kweilin before I ever saw it," my mother began, speaking Chinese. "I dreamed of jagged peaks lining a curving river, with magic moss greening the banks. At the tops of these peaks were white mists. And if you could float down this river and eat the moss for food, you would be strong enough to climb the peak. If you slipped, you would only fall into a bed of soft moss and laugh. And once you reached the top, you would be able to see everything and feel such happiness it would be enough to never have worries in your life again.

5   "In China, everybody dreamed about Kweilin. And when I arrived, I realized how shabby my dreams were, how poor my thoughts. When I saw the hills, I laughed and shuddered at the same time. The peaks looked like giant fried fish heads trying to jump out of a vat of oil. Behind each hill, I could see shadows of another fish, and then another and another. And then the clouds would move just a little and the hills would suddenly become monstrous elephants marching slowly toward me! Can you see this? And at the root of the hill were secret caves. Inside grew hanging rock gardens in the shapes and colors of cabbage, winter melons, turnips, and onions. These were things so strange and beautiful you can't ever imagine them.

6   "But I didn't come to Kweilin to see how beautiful it was. The man who was my husband brought me and our two babies to Kweilin because he thought we would be safe. He was an officer with the Kuomintang, and after he put us down in a small room in a two-story house, he went off to the northwest, to Chungking.

7   "We knew the Japanese were winning, even when the newspapers said they were not. Every day, every hour, thousands of people poured into the city, crowding the sidewalks, looking for places to live. They came from the East, West, North, and South. They were rich and poor, Shanghainese, Cantonese, northerners, and not just Chinese, but foreigners and missionaries of every religion. And there was, of course, the Kuomintang and their army officers who thought they were top level to everyone else.

8   "We were a city of leftovers mixed together. If it hadn't been for the Japanese, there would have been plenty of reason for fighting to break out among these different people. Can you see it? Shanghai people with north-water peasants, bankers with barbers, rickshaw pullers with Burma refugees. Everybody looked down on someone else. It didn't matter that everybody shared the same sidewalk to spit on and suffered the same fast-moving diarrhea. We all had the same stink, but everybody complained someone else smelled the worst. Me? Oh, I hated the American air force officers who said habba-habba sounds to make my face turn red. But the worst were the northern peasants who emptied their noses into their hands and pushed people around and gave everybody their dirty disease.

9   "So you can see how quickly Kweilin lost its beauty for me. I no longer climbed the peaks to say, How lovely are these hills! I only wondered which

hills the Japanese had reached. I sat in the dark corners of my house with a baby under each arm, waiting with nervous feet. When the sirens cried out to warn us of bombers, my neighbors and I jumped to our feet and scurried to the deep caves to hide like wild animals. But you can't stay in the dark for so long. Something inside of you starts to fade and you become like a starving person, crazy-hungry for light. Outside I could hear the bombing. Boom! Boom! And then the sound of raining rocks. And inside I was no longer hungry for the cabbage or the turnips of the hanging rock garden. I could only see the dripping bowels of an ancient hill that might collapse on top of me. Can you imagine how it is, to want to be neither inside nor outside, to want to be nowhere and disappear?

10   "So when the bombing sounds grew farther away, we would come back out like newborn kittens scratching our way back to the city. And always, I would be amazed to find the hills against the burning sky had not been torn apart.

11   "I thought up Joy Luck on a summer night that was so hot even the moths fainted to the ground, their wings were so heavy with the damp heat. Every place was so crowded there was no room for fresh air. Unbearable smells from the sewers rose up to my second-story window and the stink had nowhere else to go but into my nose. At all hours of the night and day, I heard screaming sounds. I didn't know if it was a peasant slitting the throat of a runaway pig or an officer beating a half-dead peasant for lying in his way on the sidewalk. I didn't go to the window to find out. What use would it have been? And that's when I thought I needed something to do to help me move.

12   "My idea was to have a gathering of four women, one for each corner of my mah jong table. I knew which women I wanted to ask. They were all young like me, with wishful faces. One was an army officer's wife, like myself. Another was a girl with very fine manners from a rich family in Shanghai. She had escaped with only a little money. And there was a girl from Nanking who had the blackest hair I have ever seen. She came from a low-class family, but she was pretty and pleasant and had married well, to an old man who died and left her with a better life.

13   "Each week one of us would host a party to raise money and to raise our spirits. The hostess had to serve special *dyansyin* foods to bring good fortune of all kinds—dumplings shaped like silver money ingots, long rice noodles for long life, boiled peanuts for conceiving sons, and of course, many good-luck oranges for a plentiful, sweet life.

14   "What fine food we treated ourselves to with our meager allowances! We didn't notice that the dumplings were stuffed mostly with stringy squash and that the oranges were spotted with wormy holes. We ate sparingly, not as if we didn't have enough, but to protest how we could not eat another bite, we had already bloated ourselves from earlier in the day. We knew we had luxuries few people could afford. We were the lucky ones.

15   "After filling our stomachs, we would then fill a bowl with money and put it where everyone could see. Then we would sit down at the mah jong table. My table was from my family and was of a very fragrant red wood, not what you would call rose-wood, but *hong mu*, which is so fine there's no English word for it. The table had a very thick pad, so that when the mah jong *pai* were spilled onto the table the only sound was of ivory tiles washing against one another.

16   "Once we started to play, nobody could speak, except to say '*Pung!*' or '*Chr!*' when taking a tile. We had to play with seriousness and think of nothing else but adding to our happiness through winning. But after sixteen rounds, we would again feast, this time to celebrate our good fortune. And then we would talk into the night until the morning, saying stories about good times in the past and good times yet to come.

17   "Oh, what good stories! Stories spilling out all over the place! We almost laughed to death. A rooster that ran into the house screeching on top of dinner bowls, the same bowls that held him quietly in pieces the next day! And one about a girl who wrote love letters for two friends who loved the same man. And a silly foreign lady who fainted on a toilet when firecrackers went off next to her.

18   "People thought we were wrong to serve banquets every week while many people in the city were starving, eating rats and, later, the garbage that the poorest rats used to feed on. Others thought we were possessed by demons—to celebrate when even within our own families we had lost generations, had lost homes and fortunes, and were separated, husband from wife, brother from sister, daughter from mother. Hnnnh! How could we laugh, people asked.

19   "It's not that we had no heart or eyes for pain. We were all afraid. We all had our miseries. But to despair was to wish back for something already lost. Or to prolong what was already miserable. How much can you wish for a favorite warm coat that hangs in the closet of a house that burned down with your mother and father inside of it? How long can you see in your mind arms and legs hanging from telephone wires and starving dogs running down the streets with half-chewed hands dangling from their jaws? What was worse, we asked among ourselves, to sit and wait for our own deaths with proper somber faces? Or to choose our own happiness?

20   "So we decided to hold parties and pretend each week had become the new year. Each week we could forget past wrongs done to us. We weren't allowed to think a bad thought. We feasted, we laughed, we played games, lost and won, we told the best stories. And each week, we could hope to be lucky. That hope was our only joy. And that's how we came to call our little parties Joy Luck."

21   My mother used to end the story on a happy note, bragging about her skill at the game. "I won many times and was so lucky the others teased that I had learned the trick of a clever thief," she said. "I won tens of thousands of *yuan*. But I wasn't rich. No. By then paper money had become worthless. Even toilet paper was worth more. And that made us laugh harder, to think a thousand-*yuan* note wasn't even good enough to rub on our bottoms."

Descriptive Technique Questions

1. Sensory images are very important to effective description. List at least two textures (touch), sounds, sights, tastes, and smells in the story. How do these sensory images help the reader understand the physical and emotional environment of the story's setting?

_____

_____

_____

_____

_____

_____

_____

_____

_____

_____

_____

2. Point out some examples of figurative language: simile, metaphor, and personification. How do they add to the essay's emotional impact?

_____

_____

3. How is the food in paragraphs 13 and 14 described—positively or negatively? Does this description of the food support or work against the reason the Joy Luck Club was started?

_____

_____

_____

Critical Reading Questions

1. The title of the selection is "The Joy Luck Club." How can the title be both a literal and ironic description of the women's situation?

_____

_____

_____

_____

2. A great variety of food is described at the meetings, as well as the process of cating it. What is the significance of the focus on food and how it's eaten?

_____

_____

_____

_____

_____

_____

3. There are numerous descriptions of nature. Point out three or four examples. How do they add to the essay's meaning?

_____

_____

_____

_____

Descriptive Writing Opportunities

1. Write a paragraph describing the food and table setting at a popular holiday feast. In your essay, focus on how these things might describe the family celebrating the occasion.
2. Write an essay describing some important event from your childhood. Along with similes, metaphors, and other language devices, use sensory images to focus on the dominant impression you wish to convey.

NARRATION

FOR MY INDIAN DAUGHTER

Lewis Sawaquat

> Prejudice, cultural awareness, and ethnic pride are three basic elements involved in any racial minority's world. In this essay, the author focuses on the problems caused by ethnicity, ancestry, and heritage.

Vocabulary

Before you begin to read, look up the definitions of the following words that appear in the story. The number in parentheses after each word refers to the paragraph number of the essay.

affluent (5)	backlash (4)	comeuppance (7)
forge (9)	guttural (2)	iridescent (9)
masquerade (10)	mingling (1)	unbidden (1)

For My Indian Daughter

1   My little girl is singing herself to sleep upstairs, her voice mingling with the sounds of the birds outside in the old maple trees. She is two and I am nearly 50, and I am very taken with her. She came along late in my life, unexpected and unbidden, a startling gift.

2   Today at the beach my chubby-legged, brown-skinned daughter ran laughing into the water as fast as she could. My wife and I laughed watching her, until we heard behind us a low guttural curse and then an unpleasant voice raised in an imitation war whoop.

3   I turned to see a fat man in a bathing suit, white and soft as a grub, as he covered his mouth and prepared to make the Indian war cry again. He was middle-aged, younger than I, and had three little children lined up next to him, grinning foolishly. My wife suggested we leave the beach, and I agreed.

4   I knew the man was not unusual in his feelings against Indians. His beach behavior might have been socially unacceptable to more civilized whites, but his basic view of Indians is expressed daily in our small town, frequently on the editorial pages of the county newspaper, as white people speak out against Indian fishing rights and land rights, saying in essence, "Those Indians are taking our fish, our land." It doesn't matter to them that we were here first, that the U.S. Supreme Court has ruled in our favor. It matters to them that we have something they want, and they hate us for it. Backlash is the common explanation of the attacks on Indians, the bumper stickers that say, "Spear an Indian, Save a Fish," but I know better. The hatred of Indians goes back to the beginning when white people came to this country. For me it goes back to my childhood in Harbor Springs, Mich.

5   *Theft.* Harbor Springs is now a summer resort for the very affluent, but a hundred years ago it was the Indian village of my Ottawa ancestors. My grandmother, Anna Showanessy, and other Indians like her, had their land there taken by treaty, by fraud, by violence, by theft. They remembered how whites had burned down the village at Burt Lake in 1900 and pushed the Indians out. These were the stories in my family.

6   When I was a boy my mother told me to walk down the alleys in Harbor Springs and not to wear my orange football sweater out of the house. This way I would not stand out, not be noticed, and not be a target.

7   I wore my orange sweater anyway and deliberately avoided the alleys. I was the biggest person I knew and wasn't really afraid. But I met my comeuppance when I enlisted in the U.S. Army. One night all the men in my barracks gathered together and, gang-fashion, pulled me into the shower and scrubbed me down with rough brushes used for floors, saying, "We won't have any dirty Indians in our outfit." It is a point of irony that I was cleaner than any of them. Later in Korea I learned how to kill, how to bully, how to hate Koreans. I came out of the war tougher than ever and, strangely, white.

8   I went to college, got married, lived in La Porte, Ind., worked as a surveyor and raised three boys. I headed Boy Scout groups, never thinking it odd when the Scouts did imitation Indian dances, imitation Indian lore.

9   One day when I was 35 or thereabouts I heard about an Indian powwow. My father used to attend them and so with great curiosity and a strange joy at discovering a part of my heritage, I decided the thing to do to get ready for this big event was to have my friend make me a spear in his forge. The steel was fine and blue and iridescent. The feathers on the shaft were bright and proud.

10 In a dusty state fairground in southern Indiana, I found white people dressed as Indians. I learned they were "hobbyists," that is, it was their hobby and leisure pastime to masquerade as Indians on weekends. I felt ridiculous with my spear, and I left.

11 It was years before I could tell anyone of the embarrassment of this weekend and see any humor in it. But in a way it was that weekend, for all its silliness, that was my awakening. I realized I didn't know who I was. I didn't have an Indian name. I didn't speak the Indian language. I didn't know the Indian customs. Dimly I remembered the Ottawa word for dog, but it was a baby word, *kahgee,* not the full word, *muhkaghee,* which I was later to learn. Even more hazily I remembered a naming ceremony (my own). I remembered legs dancing around me, dust. Where had that been? What had I been? "Sawaquat," my mother told me when I asked, "where the tree begins to grow."

12 That was 1968, and I was not the only Indian in the country who was feeling the need to remember who he or she was. There were others. They

had powwows, real ones, and eventually I found them. Together we researched our past, a search that for me culminated in the Longest Walk, a march on Washington in 1978. Maybe because I now know what it means to be Indian, it surprises me that others don't. Of course there aren't very many of us left. The chances of an average person knowing an average Indian in an average lifetime are pretty slim.

13   *Circle.* Still, I was amused one day when my small, four-year-old neighbor looked at me as I was hoeing in my garden and said, "You aren't a real Indian, are you?" Scotty is little, talkative, likable. Finally I said, "I'm a real Indian." He looked at me for a moment and then said squinting into the sun, "Then where's your horse and feathers?" The child was simply a smaller, whiter version of my own ignorant self years before. We'd both seen too much TV, that's all. He was not to be blamed. And so, in a way, the moronic man on the beach today is blameless. We come full circle to realize other people are like ourselves, as discomfiting as that may be sometimes.

14   As I sit in my old chair on my porch, in a light that is fading so the leaves are barely distinguishable against the sky, I can picture my girl asleep upstairs. I would like to prepare her for what's to come, take her each step of the way saying, there's a place to avoid, here's what I know about this, but much of what's before her she must go through alone. She must pass through pain and joy and solitude and community to discover her own inner self that is unlike any other and come through that passage to the place where she sees all people are one, and in so seeing may live her life in a brighter future.

Narrative Technique Questions

1. Which sentence sums up the point of the story?

_____

_____

_____

_____

_____

2. Which of the six reporter's questions does the writer use most often to develop the story? Give examples.

_____

_____

_____

3. Identify at least five transitional expressions used by the author. How do they help order the events chronologically?

_____

_____

_____

Critical Reading Questions

1. What do you think is the purpose behind Sawaquat writing this story?

_____

_____

_____

2. The author writes about an event that involved his daughter. Why does his memory of her stir within him remembrances of his own identity crises?

_____

_____

_____

3. What does the author learn about himself after attending his first pow-wow?

_____

_____

_____

Narrative Writing Opportunities

1. Write a paragraph about a particular cultural heritage. Focus on an event or celebration of that heritage.
2. Write an essay about a person arriving in a new country. How would they describe their cultural identity to their new neighbors, and how would they explain how their culture and ethnicity affects their life?

▼

KUBOTA

Garrett Hongo

Many Japanese Americans had their possessions, property, and businesses taken away from them during World War II. In this essay, Hongo retells his grandfather's experiences from that period and, in so doing, expresses the feelings and experiences of an entire group.

Vocabulary
Before you begin reading, look up the definitions of the following words that appear in the essay. The number in parentheses after each word refers to the paragraph number of the essay.

auxiliary (6)   habitually (9)   ideograms (1)

idiom (10)   injunction (12)   interstices (19)

pidgin (11)   phalanx (15)   plangent (9)

querulous (21)   stigma (14)

Kubota

1   On December 8, 1941, the day after the Japanese attack on Pearl Harbor in Hawaii, my grandfather barricaded himself with his family—my grandmother, my teenage mother, her two sisters and two brothers—inside of his home in La'ie, a sugar plantation village on Oahu's North Shore. This was my maternal grandfather, a man most villagers called by his last name, Kubota. It could mean either "Wayside Field" or else "Broken Dreams," depending on which ideograms he used. Kubota ran La'ie's general store, and the previous night, after a long day of bad news on the radio, some locals had come by, pounded on the front door, and made threats. One was said to have brandished a machete. They were angry and shocked, as the whole nation was in the aftermath of the surprise attack. Kubota was one of the few Japanese Americans in the village and president of the local Japanese language school. He had become a target for their rage and suspicion. A wise man, he locked all his doors and windows and did not open his store the next day, but stayed closed and waited for news from some official.

2   He was a *kibei,* a Japanese American born in Hawaii (a U.S. territory then, so he was thus a citizen) but who was subsequently sent back by his father for formal education in Hiroshima, Japan, their home province. *Kibei* is written with two ideograms in Japanese: one is the word for "return" and the other is the word for "rice." Poetically, it means one who returns from America, known as the Land of Rice in Japanese (by contrast, Chinese immigrants called their new home Mountain of Gold).

3   Kubota was graduated from a Japanese high school and then came back to Hawaii as a teenager. He spoke English—and a Hawaiian creole version of it at that—with a Japanese accent. But he was well liked and good at numbers, scrupulous and hard working like so many immigrants and children of immigrants. Castle & Cook, a grower's company that ran the sugarcane business along the North Shore, hired him on first as a stock boy and then appointed him to run one of its company stores. He did well, had the trust of management and labor—not an easy accomplishment in any day—married, had children, and had begun to exert himself in community affairs and excel in his own recreations. He put together a Japanese community organization that backed a Japanese language school for children and sponsored teachers from Japan. Kubota boarded many of them, in succession, in his own home. This made dinners a silent affair for his talkative, Hawaiian-bred children, as their stern *sensei,* or teacher, was nearly always at table and their own abilities in the Japanese language were as delinquent as their attendance. While Kubota and the *sensei* rattled on about things Japanese, speaking Japanese, his children hurried through their suppers and tried to run off early to listen to the radio shows.

4   After dinner, while the *sensei* graded exams seated in a wicker chair in the spare room and his wife and children gathered around the radio in the front parlor, Kubota sat on the screened porch outside, reading the local Japanese newspapers. He finished reading about the same time as he finished the tea he drank for his digestion—a habit he'd learned in Japan—and then he'd get out his fishing gear and spread it out on the plank floors. The wraps on his rods needed to be redone, gears in his reels needed oil, and, once through

with those tasks, he'd painstakingly wind on hundreds of yards of new line. Fishing was his hobby and his passion. He spent weekends camping along the North Shore beaches with his children, setting up umbrella tents, packing a rice pot and hibachi along for meals. And he caught fish. *Ulu'a* mostly, the huge surf-feeding fish known on the mainland as the jack crevalle, but he'd go after almost anything in its season. In Kawela, a plantation-owned bay nearby, he fished for mullet Hawaiian-style with a throw net, stalking the bottom-hugging, gray-backed schools as they gathered at the stream mouths and in the freshwater springs. In an outrigger out beyond the reef, he'd try for *aku*—the skipjack tuna prized for steaks and, sliced raw and mixed with fresh seaweed and cut onions, for *sashimi* salad. In Kahaluu and Ka'awa and on an offshore rock locals called Goat Island, he loved to go torching, stringing lanterns on bamboo poles stuck in the sand to attract *kumu'u*, the red goatfish, as they schooled at night just inside the reef. But in Lai'e on Laniloa Point near Kahuku, the northernmost tip of Oahu, he cast twelve- and four-teen-foot surf rods for the huge, varicolored, and fast-running *ulu'a* as they ran for schools of squid and baitfish just beyond the biggest breakers and past the low sand flats wadable from the shore to nearly a half mile out. At sunset, against the western light, he looked as if he walked on water as he came back, fish and rods slung over his shoulders, stepping along the rock and coral path just inches under the surface of a running tide.

5   When it was torching season, in December or January, he'd drive out the afternoon before and stay with old friends, the Tanakas or Yoshikawas, shop-keepers like him who ran stores near the fishing grounds. They'd have been preparing for weeks, selecting and cutting their bamboo poles, cleaning the hurricane lanterns, tearing up burlap sacks for the cloths they'd soak with kerosene and tie onto sticks they'd poke into the soft sand of the shallows. Once lit, touched off with a Zippo lighter, these would be the torches they'd use as beacons to attract the schooling fish. In another time, they might have made up a dozen paper lanterns of the kind mostly used for decorating the summer folk dances outdoors on the grounds of the Buddhist church during O-Bon, the Festival for the Dead. But now, wealthy and modern and efficient killers of fish, Tanaka and Kubota used rag torches and Colemans and cast rods with tips made of Tonkin bamboo and butts of American-spun fiberglass. After just one good night, they might bring back a prize bounty of a dozen burlap bags filled with scores of bloody, rigid fish delicious to eat and even better to give away as gifts to friends, family, and special customers.

6   It was Monday night, the day after Pearl Harbor, and there was a rattling knock at the front door. Two FBI agents presented themselves, showed iden-tification, and took my grandfather in for questioning in Honolulu. He didn't return home for days. No one knew what had happened or what was wrong. But there was a roundup going on of all those in the Japanese-American community suspected of sympathizing with the enemy and worse. My grand-father was suspected of espionage, and communicating with offshore Japan-ese submarines launched from the attack fleet days before war began. Tor-pedo planes and escort fighters, decorated with the insignia of the Rising Sun, had taken an approach route from northwest of Oahu directly across Kahuku Point and on toward Pearl. They had strafed an auxiliary air station near the fishing grounds my grandfather loved and destroyed a small gun battery there, killing three men. Kubota was known to have sponsored and harbored Japanese nationals in his own home. He had a radio. He had wholesale access to firearms. Circumstances and an undertone of racial resentment had com-bined with wartime hysteria in the aftermath of the tragic naval battle to cast suspicion on the loyalties of my grandfather and all other Japanese Ameri-cans. The FBI reached out and pulled hundreds of them in for questioning in dragnets cast throughout the West Coast and Hawaii.

7   My grandfather was lucky; he'd somehow been let go after only a few days. Others were not as fortunate. Hundreds, from small communities in Washington, California, Oregon, and Hawaii, were rounded up and, after what appeared to be routine questioning, shipped off under Justice Department orders to holding centers in Leuppe on the Navaho reservation in Arizona, in Fort Missoula in Montana, and on Sand Island in Honolulu Harbor. There were other special camps on Maui in Ha'iku and on Hawaii—the Big Island—in my own home village of Volcano.

8   Many of these men—it was exclusively the Japanese-American men suspected of ties to Japan who were initially rounded up—did not see their families again for more than four years. Under a suspension of due process that was only after the fact ruled as warranted by military necessity, they were, if only temporarily, "disappeared" in Justice Department prison camps scattered in particularly desolate areas of the United States designated as militarily "safe." These were grim forerunners of the assembly centers and concentration camps for the 120,000 Japanese-American evacuees that were to come later.

9   I am Kubota's eldest grandchild, and I remember him as a lonely habitually silent old man who lived with us in our home near Los Angeles for most of my childhood and adolescence. It was the fifties, and my parents had emigrated from Hawaii to the mainland in the hope of a better life away from the old sugar plantation. After some success, they had sent back for my grandparents who did the work of the household while my mother and father worked their salaried city jobs. My grandmother cooked and sewed, washed our clothes, and knitted in the front room under the light of a huge lamp with a bright three-way bulb. Kubota raised a flower garden, read up on soils and grasses in gardening books, and planted a zoysia lawn in front and a dichondra one in back. He planted a small patch near the rear block wall with green onions, eggplant, white Japanese radishes, and cucumber. While he hoed and spaded the loamless, clayey earth of Los Angeles, he sang particularly plangent songs in Japanese about plum blossoms and bamboo groves.

10   Once, in the mid-sixties, after a dinner during which, as always, he had been silent while he worked away at a meal of fish and rice spiced with dabs of Chinese mustard and catsup thinned with soy sauce, Kubota took his own dishes to the kitchen sink and washed them up. He took a clean jelly jar out of the cupboard—the glass was thick and its shape squatty like an old-fashioned. He reached around to the hutch below where he kept his bourbon. He made himself a drink and retired to the living room where I was expected to join him for "talk story," the Hawaiian idiom for chewing the fat.

11   I was a teenager and, though I was bored listening to stories I'd heard often enough before at holiday dinners, I was dutiful. I took my spot on the couch next to Kubota and heard him out. Usually, he'd tell me about his schooling in Japan where he learned judo along with mathematics and literature. He'd learned the *soroban* there—the abacus, which was the original pocket calculator of the Far East—and that, along with his strong, judo-trained back, got him his first job in Hawaii. This was the moral. "Study *ha-ahd*," he'd say with pidgin emphasis. "Learn read good. Learn speak da kine *good* English." The message is the familiar one taught to any children of immigrants: success through education. And imitation. But this time, Kubota reached down into his past and told me a different story. I was thirteen by then, and I suppose he thought me ready for it. He told me about Pearl Harbor, how the planes flew in wing after wing of formations over his old house in La'ie in Hawaii, and how, the next day, after Roosevelt had made his famous "Day of Infamy" speech about the treachery of the Japanese, the FBI agents had come to his door and taken him in, hauled him off to Honolulu for questioning, and held him without charge for several days. I thought he

was lying. I thought he was making up a kind of horror story to shock me and give his moral that much more starch. But it was true. I asked around. I brought it up during history class in junior high school, and my teacher, after silencing me and stepping me off to the back of the room, told me that it was indeed so. I asked my mother and she said it was true. I asked my schoolmates, who laughed and ridiculed me for being so ignorant. We lived in a Japanese-American community, and the parents of most of my classmates were the *nisei* who had been interned as teenagers all through the war. But there was a strange silence around all of this. There was a hush, as if one were invoking the ill powers of the dead when one brought it up. No one cared to speak about the evacuation and relocation for very long. It wasn't in our history books, though we were studying World War II at the time. It wasn't in the family albums of the people I knew and whom I'd visit staying over weekends with friends. And it wasn't anything that the family talked about or allowed me to keep bringing up either. I was given the facts, told sternly and pointedly that "it was war" and that "nothing could be done." *"Shikatta ga nai"* is the phrase in Japanese, a kind of resolute and determinist pronouncement on how to deal with inexplicable tragedy. I was to know it but not to dwell on it. Japanese Americans were busy trying to forget it ever happened and were having a hard enough time building their new lives after "camp." It was as if we had no history for four years and the relocation was something unspeakable.

12   But Kubota would not let it go. In session after session, for months it seemed, he pounded away at his story. He wanted to tell me the names of the FBI agents. He went over their questions and his responses again and again. He'd tell me how one would try to act friendly toward him, offering him cigarettes, while the other, who hounded him with accusations and threats, left the interrogation room. Good cop, bad cop, I thought to myself, already superficially streetwise from stories black classmates told of the Watts riots and from my having watched too many episodes of *Dragnet* and *The Mod Squad*. But Kubota was not interested with my experiences. I was not made yet, and he was determined that his stories be part of my making. He spoke quietly at first, mildly, but once into his narrative and after his drink was down, his voice would rise and quaver with resentment and he'd make his accusations. He gave his testimony to me and I held it at first cautiously in my conscience like it was an heirloom too delicate to expose to strangers and anyone outside of the world Kubota made with his words. "I give you story now," he once said, "and you learn speak good, eh?" It was my job, as the disciple of his preaching I had then become, Ananda to his Buddha, to reassure him with a promise. "You learn speak good like the Dillingham," he'd say another time, referring to the wealthy scion of the grower family who had once run, unsuccessfully, for one of Hawaii's first senatorial seats. Or he'd then invoke a magical name, the name of one of his heroes, a man he thought particularly exemplary and righteous. "Learn speak dah good Ingrish like *Mistah Inouye*," Kubota shouted. "He *lick* dah Dillingham even in debate. I saw on *terre-bision* myself." He was remembering the debates before the first senatorial election just before Hawaii was admitted to the Union as its fiftieth state. "You *tell* the story," Kubota would end. And I had my injunction.

13   The town we settled in after the move from Hawaii is called Gardena, the independently incorporated city south of Los Angeles and north of San Pedro harbor. At its northern limit, it borders on Watts and Compton, black towns. To the southwest are Torrance and Redondo Beach, white towns. To the rest of L.A., Gardena is primarily famous for having legalized five-card draw poker after the war. On Vermont Boulevard, its eastern border, there is a dingy little Vegas-like strip of card clubs with huge parking lots and flickering

neon signs that spell out "The Rainbow" and "The Horseshoe" in timed sequences of varicolored lights. The town is only secondarily famous as the largest community of Japanese Americans in the United States outside of Honolulu, Hawaii. When I was in high school there, it seemed to me that every *sansei* kid I knew wanted to be a doctor, an engineer, or a pharmacist. Our fathers were gardeners or electricians or nurserymen or ran small businesses catering to other Japanese Americans. Our mothers worked in civil service for the city or as cashiers for Thrifty Drug. What the kids wanted was a good job, good pay, a fine home, and no troubles. No one wanted to mess with the law—from either side—and no one wanted to mess with language or art. They all talked about getting into the right clubs so that they could go to the right schools. There was a certain kind of sameness, an intensely enforced system of conformity. Style was all. Boys wore moccasin-sewn shoes from Flagg Brothers, black A–1 slacks, and Kensington shirts with high collars. Girls wore their hair up in stiff bouffants solidified in hairspray and knew all the latest dances from the slauson to the funky chicken. We did well in chemistry and in math, no one who was Japanese but me spoke in English class or in history unless called upon, and no one talked about World War II. The day after Robert Kennedy was assassinated, after winning the California Democratic primary, we worked on calculus and elected class coordinators for the prom, featuring the 5th Dimension. We avoided grief. We avoided government. We avoided strong feelings and dangers of any kind. Once punished, we tried to maintain a concerted emotional and social discipline and would not willingly seek to fall out of the narrow margin of protective favor again.

14   But when I was thirteen, in junior high, I'd not understood why it was so difficult for my classmates, those who were themselves Japanese American, to talk about the relocation. They had cringed, too, when I tried to bring it up during our discussions of World War II. I was Hawaiian-born. They were mainland-born. Their parents had been in camp, had been the ones to suffer the complicated experience of having to distance themselves from their own history and all things Japanese in order to make their way back and into the American social and economic mainstream. It was out of this sense of shame and a fear of stigma I was only beginning to understand that the *nisei* had silenced themselves. And, for their children, among whom I grew up, they wanted no heritage, no culture, no contact with a defiled history. I recall the silence very well. The Japanese-American children around me were burdened in a way I was not. Their injunction was silence. Mine was to speak.

15   Away at college, in another protected world in its own way as magical to me as the Hawaii of my childhood, I dreamed about my grandfather. Tired from studying languages, practicing German conjugations or scripting an army's worth of Chinese ideograms on a single sheet of paper, Kubota would come to me as I drifted off into sleep. Or I would walk across the newly mown ball field in back of my dormitory, cutting through a street-side phalanx of ancient eucalyptus trees on my way to visit friends off campus, and I would think of him, his anger, and his sadness.

16   I don't know myself what makes someone feel that kind of need to have a story they've lived through be deposited somewhere, but I can guess. I think about *The Illiad, The Odyssey, The Peloponnesian Wars* of Thucydides, and a myraid of the works of literature I've studied. A character, almost a *topoi* he occurs so often, is frequently the witness who gives personal testimony about an event the rest of his community cannot even imagine. The sibyl is such a character. And Procne, the maid whose tongue is cut out so that she will not tell that she has been raped by her own brother-in-law, the king of Thebes. There are the dime novels, the epic blockbusters Hollywood makes into miniseries, and then there are the plain, relentless stories of witnesses who have suffered through horrors major and minor that have marked and

changed their lives. I myself haven't talked to Holocaust victims. But I've read their survival stories and their stories of witness and been revolted and moved by them. My father-in-law, Al Thiessen, tells me his war stories again and again and I listen. A Mennonite who set aside the strictures of his own church in order to serve, he was a Marine codeman in the Pacific during World War II, in the Signal Corps on Guadalcanal, Morotai, and Bougainville. He was part of the island-hopping maneuver MacArthur had devised to win the war in the Pacific. He saw friends die from bombs which exploded not ten yards away. When he was with the 298th Signal Corps attached to the Thirteenth Air Force, he saw plane after plane come in and crash, just short of the runway, killing their crews, setting the jungle ablaze with oil and gas fires. Emergency wagons would scramble, bouncing over newly bulldozed land men used just the afternoon before for a football game. Every time we go fishing together, whether it's in a McKenzie boat drifting for salmon in Tillamook Bay or taking a lunch break from wading the riffles of a stream in the Cascades, he tells me about what happened to him and the young men in his unit. One was a Jewish boy from Brooklyn. One was a foul-mouthed kid from Kansas. They died. And he *has* to tell me. And I *have* to listen. It's a ritual payment the young owe their elders who have survived. The evacuation and relocation is something like that.

17   Kubota, my grandfather, had been ill with Alzheimer's disease for some time before he died. At the house he'd built on Kamehameha Highway in Hau'ula, a seacoast village just down the road from La'ie where he had his store, he'd wander out from the garage or greenhouse where he'd set up a workbench, and trudge down to the beach or up toward the line of pines he'd planted while employed by the Work Projects Administration during the thirties. Kubota thought he was going fishing. Or he thought he was back at work for Roosevelt, planting pines as a windbreak or soilbreak on the windward flank of the Ko'olau Mountains, emerald monoliths rising out of sea and cane fields from Waialua to Kaneohe. When I visited, my grandmother would send me down to the beach to fetch him. Or I'd run down Kam Highway a quarter mile or so and find him hiding in the cane field by the roadside, counting stalks, measuring circumferences in the claw of his thumb and forefinger. The look on his face was confused or concentrated, I didn't know which. But I guessed he was going fishing again. I'd grab him and walk him back to his house on the highway. My grandmother would shut him in a room.

18   Within a few years, Kubota had a stroke and survived it, then he had another one and was completely debilitated. The family decided to put him in a nursing home in Kahuku, just set back from the highway, within a mile or so of Kahuku Point and the Tanaka Store where he had his first job as a stock boy. He lived there three years, and I visited him once with my aunt. He was like a potato that had been worn down by cooking. Everything on him—his eyes, his teeth, his legs and torso—seemed like it has been sloughed away. What he had been was mostly gone now and I was looking at the nub of a man. In a wheelchair, he grasped my hands and tugged on them—violently. His hands were still thick and, I believed, strong enough to lift me out of my own seat into his lap. He murmured something in Japanese—he'd long ago ceased to speak any English. My aunt and I cried a little, and we left him.

19   I remember walking out on the black asphalt of the parking lot of the nursing home. It was heat-cracked and eroded already, and grass had veined itself into the interstices. There were coconut trees around, a cane field I could see across the street, and the ocean I knew was pitching a surf just beyond it. The green Ko'olaus came up behind us. Somewhere nearby, alongside the beach, there was an abandoned airfield in the middle of the canes. As a child, I'd come upon it playing one day, and my friends and I kept returning

to it, day after day, playing war or sprinting games or coming to fly kites. I recognize it even now when I see it on TV—it's used as a site for action scenes in the detective shows Hollywood always sets in the islands: helicopter chasing the hero racing away in a Ferrari, or gun dealers making a clandestine rendezvous on the abandoned runway. It was the old airfield strafed by Japanese planes the day the major flight attacked Pearl Harbor. It was the airfield the FBI thought my grandfather had targeted in his night fishing and signaling with the long surf poles he'd stuck in the sandy bays near Kahuku Point.

20   Kubota died a short while after I visited him, but not, I thought, without giving me a final message. I was on the mainland, in California studying for Ph.D. exams, when my grandmother called me with the news. It was a relief. He'd suffered from his debilitation a long time and I was grateful he'd gone. I went home for the funeral and gave the eulogy. My grandmother and I took his ashes home in a small, heavy metal box wrapped in a black *furoshiki,* a large silk scarf. She showed me the name the priest had given to him on his death, scripted with a calligraphy brush on a long, narrow talent of plain wood. Buddhist commoners, at death, are given priestly names, received symbolically into the clergy. The idea is that, in their next life, one of scholarship and leisure, they might meditate and attain the enlightenment the religion is aimed at. *"Shaku Sh[[umacron]]chi,"* the ideograms read. It was Kubota's Buddhist name, incorporating characters from his family and given names. It meant "Shining Wisdom of the Law." He died on Pearl Harbor Day, December 7, 1983.

21   After years, after I'd finally come back to live in Hawaii again, only once did I dream of Kubota, my grandfather. It was the same night I'd heard HR442, the redress bill for Japanese Americans, had been signed into law. In my dream that night Kabota was "torching," and he sang a Japanese song, a querulous and wavery folk ballad, as he hung paper lanterns on bamboo poles stuck into the sand in the shallow water of the lagoon behind the reef near Kahuku Point. Then he was at a work table, smoking a hand-rolled cigarette, letting it dangle from his lips Bogart-style as he drew, daintily and skillfully, with a narrow trim brush, ideogram after ideogram on a score of paper lanterns he had hung in a dark shed to dry. He had painted a talismanic mantra onto each lantern, the ideogram for the word "red" in Japanese, a bit of art blended with some superstition, a piece of sympathetic magic appealing to the magenta coloring on the rough skins of the schooling, night-feeding fish we wanted to attract to his baited hooks. He strung them from pole to pole in the dream then, hiking up his khaki worker's pants so his white ankles showed and wading through the shimmering black waters of the sand flats and then the reef. "The moon is leaving, leaving," he sang in Japanese. "Take me deeper in the savage sea." He turned and crouched like an ice racer then, leaning forward so that his unshaven face almost touched the light film of water. I could see the light stubble of beard like a fine, gray ash covering the lower half of his face. I could see his gold-rimmed spectacles. He held a small wooden boat in his cupped hands and placed it lightly on the sea and pushed it away. One of his lanterns was on it and, written in small neat rows like a sutra scroll, it had been decorated with the silvery names of all our dead.

Narrative Technique Question

1. What do you think is the point of the story?

_____

_____

2. What introductory paragraph lead-in technique does the author use?

_____

_____

3. Point out at least five transitional expressions. How do they help to order the events chronologically?

_____

_____

_____

_____

_____

Critical Reading Questions

1. Hongo begins with the Pearl Harbor attack and then moves backward in time to talk about earlier periods in Kubota's life. How does this nonchronological positioning of events add to the story?

_____

_____

_____

_____

2. Explain what the dream sequence in the last paragraph means. How does it relate to the rest of the story?

_____

_____

_____

_____

Narrative Writing Opportunities

1. Find out about some other ethnic group that was treated as disloyal during a national conflict, and write a paragraph about one incident and its consequences in that time and place.

2. Kubota's story represents that of an entire group. Write an essay about a friend, family member, or acquaintance and the events in that person's life that represent an entire group.

EXAMPLE

BELIEVERS IN SEARCH OF PIERCING INSIGHT

D. James Romero

> Body piercing is currently the rage among America's young adults. Most people probably believe that body piercing is predominantly an act of "primitive" people. In this essay, the author pricks those balloons with a quick trip through history while commenting on just what the practice means to people today.

Vocabulary

Before you begin reading, look up the definitions of the following words that appear in the essay. The number in parentheses after each word refers to the paragraph number of the essay.

aesthetic (9)	authenticity (17)	chaste (18)
genitalia (1)	mecca (2)	nomads (1)
paradox (19)	relinquished (16)	septum (7)

Believers in Search of Piercing Insight

1   Here we are at the end of a century of scientific and technological advances so vast they may surpass the rest of humankind's history of knowledge—and cutting edge culture has some of us looking like tribal nomads ready to take some heads: barbells in our eyebrows. Studs in our chins. Hoops in our genitalia.

2   Many in California—this holy mecca of holes—say they pierce their bodies to fully realize their individuality. The body's landscape—for so long adorned with T-shirts-as-billboards, and clothing-labels-as-advertisements—becomes *their* own. Piercing is a return to flesh as fashion—and a revitalized rite of passage.

3   "If someone's under 18, it's normal behavior to get pierced," asserts pop culture expert Stuart Ewen. "It's when I see 50-year-old guys at the gym with nipple rings that I start to worry."

4   Indeed, there isn't much progressive about piercing anymore. Not when your yuppie uncle has enough hoops in his body to set off airport security. And not when state lawmakers are trying to make a note from Mom mandatory for under-18 piercing.

5   So what is a fashion-wary West Coaster to do?

6   Not to worry. There are youth cults busy at work devising new ways to anger parents and subvert the mainstream's black hole.

7   The cutting edge of piercing's "modern primitive" movement can be found at Nomad Body Piercing Studio in San Francisco. The shop specializes in tribal and ancient piercings such as stretched-out lip holes (piercing the lower lip and stretching the hole), large septum jewelry and low-hanging earlobes.

8   The term "modern primitive" was coined by Fakir Musafar, a '70s pioneer of body modification who now publishes *Body Play* magazine. The phenome-

non took off in 1989 with the publication of *Modern Primitives* (Re/Search), a book that featured photos of ancient and modern body art.

9   "It's a rejection of the modern aesthetic," says Nomad owner Kristian White. "Your body is yours. It's the one thing you have to express yourself with."

10   Extreme piercing can be found in underground pagan and gothic cults, too—sets that hang at L.A. nightclubs such as Sin-a-matic, Stigmata and Coven 13. Reports also abound of underground parties where piercing is performed and rites of pain are demonstrated as performance art.

11   Sexual piercings are the rage in L.A. body art, from the male Prince Albert (apparently, the old chap had a genital piercing—in Victorian times, no less) to the unisex nipple ring. *Body Modification E-Zine,* an online magazine, surveyed readers and found that half had their nipples pierced.

12   "It's a freaky subculture of people," says West Hollywood piercer Jennifer "Jeff" Middleton, who has square chrome hair, several piercings in her ears and one in her nose.

13   Earlier in the day, she was putting on latex gloves and preparing sterile instruments in a bright, clean second-floor room at the Gauntlet in West Hollywood. Customer Brian Lee had hoops in both ears and a tattoo on his back, so he felt the need to distinguish himself—with a pierced brow. "You want to show off what you're about," he said.

14   It took only about five minutes for Middleton to clean Lee's right eyebrow, mark it, pinch it with forceps and poke an ultra-sharp, inch-long needle through his skin: $30 please. Lee didn't flinch. Middleton explained the eight weeks of tedious healing and cleaning, but Lee just looked in the mirror and smiled when he saw the "barbell" protruding from his head.

15   "It does get trendy," said Lee, a 22-year-old club deejay. "But there will always be a new body to be pierced."

16   Culture watchers say there is something deeper going on here. The Nomad studio's White says organized religion has relinquished its grip on the minds and bodies of youth so that they may go back to pre-Christian rituals. And professor Ewen, chair of media studies at Hunter College in New York, says it is indeed a rejection of the neat, sleek, modern fashion aesthetic.

17   "This was a culture that was sold on the idea of progress since the turn of the century—clean lines, industrial aesthetic, mass-produced clothes," he says. "There's a sense of meaninglessness in this, so there's a search for meaning—a belief that other ways of life might have more authenticity than ours."

18   It is said that Roman warriors pierced body parts to show how tough they were, while Victorian women, otherwise notoriously chaste, pierced their nipples in acts of sensuality. Body modification has also been a staple of non-Western cultures for thousands of years.

19   But today, as teens and twenty-somethings try to stand out, they face the paradox of modern subculture: More people want it, more people want to make money off it, and rebellion becomes a uniform instead of a torch of individuality.

20   "Body art was an embrace against the packaged self," Ewen says. "Yet any attempt to marginalize one's self provides new grist for the style industries.

21   "The only way to battle it is to find an ideal and stick with it. At that point, you kill off the consumption process. My only solution is to buy five pairs of pants and five sweaters and never wear anything else."

22   Now that's a radical concept.

Example Technique Questions

1. Is there a thesis statement in the essay? If so, identify it. If not, what do you think is the author's thesis?

_____

_____

_____

2. What examples does the author give as reasons why people get pierced?

_____

_____

_____

3. Identify examples of the different types of piercings.

_____

_____

_____

Critical Reading Questions

1. A "nomad" is a wandering person, while a "studio" is a place. Why is "Nomad" an appropriate name for the piercing studio described in the essay?

_____

_____

_____

_____

2. What is paradoxical about piercing becoming a mainstream activity, instead of the mark of individuality that it was first intended to be?

_____

_____

_____

_____

Example Writing Opportunities

1. If you have body piercings, write a paragraph about why you decided to add to your personal appearance in this manner. If you haven't body-pierced, interview some people who have, and write a paragraph giving specific examples of the kinds of piercings each person has had done and how that personifies something about their identity.
2. The author points out that body piercing is yet another attempt by young people to anger their parents and other older people. Write an essay opposing Romero's position by using other examples of why young people body pierce.

▼

THE DON JUAN SYNDROME

JULIE CHAPA

> This essay, "The Don Juan Syndrome," was written by Julie Chapa, a freelance writer and former assistant editor of *Hispanic* magazine. In the essay, the author examines how the "Latin lover" stereotype evolved in Hollywood. Typecasting can affect actors from any ethnic background, and Chapa explores how our culture is influenced by this practice.

Vocabulary

Before you begin reading, look up the definitions of the following words that appear in the essay. The number in parentheses after each word refers to the paragraph number of the essay.

antithesis (17)	precursor (4)	primitivism (6)	psyche (2)
reincarnating (15)	stigma (19)	swarthy (1)	virile (1)

The Don Juan Syndrome

1   Since the days of early cinema, Latin men have portrayed some of the most virile, passionate, and forbidden characters on the screen. With their swarthy good looks and smoldering eyes, these "Latin lovers" have caused female moviegoers to swoon for decades. But unlike his blond counterpart, the Latin lover was generally not cast in the leading role. He played the rogue to the Anglo gentleman. He was, however, suave and more than able to captivate even the strongest screen siren. Early screen actors such as Rudolph Valentino, Ramón Novarro, and Gilbert Roland invariably set the stage for today's Latino film roles.

2   While the Latin lover stereotype seems like a whimsical characterization that only existed on the big screen decades ago, its effects have seeped into the American psyche, forcing Latinos, especially those in the film industry, into a smothering, tight mold. Although no stereotype should be deemed acceptable, some argue that the Latin lover image is just a step above the other stereotypes today's Latino actors have to play—drug runners, gang members, and crime lords.

The Roots of the Latin Lover

3   The Latin lover character evolved from other stereotypes, which were seemingly much worse. Throughout cinematic and television history, Latinos have been relegated to portraying several stereotypes, according to Charles Ramírez Berg, professor of radio-television-film at the University of Texas at Austin, in the *Howard Journal of Communications*. Some have been comic characters, such as the "male buffoon" incarnated as Sergeant Garcia in Walt Disney's *Zorro* series and Leo Carrillo's Pancho in *The Cisco Kid* television series of the early fifties. Carrillo made a career of playing the buffoon, especially in his various film portrayals of the thirties. The buffoon character usually utilized his broken English or feisty temper for comic relief.

4   Another unlikely precursor of the Latin lover is the "bandido." A series of early films, including *Tony the Greaser* (1911) and *The Greaser's Revenge* (1914) conceived the bandido stereotype—the greasy and/or slovenly rapist, thief, drunk, or murderer. Ramírez Berg writes that the bandido stereotype not only over-simplifies Latinos—the very definition of stereotype—but also "reinforces the cleanliness, sobriety, sanity, overall decency, and moral rectitude of the WASP in the white hat." Consciously or not, movie studios used the bandido to reaffirm white America's values and morality.

5   Changing the image of Latinos from murderous greasers to the passionate, suave lover resulted from the loss of what the film industry sought from the beginning—money. The "greaser" movies were not embraced by all. They were virulently anti-Mexican. After ignoring a written protest from the Mexican government in 1919, Hollywood suffered a blow in 1922 when films promoting such stereotypes were banned south of the border. Hollywood's response? The "greaser" became the citizen of fictitious Latin American countries. This aura of mystery added a touch of romanticism to the character and became one of the reasons for the birth of the Latin lover image.

6   According to Victoria Thomas, author of *Hollywood's Latin Lovers* (Santa Monica: Angel City Press, 1998), another reason was American audiences' fascination with primitivism. "The Latin lover was created for a non-Latino audience," she says. "Latin men were a passport to the forbidden." Swashbuckling heroes were venturing into previously unchartered territory in theaters, a reflection of the real-life spirit of adventure that was sweeping across the United States. "Although the portrayal has a tang of racism, it reveals the colonial attitude of the European meeting the indigenous," continues Thomas.

Early Screen Heartthrobs

7   While most consider Italian Rudolph Valentino as the founder of the Latin lover persona, the true architect of the role was Antonio Moreno. Born Antonio Garrido Monteagudo y Moreno in Madrid, Moreno began his career in 1912 in the one-reeler *Voice of the Million*. Because of his dark features and expressive face, which "read" well on camera, he was considered a natural for early films being produced under difficult conditions and with primitive equipment. By 1923 he was Paramount's leading man. That same year, his much-publicized marriage to oil heiress Daisy Canfield Danziger gave his already successful career a boost. Later that year, his three most successful films—*The Trail of the Lonesome Pine, The Spanish Dancer,* and *My American Wife*—were released, elevating demand for motion pictures with dark, dangerous men.

8   Following close behind Moreno was the steamy Ramón Novarro. The actor, nicknamed Ravishing Ramón, caused a furor throughout his career, offering audiences scene-stealing performances. It usually wasn't his acting that caused the distraction. In *Ben-Hur* (1926), moviegoers were treated to visions of the bare-chested Novarro as the legendary charioteer. More scan-

dalous than that was his appearance as the sarong-clad lead in *The Pagan* (1929). Born José Ramón Gil Samaniegos in 1899 in Durango, Mexico, Novarro's ambition led him and his brother to California with only $10 between them. To help support his mother and twelve younger siblings, Novarro took a variety of odd jobs as a grocery clerk, busboy, and theater usher, among others. A talented dancer and singer, he had no trouble finding work as a studio dance extra. He appeared in myriad films, but his first big break came in 1921 when he was discovered by director Rex Ingram, who cast him in *The Four Horsemen of the Apocalypse*, also starring Valentino. Ingram then approached Novarro about a role that would showcase Novarro's Adonis-like qualities. As Rupert von Hentzau in 1922's *The Prisoner of Zenda* and with Valentino's untimely death that same year, the title of Hollywood's premier Latin lover was bestowed upon Novarro. Responsible for more than one case of "front row fainting," Novarro's sizzling scenes and exotic roles made him one of the most popular Mexican actors in American cinema history.

9   Along with Valentino, Moreno and Novarro unknowingly set the precedent for the future of Latino screen roles. Although the role opened the door for many Hispanic actors, including Gilbert Roland, Ricardo Montalbán, Cesar Romero, and Fernando Lamas, the Latin playboy image has been rather difficult to shake. Many modern-day Latino actors, most notably Andy Garcia and Jimmy Smits, have played "exotic" romantic leads but have also successfully avoided being typecast, thanks to their box-office appeal.

Rejecting the Lover

10   For lesser-known actors trying to make their big break, the Latin lover image has made the road to stardom all the more frustrating. Manny Alfaro, an actor and executive director of the Hispanic Organization of Latin Actors (HOLA), says he has learned not to have a knee-jerk reaction to typecasting. "I'm more [incensed] when Latinos are left out," he says.

11   HOLA, based in New York, lists as its objective "to gain an accurate, educated, and nonstereotypical portrayal of Hispanic culture and its people through the arts and media." To achieve this objective, HOLA helps its members by providing talent referrals, professional workshops, and by publishing the *HOLA Pages*, a directory of Hispanic talent.

12   Nonetheless, typecasting Latinos in Hollywood still exists, partly because of the needs of audiences. According to actor James Borrego, who has worked on various film projects, including *Lone Star* (1996), American audiences have more control over the situation than actors do. "As an audience member, if you don't like the casting choices, you don't go see it," he says. "For actors, it's different. What are you going to do if that's the only game in town?"

13   Another factor lies in *who* is making the film. The "greaser" continued to appear in motion pictures well into the seventies in films such as *Duck, You Sucker* (1972), *Bring Me the Head of Alfredo Garcia* (1974), and *Boulevard Nights* (1979). When Latino filmmakers gained visibility in the early eighties with films like Luis Valdez's *Zoot Suit* (1981), more realistic, acceptable portrayals of Latinos in films made it to the silver screen. But even these early films were blasted, as Clint C. Wilson II and Félix Gutierrez write in *Race, Multiculturalism, and the Media* (Thousand Oaks: Sage Publications, 1995), for their "perceived glorification of the drug culture, sexist orientation, and nontraditional lifestyle of the featured characters."

14   It wasn't until the late eighties that Latinos were recognized as members of mainstream culture with the release of highly acclaimed motion pictures like Valdez's *La Bamba* (1987), an account of the life of Richie Valens, a Latino rock and roller of the fifties; and Ramon Menendez's *Stand and Deliver* (1988),

recounting the true story of inspirational Mexican American math teacher Jaime Escalante. However, according to Wilson and Gutierrez, who also penned *Minorities and the Media* (Beverly Hills: Sage Publications, 1985), films in general still portray Latinos as hoodlums and drug runners.

15　　Many Latinos actors rode in on the wave of Latino films of the late seventies and early eighties, including Edward James Olmos, Cheech Marin, and Andy Garcia. For the most part, their characters bore no resemblance to the stereotypical Latin lover. Many of today's Latino stars got their breaks by reincarnating the "greaser," who, in today's films, has evolved into the drug lord and gang member. One of today's hottest Hispanic actors, Garcia, has played a few modern-day "greaser" roles, including his sadistic gangster role in *Eight Million Ways to Die* (1986). (Not all of Garcia's gangster portrayals have been Latinos; some have been Italians.) Like most of today's Latino actors, however, he has successfully steered clear of Latin lover roles. "Today Latin actors won't play it," says author Thomas, because of the fear of being limited in acting choices.

16　　Garcia, born Andrés Arturo Garcia-Menéndez in Havana, Cuba, immigrated to the United States in 1961 at the age of five. The extremely private actor refuses to play by Hollywood's rules, keeping reporters at bay about his family life and refusing to do nude scenes. So determined is Garcia to avoid the Latin lover label, that he has reportedly refused to continue auditions when asked to remove his shirt.

Embracing the Lover

17　　The antithesis of Garcia, Spanish heartthrob Antonio Banderas has made a career of resurrecting the Latin lover role. Making his debut in Spanish writer-director Pedro Almodóvar's films, including *Labyrinth of Passion* (1983), *Law of Desire* (1986), and *Women on the Verge of a Nervous Breakdown* (1988), this sultan of sweat, who had previously appeared in various screen roles, exploded on the scene in his first starring role in an American film, Robert Rodriguez's *Desperado* (1995). Later that year, he costarred in *Assassins* with Sylvester Stallone. Since then, Banderas has appeared in many testosterone-driven roles, most recently in *The Mask of Zorro* (1998). In a recent *Los Angeles Times* interview, Banderas said of his sex-symbol status, "I don't care. It doesn't bother me and doesn't make me feel like a superhero."

18　　While the character of the Latin lover is not as prevalent in films today as it was seventy years ago, Hispanic men in general are still feeling the effects. "Obviously when you have Latin features—a dark complexion and different hair type—you are placed in a special category," explains actor Fred Estrada. "Usually the only category [other than that of the Latin lover] you get called in for is the homeboy with the accent." Estrada has stopped playing to the stereotype and describes his acting style as playing basically himself. "I'm educated. I don't have an inner-city accent. But when I'm auditioning I frequently hear, 'Can you have more of an accent?' or '. . . more of a lisp?'"

19　　Estrada, who has appeared on ABC soaps *General Hospital* and *Port Charles*, also finds himself being type-cast in his day-to-day life as well as in his acting roles. As licensed New York attorney, Estrada says that the stigma of being a "Latin playboy" haunted him throughout his legal career. "In law school, people were always calling me to find out where the parties were. No one ever asked me to be in their study groups." Estrada also says he also experienced discrimination and sexual harassment because of his looks. "As an attorney, I had five assignments cut short because of jealousy." The frustration of not being taken seriously has followed the 30-year-old actor into his new career. "The 'ladies man' stereotype definitely hurts Latin nonactors," he says, emphatically.

20   It is quite possible that the Latin lover is a character that will never fully go away. After all, he's not all bad. Among his redeeming qualities is his attractiveness. As Borrego reminds us, "In film and media, the emphasis is on sex appeal. It's about gorgeous people. If you're going to make it [as an actor], you have to have sex appeal." While that in itself is not a bad thing, "it unfortunately gives us an unrealistic representation [of people]," he continues. "While no stereotypes are better than others, today they are not as overt as they used to be. Today's characters are more stylized. It's now possible to *like* villains. They're no longer just ugly bandits—they can be slick dudes." Alfaro also offers hope for the future of Latino roles. "Things are changing," he says. "It's coming—it's just slow."

Example Technique Questions

1. Is there a thesis statement in the essay? If so, identify it.

_____

_____

_____

_____

_____

2. Point out examples of the historical stereotypes from which modern stereotypes have evolved.

_____

_____

_____

3. Point out some examples of modern stereotypes.

_____

_____

_____

Critical Reading Questions

1. What is the "Don Juan Syndrome"?

_____

_____

_____

_____

2. How does the author indicate that the stereotype of the "Latin Lover" is changing?

_____

_____

_____

_____

3. How does the author indicate that the stereotype is being resurrected?

_____

_____

_____

_____

Example Writing Opportunities

1. Write a paragraph focusing on a specific type of role you have noticed in the movies. Use examples to support your topic sentence.
2. Using the topic of your paragraph in exercise 1, write an essay. Expand your ideas to include several roles. Use specific examples in the body paragraphs to support your thesis statement.

CLASSIFICATION

▼

SINGLE WHITE FEMALE

Viet D. Dinh

Relationships are difficult enough without opposition from parents and friends because a partner is a different race. In this essay, Dinh expresses his dismay that race is often still an objection where marriage is concerned.

Vocabulary
Before you begin reading, look up the definitions of the following words that appear in the essay. The number in parentheses after each word refers to the paragraph number of the essay.

absolved (23)	bequeathed (21)	conflagration (23)
innocuous (17)	opprobrium (16)	proxy (18)
talisman (21)	surreptitiously (12)	

Single White Female

1 Mary and I met in my senior year of high school at a weekend speech and debate tournament in northern California. By chance, I stopped at an afternoon storytelling competition and listened to her recite passages from *Jonathan Livingston Seagull*. We fell in love—quickly, foolishly. Each day after watching each other compete, we'd sneak into San Francisco for dinner in Chinatown (my choice) or Ghiradelli Square (hers) and a stroll through North Beach to Coit Tower.

2 About a week later, Mary's mother asked about her new boyfriend on the drive to school.

3 "I hear you've met a new boy."

4 "Yes."

5 "Is he Catholic?"

6 "Yes."

7 "College?"

8 "Yes, he's going to Harvard."

9 Her mother smiled, "Well, good. What's his name?"

10 "Viet," Mary answered, wittily adding a pronunciation tip, "as in Vietnam."

11 "I'm sorry, Mary, tell him you can't see him anymore."

12 That was the end. I saw Mary only a few times after she told me this story, mostly to talk about what happened. She wondered why we didn't continue surreptitiously; I tried to understand what motivated her mother's response. Mary offered (inexplicably) that her mother was from Indiana, and argued that she really was not racist, that if I were to apply for a job at her real estate office she probably would hire me.

13 I met Mary's mother once, years later. I worked as a real estate developer and wanted to buy some land in the area. More as an excuse than out of necessity, I called up to schedule a tour of her listings. She never placed me, and after an hour in her car, I began to accept that Mary was right. Her mother was not a racist—at least not in the sense that I had imagined in high school. She was comfortable with me. Nothing in her manner betrayed nervousness or artificial cordiality.

14 That revelation only made my question harder to answer. What motivates an otherwise intelligent person to inflict such pain on such a seemingly irrational basis? She is not racist, yet cannot tolerate her daughter dating an Asian. Why is love, or sex, so special?

15 The question presents itself frequently. Open any magazine to the personal ads and one finds exposed on every page the impulse that Mary's mother displayed. Single White Female seeking same; Divorced Black Male, professional, seeking compatible companion; Gay White Male seeking mate; Asian Woman seeking a gentleman. The open invitation to judge based on race extends shamelessly across all social barriers, from *New York Review of Books* intellectuals to *Village Voice* bohemians to *Washingtonian* power brokers.

16 Such open reliance on racial qualifications is hard to reconcile with moral and social opprobrium accorded to racism and the suspicion of racial classifications in the post–Civil Rights era. In most cases, race cannot legally be a factor in hiring or firing, in buying or selling, in admission or rejection. Even an acknowledgment that one's friends or associates are only of a particular race gives pause and sometimes has derailed otherwise promising public careers. Yet romantic race-typing persists, explicitly and pervasively, not noticed and hardly questioned.

17   Maybe the designation of one's race in a personal ad is innocuous. The ad, after all, attempts to convey a full (maybe even inflated) picture of its owner, and race is simply part of the picture, like a glimpse of someone walking down the street or eating in a restaurant. But to offer race as part of that verbal picture is to recognize, and approve, that race matters when one judges a stranger for compatibility and attraction. Why?

18   For one thing, the racial designation may be shorthand for a number of cultural and ethnic traits that cannot be fully captured in a short ad or a quick glimpse. But to accept race as proxy for personal characteristics is to succumb to exactly the impulse that one finds reprehensible in racism: the blind acceptance of generalized biases without regard to individual qualities. It is not justifiable (both factually and morally) to assume that a black man likes jazz or that an Asian woman is petite any more than to say that black men are muggers or Asian women are submissive.

19   Moreover, race is just one arbitrary level of generalization. If it is a "package" of personal characteristics that one is looking for, that mix need not be determined by race. Asian Male describes very little of who I am, the differences among Asian cultures being large. Southeast Asian is closer, but then why not Vietnamese, or South Vietnamese? Better yet, why not simply Male?

20   When I told my sister that I don't discriminate in my romantic decisions, she replied, "Maybe you're just not very discriminating." Race-typing, she argued, flows from the natural desire to preserve one's culture in a pluralistic society. She feared that in searching for an American, I would stop being Vietnamese.

21   But this argument assumes that culture is something timeless, a neverchanging talisman that has been begotten and bequeathed and is to be passed on forever. That is hardly the case. Any immigrant who returns to his native country can readily observe the chasm that only a few years' absence has forged between him and the culture that he had nostalgically and unrequitedly loved. People change, traditions evolve, and institutions adapt. To assume that one's "culture" could remain unchanged is to ignore that what defines culture is simply a dynamic and complex process of human and natural interaction.

22   I do not deny that I am Vietnamese, that I have a distinct cultural heritage in which to take pride. It is precisely that pride which makes me willing to share my culture, not to lock it away in a tower of racial chastity. Whatever is lost in authenticity I hope is gained doubly in wider acceptance and deeper appreciation.

23   Perhaps romantic race-typing can be absolved as a Darwinian strategy to perpetuate one's genetic longevity. A friend confesses to having felt a tinge of alarm when her then-fiancé casually remarked that their children would look like him, since his Jamaican genes would dominate her recessive white ones. Such a reaction, natural as it may be, is only valid if the animating desire for racial purity is itself justifiable. At another time or in a different place, racial homogeneity may have been an effective means of preservation and survival. But in America's multiracial 1990s, where the danger is not of racial extinction but of ethnic conflagration, racial husbandry is as unwise as it is indefensible.

24   After my relationship with a Vietnamese woman ended when we could find little in common, I recently began seeing someone new, a white woman. Often when we walk hand in hand down Capitol Hill or through the Boston Common, we smile at the people who hold us in their stares. I think I will stop wondering about Mary's mother when I can be confident that the heads that turn do so because of my girlfriend's beauty or our apparent happiness together.

Classification Technique Questions

1. The author states that Mary's mother "was not a racist—at least not in the sense that I had imagined." How does he classify her as a racist?

_____

_____

_____

2. According to the author, in what categories of life is it no longer acceptable to use race as an issue?

_____

_____

3. What other categories can you think of that might fit in the essay?

_____

_____

_____

Critical Reading Questions

1. Can you find a thesis statement? If so, identify it. If not, what do you think is the main idea of the essay?

_____

_____

_____

_____

2. How does the author's sister defend choosing a partner using discriminatory practices?

_____

_____

_____

Classification Writing Opportunities

1. Write a paragraph in which you classify a group of people by their religious beliefs.
2. Write an essay in which you classify people by how they dress or by the food they eat.

CONFESSIONS OF AN EX-SMOKER

Franklin Zimring

> Addiction is an increasing problem in America. This includes addiction to heroin, sugar, caffeine, sex, food, and alcohol. But for many people, the addiction to nicotine seems harder to break than almost any other. Some heroin addicts have stated that it was easier for them to give up heroin than it was for them to stop smoking.

Vocabulary

Before you begin reading, look up the definitions of the following words that appear in the essay. The number in parentheses after each word refers to the paragraph number of the essay.

anecdotal (4)	brimstone (2)	nil (5)
excoriate (10)	fervor (3)	tenuous (3)
proselytizing (7)	recidivist (3)	watershed (1)
unmitigated (6)	vitriolic (4)	
zealot (1)	cessation (1)	

Confessions of an Ex-Smoker

1   Americans can be divided into three groups—smokers, nonsmokers and that expanding pack of us who have quit. Those who have never smoked don't know what they're missing, but former smokers, ex-smokers, reformed smokers can never forget. We are veterans of a personal war, linked by that watershed experience of ceasing to smoke and by the temptation to have just one more cigarette. For almost all of us ex-smokers, smoking continues to play an important part in our lives. And now that it is being restricted in restaurants around the country and will be banned in almost all indoor public places in New York State starting next month, it is vital that everyone understand the different emotional states cessation of smoking can cause. I have observed four of them; and in the interest of science I have classified them as those of the zealot, the evangelist, the elect and the serene. Each day, each category gains new recruits.

2   Not all antitobacco zealots are former smokers, but a substantial number of fire-and-brimstone opponents do come from the ranks of the reformed. Zealots believe that those who continue to smoke are degenerates who deserve scorn not pity and the penalties that will deter offensive behavior in public as well. Relations between these people and those who continue to smoke are strained.

3   One explanation for the zealot's fervor in seeking to outlaw tobacco consumption is his own tenuous hold on abstaining from smoking. But I think part of the emotional force arises from sheer envy as he watches and identifies with each lung-filling puff. By making smoking in public a crime, the zealot seeks reassurance that he will not revert to bad habits; give him strong social penalties and he won't become a recidivist.

4   No systematic survey has been done yet, but anecdotal evidence suggests that a disproportionate number of doctors who have quit smoking can be found among the fanatics. Just as the most enthusiastic revolutionary tends

to make the most enthusiastic counterrevolutionary, many of today's vitriolic zealots include those who had been deeply committed to tobacco habits.

5   By contrast, the antismoking evangelist does not condemn smokers. Unlike the zealot, he regards smoking as an easily curable condition, as a social disease, and not a sin. The evangelist spends an enormous amount of time seeking and preaching to the unconverted. He argues that kicking the habit is not *that* difficult. After all, *he* did it; moreover, as he describes it, the benefits of quitting are beyond measure and the disadvantages are nil.

6   The hallmark of the evangelist is his insistence that he never misses tobacco. Though he is less hostile to smokers than the zealot, he is resented more. Friends and loved ones who have been the targets of his preachments frequently greet the resumption of smoking by the evangelist as an occasion for unmitigated glee.

7   Among former smokers, the distinctions between the evangelist and the elect are much the same as the differences between proselytizing and non-proselytizing religious sects. While the evangelists preach the ease and desir- ability of abstinence, the elect do not attempt to convert their friends. They think that virtue is its own reward and subscribe to the Puritan theory of pre- destination. Since they have proved themselves capable of abstaining from tobacco, they are therefore different from friends and relatives who continue to smoke. They feel superior, secure that their salvation was foreordained. These ex-smokers rarely give personal testimony on their conversion. They rarely speak about their tobacco habits, while evangelists talk about little else. Of course, active smokers find such blue-nosed behavior far less offensive than that of the evangelist or the zealot, yet they resent the elect simply because they are smug. Their air of self-satisfaction rarely escapes the notice of those lighting up. For active smokers, life with a member of the ex- smoking elect is less stormy than with a zealot or evangelist, but it is subtly oppressive nonetheless.

8   I have labeled my final category of former smokers the serene. This classification is meant to encourage those who find the other psychic styles of ex-smokers disagreeable. Serenity is quieter than zealotry and evangelism, and those who qualify are not as self-righteous as the elect. The serene ex- smoker accepts himself and also accepts those around him who continue to smoke. This kind of serenity does not come easily nor does it seem to be an immediate option for those who have stopped. Rather it is a goal, an end stage in a process of development during which some former smokers progress through one or more of the less-than-positive psychological points en route. For former smokers, serenity is thus a positive possibility that exists at the end of the rainbow. But all former smokers cannot reach that promised land.

9   What is it that permits some former smokers to become serene? I think the key is self-acceptance and gratitude. The fully mature former smoker knows he has the soul of an addict and is grateful for the knowledge. He may sit up front in an airplane, but he knows he belongs in the smoking section in back. He doesn't regret that he quit smoking, nor any of his previous adven- tures with tobacco. As a former smoker, he is grateful for the experience and memory of craving a cigarette.

10   Serenity comes from accepting the lessons of one's life. And ex-smokers who have reached this point in their world view have much to be grateful for. They have learned about the potential and limits of change. In becoming the right kind of former smoker, they developed a healthy sense of self. This former smoker, for one, believes that it is better to crave (one hopes only occasionally) and not to smoke than never to have craved at all. And by accepting that fact, the reformed smoker does not need to excoriate, envy or disassociate himself from those who continue to smoke.

Classification Technique Questions

1. Into what classifications does the author divide all Americans?

   _____

   _____

   _____

2. Into what classifications does the author divide ex-smokers, and how does the author characterize each type?

   _____

   _____

   _____

   _____

   _____

   _____

3. Does the author use many transitional expressions? If so, identify them, and explain how they help order the information chronologically. If not, which ones would have been effective, and where would you place them?

   _____

   _____

   _____

Critical Reading Questions

1. What is the essay's purpose, and how does classification help achieve the purpose?

   _____

   _____

   _____

   _____

   _____

   _____

2. How does the author differentiate between the types of ex-smokers?

_____

_____

_____

3. Whether you are an ex-smoker or not, do you agree with the author's conclusion in paragraph 10 that "Serenity comes from accepting the lessons of one's life"? Explain.

_____

_____

_____

Classification Writing Opportunities

1. Write a paragraph about things that people are addicted to. Whether you write about a single addiction or multiple addictions, try to classify them by type, i.e., food, drug, behavior, etc. The classification should help identify, explain, and clarify the point you are trying to make about the addiction.
2. Write an essay explaining the consequences of an addiction. Classify the consequences into categories (physical, psychological, social, etc.) to help you explain the points you make about the consequences.

PROCESS

▼ INTERNET JOB SEARCH

A. C. "Buddy" Krizan, Patricia Merrier, Carol Larson Jones, and Jules Harcourt

The Internet has become an integral part of doing business around the world. Millions of people, both those who already have jobs and those who do not, are using the Internet to search for new positions. The authors share invaluable insights and strategies to facilitate a job-seeker's search experience.

Vocabulary
Before you begin reading, look up the definitions of the following words that appear in the essay. The number in parentheses after each word refers to the paragraph number of the essay.

advent (1)	cyberspace (2)	URL (2)	diversity (4)
links (2)	home page (2)	potential (6)	confidentiality (6)

Internet Job Search

1   With the advent of the Internet, you now have a new method for seeking your career position and making worthwhile connections. The Web has now opened up a new arena of job hunting for you. The Web can be used for accessing information on how to conduct a job search on the Web, how to develop an online resume, how to learn about the various companies, and which companies have openings in your field.

2   To begin the cyberspace job search you must first have a computer with access to the Web. A good place to start your job search is on your career center's home page, which will have links to the necessary resources. Your career center may be located through the Catapult Career Offices Home Pages: Index at **http://www.jobweb.org/catapult/homepage.htm** or through Jobtrak, which has partnered with over 500 college and university career centers nationwide. The URL for this Web site is **http://www.jobtrak.com/**. Jobtrak has job listings for full-time jobs, part-time jobs, temporary jobs, and internships. Jobtrak has information on career fairs, resume development, job searches, and top recruiters, too.

3   The Riley Guide Web site, which was developed by Worcester Polytechnic Institute's librarian Margaret F. Riley Dikel (the grandmother of resources for job seekers), is a site with information of employment opportunities and job resources on the Internet. This site, found at **http://www.dbm.com/ jobguide,** has information ranging from the basic use of the Internet to incorporating the Internet into your job search to online job application procedures to recruiting online. This Web site includes all the current information on searching for positions on the Web.

4   Additional sites that can be accessed on the Web include the following:

Career Magazine. **http://www.careermag.com.** This Web site is an online career magazine with information on job openings, employers, resume banks, job fairs, and various articles on current topics such as diversity in the workplace.

CareerMosaic. **http://careermosaic.com.** This Web site is popular with college students because it has a jobs database, a "usenet" to perform searches of jobs listed in regional and occupational newsgroups, an online job fair, career resource center, and an international gateway to link to *CareerMosaic* sites around the world. This Web site strives to be a valuable source to both the employer and the job seeker.

E-Span: Interactive Employment Network. **http://www.espan.com.** E-Span has as its motto "The Right Person for the Job and the Right Job for the Person." This site offers job-search information and job listings.

JobDirect. **http://www.jobdirect.com.** JobDirect connects entry-level job seekers with employers who want qualified applicants. This Web site will help students find summer jobs, internships, or career positions.

Monster Board. **http://www.monster.com.** One of the most popular Web sites for job seekers, the Monster Board offers a variety of hyper-text links to job-search resources and connections to job listings.

Online Career Center. **http://www.occ.com.** Online is a nonprofit job-research home page sponsored by employer organizations and includes information on companies and job listings.

5   The U.S. Government's official Web site for jobs and employment information can be located at **http://www.usajobs.opm.gov/**. America's Job

Bank, which will also list jobs that can be found in the 50 states, can be viewed at **http://www.ajb.dni.us**. The home page of the White House is another site for job openings in the United States; the address is **http://www.whitehouse .gov/wh/welcome.html.**

6   The above is a listing of just a few of the Web site addresses for job searching online. You may contact your career center staff or Internet directory indexes for additional sites since new ones are added regularly. As you surf the Internet and the many career-related sites, remember to select sites that are current, look out for sales pitches, check the fees for listing your resume, be selective in contacting the potential employer, and ask what type of confidentiality or privacy protection for your resume is offered. The job search on the Web is just another tool to assist you in locating your career position.

Process Technique Questions

   1. Why do the authors consider the Internet an important tool for conducting a job search?

_____

_____

_____

_____

_____

   2. Some of the process information is in the form of lists while other information is in the form of paragraphs. Which is the easier format to read and understand? Why?

_____

_____

   3. Can you think of any other steps in the process of job searching that need to be added to the steps in this essay?

_____

_____

Critical Reading Questions

   1. Is there a thesis statement with an essay map? If so, identify it.

_____

_____

_____

_____

2. What benefit does the essay map have for the reader?

_____

_____

_____

3. The authors mention a number of websites that job seekers can access. Which do you think is the most valuable? Explain.

_____

Process Writing Opportunities

1. Write a process paragraph about the most difficult part of job searching. You can write about searching on the Internet or by some other method, like going from business to business filling out applications and attempting to get interviews.

2. Let's say you have been granted an interview. Write a process essay about how you would go about preparing for the interview. You should consider using an essay map to organize your essay into three or more steps in the process.

MANAGING YOUR TIME

Edwin Bliss

The lack of good time-management skills is at the heart of many failures and jobs not well done. In this essay, the author lays out the steps necessary for using your time more effectively.

Vocabulary

Before you begin reading, look up the definitions of the following words that appear in the essay. The number in parentheses after each word refers to the paragraph number of the essay.

allocate (3)	chaotic (8)	constituents (1)
delegate (15)	differentiates (17)	invariably (4)
irretrievably (19)	isometric (5)	neurotic (9)
omission (9)	piecemeal (4)	procrastination (11)

Managing Your Time

1   I first became interested in the effective use of time when I was an assistant to a U.S. Senator. Members of Congress are faced with urgent and conflicting demands on their time—for committee work, floor votes, speeches, interviews, briefings, correspondence, investigations, constituents' problems, and the need to be informed on a wide range of subjects. The more successful

Congressmen develop techniques for getting maximum benefit from minimum investments of time. If they don't, they don't return.

2   Realizing that I was not one of those who use time effectively, I began to apply in my own life some of the techniques I had observed. Here are ten I have found most helpful.

Plan.

3   You need a game plan for your day. Otherwise, you'll allocate your time according to whatever happens to land on your desk. And you will find yourself making the fatal mistake of dealing primarily with problems rather than opportunities. Start each day by making a general schedule, with particular emphasis on the two or three major things you would like to accomplish—including things that will achieve long-term goals. Remember, studies prove what common sense tells us: The more time we spend planning a project, the less total time is required for it. Don't let today's busywork crowd planning-time out of your schedule.

Concentrate.

4   Of all the principles of time management, none is more basic than concentration. People who have serious time-management problems invariably are trying to do too many things at once. The amount of time spent on a project is not what counts: It's the amount of *uninterrupted* time. Few problems can resist an all-out attack; few can be solved piecemeal.

Take Breaks.

5   To work for longer periods without taking a break is not an effective use of time. Energy decreases, boredom sets in, and physical stress and tension accumulate. Switching for a few minutes from a mental task to something physical—isometric exercises, walking around the office, even changing from a sitting position to a standing position for a while—can provide relief.

6   Merely resting, however, is often the best course, and you should not think of a "rest" break as poor use of time. Not only will being refreshed increase your efficiency, but relieving tension will benefit your health. Anything that contributes to health is good time management.

Avoid Clutter.

7   Some people have a constant swirl of papers on their desks and assume that somehow the most important matters will float to the top. In most cases, however, clutter hinders concentration and can create tension and frustration—a feeling of being "snowed under."

8   Whenever you find your desk becoming chaotic, take time out to reorganize. Go through all your papers (making generous use of the wastebasket) and divide them into categories: (1) Immediate action, (2) Low priority, (3) Pending, (4) Reading material. Put the highest priority item from your first pile in the center of your desk, then put everything else out of sight. Remember, you can think of only one thing at a time, and you can work on only one task at a time, so focus all your attention on the most important one. A final point: Clearing the desk completely, or at least organizing it, each evening should be standard practice. It gets the next day off to a good start.

Don't Be a Perfectionist.

9   There is a difference between striving for excellence and striving for perfection. The first is attainable, gratifying and healthy. The second is often unattainable, frustrating and neurotic. It's also a terrible waste of time. The

stenographer who retypes a lengthy letter because of a trivial error, or the boss who demands such retyping, might profit from examining the Declaration of Independence. When the inscriber of that document made two errors of omission, he inserted the missing letters between the lines. If this is acceptable in the document that gave birth to American freedom, surely it would be acceptable in a letter that will be briefly glanced at en route to someone's file cabinet or wastebasket.

Don't Be Afraid to Say No.

10   Of all the time-saving techniques ever developed, perhaps the most effective is frequent use of the word *no*. Learn to decline, tactfully but firmly, every request that does not contribute to your goals. If you point out that your motivation is not to get out of work but to save your time to do a better job on the really important things, you'll have a good chance of avoiding unproductive tasks. Remember, many people who worry about offending others wind up living according to other people's priorities.

Don't Procrastinate.

11   Procrastination is usually a deeply rooted habit. But we can change our habits provided we use the right system. William James, the father of American psychology, discussed such a system in his famous *Principles of Psychology,* published in 1890. It works as follows:

1. Decide to start changing as soon as you finish reading this article, while you are motivated. Taking that first step promptly is important.
2. Don't try to do too much too quickly. Just force yourself right now to do one thing you have been putting off. Then, beginning tomorrow morning, start each day by doing the most unpleasant thing on your schedule. Often it will be a small matter: an overdue apology; a confrontation with a fellow worker; an annoying chore you know you should tackle. Whatever it is, do it before you begin your usual morning routine. This simple procedure can well set the tone for your day. You will get a feeling of exhilaration from knowing that although the day is only 15 minutes old, you have already accomplished the most unpleasant thing you have to do all day.

12   There is one caution: Do not permit any exceptions. William James compared it to rolling up a ball of string; a single slip can undo more than many turns can wind up. Be tough with yourself, for the first few minutes of each day, for the next two weeks, and I promise you a new habit of priceless value.

Apply Radical Surgery.

13   Time-wasting activities are like cancers. They drain off vitality and have a tendency to grow. The only cure is radical surgery. If you are wasting your time in activities that bore you, divert you from your real goals, and sap your energy, cut them out, once and for all.

14   The principle applies to personal habits, routines, and activities as much as to ones associated with your work. Check your appointment calendar, your extracurricular activities, your reading list, your television viewing habits, and ax everything that doesn't give you a feeling of accomplishment or satisfaction.

Delegate.

15   An early example of failure to delegate is found in the Bible. Moses, having led his people out of Egypt, was so impressed with his own knowledge

and authority that he insisted on ruling personally on every controversy that arose in Israel. His wise father-in-law, Jethro, recognizing that this was poor use of a leader's time, recommended a two-phase approach: First, educate the people concerning the laws; second, select capable leaders and give them full authority over routine matters, freeing Moses to concentrate on major decisions. The advice is still sound.

16   You don't have to be a national leader or a corporate executive to delegate, either. Parents who don't delegate household chores are doing a disservice to themselves and their children. Running a Boy Scout troop can be as time-consuming as running General Motors if you try to do everything yourself. One caution: Giving subordinates jobs that neither you nor anyone else wants to do isn't delegating, it's assigning. Learn to delegate the challenging and rewarding tasks, along with sufficient authority to make necessary decisions. It can help to free your time.

Don't Be a "Workaholic."

17   Most successful executives I know work long hours, but they don't let work interfere with the really important things in life, such as friends, family and fly fishing. This differentiates them from the workaholic who becomes addicted to work just as people become addicted to alcohol. Symptoms of work addiction include refusal to take a vacation, inability to put the office out of your mind on weekends, a bulging briefcase, and a spouse, son or daughter who is practically a stranger.

18   Counseling can help people cope with such problems. But for starters, do a bit of self-counseling. Ask yourself whether the midnight oil you are burning is adversely affecting your health. Ask where your family comes in your list of priorities, whether you are giving enough of yourself to your children and spouse, and whether you are deceiving yourself by pretending that the sacrifices you are making are really for them.

19   Above all else, good time management involves an awareness that today is all we ever have to work with. The past is irretrievably gone, the future is only a concept. British art critic John Ruskin had the word "TODAY" carved into a small marble block that he kept on his desk as a constant reminder to "Do It Now." But my favorite quotation is by an anonymous philosopher:

> Yesterday is a canceled check.
> Tomorrow is a promissory note.
> Today is ready cash. Use it!

Process Technique Questions

1. In your own words, explain the ten-step process for achieving effective time-management skills. Limit each explanation to no more than two sentences.

_____

_____

_____

_____

2. In your opinion, which of the steps is the most important? Explain.

_____

_____

_____

_____

3. Can you think of any additional steps in the process that might be helpful for better time management?

_____

_____

_____

_____

Critical Reading Questions

1. Why does the author place so much importance on good time-management skills?

_____

_____

_____

_____

_____

2. At the end of the essay, the author gives his favorite quotation. Explain how the quotation supports his point about time management.

_____

_____

_____

Process Writing Opportunities

1. Since you are a college student, write a paragraph describing a process that would help you become a more effective student. Connect your ideas with proper transitional expressions, so that your steps do not appear as an unconnected list.

2. Sometimes we can learn more effectively if we discover what *not* to do. Write a humorous essay describing the steps in a process designed to make you a terrible student.

COMPARISON AND CONTRAST

▼ A BATTLE OF CULTURES

K. Connie Kang

America is a multicultural nation, yet people from varying backgrounds still find it hard to communicate with each other even though we speak a common language. In this essay, Kang suggests that for a multicultural nation to work, we need "cultural insight."

Vocabulary

Before you begin reading, look up the definitions of the following words that appear in the essay. The number in parentheses after each word refers to the paragraph number of the essay.

bicultural (3)	bilingual (3)	brusque (4)
chided (10)	interethnic (5)	ethos (16)
gregarious (9)	inclination (10)	orientation (15)
prestigious (12)	retort (10)	sporadic (4)
volatile (1)		

A Battle of Cultures

1   A volatile inner-city drama is taking place in New York where blacks have been boycotting Korean groceries for four months.

2   The recent attack on three Vietnamese men by a group of blacks who mistook them for Koreans has brought this long-simmering tension between two minority groups to the world's attention. Korean newspapers from San Francisco to Seoul have been running front-page stories. Non-Asian commentators around the country, whose knowledge of Korea may not be much more than images from the Korean war and the ridiculous television series *M.A.S.H.*, are making all sorts of comments.

3   As I see it, the problem in the Flatbush area of Brooklyn started with cultural misunderstanding and was compounded by a lack of bilingual and bicultural community leaders to intervene quickly.

4   Frictions between Korean store owners in New York and blacks had been building for years. Korean merchants have been complaining about thefts. On the other hand, their black customers have been accusing immigrant store owners of making money in their neighborhoods without putting anything back into the community. They have also complained about store owners being brusque. Over the past eight years, there have been sporadic boycotts but none has lasted as long as the current one, which stemmed from an accusation by a black customer in January that she had been attacked by a store employee. In defense, the store owner has said the employee caught the woman stealing.

5   The attack on the Vietnamese on May 13 wasn't the first time one group of Asians has been mistaken for another in America. But the publicity surrounding the case has made this unfortunate situation a case study in interethnic tension.

6   What's missing in this inner-city drama is cultural insight.

7   What struck me more than anything was a recent remark by a black resident: "The Koreans are a very, very rude people. They don't understand you have to smile."

8   I wondered whether her reaction would have been the same had she known that Koreans don't smile at Koreans either without a reason. To a Korean, a smile is not a facial expression he can turn on and off mechanically. Koreans have a word for it—mu-ttuk-ttuk-hada" (stiff). In other words, the Korean demeanor is "myu-po-jung"—lack of expression.

9   It would be an easy thing for blacks who are naturally friendly and gregarious to misunderstand Korean ways.

10   As a Korean American I've experienced this many times. Whenever I'm in Korea, which is often, I'm chided for smiling too much. "Why do you smile so easily? You act like a Westerner," people tell me. My inclination is to retort: "Why do you always have to look like you've got indigestion?" But I restrain myself because I know better.

11   In our culture, a smile is reserved for people we know and for a proper occasion. Herein lies a big problem when newcomers from Korea begin doing business in America's poor inner-city neighborhoods.

12   Culturally and socially, many newcomers from Korea, like other Asian immigrants, are ill-equipped to run businesses in America's inner cities. But because they are denied entry into mainstream job markets, they pool resources and open mom-and-pop operations in the only places where they can afford it. They work 14 and 15 hours a day, seven days a week, dreaming of the day when their children will graduate from prestigious schools and make their sacrifices worthwhile.

13   From the other side, inner-city African Americans must wonder how these new immigrants find the money to run their own businesses, when they themselves can't even get a small loan from a bank. Their hope of getting out of the poverty cycle is grim, yet they see newcomers living in better neighborhoods and driving new cars.

14   "They ask me, 'Where do you people get the money to buy a business?'" Bong-jae Jang, owner of one of the grocery stores being boycotted, told me. "How can I explain to my neighbors in my poor English the concept of our family system, the idea of 'kye' (uniquely Korean private money-lending system), our way of life?"

15   I think a little learning is in order on both sides. Korean immigrants, like other newcomers, need orientation before they leave their country as well as when they arrive in the United States. It's also important for Korean immigrants, like other Asians who live in the United States, to realize that they are indebted to blacks for the social gains won by their civil rights struggle. They face less discrimination today because blacks have paved the way. Instead of looking down on their culture, it would be constructive to learn their history, literature, music, and values and see our African American brothers and sisters in their full humanity.

16   I think it is also important to remind ourselves that while the Confucian culture has taught us how to be good parents, sons and daughters and how to behave with people we know, it has not prepared us for living in a democracy. The Confucian ethos lacks the value of social conscience, which makes democracy work.

17   It isn't enough that we think of educating our children and send them to the best schools. We need to think of other peoples' children, too. Most of all, we need to be more tolerant of other peoples' cultures. We need to celebrate our similarities as well as our differences.

18   Jang, the grocer, told me this experience has been painful but he has learned an important lesson. "We Koreans must learn to participate in this

society," he said. "When this is over, I'm going to reach out. I want to give part-time work to black youths."

19   He also told me that he has been keeping a journal. "I'm not a writer but I've been keeping a journal," he said. "I want to write about this experience someday. It may help someone."

20   By reaching out, we can make a difference. The Korean grocer's lesson is a reminder to us all that making democracy work in a multicultural society is difficult but we have no choice but to strive for it.

Compare and Contrast Technique Questions

1. Point out several cultural differences that make it difficult for African Americans and Korean Americans to get along.

_____

_____

_____

_____

_____

_____

_____

_____

2. What type of cultural misunderstandings does the author give as reasons for the long-standing problems between Korean Americans and African Americans?

_____

_____

_____

Critical Reading Questions

1. What is the essay's purpose?

_____

_____

_____

_____

2. Why are Korean Americans indebted to African Americans? How does Kang suggest that comparing the two cultures would help the two communities get along better?

_____

_____

_____

_____

_____

_____

Comparison and Contrast Writing Opportunities

1. Write a paragraph comparing the similarities or contrasting the differences between two ethnic groups living in the same community. As you write, comment on how those similarities or differences affect relationships within the community.

2. Many families or groups (associations, clubs, churches, etc.) are composed of people of more than one ethnic background. Write an essay comparing the similarities and contrasting the differences of the cultural characteristics within a family or group. As you write, comment on how the similarities and differences cause harmony and dissension between the members.

▼

TWO WAYS TO BELONG IN AMERICA

Bharati Mukherjee

Like much of her writing, this essay by Mukherjee involves immigrants. "Two Ways to Belong in America," originally published in The *New York Times,* September 22, 1996. As you read the essay, notice how she engages your interest by moving from particular events to the general as she relates personal observations and universal beliefs.

Vocabulary

Before you begin reading, look up the definitions of the following words that appear in the essay. The number in parentheses after each word refers to the paragraph number of the essay.

ancestral (12)	curtailing (8)	expatriate (11)
hysteria (10)	looming (6)	mongrelization (5)
mythic (7)	opting (5)	quota (5)
referendum (13)	renouncing (5)	scrutiny (7)
subtext (9)		

Two Ways to Belong in America

1   This is a tale of two sisters from Calcutta, Mira and Bharati, who have lived in the United States for some 35 years, but who find themselves on different sides in the current debate over the status of immigrants. I am an American citizen and she is not. I am moved that thousands of long-term residents are finally taking the oath of citizenship. She is not.

2   Mira arrived in Detroit in 1960 to study child psychology and pre-school education. I followed her a year later to study creative writing at the University of Iowa. When we left India, we were almost identical in appearance and attitude. We dressed alike, in saris; we expressed identical views on politics, social issues, love and marriage in the same Calcutta convent-school accent. We would endure our two years in America, secure our degrees, then return to India to marry the grooms of our father's choosing.

3   Instead, Mira married an Indian student in 1962 who was getting his business administration degree at Wayne State University. They soon acquired the labor certifications necessary for the green card of hassle-free residence and employment.

4   Mira still lives in Detroit, works in the Southfield, Mich., school system, and has become nationally recognized for her contributions in the fields of pre-school education and parent-teacher relationships. After 36 years as a legal immigrant in this country, she clings passionately to her Indian citizenship and hopes to go home to India when she retires.

5   In Iowa City in 1963, I married a fellow student, an American of Canadian parentage. Because of the accident of his North Dakota birth, I bypassed labor-certification requirements and the race-related "quota" system that favored the applicant's country of origin over his or her merit. I was prepared for (and even welcomed) the emotional strain that came with marrying outside my ethnic community. In 33 years of marriage, we have lived in every part of North America. By choosing a husband who was not my father's selection, I was opting for fluidity, self-invention, blue jeans and T-shirts, and renouncing 3,000 years (at least) of caste-observant, "pure culture" marriage in the Mukherjee family. My books have often been read as unapologetic (and in some quarters overenthusiastic) texts for cultural and psychological "mongrelization." It's a word I celebrate.

6   Mira and I have stayed sisterly close by phone. In our regular Sunday morning conversations, we are unguardedly affectionate. I am her only blood relative on this continent. We expect to see each other through the looming crises of aging and ill health without being asked. Long before Vice President Gore's "Citizenship U.S.A." drive, we'd had our polite arguments over the ethics of retaining an overseas citizenship while expecting the permanent protection and economic benefits that come with living and working in America.

7   Like well-raised sisters, we never said what was really on our minds, but we probably pitied one another. She, for the lack of structure in my life, the erasure of Indianness, the absence of an unvarying daily core. I, for the narrowness of her perspective, her uninvolvement with the mythic depths or the superficial pop culture of this society. But, now, with the scapegoating of "aliens" (documented or illegal) on the increase, and the targeting of long-term legal immigrants like Mira for new scrutiny and new self-consciousness, she and I find ourselves unable to maintain the same polite discretion. We were always unacknowledged adversaries, and we are now, more than ever, sisters.

8   "I feel used," Mira raged on the phone the other night. "I feel manipulated and discarded. This is such an unfair way to treat a person who was

invited to stay and work here because of her talent. My employer went to the I.N.S. and petitioned for the labor certification. For over 30 years, I've invested my creativity and professional skills into the improvement of *this* country's pre-school system. I've obeyed all the rules, I've paid my taxes, I love my work, I love my students, I love the friends I've made. How dare America now change its rules in midstream? If America wants to make new rules curtailing benefits of legal immigrants, they should apply only to immigrants who arrive after those rules are already in place."

9   To my ears, it sounded like the description of a long-enduring, comfortable yet loveless marriage, without risk or recklessness. Have we the right to demand, and to expect, that we be loved? (That, to me, is the subtext of the arguments by immigration advocates.) My sister is an expatriate, professionally generous and creative, socially courteous and gracious, and that's as far as her Americanization can go. She is here to maintain an identity, not to transform it.

10   I asked her if she would follow the example of others who have decided to become citizens because of the anti-immigration bills in Congress. And here, she surprised me. "If America wants to play the manipulative game, I'll play it too," she snapped. "I'll become a U.S. citizen for now, then change back to Indian when I'm ready to go home. I feel some kind of irrational attachment to India that I don't to America. Until all this hysteria against legal immigrants, I was totally happy. Having my green card meant I could visit any place in the world I wanted to and then come back to a job that's satisfying and that I do very well."

11   In one family, from two sisters alike as peas in a pod, there could not be a wider divergence of immigrant experience. America spoke to me—I embraced the demotion from expatriate aristocrat to immigrant nobody, surrendering those thousands of years of "pure culture," the saris, the delightfully accented English. She retained them all. Which of us is the freak?

12   Mira's voice, I realize, is the voice not just of the immigrant South Asian community but of an immigrant community of the millions who have stayed rooted in one job, one city, one house, one ancestral culture, one cuisine, for the entirety of their productive years. She speaks for greater numbers than I possibly can. Only the fluency of her English and the anger, rather than fear, born of confidence from her education, differentiate her from the seamstresses, the domestics, the technicians, the shop owners, the millions of hard-working but effectively silenced documented immigrants as well as their less fortunate "illegal" brothers and sisters.

13   Nearly 20 years ago, when I was living in my husband's ancestral homeland of Canada, I was always well-employed but never allowed to feel part of the local Quebec or larger Canadian society. Then, through a Green Paper that invited a national referendum on the unwanted side effects of "nontraditional" immigration, the Government officially turned against its immigrant communities, particularly those from South Asia.

14   I felt then the same sense of betrayal that Mira feels now. I will never forget the pain of that sudden turning, and the casual racist outbursts the Green Paper elicited. That sense of betrayal had its desired effect and drove me, and thousands like me, from the country.

15   Mira and I differ, however, in the ways in which we hope to interact with the country that we have chosen to live in. She is happier to live in America as an expatriate Indian than as an immigrant American. I need to feel like a part of the community I have adopted (as I tried to feel in Canada as well). I need to put roots down, to vote and make the difference that I can. The price that the immigrant willingly pays, and that the exile avoids, is the trauma of self-transformation.

Compare and Contrast Technique Questions

1. How is the essay organized, in the point-by-point or block method?

_____

_____

_____

2. What are the two ways to belong in America? Are the two ways being compared or contrasted?

_____

_____

_____

Critical Reading Questions

1. What is the essay's thesis?

_____

_____

_____

_____

_____

2. Why does the author say that she and her sister stayed "sisterly," but really probably pitied each other?

_____

_____

_____

_____

Comparison and Contrast Writing Opportunities

1. Write a paragraph comparing or contrasting American culture from the perspective of someone who has lived here for a long time and from the perspective of a newly arrived immigrant.

2. Pretend your job forces you to move to another country for a long period of time. Write a comparison or contrast essay describing whether you would be more like Mukherjee or her sister.

DEFINITION

IN ALL WAYS A WOMAN

Maya Angelou

In this essay, "In All Ways a Woman," by Maya Angelou, the noted writer and poet explores the many definitions of a woman. Some of the definitions are negative, and the definitions vary from group to group and change throughout the years. Despite these definitional roadblocks, the author offers a definition for women that will help them attain success in life.

Vocabulary

Before you begin reading, look up the definitions of the following words that appear in the essay. The number in parentheses after each word refers to the paragraph number of the essay.

aloof (1)	amiability (9)	fickle (1)	frivolous (1)
inane (2)	imperative (8)	misnomer (6)	parlance (5)
rectitude (5)	rectoress (5)	therapeutic (9)	unabated (10)

In All Ways a Woman

1   In my young years I took pride in the fact that luck was called a lady. In fact, there were so few public acknowledgments of the female presence that I felt personally honored whenever nature and large ships were referred to as feminine. But as I matured, I began to resent being considered a sister to a changeling as fickle as luck, as aloof as an ocean, and as frivolous as nature.

2   The phrase "A woman always has the right to change her mind" played so aptly into the negative image of the female that I made myself a victim to an unwavering decision. Even if I made an inane and stupid choice, I stuck by it rather than "be like a woman and change my mind."

3   Being a woman is hard work. Not without joy and even ecstasy, but still relentless, unending work. Becoming an old female may require only being born with certain genitalia, inheriting long-living genes and the fortune not to be run over by an out-of-control truck, but to become and remain a woman command the existence and employment of genius.

4   The woman who survives intact and happy must be at once tender and tough. She must have convinced herself, or be in the unending process of convincing herself, that she, her values, and her choices are important. In a time and world where males hold sway and control, the pressure upon women to yield their rights-of-way is tremendous. And it is under those very circumstances that the woman's toughness must be in evidence.

5   She must resist considering herself a lesser version of her male counterpart. She is not a sculptress, poetess, authoress, Jewess, Negress, or even (now rare) in university parlance a rectoress. If she is the thing, then for her own sense of self and for the education of the ill-informed she must insist with rectitude in being the thing and in being called the thing.

6   A rose by any other name may smell as sweet, but a woman called by a devaluing name will only be weakened by the misnomer.

7   She will need to prize her tenderness and be able to display it at appropriate times in order to prevent toughness from gaining total authority and to avoid becoming a mirror image of those men who value power above life, and control over love.

8   It is imperative that a woman keep her sense of humor intact and at the ready. She must see, even if only in secret, that she is the funniest, looniest woman in her world, which she should also see as being the most absurd world of all times.

9   It has been said that laughter is therapeutic and amiability lengthens the life span.

10   Women should be tough, tender, laugh as much as possible, and live long lives. The struggle for equality continues unabated, and the woman warrior who is armed with wit and courage will be among the first to celebrate victory.

Definition Technique Questions

1. How many definitions of "woman" does the author give as examples?

_____

_____

2. Is there an identifiable thesis statement? If so, identify it, and give reasons to support your choice.

_____

_____

_____

3. In several paragraphs, the author defines through the technique of comparison/contrast. Identify the paragraphs, and explain whether she is using comparison or contrast.

_____

_____

_____

Critical Reading Questions

1. How does the title help support the variety of definitions given in the essay?

_____

_____

_____

_____

2. What definition of a woman does the author offer that will help women succeed in whatever endeavor they attempt?

_____

_____

_____

_____

_____

Definition Writing Opportunities

1. Write a paragraph defining the type of people living in a particular area of a city or a larger area, such as a region of the country. Use the labels others give them, and explain the negative meanings of those labels.

2. Angelou suggests that negative labels given to women can be used by women in a positive way. Write an essay defining how the terms you used in the paragraph you wrote in exercise 1 might be used positively by the groups given those labels.

▼

A MAGIC CIRCLE OF FRIENDS

Elvira M. Franco

> You might think that a forty-year-old returning to school would stand out like a sore thumb amid the twenty-somethings. But the author of this essay found a group of students her own age with similar backgrounds and with similar fears. Instead of forcing their new school environment to conform to their own experiences, the group allows their experience to help establish new ideas about life and friendships.

Vocabulary

Before you begin reading, look up the definitions of the following words that appear in the essay. The number in parentheses after each word refers to the paragraph number of the essay.

abrading (9)	bolstered (12)	brash (7)
cajole (14)	camaraderie (7)	depleted (3)
exhilarating (7)	ignited (5)	multifaceted (11)
orthopedic (5)	pangs (15)	prominent (5)
unique (1)		

A Magic Circle of Friends

1   Older than forty and starting from scratch: I thought I was a unique item, but as soon as I peeked out of my shell I found a sea of women in similar positions.

2   The little child in us has grown mature and middle-aged, almost to our surprise. We share a fear that sits in the back of the mind like a spider ready to pounce, but we've also developed determination, almost like a religion.

3   We know we have friends; at least, I know my friends are with me, if not always, at least most of the time. And most of the time I need them, and they me. We reach over the phone lines for that word of comfort, the encouragement we need to go on when our own store of willpower has become depleted.

4   Returning to school, I found my friends were my best fans. In spite of their own insecurities, they never failed to offer me the cheering I often needed to rewrite a paper one more time or to stay up one last half-hour to re-read a difficult chapter.

5   After classes we would go to a diner, a bunch of over-forty class-mates. Working together on a project that we felt strongly about ignited a part of us we did not know existed. While we were quite far from orthopedic shoes, bifocals were prominent. Underneath the artful makeup, we would measure the wrinkles on each other's cheeks across the table, almost as if these lines could form a cord to link us.

6   It was a good time. For years, in a locked-up corner of our minds, we had held the unspoken fear that we might actually be brain-dead. We were finally giving ourselves permission to celebrate our minds.

7   For some, it was a return to the carefree years of college. For others, a first-time discovery that learning can be both fun and exhilarating. Besides the intellectual surprises, we found joy in each other's company, and we delved in this new-found camaraderie with an intensity we did not know we could achieve outside of love and pregnancies. We were, and are, proud of our ages. The only woman in the group who was under thirty struck most of us as brash, angry, and, frankly, quite inappropriate. We were probably insensitive to her needs, but somehow we failed to find out how she felt in our midst and were almost relieved when she found excuses for not joining our study sessions.

8   We ended up treating her almost like a daughter, and doing for her what most of us have been doing for our own daughters: that is, picking up the slack. The hidden bonus was that now we could continue to do things our way, which, we all knew, was the best anyway. Things were smoother when she was not around: the rest of us would always agree, and even our disagreements were somehow smooth and enjoyable.

9   We had, in fact, created a sort of bubble around us, a magic circle that follows us still and says we are bright, successful, caring, ambitious, and, finally, ready to change the world. We will not do it, as we might have been ready to do at twenty, pushing and fighting and abrading.

10   We will do it instead at a slower pace, because, along the way, we have learned lessons both small and big: for example, that the world is in no hurry to be changed and that we will have a better shot at it after a good night's sleep. We may not complete our plans by tomorrow, or even by the end of the week, because the details of our lives may interfere, such as a child home from college, or a neighbor's emergency.

11   Our goals may not even be achieved exactly as originally planned, and that is fine, too, because time has also brought us a sense of flexibility and an

appreciation for the serendipitous properties of practically any action. The end product could turn out to be infinitely more complex, and in its way more perfect, more multifaceted and rich, than what we had first envisioned. The process is in itself an achievement.

12   They call us "late bloomers," they call us "returnees." We are sought by schools, thanks to the sheer numbers we represent, not to mention the life experience and the common sense that even the least bright among us brings to the classroom. We feel flattered and surprised, and our ego is bolstered by the realization that we are indeed quite capable.

13   There are fears, too ("Will it all make sense at some point?" "What if I'll never be able to get a decent job?"), but they are kept for only a few pairs of ears, where we know we will find support and understanding.

14   Graduation comes: the last papers have been handed in with trepidation, the test booklets carrying in their pages the very essence of our knowledge closed for the last time. Goodbyes, with promises and some tears, even a photograph to keep as souvenir. We've made it: watch out world, here come the mothers and the grandmothers, ready to push, cajole, smile, and negotiate to achieve those goals we did not have a chance to effect the first time around.

15   We may just be beginning to feel a few arthritic pangs in our toes and fingers, but with our hair neatly streaked and some expensive dental work, we know we still look good. We know we are still strong, smart, vital, and, most especially, ready to work. This time around we will make a big difference. We know, because, for sure, we already are different.

Definition Technique Questions

1. Why does Franco define her group as a "magic circle"?

_____

_____

_____

_____

2. What is the simile in paragraph 2? What is the fear the author shares with her friends?

_____

_____

_____

_____

Critical Reading Questions

1. The author defines herself and her friends and others like them as "late bloomers" and "returnees." Why do schools seek them out as part of their student body?

_____

_____

_____

_____

_____

_____

2. Why didn't Franco and her group of forty-year-olds have a chance to reach their goals earlier in life? How will their education help them achieve their goals this time around?

_____

_____

_____

_____

Definition Writing Opportunities

1. Write a paragraph defining two groups that compete with each other, either in school or on the job.
2. Write an essay about your circle of friends. What were the circumstances under which you met? How have you supported each other during crises? Is your group still together, or has it broken up? Why?

CAUSE AND EFFECT

SPANGLISH SPOKEN HERE

Janice Castro

> In this essay, "Spanglish Spoken Here," which originally appeared in _Time,_ July 8, 1998, the author explores the causes and effects that the burgeoning Hispanic population has had on our language. Many citizens, having Standard American English as their first language, know some Spanish words and phrases, and some immigrants, having Spanish as their first language, know some Standard American English words and phrases. When people speak a language that is a mixture of both, a new language, Spanglish, develops.

Vocabulary

Before you begin reading, look up the definitions of the following words that appear in the essay. The number in parentheses after each word refers to the paragraph number of the essay.

bemused (1)   context (5)   gaffes (10)   inadvertently (10)

linguistics (2)   mode (2)   patter (3)   syntax (3)

Spanglish Spoken Here

1   In Manhattan a first-grader greets her visiting grandparents, happily exclaiming, "Come here, *siéntate!*" Her bemused grandfather, who does not speak Spanish, nevertheless knows she is asking him to sit down. A Miami personnel officer understands what a job applicant means when he says "*Quiero un* part time." Nor do drivers miss a beat reading a billboard alongside a Los Angeles street advertising CERVEZA—SIX-PACK!

2   This free-form blend of Spanish and English, known as Spanglish, is common linguistic currency wherever concentrations of Hispanic Americans are found in the U.S. In Los Angeles, where 55% of the city's 3 million inhabitants speak Spanish, Spanglish is as much a part of daily life as sunglasses. Unlike the broken-English efforts of earlier immigrants from Europe, Asia, and other regions, Spanglish has become a widely accepted conversational mode used casually—even playfully—by Spanish-speaking immigrants and native-born Californians alike.

3   Consisting of one part Hispanicized English, one part Americanized Spanish and more than a little fractured syntax, Spanglish is a bit like a Robin Williams comedy routine: a crackling line of cross-cultural patter straight from the melting pot. Often it enters Anglo homes and families through the children, who pick it up at school or at play with their young Hispanic contemporaries. In other cases, it comes from watching TV; many an Anglo child watching *Sesame Street* has learned *uno dos tres* almost as quickly as one two three.

4   Spanglish takes a variety of forms, from the Southern California Anglos who bid farewell with the utterly silly "*hasta la* bye-bye" to the Cuban-American drivers is Miami who *parquean* their *carros*. Some Spanglish sentences are mostly Spanish, with a quick detour for an English word or two. A Latino friend may cut short a conversation by glancing at his watch and excusing himself with the explanation that he must "*ir al* supermarket."

5   Many of the English words transplanted in this way are simply handier than their Spanish counterparts. No matter how distasteful the subject, for example, it is still easier to say "income tax" than *impuesto sobre la renta*. At the same time, many Spanish-speaking immigrants have adopted such terms as VCR, microwave and dishwasher for what they view as largely American phenomena. Still other English words convey a cultural context that is not implicit in the Spanish. A friend who invites you to *lonche* most likely has in mind the brisk American custom of "doing lunch" rather than the languorous afternoon break traditionally implied by *almuerzo*.

6   Mainstream Americans exposed to similar hybrids of German, Chinese or Hindi might be mystified. But even Anglos who speak little or no Spanish are somewhat familiar with Spanglish. Living among them, for one thing, are 19 million Hispanics. In addition, more American high school and university students sign up for a Spanish than for any other foreign language.

7   Only in the past ten years, though, has Spanglish begun to turn into a national slang. Its popularity has grown with the explosive increases in U.S. immigration from Latin American countries. English has increasingly collided with Spanish in retail stores, offices and classrooms, in pop music and on street corners. Anglos whose ancestors picked up such Spanish words as *rancho, bronco, tornado* and *incommunicado*, for instance, now freely use such Spanish words as *gracias, bueno, amigo* and *por favor*.

8   Among Latinos. Spanglish conversations often flow easily from Spanish into several sentences of English and back gain. "It is done unconsciously," explains Carmen Silva-Corvalan, a Chilean-born associate professor of linguistics at the University of California who speaks Spanglish with relatives and neighbors. "I couldn't even tell you minutes later if I said something in Spanish or English."

9   Spanglish is a sort of code for Latinos: the speakers know Spanish, but their hybrid language reflects the American culture in which they live. Many lean to shorter, clipped phrases in place of the longer, more graceful expressions their parents used. Says Leonel de la Cuesta, an assistant professor of modern languages at Florida International University in Miami: "In the U.S., time is money, and that is showing up in Spanglish as an economy of language." Conversational examples: *taipiar* (type) and *winshi-wiper* (windshield wiper) replace *escribir a máquina* and *limpiaparabrisas*.

10   Major advertisers, eager to tap the estimated $134 billion in spending power wielded by Spanish-speaking Americans, have ventured into Spanglish to promote their products. In some cases, attempts to sprinkle Spanish through commercials have produced embarrassing gaffes. A Braniff airlines ad that sought to tell Spanish-speaking audiences that they could settle back *en* (in) luxuriant *cuero* (leather) seats, for example, inadvertently said they could fly without clothes (*encuero*). A fractured translation of the Miller Lite slogan told readers the beer was "Filling, and less delicious." Similar blunders are often made by Anglos trying to impress Spanish-speaking pals. But if Latinos are amused by mangled Spanglish, they also recognize these goofs as a sort of friendly acceptance. As they might put it, *no problema*.

Cause and Effect Technique Questions

1. The author's last name is Castro, and she uses many Spanish words and phrases. For whom do you think she is writing?

_____

_____

_____

2. The author ends the essay with a Spanglish expression *no problema*. How does her doing this help develop the point she is making about Spanglish?

_____

_____

_____

Critical Reading Questions

1. What are the positive effects of learning to speak a second language?

_____

_____

_____

2. What is the main economic effect of the expanding number of Hispanics in America?

_____

_____

Cause and Effect Writing Opportunities

1. Write a paragraph about the effects of learning another language.
2. Write an essay about the cultural benefits that America has gotten from the influx of a particular culture. Food, music, art, language, business, and religion are just some of the elements you might want to include in your essay.

▼

WHY WE CRAVE HORROR MOVIES

Stephen King

For the most part, people's lives are filled with fears about their jobs, paying the bills, their children, and a variety of crimes against people and property. Yet society doesn't respond well to those making their fears public. They are often seen as unbalanced, or troublemakers, or social misfits. Where do people go to release their pent up fears? In this essay, the master of the macabre reveals his thoughts about why people are drawn to accounts of horror.

Vocabulary

Before you begin reading, look up the definitions of the following words that appear in the essay. The number in parentheses after each word refers to the paragraph number of the essay.

anarchistic (11)	asylum (1)	depleted (3)
exalted (9)	innately (4)	menaced (6)
morbidity (12)	mythic (7)	normality (4)
penchant (7)	province (3)	remonstrance (10)
sanctions (10)	squinch (1)	status quo (9)
voyeur (6)		

Why We Crave Horror Movies

1   I think that we're all mentally ill; those of us outside the asylums only hide it a little better—and maybe not all that much better, after all. We've all known people who talk to themselves, people who sometimes squinch their faces into horrible grimaces when they believe no one is watching, people who have some hysterical fear—of snakes, the dark, the tight place, the long drop . . . and, of course, those final worms and grubs that are waiting so patiently underground.

state the obvious (points) first

2   When we pay our four or five bucks and seat ourselves at tenth-row center in a theater showing a horror movie, we are daring the nightmare.

3   Why? Some of the reasons are simple and obvious. To show that we can, that we are not afraid, that we can ride this roller coaster. Which is not to say that a really good horror movie may not surprise a scream out of us at some point, the way we may scream when the roller coaster twists through a complete 360 or plows through a lake at the bottom of the drop. And horror movies, like roller coasters, have always been the special province of the young; by the time one turns 40 or 50, one's appetite for double twists or 360-degree loops may be considerably depleted.

4   We also go to reestablish our feelings of essential normality; the horror movie is innately conservative, even reactionary. Freda Jackson as the horrible melting woman in *Die, Monster, Die!* confirms for us that no matter how far we may be removed from the beauty of a Robert Redford or a Diana Ross, we are still light-years from true ugliness.

5   And we go to have fun.

6   Ah, but this is where the ground starts to slope away, isn't it? Because this is a very peculiar sort of fun, indeed. The fun comes from seeing others menaced—sometimes killed. One critic has suggested that if pro football has become the voyeur's version of combat, then the horror film has become the modern version of the public lynching.

7   It is true that the mythic, "fairy-tale" horror film intends to take away the shades of gray. . . . It urges us to put away our more civilized and adult penchant for analysis and to become children again, seeing things in pure blacks and whites. It may be that horror movies provide psychic relief on this level because this invitation to lapse into simplicity, irrationality, and even outright madness is extended so rarely. We are told we may allow our emotions a free rein . . . or no rein at all.

8   If we are all insane, then sanity becomes a matter of degree. If your insanity leads you to carve up women, like Jack the Ripper or the Cleveland Torso Murderer, we clap you away in the funny farm (but neither of those two amateur-night surgeons was ever caught, heh-heh-heh); if, on the other hand, your insanity leads you only to talk to yourself when you're under stress or to pick your nose on your morning bus, then you are left alone to go about your business . . . though it is doubtful that you will ever be invited to the best parties.

9   The potential lyncher is in almost all of us (excluding saints, past and present; but then, most saints have been crazy in their own ways), and every now and then, he has to be let loose to scream and roll around in the grass. Our emotions and our fears form their own body, and we recognize that it demands its own exercise to maintain proper muscle tone. Certain of these emotional muscles are accepted—even exalted—in civilized society; they are, of course, the emotions that tend to maintain the status quo of civilization itself. Love, friendship, loyalty, kindness—these are all the emotions that we applaud, emotions that have been immortalized in the couplets of Hallmark cards and in the verses (I don't dare call it poetry) of Leonard Nimoy.

10   When we exhibit these emotions, society showers us with positive reinforcement; we learn this even before we get out of diapers. When, as children, we hug our rotten little puke of a sister and give her a kiss, all the aunts and uncles smile and twit and cry, "Isn't he the sweetest little thing?" Such coveted treats as chocolate-covered graham crackers often follow. But if we deliberately slam the rotten little puke of a sister's fingers in the door, sanctions follow—angry remonstrance from parents, aunts and uncles; instead of a chocolate-covered graham cracker, a spanking.

11   But anticivilization emotions don't go away, and they demand periodic exercise. We have such "sick" jokes as, "What's the difference between a truckload of bowling balls and a truckload of dead babies?" (You can't unload

a truckload of bowling balls with a pitchfork . . . a joke, by the way, that I heard originally from a ten-year-old.) Such a joke may surprise a laugh or a grin out of us even as we recoil, a possibility that confirms the thesis: If we share a brotherhood of man, then we also share an insanity of man. None of which is intended as a defense of either the sick joke or insanity, but merely as an explanation of why the best horror films, like the best fairy tales, manage to be reactionary, anarchistic, and revolutionary all at the same time.

12   The mythic horror movie, like the sick joke, has a dirty job to do. It deliberately appeals to all that is worst in us. It is morbidity unchained, our most base instincts let free, our nastiest fantasies realized . . . , and it all happens, fittingly enough, in the dark. For those reasons, good liberals often shy away from horror films. For myself, I like to see the most aggressive of them— *Dawn of the Dead,* for instance—as lifting a trap door in the civilized forebrain and throwing a basket of raw meat to the hungry alligators swimming around in that subterranean river beneath.

13   Why bother? Because it keeps them from getting out, man. It keeps them down there and me up here. It was Lennon and McCartney who said that all you need is love, and I would agree with that.

14   As long as you keep the gators fed.

Cause and Effect Technique Questions

1. Is there an identifiable thesis statement that clarifies the cause and effect nature of our craving for horror movies?

2. Point out one metaphor and one simile wherein King compares horror movies to something else.

Critical Reading Questions

1. In King's opinion, why do people enjoy being scared (the effect) by watching horror movies (the cause)?

2. In the last line of the essay, King says, "As long as you keep the gators fed." What does he mean by this?

_____

_____

_____

_____

_____

Cause and Effect Writing Opportunities

1. Horror movies are not the only type of film in which murder and mayhem take place. Choose another type of film and write a paragraph showing the cause and effect relationship that exists between it and the viewing public.

2. King states that there is a certain amount of insanity in the American population. Write an essay pointing out the causes and effects of an insane society.

PERSUASION

JUST SAY NO TO RANDOM DRUG TESTING

David Rocah

> This essay, written by American Civil Liberties Union attorney David Rocah, recounts a case he was to defend involving a Ridgefield Park High School student who was forbidden to play football because he refused to be randomly drug tested. The case never went to trial because the school district revoked their earlier policy on the advice of a judge who said there wasn't sufficient evidence of a widespread drug problem to warrant the enforcement of such a policy.
>
> In the next essay that follows, by former news writer and editor Claude Lewis, a contrary position is represented. Lewis believes that all students, not just athletes, should be randomly drug tested.

Vocabulary
Before you begin reading, look up the definitions of the following words that appear in the essay. The number in parentheses after each word refers to the paragraph number of the essay.

affidavits (7)	bedrock (14)	coercing (8)	embodies (4)
illicit (1)	platitudes (14)	presumption (2)	toll (5)

Just Say No to Random Drug Testing

In our system, state-operated schools may not be enclaves of totalitarianism. School officials do not possess absolute authority over their students. Students in school as well as out of school are "persons" under our Constituttion.

—JUSTICE ABE FORTAS, *Tinker v. Des Moines* (1969)

1   Ridgefield Park, like at least nine other school districts in New Jersey, recently decided that it would not permit its junior and senior high school students to participate in interscholastic sports unless they agreed to have their urine tested for traces of certain illicit drugs at random intervals during the athletic season. Because we believe that this intrusive and demeaning search of students' bodily fluids violates fundamental constitutional principles, the American Civil Liberties Union of New Jersey is representing a student and his parents in a legal challenge to the Ridgefield Park program.

2   One of the fundamental features of our legal system is that we are presumed innocent of any wrongdoing unless and until the government proves otherwise. Random drug testing of student athletes turns this presumption on its head, telling students that we assume they are using drugs until they prove to the contrary with a urine sample. The overwhelming majority of student athletes in Ridgefield Park, and throughout New Jersey, are law abiding citizens, and there is no basis in law or logic to presume otherwise or to treat them worse than accused criminals.

3   An equally cherished constitutional command is the rule that government officials may not search us without an adequate reason. Thus, for example, even though we know there is a drug problem in our society, we do not allow the police to randomly stop us on the street to see if we are carrying drugs.

4   The constitutional prohibition against "unreasonable" searches also embodies the principle that merely belonging to a certain group is not a sufficient reason for a search, even if many members of that group are suspected of illegal activity. Thus, for example, even if it were true that most men with long hair were drug users, the police would not be free to stop all long haired men and search them for drugs.

5   Unfortunately, many school officials concerned about drug use by students seem willing to ignore these principles. There is no doubt that the concern is well placed, and it is one that we share. Drug use is a scourge on our society, exacting a terrible toll in lost lives. And no one is arguing that we should tolerate students' use of illegal drugs. But zero tolerance for drugs should not lead us to have zero tolerance for constitutional limits. Sadly, that is exactly what is happening.

6   Parents and school officials currently have a wide variety of tools at their disposal to address drug use by students. Educating students about the dangers of drug use can be highly effective. A recent study by the Parent's Resource Institute for Drug Education shows that students who are warned about drugs by their parents use them 30 percent less often than those who are not, and students who said their parents set "clear rules" regarding drugs used them 57 percent less than those whose parents did not.

7   In addition, school officials currently have the power to require any student whom they reasonably suspect of using drugs to submit to a drug test. Indeed, if the affidavits submitted in court by the Ridgefield Park School Board are to be believed, school officials there have been grossly irresponsible in failing to act when they had reason to suspect particular students were

using drugs. Not only did they not conduct drug tests, there is no indication that they even informed the parents of their suspicions.

8   Acting on the basis of individual suspicion ensures both that hundreds of innocent children are not subjected to a degrading search, and demonstrates that school officials care about all students who use drugs, not just student athletes. The Board also could have implemented a truly voluntary drug testing program, rather than coercing parents to consent by denying their children the opportunity to participate in interscholastic athletics. Had the Board done so, it is likely that no one would have objected, and the ACLU could not and would not have challenged it.

9   Given these tools, which, when employed vigorously can be an effective and constitutional means of dealing with drug use by the entire student body, why are school districts resorting to random drug testing of athletes? Because they improperly read a 1995 U.S. Supreme Court decision as giving them carte blanche. In a case involving a school district in Vernonia, Oregon, the Court decided that the district could constitutionally require student athletes to submit to random drug testing where officials testified that they were no longer able to maintain discipline in the school system because of a culture of pervasive drug use and disrespect for authority, and where student athletes were the leaders of the drug culture.

10   Are the parents and administrators in Ridgefield Park prepared to admit that they cannot maintain order and discipline in their schools? There is no evidence of this, and we would be surprised if it were so. Ridgefield Park has a fine school system, which sent 73 percent of its graduates to college last year.

11   Are student athletes leaders of the drug culture? Although the Ridgefield Park School Board's court papers scandalously attempted to portray its student athletes as a pack of drug addled alcoholics, these same athletes won state championships in football for the past two years. Nationally, student athletes have been found to have higher academic achievement and fewer disciplinary problems than non-athletes, due in large part to the tremendous discipline required to balance a full academic program and the time demanded by practice and competition schedules. Singling out athletes in New Jersey because of a problem in Vernonia, Oregon, is both ridiculous and unfair.

12   School officials argue that random drug testing will deter drug use. But students should not use drugs because they are harmful and illegal, not because they might get caught. Moreover, random drug testing simply encourages students to defer drug use until after the athletic season is completed, rather than completely refraining from drug use.

13   School officials also argue that participating in interscholastic athletics is a privilege, not a right, and that they may therefore impose any conditions on the exercise of that privilege that they see fit. This ignores the well established constitutional doctrine that the government may not condition the receipt of a governmental benefit on the waiver of constitutional rights. Just as a school could not condition participation in interscholastic athletics on students giving up their right to free speech, they also may not condition participation on students giving up their right to be free from unreasonable searches.

14   Some also argue that students who aren't doing anything wrong have nothing to fear. This ignores the fact that what they fear is not getting caught, but the loss of dignity and trust that the drug test represents. And we should all be afraid of government officials who believe that a righteous cause warrants setting aside bedrock constitutional protections. The lesson that our schools should be teaching is respect for the Constitution and for students' dignity and privacy, not a willingness to treat cherished constitutional principles as mere platitudes.

NAÏVE COURT DIDN'T GO FAR ENOUGH WITH DRUG TESTING

Claude Lewis

Vocabulary

Before you begin reading, look up the definitions of the following words that appear in the essay. The number in parentheses after each word refers to the paragraph number of the essay.

antithesis (3)	botched (1)	demise (5)	depraved (5)
draconian (2)	errant (7)	irony (9)	valid (10)

Naïve Court Didn't Go Far Enough with Drug Testing

1   This nation has so badly botched the war on drugs that I find myself in painful agreement with a Supreme Court ruling that public schools can require students to take drug tests as a condition of playing sports.

2   Indeed, my concern for an end to the devastation of drug abuse and addiction is so great that I find myself wondering why such tests should be restricted to athletes. Why not apply the pain all at once and permit random testing of all students? If such draconian solutions are necessary, why single out those who play sports? What about the millions of other students who don't? Should they not be required to undergo random drug tests?

3   Random drug testing is the antithesis of a free society. Yet, I am persuaded that since the drug problem is so pervasive, destructive and corrupt, and since the government has failed so miserably for so long in ending its corrosive effects, we have few alternatives other than poking our noses in places where they don't belong.

4   When it comes to drugs, we have reached a point where the only cure may have to be worse than the disease. We "must" take the strongest possible action to protect the young and the unsuspecting.

5   Most American have never seen firsthand the powerful and depraved activity in the world of illicit drugs. I have talked with addicts for years and have witnessed the demise and deaths of countless young men and women who were unable to end their enslavement.

6   I have seen young people with old faces, the result of persistent experimenting with drugs. Because government has failed at containing addiction and our nation has no sure method of treating the army of addicts living among us, extreme measures must be adopted.

7   No longer is it possible, if it ever was, to accept the pathetic lie that drug addicts exist mainly in the inner city. The problem has grown so great that in almost any community, children and errant adults can locate drugs within a half-hour of their homes.

8   If the court's decision is, as some say, a victory, it is one of the saddest victories I can imagine. It is distressing that we must resort to limiting Fourth Amendment privacy rights to student athletes in order to protect them from the danger of drugs. Students spend more time in school than in any other institution outside their homes. And it is the school where initial exposure to illegal drugs often takes place.

9   The irony in all this is that it is not the students who have failed, but the adults who are responsible for them. In Washington, the court's ruling was met with wide acceptance among young athletes.

10   Others argue if there's no reason to suspect illegal drug use, students should not be subjected to random testing. Such notions were valid in another era. No more.

11   How else do we begin to get at the problem? Drug education is good but won't provide a total solution. Education must be a part of the solution along with other firm approaches. Few of us come new to this problem. America is one of the world's most drug-dependent nations and the problem threatens to grow worse.

12   An enormous number of crimes committed every year—from petty thefts to bank robberies to murders—are connected to addiction.

13   Supreme Court Justice Sandra Day O'Connor holds a naïve notion on the matter, calling the collection of urine samples "particularly destructive of privacy and offensive to personal dignity."

14   What could be more offensive to personal dignity than addiction itself? The court's ruling may contain some frightening implications, but not nearly as frightening as the growing new armies of addicts who will poison the future of many young people for generations.

Persuasion Technique Questions

1. Both Rocah and Lewis use evidence to support their points of view. Which essay's evidence seems the most convincing? Why?

_____

_____

_____

_____

2. Is there a thesis statement in each essay? If so, identify them.

_____

_____

_____

_____

Critical Reading Questions

1. David Rocah suggests that most students and student athletes do not take drugs; therefore, he argues that a random drug testing policy is not necessary. Do you agree or disagree?

_____

_____

_____

2. Claude Lewis, on the other hand, says that the court's decision that public schools can randomly drug test athletes is a sad victory. How can a victory be sad?

_____

_____

_____

_____

3. Even though these two essays are on different sides of the issue, can you suggest a way that a compromise can be reached?

_____

_____

_____

_____

Persuasion Writing Opportunities

1. Write a persuasive paragraph defending or attacking random drug testing for high school athletes.
2. Write a persuasive essay supporting or rejecting the idea that random drug testing of all high school students will decrease drug use among them.

▼

WHY I HUNT

Dan Sisson

> This essay by Dan Sisson and the one that follows by Steve Ruggeri are clearly persuasive and representative of groups on either side of the gun issue. As you read each writer's position, notice that they concede points to the other side, yet these concessions actually make their own positions stronger. Being fair to your opponent can be an effective technique in persuasive writing.

Vocabulary
Before you begin reading, look up the definitions of the following words that appear in the essay. The number in parentheses after each word refers to the paragraph number of the essay.

aesthetic (13)	anachronism (4)	articulated (11)
banal (7)	clichés (1)	corollary (6)
leper (3)	ponder (17)	

Why I Hunt

1   Hunting implies a relationship between man and animal, and as in any relationship, the layers of meaning that make it unique cannot be reduced to a single proposition or a simple-minded set of clichés.

2   Yet that is what has happened in the United States, where the debate between hunters and anti-hunters has been reduced to one question: How can anyone justify killing any animal?

3   As a hunter, I have felt hostility from people I know and respect who are anti-hunters. I have been told that killing any animal, except in self-defense, is immoral; and I have been characterized as a social leper who belongs to a more primitive age.

4   But this view of the hunter as an anachronism ignores the histories of science and of humankind. It conveniently blots out the fact that in nature every species, no matter how big or small, is either predator or prey, the hunter or the hunted. This—not the preservation of all life at any cost—is the dynamic of existence on our planet.

5   In all predator relationships there is an inequality between the hunter and the hunted. The belief that all creatures have an equal right to life, and that therefore all killing is immoral, is a fallacy without precedent in science or the natural world.

6   The conviction of the anti-hunter that killing any animal is wrong may be based on the misguided concept that equality between hunter and hunted is the corollary of equality before the law. The equality of men and their right to life are *artificial* constructs of constitutional government and hold true only in the most civilized nations.

7   For me the essence of hunting is not the indulgence of the instinct to kill, nor is it to be found in the instant one kills. In fact, killing is no more necessary to a successful hunt than catching a fish is to a good fishing trip. If every hunt ended in a successful kill, hunting would be both boring and banal.

8   The essence of hunting for me is to pursue the animal ethically and in a manner that makes the possibility of killing or capturing it a genuine challenge. There is no certainty of killing when I hunt. Indeed, the *uncertainty* is what makes the sport interesting.

9   I accept limits on my ability to kill. The hunting seasons are carefully constructed so as to make the wit of the hunter and the cunning of the animal more truly competitive.

10   That is why we limit seasons to several days or weeks a year, limit the use of baits to lure unwary animals and birds, and limit the number of animals we kill, their size and age and sex. We limit our behavior by law in order to pursue game ethically and to make the challenge even more difficult. These odds I take on happily, knowing the elk herds will continue to flourish. Those who refuse to accept the odds—the poachers—are not hunters, they are outlaws.

11   Hunting is a complex activity involving undercurrents that are rarely articulated, but that nevertheless form the basis for one's actions. One of these unstated values is the attempt to establish a strong ethical position in life. Few activities in this world test ethical standards as does hunting.

12   There are no witnesses in the wilderness. The hunter knows in his conscience whether he has compromised the sportsman's standards. For an ethical hunter, hypocrisy and hunting are incompatible.

13   I have asserted that hunting involves much more than the act of killing. I hunt to nourish my aesthetic appreciation of nature; being in the field six months a year allows me to experience, personally, the most beautiful parts of America.

14   I hunt for food, and I do not choose to delegate my right to obtain it to a slaughterhouse. My friends go to supermarkets and buy packaged beef and lamb. I go into the wilderness and kill elk, venison, and wildfowl. Is there a moral difference between a cow being killed for market and a deer for my freezer?

15   I hunt because it deepens my relationship with my son. We have literally spent years in duck blinds, on deer stands, and around campfires—talking. I would not trade those conversations for anything on Earth.

16   I hunt because I can contribute to conservation directly. Last year I raised 5,000 valley quail. I killed 49 of them. This reflects a traditional value of giving more to the land and the environment than you take from it. How many anti-hunters can make a similar claim?

17   I hunt to simplify my life, away from the noise and the pollution of urban environments. What better way to ponder John Muir's axiom that every star is connected to every other star in the universe than by starlight after a day in the wilderness?

18   All this is why I hunt.

WHY I DON'T HUNT

Steve Ruggeri

Vocabulary
Before you begin reading, look up the definitions of the following words that appear in the essay. The number in parentheses after each word refers to the paragraph number of the essay.

compunction (4)	credo (7)	diversion (2)
rigors (2)	solicitous (5)	visceral (4)
wantonly (9)		

Why I Don't Hunt

1   Why did I hunt? From the time I was 12 until shortly after my 18th birthday, I pumped lead at the furred and feathered from Maine to Pennsylvania. I was the youngest member of the Newport Rifle Club in Rhode Island, where I was trained and disciplined as a small-bore competitive shooter. I was tutored by masters of the art, and I was given numerous opportunities to engage in my sport.

2   Despite my enthusiasm, I sought diversion from the rigors of competitive shooting. Trap and skeet shooting introduced me to moving targets, but I was anxious to sight down a barrel at animate ones. I looked forward to the pleasure of seeing birds plummet earthward. I knew I would delight in the contortions of small game, the end-over-end tumbling after the rabbit felt the sting of my .22. And I was confident that I would shrug and say, "Better luck, next buck," should I miscalculate shot placement and merely blow the lower jaw completely off a deer.

3   I didn't disappoint myself. I reveled in killing, maiming, bloodletting, and gutting. Never did I have the slightest thought regarding carrying capacity, overbrowsing, population dynamics, or any other game-management concept. The arguments that hunters advanced in defense of their sport were

alien to me. I hunted in order to kill; I did not kill in order to have "the hunting experience."

4   Why did I stop? Social expedience: My pastime was deemed unacceptable by a circle of high-school mates from whom I sought acceptance. Would I have ever experienced an after-kill crisis of conscience of such emotional magnitude that I would hurl my weapon into the nearest lake? No, I was incapable of the visceral compunction that has triggered the moral rebirth of many who formerly exploited animals.

5   A couple of years after my guns had been silenced by peer pressure, I was dining on a hamburger so rare that the blood still appeared to be coursing through the animal tissue. While hurrying to finish so as not to be late for my cat's appointment with the vet, I was seized by the realization of how utterly inconsistent it was for me to be so solicitous of a cat, yet have no regard for the cow I was devouring.

6   Pain is pain, I reasoned, whether felt by the family feline or by the unknown steer shackled and hoisted above the killing-room floor. It became morally imperative for me to end my complicity in the infliction of any gratuitous pain and suffering upon either wild or domesticated animals. This ethical awakening led to extensive research and reading that enlightened me further as to the magnitude of our exploitation of nonhuman animals, and reaffirmed my resolve to embrace an ethic of moral consideration for all animal species. I recognized that my decision to stop hunting years earlier had been correct, though made for the wrong reason.

7   Why don't I hunt? I could allude to the fruits of exhaustive research into the ecological and biological consequences of hunting, and to the collective insight of biologists, ecologists, and naturalists who challenge the prevailing wildlife-management dogma. Yet, fundamentally, the answer can be expressed in simple moral terms: Hunting is wrong, and should be acknowledged to be so not only by those who espouse the strict precepts of the animal-rights credo, but by those who hold a common sense of decency, respect, and justice. When we have exposed the specious reasoning of the hunters' apologists and stripped their sport of its counterfeit legitimacy, the naked brutality of hunting defines itself: killing for the fun of it.

8   Although my current occupation requires attention to a wide array of animal issues, the subject of hunting is the predominant focus of my work. If I find my energy or motivation waning during the course of a day's work, I merely conjure up the image of my former self as a slayer of wildlife. The memory of stalking targets on the hoof or wing infuses me with renewed vigor in my labor against blood sports.

9   But obviously, no amount of dedication or energy expanded will atone for the suffering and death I visited upon the scores of animals I wantonly killed.

Persuasion Technique Questions

1. Identify the thesis statement in each essay. What are the main differences?

_____

_____

_____

_____

_____

_____

_____

_____

_____

_____

2. Which essay contains the most persuasive evidence? Explain.

_____

_____

_____

_____

_____

Critical Reading Questions

1. What logical fallacies can you find in each essay? Explain how you think they detract from each essay's effectiveness.

_____

_____

_____

_____

_____

2. Even though these essays are on different sides of the issue, can you suggest a way that a compromise can be reached?

_____

_____

_____

_____

Persuasion Writing Exercises

1. Write a paragraph either defending or attacking hunting.
2. Hunting is only one activity that has an impact on the environment. Write a persuasive essay about how another activity adversely affects the environment: off-road racing (including motorcross biking and snowmobiling), camping, canoeing, and skiing are just a few examples.

LIMITED ANSWER KEY

Chapter 2

PRACTICE 1

1. Paragraph 2, sentence 3, and sentence 12: gene therapy might evolve to allow scientists to alter a fertilized egg in ways that differ from how it would have developed naturally.

3. Paragraph 2: Dr. Anderson of USC stated that within just a few years he would ask the National Institutes of Health for permission to alter the genes of a fetus with an inherited disease. Paragraph 3: Many scientists agree that gene therapy is an ethical procedure. Paragraph 5: Researchers are already experimenting with introducing gene self-destruct cells in cells that become eggs and sperm.

Chapter 3

Answers will vary in all the practices.

Chapter 4

PRACTICE 1

1. Reading a newspaper each day <u>is important because it keeps you informed about current events.</u>

3. Working while going to school <u>should teach young people responsibility</u>.

5. The Beatles <u>remain popular</u>, <u>even after their breakup decades ago, because of their versatile musical style.</u>

PRACTICE 2

2. <u>The aging process, talented newcomers, and constant travel</u> make maintaining a sports career a difficult lifestyle.

4. A successful career often hinges upon <u>hard work, dedication, and intelligence</u>.

PRACTICE 3

1. <u>Fruits</u> <u>are a good source for vitamin C.</u> (The essay map is missing.)

3. Many <u>students</u> <u>make college a worthwhile experience</u> by <u>joining fraternities and sororities, playing intramural sports, and participating in student government.</u> (All elements are present.)

5. <u>Styling, construction, and value</u> make <u>the Breitling</u> <u>a popular wristwatch for collectors.</u> (All the elements are present.)

7. <u>Skydiving and bungee jumping</u> <u>are dangerous activities.</u> (The essay map is missing.)

9. *Star Trek* <u>has been a long-running television series</u> because of <u>special effects, interesting characters, and fascinating stories.</u> (All the elements are present.)

PRACTICE 4
Answers will vary.

PRACTICE 5
Answers will vary.

Chapter 5

Answers will vary in all the Practices.

Chapter 6

Answers will vary in all the Practices.

Chapter 7

Answers will vary in all the Practices.

Chapter 8

Answers will vary in all the Practices.

Chapter 9

PRACTICE 1
Answers will vary.

PRACTICE 2
1. Cybersex is becoming a popular activity.
3. Binge drinking at parties is increasing.
5. A positive attitude can help fight illness.

Chapter 10

Answers will vary in all the Practices.

Chapter 11

Answers will vary in all the Practices.

Chapter 12

Answers will vary in all the Practices.

Chapter 13

Answers will vary in all the Practices.

Chapter 14

PRACTICE 1
Answers will vary.

PRACTICE 2
2. The problem is one of *coincidence*. The problem may have nothing to do with overeating or being exposed to cold weather on a walk. It would be unusual for the person never to have overeaten on other holidays. Did the person become sick then? Most likely the person is exposed to cold weather during the winter months on other occasions, such as playing in the snow with family or friends, waiting for a bus, or walking the dog. Did illness occur after these events? If the answer is no, then the cause lies elsewhere. A good candidate would be an allergy to a specific food such as turkey, cranberries, or pumpkin pie, foods that are commonly eaten on holidays.

Chapter 15

PRACTICE 1
Answers will vary, but sample responses are provided.
1. Pro: Selling cigarettes to teens under eighteen years of age should be legalized.
   Con: Teens under eighteen years of age should not be permitted to buy cigarettes.
3. Pro: Organized prayer should be permitted in public schools to promote morality.
   Con: To ensure the separation of church and state, organized prayer should not be allowed in public schools.
5. Pro: All eighteen-year-olds should be drafted into the armed services.
   Con: Eighteen-year-olds should not be drafted into military service.
7. Pro: The government should require periodic safety inspections for automobiles.
   Con: The government should not require periodic safety inspections for automobiles.
9. Pro: The income tax must be increased.
   Con: The income tax must not be increased.

PRACTICE 4
2. Either-or
5. Red herring

Chapter 17

PRACTICE
Essay responses will vary. Key terms:
2. evaluate
4. contrast

Chapter 18

Answers will vary in all the Practices.

GLOSSARY

Absolute phrase: a group of words consisting of a noun or pronoun and a **participle** (not the regular verb form) plus any other completing words. Absolute phrases modify the entire sentence and cannot be punctuated as a complete sentence.

Abstract language: general words that refer to ideas or concepts that cannot be perceived through the senses.

Action verb: a verb that states what a subject does (in the past, present, or future tense).

Active voice: a verb form in which the subject of the sentence does the acting (using an action verb or a transitive verb).

Adjective: a word that modifies (or describes) a noun or pronoun. Adjectives usually come before the nouns they describe, but they can also follow the noun (in the predicate of the sentence).

Adverb: a word that modifies (describes) a verb, an adjective, or another adverb. Often adverbs end in –*ly*. Many adverbs answer the question *where, how,* or *when.*

Adverbial conjunction: a word that often follows a semicolon to explain how or in what way the two clauses joined by the semicolon are logically related.

Antecedent: the **noun** to which a **pronoun** refers in a sentence.

Apostrophe: a punctuation mark used to indicate contractions (isn't) or possession/ownership (Anna's papers).

Appositive: a word or phrase that renames the preceding word or phrase. Appositive phrases are often called noun phrases.

Argument: developing a topic by persuading the audience to agree with, or be convinced by, a particular point of view.

Article: a type of word that introduces a noun and indicates whether it is specific or countable. Frequently used articles are *a, an, the.*

Audience: who you are writing for. This could be a professor, a classmate, a boss, a co-worker, or even a member of a club to which you belong.

Background character: a character that serves as part of the scene or setting but is not developed.

Block citation: a quotation of five or more typed lines separated from the text by being indented ten spaces from the left margin and followed with parenthetical citation of the source.

Body paragraphs: the central section of an essay that explains the thesis statement of the essay.

Brackets: punctuation marks used in quoted material to set apart editorial explanations. (The dean wrote, "All faculty must teach sumer [sic] school.")

Brainstorming: a form of freewriting in which the writer lists thoughts freely, at random.

Causal chain: a series of events that can develop; the relationships that exist between events.

Causal relationship: the connection between cause and effect.

Cause-effect: an organization system that examines why something happens or the consequences stemming from causes.

Central character: a character presented as complicated, multidimensional (round), and essential to the plot and theme of a literary work.

Chronological order: an organization system for events according to how they occur in order of time. This order is used most often in narratives, process analysis, and cause-effect essays.

Chronological plot: a story line of events presented in order of time (chronological order).

Class definition: the indication of a word's meaning by its placement in a broad class of similar things that readers will readily understand. A class definition usually includes a specific detail that distinguishes the original term or word from the others in the class.

Classification: an organization system that divides the subject matter into categories determined by one criterion or basis for grouping.

Clause: a group of related words containing both a subject and a verb. Clauses are either **independent** or **dependent.** They also can be **restrictive** or **nonrestrictive.**

Climax: the point at which the protagonist learns a truth that forever changes the character or the action of the plot; the moment of highest tension that soon leads to falling action.

Clustering: a type of prewriting in which the writer explores and organizes thoughts in a chart that begins with putting the main topic in a circle in the center of the page, then connecting related ideas (in smaller circles) with lines (branches).

Coherence: a quality in which the relationship between ideas is clear throughout a paragraph or essay.

Coincidence: two or more events that occur around the same time but with no direct cause-effect relationship.

Colon: a punctuation mark most often used to show that a list or explanation will follow. (Eat plenty of green vegetables: broccoli, spinach, and cabbage, for example.)

Comma: a punctuation mark used for separating ideas, independent clauses, and items in a list, and for enclosing descriptive phrases.

Comma splice: a sentence containing two independent clauses incorrectly joined by a comma.

Comparison-contrast: an organization system showing similarities (comparisons) and differences (contrasts) between two or more subjects or topics. The organization can be blocked by topic or point by point by criteria.

Complex sentence: a sentence that contains an independent clause and a dependent clause.

Complication: a plot element that introduces a problem or conflict to stimulate a reader's interest.

Compound verb (predicate): a predicate (the part of the sentence containing the verb) containing two or more verbs.

Compound sentence: a sentence consisting of two or more independent clauses.

Compound subject: two or more simple subjects joined by a coordinating conjunction.

Concluding paragraph: the paragraph that ends an essay and gives a sense of completeness.

Conclusion: the last sentence of a paragraph or the last paragraph of an essay that ties together the preceding ideas.

Concrete language: particular, specific words used to portray the unique complex nature of the real world.

Conjunction: a joining word or phrase (see **coordinating conjunction, adverbial conjunction,** and **subordinating conjunction**).

Connotative language: use of words that have (or develop) associations and implications apart from their explicit sense.

Controlling idea or attitude: the focus concerning the topic or how the author feels about the topic.

Coordinating conjunction: a word that joins grammatically equal structures. The most frequently used are *and, but, or, yet, for, nor, so.*

Coordination: joining two or more grammatically equal structures, most often with a coordinating conjunction or a semicolon.

Countable nouns: nouns that can be either singular or plural.

Criterion: the standard used to classify things (basis for grouping, evaluating, comparing, and contrasting).

Cross-examination: a prewriting technique used to discover ideas about a topic. You can interview yourself or a partner by using sets of questions regarding definition, relationship, compare and contrast, testimony, and circumstances.

Dangling modifier: a descriptive phrase or clause that does not modify (describe) any word or phrase in a sentence.

Dash: a punctuation mark used to set apart parenthetical information that needs more emphasis than would be indicated by parentheses. (Irina's professor—a dynamic sociology teacher—helped her understand American society.)

Definition: an organization system that explains the meaning of a term or concept using a variety of strategies (examples, contrast, description, etc.).

Definition by negation: saying what a given word or term *is not* before saying what the word or term *actually is.*

Demonstrative pronoun: a pronoun used to point out or specify certain people, places, or things (*this, that, these, those*).

Denotative language: use of words in their accepted, dictionary-defined sense.

Dependent clause: a group of words with a subject and verb but which cannot stand alone and must be joined to an independent clause to complete its meaning. Most dependent clauses begin with subordinating conjunctions or relative pronouns.

Description: the mode of writing that develops a topic through the use of vivid sensory detail.

Developing character: a character that undergoes change during the course of a literary work.

Direct object: the word or words (usually nouns or pronouns) following and receiving the action of an action verb.

Directional process: the explanation of how to do something. The intent of directional process writing is to enable the readers to do something (to duplicate some process) after they have followed the directions.

Dominant impression: the overall feeling or emotional response the writer wants the reader to take away from descriptive writing.

Drafting: a draft is another word for *version*. Several versions of a paper should be written until the topic is explored, organized, and expressed for optimum clarity.

Editing: one of the final steps in the writing process during which the writer checks the draft of the essay for misspelled words, grammatical errors, missing words, and other errors.

Essay: an organized written work on a topic in a series of paragraphs, including an introduction that attracts the reader's attention and states the thesis of the essay; body paragraphs that present the supporting points of the thesis and develop them with facts, details, and examples; and a conclusion that summarizes the ideas and coherently ends the work.

Essay map: in the thesis statement of an essay, the indication of the subtopics that the essay will cover.

Example: an instance or case used to illustrate or explain a point.

Exposition: informative writing. In a literary work, it introduces the audience to the universe of the fictional work, the characters and their interrelationships, and the narrator's point of view.

Expository writing (exposition): informative writing, the primary purpose of which is to explain a concept.

Extended definition: a definition explained in several sentences or a paragraph by means of any one mode of development or any combination of the modes of development: description, narration, example, classification, process, comparison and contrast, and cause and effect.

Fact: a statement that can be proven to be true.

Falling action: in the plot line, the diminishing of tension and release of emotion following the climax.

Figurative language: the device of describing a person or thing in terms usually associated with something very different.

Flashback: a plot device that interrupts the chronological sequence to introduce a past episode.

Flat character: a character portrayed as representative, incomplete, or not complex—a type rather than an individual.

Foreshadowing: a hint or suggestion of what will come later.

Fragment: an incomplete sentence because it is missing a subject or verb or the verb is incomplete; a dependent clause not attached to an independent clause.

Frame: an introduction to or explanation for a quotation. The frame states the name of the person quoted, the person's title or expertise, or a brief comment on the quotation's content. This information can be placed before the quotation, after the quotation, or in the middle of the quotation.

Freewriting: writing that is used to explore ideas without concern for grammar, spelling, or organization.

Future tense: a tense used to indicate action or being that has not yet occurred.

Gerund: the *–ing* form of a verb that functions as a noun in a sentence.

Gerund phrase: a **gerund** and its completing words.

Helping verb: a part of the verb before the main verb, conveying information about tense. Helping verbs usually are forms of *have, be, do, will.*

Hyphen: a punctuation mark used to join descriptive adjectives before a noun, to join compound words, to attach some prefixes, or to separate syllables at the end of a line.

Image/imagery: a word, phrase, or figure of speech (such as a simile or metaphor) addressing the senses, suggesting sounds, smells, sights, feelings, tastes, or actions.

Indefinite pronoun: a pronoun used to refer to general or indeterminate people, places, or things (*everyone, everybody, someone, somebody, everything, something, nothing, anyone*).

Independent clause: a clause that can stand alone as a sentence, containing a complete subject and verb.

Indirect object: a noun or pronoun following a verb that receives a direct object. (Jane gave *her* the book.)

Infinitive phrase: a group of words consisting of *to* plus a verb and its completing words. An infinitive phrase can function as a noun, adjective, or adverb.

Informational process: the explanation of how something was made, how an event occurred, or how something works.

Interrupter: a clause or phrase that clarifies or provides additional meaning.

In-text citation: quoted material of no more than three or four typed lines incorporated into the text of the paper rather than set apart in block form. This material should be followed by parentheses containing the author's name and the page number of the source.

Introductory paragraph: the paragraph that introduces the reader to the topic of an essay.

Introductory sentence: the sentence that often precedes the thesis statement. The purpose of introductory sentences is to catch the reader's attention and clarify your **tone.**

Inverted plot: a plot pattern in which events are portrayed out of sequence.

Irony: a verbal device that expresses a contrast between what is said and what is meant.

Irregular verb: a verb that does not form the past tense by adding *–ed* or *–d*. Some verbs do not change forms at all, or they form the past tense by changing the spelling of the entire word (stem-changing verbs).

Linking verb: a verb that does not express action but links the subject to the word or words that describe the subject. The most common linking verbs are forms of *be.*

Listing: a prewriting technique used to discover ideas about a topic. Th topic is written at the top of a blank piece of paper, and the writer writes down a list of ideas associated with the topic. This technique also is called *free association.*

Literary analysis: an interpretation or discussion of one or more works of literature. Literary analysis often takes a persuasive approach; the writer takes a position about some aspect of the work and defends it.

Main idea: the writer's basic approach to the subject. It is the problem to be solved or the issue being raised for consideration.

Main verb: the most important word in a verb phrase, usually conveying the action of the sentence.

Metaphor: a way to describe a topic in terms of another concept (love is *a rose*).

Modes of development: the different viewpoints from which to write about a topic: description, narration, example, classification, process, comparison and contrast, definition, cause and effect, persuasion.

Modifier: a word or group of words that functions as an adjective or adverb (providing description).

Motif: a recurring thematic element in an artistic or literary work.

Narration: a story, usually told in chronological order, usually building to a climax and then resolving.

Nonrestrictive clause: a clause that is not essential to complete the meaning of a sentence. If you remove a nonrestrictive clause from a sentence, the basic meaning of the sentence will remain clear.

Noun: a word that stands for a person, place, or thing. It can be singular or plural.

Noun clause: a clause functioning as a noun, usually beginning with *a, the, what, where, why,* or *when.*

Object: a word or words (usually nouns or pronouns) following prepositions, action verbs, and words formed from verbs (participles, infinitives).

Objective description: factual description, using sensory details of what is seen, heard, tasted, smelled, or touched without any emotional response or interpretation.

Oxymoron: a verbal device in which two contradictory words are used together to enhance meaning ("sweet sorrow"); a condensed form of **paradox.**

Paradox: a statement that at first appears to be a contradiction but upon study makes sense.

Paragraph: a group of sentences that discuss or develop a topic.

Parallel construction (parallelism): the repetition of the same grammatical structure for coherence or emphasis.

Paraphrase: restating someone's ideas in your own words and sentence structure (not directly quoting the other person's words).

Parenthesis: a mark of punctuation used to set off specific details giving additional information, explanations, or qualifications of the main idea in a sentence. *Many students name famous athletes as heroes (Barry Bonds and Mia Hamm, for example).*

Participial phrase: a group of words consisting of a participle and its completing words.

Participle: a verb form ending in *–ed* or *–ing* that is used as an adjective or used with helping verbs to form present perfect or past perfect forms. See **past participle** and **present participle.**

Passive voice: a verb form chosen when the actor of the sentence is not important or when the writer wishes to avoid naming the subject. In the passive voice, the object of an active verb becomes the subject of a passive verb (*be* + past participle).

Past participle: a verb form used to help form the present perfect and past perfect tenses and the passive voice. Past participles usually end with *–d, –ed,* or *–en.*

Past perfect tense: a tense used to describe past action or events occurring prior to a later time in the past. The past perfect is formed from *had* and the verb's past participle form.

Past tense: a tense used to discuss completed past actions. All **regular verbs** in the past tense end in *–ed.*

Period: a punctuation mark that is used to end a complete statement or is included in an abbreviation.

Personal pronoun: a pronoun that refers to a specific person or thing (*I, me, you, he, him, she, her, it, we, us, they, them*). There are three forms, depending on how the personal pronoun is used in a sentence:

subjective (used as a subject), objective (used as an object), or possessive (used to indicate possession or ownership).

Personification: a form of metaphor in which nonhuman things are given human characteristics.

Persuasion: argument that seeks to convince others of the rightness of a belief, point of view, or course of action.

Phrase: a group of related words missing a subject or verb, or both. Phrases are used in sentences to complete thoughts or add descriptive detail; they may be restrictive or nonrestrictive. See **prepositional phrase, participial phrase, gerund phrase, infinitive phrase,** and **absolute phrase.**

Phrasal verb: a two-word or three-word expression that combines a verb with another word, changing the meaning (such as *pick it up*).

Plagiarism: presenting someone else's ideas or words as if they are your own.

Point of the story: in narrative writing, what is interesting about the subject.

Predicate: the part of the sentence containing the verb, making a statement or asking a question about the subject.

Preposition: a word that connects a noun or pronoun to the rest of the sentence, often showing location or time. Frequently used prepositions are *in, on, over, before, after*.

Prepositional phrase: a phrase that contains a preposition and its object (e.g., *in the car* or *on the table*).

Present participle: a verb form ending in *–ing* that is used to help form the **progressive tenses** and that may be used as an adjective.

Present perfect tense: a tense used to describe an action or condition that started in the past and continues up to the present. The tense is formed by combining *has* or *have* and the past participle.

Present tense: a tense used to discuss habitual actions, facts, or conditions that are true of the present.

Prewriting: the step in the writing process in which the writer thinks about the topic, purpose, and audi-

ence and explores ideas for development through **brainstorming, clustering,** or **freewriting.**

Process: a series of actions leading to a concluding point.

Process analysis: an organizational structure that explains how to do something or how something works.

Progressive tense: a tense that discusses actions that are or were happening or are planned for the future. This tense is formed by adding a form of the verb *be* (*is, am, are*) to a verb ending in *–ing*.

Pronoun: a word that takes the place of, or refers to, a noun. The word or phrase that the pronoun refers to is the **antecedent** of the pronoun. See **personal pronoun, relative pronoun, demonstrative pronoun, indefinite pronoun,** and **reflexive pronoun.**

Proofreading: checking the final draft for spelling, punctuation, sentence fragments, and grammar.

Question mark: the punctuation mark that ends a direct question.

Reflexive pronoun: a pronoun ending in *–self* or *–selves* that is used to indicate action performed to or on the antecedent.

Regular verb: a verb ending in *–ed* in the past tense or past participle, or forming its third-person singular form by adding *–s* or *–es*.

Relative clause: a clause that functions as an adjective and begins with a **relative pronoun** (*who, whom, which, that*).

Relative pronoun: a pronoun used to introduce a qualifying or explanatory clause (*who, whom, which, that, whoever, whichever*).

Resolution (*denouement*): the section of the plot line in which the complications are resolved, but not necessarily in a satisfactory way when compared to the traditional legal or moral values of society.

Restrictive clause: a clause that is essential to identify nouns or to complete the meaning. These clauses follow the nouns or ideas they modify. No commas are used to offset restrictive clauses.

Revising: rewriting drafts for both content and organization.

Rising action: a plot element in which increased emotional effect is created by additional events or ramifications from the original action, creating complications for the protagonist.

Round character: a character presented as a complicated, multidimensional individual.

Run-on sentence: a sentence containing two or more independent clauses with nothing that joins them together (a serious grammatical error).

Semicolon: a mark of punctuation that usually joins two independent clauses; it occasionally is used to separate items in a series containing internal commas.

Sensory image: descriptive writing utilizing or evoking the five senses: sight, touch, smell, sound, and taste.

Sentence: a complete statement or question containing a subject and a verb and expressing a complete thought.

Setting: the location within a literary work, consisting of both spatial (house, community, region, country) and cultural qualities (social, moral, economic, political, psychological). The setting can create an atmosphere, playing on our feelings about certain locations.

Simile: a comparison using *like* or *as* (My love is *like a rose*).

Simple definition: a brief explanation such as found in a dictionary. There are three types of simple definition: definition by synonym, class, and negation.

Static character: a character that remains essentially unchanged throughout a literary work.

Subject: the topic (who or what) about which a clause makes a statement or asks a question. Usually the subject is a noun or pronoun, and usually the subject precedes the verb.

Subjective description: description that creates an easily identifiable emotion or impression. This type of description communicates the writer's emotional response to what he or she encounters.

Subject-verb agreement: Subjects and verbs should agree in number. Thus, singular subjects require verbs with singular endings, and plural subjects require verbs with plural endings.

Subordinating conjunction: a word that joins two clauses by making one clause dependent on the other (independent) clause. (Examples: *although, after, because, while*.)

Subordination: joining a dependent clause to an independent clause.

Support sentence: a sentence that explains, clarifies, or defines the subject stated in the topic sentence.

Supporting character: a character who is not the main protagonist but who supports the main characters and may be round or complex.

Symbol: an object, person, image, word, or event that represents more than the literal significance of the term, often evoking complex ideas or themes in literary works.

Synonym: a word with the same, or close to the same, meaning as another word.

Synonym definition: defines a word by supplying another (often simpler) word that means the same thing.

Tense: the form of the verb that shows when in time an action occurred (present, past, future).

Theme: the central meaning, purpose, or dominant idea of a literary work.

Thesis statement: one or more sentences, usually included in the introduction, that state the main idea of an essay and often outline the subtopics of the essay (**essay map**).

Three-item essay map: three items listed in a thesis statement that will support the thesis.

Tone: the author's implied attitude toward the reader or the places, people, and events in a literary work, revealed by the style and word choice.

Topic: the subject or focus of a paragraph or essay.

Topic sentence: a sentence stating the main idea of a paragraph.

Transitional expression: a word or phrase explaining how or in what way two ideas are related. These are often **adverbial conjunctions.**

Uncountable nouns: nouns that represent an idea or concept that cannot be counted (water, air) and cannot be made plural.

Unity: a clearness, coherence, and consistency in the purpose, theme, or organization of a literary work.

Verb: a word indicating action, feeling, or being. The form of the verb can indicate the time of the action: present, past, or future (**tense**).

Works cited list: a list of the reference works referred to in a research paper and cited parenthetically in MLA form.

CREDITS

Text Credits

Maya Angelou, "In All Ways a Woman" from *Wouldn't Take Nothing for My Journey Now* by Maya Angelou. Copyright © 1993 by Maya Angelou. Used by permission of Random House, Inc.

Sharon Begley, "Designer Babies" from *Newsweek*, November 9, 1998. Copyright © 1998 Newsweek, Inc. All rights reserved. Reprinted by permission.

Edwin C. Bliss, "Managing Your Time." Reprinted with the permission of Scribner, an imprint of Simon & Schuster Adult Publishing Group, from *Getting Things Done: The ABC's of Time Management* by Edwin C. Bliss. Copyright © 1976 by Edwin C. Bliss.

Judy Brady, "Why I Want a Wife," originally published in *Ms.* magazine, 1971. Reprinted by permission of the author.

Janice Castro, "Spanglish Spoken Here," *Time*, July 8, 1998. Copyright © *Time*, Inc. Reprinted by permission.

Viet D. Dinh, "Single White Female," *Reconstruction*, Vol. 2, No. 3, 1994. Copyright © 1994. Reprinted by permission of Viet D. Dinh.

Barbara Ehrenreich, "The Ecstasy of War" from *Blood Rites: Origins and History of the Passions of War*. Copyright © 1997 by Barbara Ehrenreich. Reprinted by permission of Henry Holt and Company, LLC.

Elvira M. Franco, "A Magic Circle of Friends." Originally published in *The New York Times*, January 28, 1990. Reprinted by permission of the author.

Robert Frost, "After Apple Picking," 1914.

Sydney J. Harris, "A Jerk Can't See Himself as Others Do," *Last Things First* by Sydney J. Harris. Copyright © 1957, 1958, 1959, 1960 by the Chicago Daily News and General Features Corporation.

Copyright © 1961 by Sydney J. Harris. Reprinted by permission of Houghton Mifflin Company. All rights reserved.

Bud Herron, "Cat Bathing as Martial Art." First published in the *Franklin Daily Journal* (Indiana), 1984. Reprinted by permission of the author.

Garret Hongo, "Kubota." Reprinted by permission of the author.

Charisse Jones, "Light Skin versus Dark." Originally published in *Glamour*, October 1995. Reprinted by permission of the author.

Connie Kang, "A Battle of Cultures," from *Asian Week*, May 25, 1990. Reprinted with the permission of the author.

Eric Kim, "Have You Ever Met an Asian Man You Thought Was Sexy?" Originally published in *Glamour*, March 1995. Reprinted by permission of the author.

Stephen King, "Why We Crave Horror Movies." Originally appeared in *Playboy* (1982). Reprinted with permission. Copyright © Stephen King. All rights reserved.

Harold Krents, "Darkness at Noon." Originally published in *The New York Times*, May 26, 1976. © 1976 The New York Times Co. Reprinted by permission.

A.C. "Buddy" Krizan et al., "Internet Job Search." From *Business Communication*, 4th edition by Krizan/Merrier/Jones/Harcourt. Copyright © 1999. Reprinted with permission of South-Western, a division of Thomson Learning: www.thomsonrights.com. Fax 800-730-2215.

Bharati Mukherjee, "Two Ways to Belong in America." Originally published in *The New York Times*, September 22, 1996. Copyright © 1996 by The New York Times Co. Reprinted by permission.

INDEX